Speaking for the people asks us to think again about the role of party in late nineteenth and early twentieth-century popular politics. By focusing critical attention on the problematic nature of politicians' claims to represent others, it challenges conventional ideas about both the rise of class politics and the triumph of party between 1867 and 1914. Popular Toryism, the problems of Liberal unity and the growth of Labour are all examined from fresh perspectives. The book emphasises the strongly gendered nature of party politics before the First World War, and suggests that historians have greatly underestimated the continuing importance of the 'politics of place'. Most importantly, however, *Speaking for the people* argues that we must break away from teleological notions such as the 'modernisation' of politics, the taming of the 'popular', or the rise of class. Only then will we understand the shifting currents of popular politics. The book as a whole represents a major challenge to the ways in which historians and political scientists have studied the interaction between party politics and popular political cultures.

Speaking for the people

Speaking for the people

Party, language and popular politics in England, 1867–1914

Jon Lawrence

University of Liverpool

CAMBRIDGE
UNIVERSITY PRESS

PUBLISHED BY THE PRESS SYNDICATE OF THE UNIVERSITY OF CAMBRIDGE
The Pitt Building, Trumpington Street, Cambridge CB2 1RP, United Kingdom

CAMBRIDGE UNIVERSITY PRESS
The Edinburgh Building, Cambridge CB2 2RU, United Kingdom
40 West 20th Street, New York, NY 10011–4211, USA
10 Stamford Road, Oakleigh, Melbourne 3166, Australia

© Cambridge University Press 1998

First published 1998

Printed in the United Kingdom at the University Press, Cambridge

Typeset in 10/12pt Plantin   [SE]

A catalogue record for this book is available from the British Library

Library of Congress cataloguing in publication data

Lawrence, Jon.
   Speaking for the people : party, language, and popular politics in
England, 1867–1914 / Jon Lawrence.
         p.   cm.
   Includes bibliographical references and index.
   ISBN 0 521 47034 X
      1. Great Britain – Politics and government – 1837–1901.   2. English
language – Political aspects – Great Britain.   3. Great Britain –
Politics and government – 1901–1936.   4. Political parties – Great
Britain – History.   5. Popular culture – Great Britain – History.
6. Political oratory – Great Britain.   I. Title.
DA560.L29   1998
324′.0941′09034–dc21   97–30166   CIP

ISBN 0 521 47034 X hardback

To Ronald John Lawrence
born Bristol, 14 November 1926
and Doreen May Lawrence
born Bristol, 8 May 1927

Contents

Figures

Acknowledgements

This book has been a long time in the making. When I began working on English popular politics Margaret Thatcher had only just won her second term, John Major was a nobody (no change there), and Tony Blair was little more than a child. Almost a decade and a half later I would like to take this opportunity to thank friends and colleagues who have helped me to think through the problems addressed in this book. Particular mention must go to Steve Tolliday, Alastair Reid, Martin Daunton and Pat Thane for the generous way they encouraged and supported me at times during the 1980s when my confidence was so low that teacher training (or even the City) seemed preferable to a jobless future in academia.

Like most historians of my generation I have enjoyed a variety of institutional homes over the past decade: King's College, Cambridge, the Institute of Historical Research, the Cambridge History Faculty, East London Polytechnic (as was), University College London, and since October 1993 the History Department at Liverpool. At each I have found a pleasant, supportive environment in which to undertake my research. No less importantly, during these years of semi-nomadism I have learned much from arguing through my obsessions and my hunches with fellow historians. It is this, rather than dry days in dusty archives, which makes history fun for me – so thanks again to Sally Alexander, Eugenio Biagini, Peter Claus, Krista Cowman, David Feldman, Steve Fielding, Jon Fulcher, Ewen Green, Adrian Gregory, David Jarvis, Paul Johnson, Patrick Joyce, Ross McKibbin, Jon Parry, Jean-Louis Robert, Mike Savage, John Shaw, Nick Stargardt, Duncan Tanner, Deborah Thom, Amanda Vickery and Jay Winter.

Since I would hate anyone to send me a whole manuscript to read (publishers offering decent fees excepted), I have resisted the temptation of boosting 'Parcel Farce' profits by posting *Speaking for the people* to every corner of the globe for feedback. I am, however, very grateful to John Belchem, Andy Davies, James Vernon and Andy Wood for taking the time to read and comment upon individual chapters. Two people have read substantial chunks of the text and deserve special mention. Miles Taylor, always the sharpest (and therefore the most useful) of critics, read the whole of Part III, helping me greatly to tighten up its arguments. Jane Elliott, no less stern a critic, has read most chapters while they were still hot from the printer, and her influence on *Speaking for the people* has been profound. Finally, I must thank Gareth Stedman Jones, my supervisor in the 1980s, and always an inspiring influence.

Many institutions and their staff have been kind enough to help facilitate the research for this volume, and I am pleased to be able to record my sincere thanks to them. Special thanks must go to the hard-worked staff of Wolverhampton Reference Library, who must have grown sick of the sight of me during the mid-1980s, and to Liz Rees in particular, then borough archivist at Wolverhampton, who was always both helpful and informative. The staff of Cambridge University Library have always displayed a similar faultless professionalism, and I must thank them for making the UL such a pleasant place to work. I must also thank the archivists and staff of the following institutions for allowing me to consult manuscript material in their possession: the British Library of Political and Economic Science, Bristol University Library (Special Collections), the British Library Manuscript Reading Room, the Bishopsgate Institute, and the Club and Institute Union, and the staff at the many other libraries where I have worked over the past fourteen years including the Sydney Jones Library (Liverpool), Birmingham Reference Library, Birmingham University Library, the John Rylands Library (Manchester University), the British Newspaper Library (Colindale), the Senate House Library (London), Manchester Central Library, and the Modern Records Centre (Warwick). I would also like to acknowledge the financial support I have received while undertaking my research. Particular mention must go to the British Academy, for granting me a state studentship in the 1980s, and then a Post-Doctoral Research Fellowship at University College London during 1992–93, and to Jay Winter for understanding that a 'research assistant' should not be a research slave. I would also like to acknowledge Liverpool University's Research Development Fund for funding the analyses of urban election results referred to in Chapter 8. Finally, I would like to thank Richard Fisher for his faith in the project and his patience in seeing it through to completion.

Liverpool
July 1997

Abbreviations

ASE	Amalgamated Society of Engineers
BL	British Library
BLPES	British Library of Political and Economic Science
CCSR	Centre for Census and Survey Research
CIU	Club and Institute Union
CUL	Cambridge University Library
GWR	Great Western Railway
ILP	Independent Labour Party
LCC	London County Council
LRC	Labour Representation Committee
NAC	National Administrative Council (ILP)
NEC	National Executive Committee (Labour)
NUBSO	National Union of Boot and Shoe Operatives
NUC	National Union of Clerks
PLP	Parliamentary Labour Party
RCA	Railway Clerks Association
SDF	Social Democratic Federation
SDP	Social Democratic Party
TUC	Trades Union Congress
WRL	Wolverhampton Reference Library

Introduction

I

Like many histories this is a work shaped in large measure by the idiosyncrasies of its author. Unlike many histories it makes no attempt to pass off a necessarily personal perspective as a definitive or comprehensive study of its subject. The account which follows of English popular politics in the half century before the First World War is partial, not simply because the subject is so vast and multifaceted that no 'final' word would be possible, but because it has been written by a 'situated author'. My efforts to make sense of the stories I have been told about my own past, and about the lives of my parents and grandparents, have necessarily influenced the ways in which I have thought about the past as a professional historian – so too have the stories I have told myself to give shape and meaning to my experiences. Rather than deny this interaction between making the self and making history I wish to celebrate it. Historical inquiry should emerge out of critical engagement with the 'myths we live by', as much as with historiographical debate.[1]

Part I, 'Rethinking popular politics', maps out the historiographical and methodological location of the present study in fairly conventional terms; this introduction offers a more personal chart of the same terrain. Since much of part I is concerned with criticising historical accounts of class and 'class politics', I should perhaps begin by emphasising that the last thing I wish to suggest is that perceptions of class and class difference have had no impact on the development of English popular politics. If years spent being bussed across Bristol to enjoy the benefits of a grammar school education did not teach me both the importance, and the ambiguities, of class identity, then growing up in a staunchly Tory working-class home certainly did. Rejecting my parents' politics from an early age, I was

---

[1] Raphael Samuel and Paul Thompson (eds.), *The myths we live by* (London, 1990). For attempts to rethink objectivity in the light of the postmodernist critique of universal rationality and meaning, see Wolfgang Natter, Theodore Schatzki and John Paul Jones (eds.), *Objectivity and its other* (New York, 1995), intelligently reviewed by Mark Bevir in *History and Theory*, 35 (1996), pp. 391–401.

none the less conscious that these politics had played their part in shaping my own identity. At the same time, in trying to understand the origins, the rationale, and above all the tensions of my parents' Toryism, I became suspicious of superficial assumptions about the relationship between social class and politics. This suspicion intensified when I later discovered that when I was born, in 1961, my father had been as staunchly, dogmatically Labour as he now was Tory. That he had worked for the Co-op, that he had remained unmoved by post-war affluence, and that he still cherished memories of Cripps and Stockwood as champions of east Bristol's poor in the 1930s. To this day I cannot fully explain his shift of allegiance – perhaps he cannot either – but I doubt whether his attitudes have changed greatly since the early 1960s. Those attitudes are no more naturally Tory than Labour – yet this shift of allegiance occurred, and has never been reversed.

My mother's politics, though worn more lightly, have been more constant. Like Carolyn Steedman's mother in *Landscape for a good woman*, her aspirations and her dreams found no echo in the ethos of post-war Labour politics.[2] She hankered, not for comfort or 'equality of opportunity', but for glamour and for luxury – for more than a celluloid glimpse of the delights of Hollywood or 'High society'. But she lived in the knowledge, not only that her dreams were 'mere' fancies, but that it was 'wrong' to want what she could not have. Here was a Conservatism that was easier to understand, shaped as it was by a reaction against Labour's concerns with production and *collective* consumption, but still it had no history. My parents had both grown up in working-class and strongly Labour households in east Bristol. Why, I asked myself, had they subsequently turned their backs on Labour – my mother as soon as she could vote in 1950, my father at some point in the early 1960s? It was this puzzle which first encouraged me to embark on a PhD – my project, I felt sure, must be to understand the culture of Labour politics my parents had grown up within during the 1930s. My father remembered joining a children's march through the streets of St George at the 1931 election – he was only four, but his support for Cripps still earnt him a bag of sweets. He also remembered local Labour councillors who could always be relied upon for advice or help in times of adversity. From such accounts it seemed as though Labour was deeply enmeshed in people's daily life, and that its leaders really did speak (as they claimed) for the local community. But was this simply a romantic reconstruction of the past, perhaps even a retelling of Labour's own myths about itself in east Bristol? After all, Cripps had survived by less than 500 votes in 1931.

---

[2] Carolyn Steedman, *Landscape for a good woman: a story of two lives* (London, 1986).

As is the way with PhDs, especially ones begun before government funding bodies focused their attention on swift completion rates, my research eventually veered away, not only from Cripps and east Bristol, but from the whole problem of understanding partisanship between the wars. The more I studied inter-war party politics, the more I became convinced of the need to rethink our understanding of the forces which had shaped party politics in the period between the introduction of (male) household suffrage in 1867, and the First World War. Not only had this period seen the beginnings of independent Labour politics, but it was also said to have witnessed the 'triumph of party' – and with it the emergence of more national, programmatic and truly 'modern' politics. I had serious doubts about our historical understanding of both phenomena. But even though this engagement with the historiography of English popular politics altered the focus of my study, it did not lead me to abandon many questions originally formulated to decode the Labour culture my parents must have known during the 1930s. I still wanted to know how politicians had understood the claim to *represent*, and to analyse the different ways they had gone about trying to articulate that claim. I still wanted to explore the relationship between popular understandings of class and the languages of class articulated by political parties. And I still wanted to explore the relationship between local identities and partisanship. What factors might shape the emergence of a strong sense of communal identity, and under what circumstances might the idea of 'community' or 'locality' take a decidedly partisan form? Did party discourse conjure up the 'politics of place', or were the physical and demographic characteristics of a district of primary importance to their success?[3]

No less than my interest in class, this interest in locality has strong personal roots. In part this fascination has doubtless been shaped by the romantic perspective of the forced exile – it is now nearly twenty years since I left Bristol. But my interest in the 'politics of place' has also been shaped by involvement in party politics since my 'exile'. Living in the Romsey district of Cambridge during the 1980s I was intrigued to find that political activism gave me access to a version of 'community' rooted not in blood and dialect (my cherished symbols of Bristolian identity), but in party. Labour politicians had represented Romsey continuously since 1919 (but for a brief hiccup at a by-election in 1982 when the SDP

[3] For explorations of this theme, see Marie Dickie, 'Town patriotism in Northampton, 1918–1939: an invented tradition?', *Midland History*, 17 (1992), pp. 109–17; David Gilbert, 'Community and municipalism: collective identity in late-Victorian and Edwardian mining towns', *Journal of Historical Geography*, 17 (1991), pp. 257–70, and 'Imagined communities and mining communities', *Labour History Review*, 60, 2 (1995), pp. 47–55. Also David Cannadine, 'The transformation of civic ritual in modern Britain: the Colchester oyster feast', *Past and Present*, 94 (1982), pp. 107–30.

band-wagon rolled into the ward), and for generations the district had been affectionately known as 'Red Romsey'. Myths of community and myths of party appeared inter-twined. By the late 1980s only one Labour councillor was a native of the ward, and he no longer lived there. But this mattered little. Labour's claim to represent the community rested not on birth-rights but on historical tradition and on its activists' knowledge of the ward and its problems (Labour's three 'outsider' councillors all lived in the ward). The party, and its local leaders, thus had every incentive to perpetuate the myth of 'Red Romsey', though by the 1980s it had clearly worn very thin. Nothing could disguise the low turnouts recorded in the ward, nor the alarming fluctuations in the Labour vote from year to year. Rapid turnover of population weakened both party resources, and the relevance of any appeal to identification with 'Red Romsey'. Apart from in a few core streets, few people had any sense that they even lived in a place called 'Romsey', whilst others who did live in 'historic' Romsey had recently been shunted into an adjacent, highly marginal ward in a cunning piece of gerrymandering which had cut across the 'politics of place' (it was rumoured that these voters proved much more reluctant to turn out in their new ward).

But even if the myth of 'Red Romsey' had not been unravelling in the 1980s, it was clear to me that at its centre lay one of the great tensions of party politics. The Romsey Labour party wished to present itself as the embodiment of an active, radical and cohesive local community ('Red Romsey'), but it also longed for such a community to exist outside the narrow, and generally rather alienating, confines of formal party structures. The problem was that by claiming to be the authentic 'voice of Romsey', the party not only tended to deny the legitimacy (or 'representativeness') of other voices, but it actively discouraged their articulation. Political influence and power may have been sought for the best of motives – to bring material improvements to the lives of people who lacked influence and power – but it was difficult to escape the conclusion that Labour's project of improving the lives of others (however benign in its intentions) was itself disempowering.

Moving to Liverpool in the early 1990s did nothing to challenge my sense of the tensions at the heart of party. It did, however, confirm my conviction that whilst these tensions might have a common source in the ambiguous nature of the claim 'to represent', the problems of party were not timeless and immutable. The relationship between politicians and those they claim to represent must always be studied within the context of time and place. Liverpool was not Cambridge; the late twentieth century is not Edwardian England. It did not take me long to realize that whilst political myths about 'community' were no less important in Liverpool than in Romsey, these myths could not easily accommodate a southern, and by now decidedly middle-class, white male. And hence the paradox that whilst I now lived on a street that was more genuinely communal and inclusive than any I had known in Cambridge – so much so that it is almost a parody of the romanticised view of community – I none the less felt cut off from the conceptions of 'community' embedded in *political* mythology. Nor, it seemed to me, could party provide a point of access to this mythology (as it had in Romsey), since, on my reading at least, party appeared a largely peripheral force – its power to forge new myths blunted by extreme instrumentalism thanks to the jobbery and clientism practised by all parties for generations.

These, then, are the personal influences which I feel have done most to shape the present study. I am conscious that in discussing them in this manner I lay myself open to many charges: that I wish to close down the scope for alternative readings of my text, that I naively believe one can know one's 'true' self, or that I have no interest in historical 'truth' (ie. in offering the most convincing interpretation of the past which can be constructed from available sources). Naturally I would refute such charges, but not more strongly than I would refute the suggestion that my reading of late Victorian and Edwardian popular politics is somehow 'definitive' – that it is, in effect, the only interpretation of the subject possible. Such a claim would be at least as imperious as the politician's claim to represent a community.

II

We move now from the confessional to the 'user guide', since I would like (briefly) to explain the structure of the present volume, mindful that in these hard-pressed times it is becoming increasingly rare for a monograph to be read from cover to cover. Part I, as suggested, contains much that one might normally expect to find in a lengthy introduction. Reviewers in a hurry to find rash statements about the underlying assumptions of the book may choose to skip chapters 1 and 2 (which examine the problems inherent in arguments about, respectively, the 'rise of class politics', and the 'homogenisation' of working-class life), and move straight to chapter 3. Besides offering a critical assessment of recent trends in the history of nineteenth-century popular politics, this chapter ends by explaining at some length the approach to popular politics which has informed the present study. Particular attention is given to interrogating the ambiguities at the heart of the claim to 'represent' – the claim, that is, to 'speak for the people'.

Part II uses a case-study of popular politics in Wolverhampton to explore the ambiguities and tensions of party politics at greater length. The intention here is not to argue for the 'typicality' of Wolverhampton, but rather to use the in-depth local study to explore the dynamics of urban popular politics in a manner deeper and more contextualised than is possible through a general survey of many cases. The latter approach may appear more definitive, but in truth it must rely either on the questions pursued by other researchers, or on whistle-stop tours of the country's archives. There is nothing wrong with this, of course – I rely on such strategies myself in part III which looks at party politics on a national scale – but it does seem unfortunate that historical fashion has turned so resolutely against the local study since the 1970s. In part, this probably reflects little more than the commercial realities of academic publishing (after all, regional and local history journals continue to flourish, apparently oblivious of 'fashion'). But there are other reasons. On the one hand there is the ever-present danger of slipping into 'mere antiquarianism', on the other the trap of drawing unsustainable conclusions from the particular to the universal. In recent years, however, there has been a significant revival of interest in the ways in which locality has helped shape political cultures and party allegiance.[4] And whilst this revival has as yet spawned few detailed case studies of popular politics, it has highlighted the need for extensive new research into the 'politics of locality' which recognises, rather than disguises, the peculiarities of place.[5]

This is the approach adopted in the case-study of Wolverhampton presented here. The intention is to examine the shifting fortunes of party within a framework which is sensitive both to local social, economic and cultural context, and to the impact of developments at the national level. Local politics are seen not as the antithesis of Westminster politics, but as a specific, and electorally very important, facet of the 'party game'. This case study is therefore able to explore the vital question of how national politics were refracted through local political cultures and traditions, and how this process of mediation helped to shape patterns of allegiance within a constituency. In chapter 4 attention is focused on the long period of Liberal hegemony in Wolverhampton between 1832 and 1885. In Wolverhampton, it is argued, popular liberalism developed in spite of, rather than because of, the actions of the local Liberal leaders, whose

---

[4] See especially John Agnew, *Place and politics: the geographical mediation of state and society* (Boston, Mass., 1987); Mike Savage, 'Political alignments in modern Britain: do localities matter?', *Political Geography Quarterly*, 6 (1987), pp. 53–76, and 'Urban history and social class: two paradigms', *Urban History*, 20 (1993), pp. 61–77; Duncan Tanner, *Political change and the Labour party, 1900–1918* (Cambridge, 1990).

[5] A notable exception is Michael Savage, *The dynamics of working-class politics: the labour movement in Preston, 1880–1940* (Cambridge, 1987).

greatest concern appeared to be to guard their oligarchic control of the local party. Chapter 5, examines the rise of popular Toryism in Wolverhampton in the later nineteenth century, demonstrating the considerable appeal of the party's claim to defend male leisure culture from the interference of nonconformist Liberalism. This chapter also shows how the rise of popular Toryism determined both the context and the tenor of early Labour politics in Wolverhampton. Concluding this section, chapter 6 focuses in detail on pre-war Labour politics, and in particular on the tensions inherent in the party's claim to represent a heterogeneous social constituency. It is shown both that few Labour activists lived in the older, more solidly working-class parts of the town, and that the politics they embraced tended to marginalise both women and the urban poor – two constituencies vital for the party's long-term political success.

In part III, the focus shifts from local to national, but still the central concern is to explore the problems of party. Each chapter can be read as a free-standing essay on an aspect of party before 1914, but taken together they are intended to show how problematising the role of party can provide new insights into the shifting currents of popular politics in the late nineteenth and early twentieth centuries. Chapter 7 offers a sustained critique of the idea of the 'triumph of party' in the years between the Second Reform Act and the First World War. In fact, it is suggested, the power of party remained strictly circumscribed, not least because politicians themselves continued to show a surprising degree of tolerance towards robust forms of popular politics such as the disruption of political meetings or the symbolic 'conquest' of public space. Popular politics remained far from 'tamed' before 1914, a point which perhaps helps to explain why so many politicians remained fearful about the implications of mass democracy. Chapter 8 looks in detail at the problems facing the Liberal party in the twenty years between the Home Rule split of 1886 and the landslide victory of 1906. The discussion is intended to complement my analysis of Tory hegemony during the same period published elsewhere.[6] It focuses both on dissension within the Liberal coalition, and on the specific problems faced by party propagandists searching for a popular voice with which to counter the strident appeals of Tory populism, and its critique of their party's 'nonconformist agenda'. It is argued that the nadir in Liberal electoral fortunes came in 1895, rather than in 1886 or even 1900, and that reactions to this defeat, particularly within the labour movement, did much to shape the subsequent development of

---

[6] See Jon Lawrence, 'Class and gender in the making of urban Toryism, 1880–1914', *English Historical Review*, 108 (1993), pp. 629–52.

English popular politics. Liberalism was increasingly perceived as a spent force, both electorally and ideologically, but with the workers apparently in thrall to Toryism and jingoism, few within the Labour movement felt confident about the prospects for popular politics. Hence the growing conviction of many socialists that social reform must take precedence over political reform – not because economic equality was more important than political equality, but because such reforms were seen as the only means of creating a rational democracy. The final chapter, which focuses specifically on Labour politics, explores these themes in greater depth. It examines the importance of the 'politics of place' to the party's faltering first steps, suggesting that Labour found it very difficult to develop a natural, 'organic' relationship with its putative constituency. It also charts the rapid decline of anti-party traditions within Labour politics before 1914, and concludes by offering a critical reading of Labour autobiography and popular biography. The aim here is to identify the myths which helped to shape the early Labour party, in order to shed new light on how Labour activists perceived their mission to 'speak for the people' (and how they legitimated that mission in the face of frequent popular rejection).

Part I

Rethinking popular politics

1   From the rise of 'demos' to the 'rise of class'

I

By the late nineteenth century there was a broad consensus among historians and political commentators that British history had been characterised by the slow, but inexorable growth of constitutional liberties and democratic influence. In particular, few doubted that the nineteenth century had witnessed a continual strengthening of popular political forces – of 'the masses' or 'the Democracy' – although there was considerable disagreement about the desirability of this trend.[1] Radicals such as John Richard Green placed the English 'common people' at the centre of their story of the growth of liberty and freedom,[2] whereas mainstream Liberal writers tended to place greater emphasis on the constitutional and legislative reforms of progressive leaders,[3] and Conservative writers tended to lament the slow erosion of historic elements of the constitution by politicians who misrepresented the true instincts of the English people.[4]

[1] Asa Briggs, 'The language of "mass" and "masses" in nineteenth-century England', in David E. Martin and David Rubinstein (eds.), *Ideology and the labour movement: essays presented to John Saville* (London, 1979), pp. 62–83.

[2] John Richard Green, *A short history of the English people* (London, 1874) – although even Green often placed more emphasis on the achievements of 'the missionary, the poet, the printer, the merchant or the philosopher' (*ibid.*, p. x) than on the aspirations of 'the poor stockinger'. For a discussion of Green's influence on British Radical historiography, see Raphael Samuel, 'British Marxist historians, 1880–1980: part one', *New Left Review*, 120 (March–April 1980), pp. 37–42.

[3] T. E. May, *The constitutional history of England since the accession of George the Third, 1760–1860*, 2 vols. (London, 1861–63); William Stubbs, *The constitutional history of England in its origin and development*, 3 vols. (Oxford, 1866); Walter Bagehot, *The English constitution* (London, 1867).

[4] For many, Edmund Burke's *Reflections on the revolution in France* (1790) remained the classic statement of the conservative position, despite its author's Whig connections. Other key statements of the Conservative constitutionalist position are to be found in William Hutcheon (ed.), *Whigs and Whiggism: political writings by Benjamin Disraeli* (London, 1913), which includes the essays 'Peers and people' (1835), 'Vindication of the English constitution in a letter to a noble and learned lord' (1835), 'The letters of Runnymede' (1836) and 'The spirit of Whiggism' (1836); and in John Colmer (ed.), *The collected works of Samuel Taylor Coleridge, volume 10: On the Constitution of the Church and State* (1829; London, 1976).

Perhaps understandably, disagreements were often sharpest over contemporary politics, and in particular over the consequences of the electoral reforms of 1867 and 1884–5. While Henry Jephson could write
approvingly of the 1870s and 1880s as marking the final stage in the 'rise
of the Platform', less sanguine writers such as Moisei Ostrogorski deeply
lamented the corruption of political life associated with the emergence of
the mass party.[5] Few doubted that the growth of political democracy
('the rise of demos') had been a century-long process with its roots in the
metropolitan Radicalism of the late eighteenth century, the struggle for
manhood suffrage after the Napoleonic wars, and above all the Chartist
campaigns of the 1830s and 1840s. However, this emphasis on the
continuity of Radical politics began to wane after the First World War,
with the gradual emergence of a new labour historiography which saw the
1880s as a period of political discontinuity marked by the beginnings of
the 'rise of class politics'. Even so, the influence of earlier Radical historiographies remained profound, not least in the continued emphasis on the
progressive and democratic credentials of the English 'common people'.
This radical populism only lost its hold over the historiography of
popular politics in the late 1960s and 1970s – the true heyday of 'the rise
of class' as an explanatory framework for modern British politics. As the
ensuing discussion seeks to demonstrate, it is only by understanding the
historical origins of this all pervasive model of modern popular politics
that we can begin to appreciate its inherently constructed and contestable
nature.

II

Labour historiography more or less began with Sidney and Beatrice
Webb's major studies of trade unionism and cooperation during the
1890s.[6] For the Webbs, however, the dramatic events of 1889–93 – the
growth of 'New Unionism' and of trade union collectivism – marked not a
radical break with earlier traditions, but 'only another manifestation of
the same deep-rooted belief in the essential Brotherhood of Labour'.[7] If
anything the pioneering social histories of Barbara and John Hammond
such as *The village labourer* were even more firmly rooted within estab-

---

[5] Henry Jephson, *The platform: its rise and progress*, 2 vols. (London, 1892);
Moisei Ostrogorski, *Democracy and the organisation of political parties*, 2 vols. (London,
1902).

[6] See Beatrice Webb, *The co-operative movement in Great Britain* (London, 1891); Beatrice
and Sidney Webb, *The history of trade unionism* (London, 1894); and *Industrial democracy*
(London, 1897). Also Royden Harrison, 'Sidney and Beatrice Webb', in Carl Levy (ed.),
Socialism and the intelligentsia, 1880–1914 (London, 1987), pp. 35–89.

[7] Webbs, *History of trade unionism*, p. 477.

lished historiographical traditions.[8] Like the Webbs, the Hammonds'
novelty lay more in their choice of subject matter (in their case popular
experiences of industrialisation, in the Webbs' case the institutions of
working-class life), than in their wider interpretative framework. Indeed
both the Webbs and the Hammonds tapped into Liberal, as well as the
Radical, historiographical traditions. Not only did they stress the
continuity of nineteenth-century popular politics, but they also acknowledged that progressive statesmen and free institutions had played a
crucial part in ameliorating the hardships of industrialisation.[9]

It is therefore only after the First World War that one can talk of the
emergence of a distinctive 'Labour' historiography (with a capital 'L')
which offered a re-interpretation of the basic chronology of nineteenth-
century popular politics. By the late 1920s, when the American scholar
Frances Gillespie published her major study *Labor and politics in England*,
with its sophisticated restatement of the continuity thesis, British labour
historians were already beginning to argue for the radical *discontinuity* of
nineteenth-century popular politics.[10] Increasingly labour historians
divided the century into three distinct phases of political activity: a militant, semi-revolutionary phase culminating in the Chartist campaigns of
the 1830s and 1840s; a quiescent mid-Victorian phase characterised by
collaboration between labour and capital, radical and liberal; and a second
phase of militancy beginning in the 1880s and culminating in the formation of a trade union-based Labour party at the turn of the century.[11] For
inter-war writers such as Theodore Rothstein, T. A. Jackson, A. L. Morton
and G. D. H. Cole it was important to establish a radical, but unambiguously non-Liberal, genealogy for contemporary socialist and Labour politics.[12] This meant stressing the class character and intuitive socialism of

---

[8] John and Barbara Hammond, *The village labourer, 1760–1832: a study in the government of
England before the Reform Bill* (London, 1911); *The town labourer, 1760–1832: the new
civilization* (London, 1917); *The skilled labourer, 1760–1832* (London, 1919); *The age of the
Chartists, 1832–1854: a study of discontent* (London, 1930); *The bleak age* (London, 1934).

[9] See John and Barbara Hammond, *The bleak age*, p. 121; Fabian tract No. 11 [Sidney
Webb], *The workers' political programme* (London, 1890); and for Fabian attitudes to the
state and social progress more generally, see the discussion in Jon Lawrence, 'Popular
Radicalism and the Socialist revival in Britain', *Journal of British Studies*, 31 (1992), pp.
163–86, esp. pp. 179–85. Also of interest is Joseph Clayton, *Leaders of the people: studies in
democratic history* (London, 1910).

[10] Frances Gillespie, *Labor and politics in England, 1850–1967* (Durham, N. Carolina, 1927).

[11] The influence of the 'three-phase' model of nineteenth-century popular politics is discussed at greater length in Lawrence, 'Popular Radicalism'.

[12] Theodore Rothstein, *From Chartism to Labourism: historical sketches of the English working-
class movement* (London, 1929); A. L. Morton, *A people's history of England* (London,
1938); T. A. Jackson, *Trials of British freedom: being some studies in the history of the fight for
democratic freedom in Britain* (London, 1940); G. D. H. Cole, *A short history of the English
working-class movement, 1789–1927*, 3 vols. (London, 1925–7); and *British working-class politics, 1832–1914* (London, 1941).

both early nineteenth-century popular protest, and late nineteenth-century independent Labour politics. Given that the Labour party found it difficult to win majority (let alone hegemonic) support among manual workers between the wars,[13] it should be clear that for these writers establishing the 'rise of class politics' thesis was as much about legitimising current political struggles as about analyzing past politics.

Although G. D. H. Cole was undoubtedly the most influential labour historian of the inter-war period, he did little to extend the methodological legacy of pioneers such as the Webbs or the Hammonds. His overall approach owed most to the Webbs, and his histories of the 'working-class movement' are essentially histories of the collective institutions of working-class life. The primary influence on Cole appears to have been the positivist reductionism then fashionable within the emergent discipline of economic history.[14] His reading of Marx, an acknowledged influence, was strongly positivist so that his approach to social change and causality was essentially linear rather than dialectic.[15] As a result, Cole's histories eschew the Hammonds' interest in popular beliefs and aspirations, and offer instead rather bland assertions about the relationship between standards of living and popular politics. For Cole poverty and hunger bred revolt, growing prosperity bred quiescence or reformism. Hence each volume of his *Short history of the British working class movement* ends with a brief survey of working-class living standards which is offered as an explanation of the preceding historical narrative.[16] For Cole economic determinism was pretty well absolute: his readers were asked 'to bear in mind, at every stage, the economic forces to which the political movements arose as a response'.[17]

III

After the Second World War, the 'three phase' model of nineteenth-century popular politics gradually became entrenched in both liberal and

[13] See Geoffrey Fry, 'A reconsideration of the British General Election of 1935 and the electoral revolution of 1945', *History*, 76, 246 (1991), pp. 43–55; John Turner, *British politics and the Great War: coalition and conflict, 1915–1918* (New Haven, Conn., 1992), ch. 11; Duncan Tanner, 'Class voting and radical politics: the Liberal and Labour parties, 1910–1931' in Jon Lawrence and Miles Taylor (eds.), *Party, state and society: electoral behaviour in Britain since 1820* (Aldershot, 1997).

[14] For discussion of this influence, see Gareth Stedman Jones, 'History: the poverty of empiricism', in R. Blackburn (ed.), *Ideology in social science: readings in critical social theory* (London, 1972), pp. 97–107, and Richard Johnson, 'Culture and the historians', in J. Clarke, C. Critcher and R. Johnson (eds.), *Working-class culture: essays in history and theory* (London, 1979), pp. 44 and 49–53.

[15] See G. D. H. Cole, *What Marx really meant* (London, 1934), esp. pp. 7–45. Also *A history of socialist thought*, vol. 2, *Marxism and Anarchism, 1850–1896* (London, 1954), pp. 267–314.

[16] See Cole, *A short history*, I, pp. 175–88; II, pp. 187–96; and III, pp. 217–26.

[17] G. D. H. Cole, *British working-class politics*, p. 10.

socialist historiographies. A new generation of Marxist historians, connected with the Communist Party Historians' Group and the journal
Modern Quarterly, played a crucial role in this process.[18] Although the key
controversies of post-war Marxist historiography focused on the seventeenth rather than the nineteenth century, the work of Eric Hobsbawm
and Edward Thompson on nineteenth-century labour history more or
less established the new orthodoxy of discontinuity. In early works such as
Labour's turning point (1948), and essays such as 'Trends in the British
labour movement' (1949), 'Economic fluctuations and some social movements' (1952) and 'The labour aristocracy' (1954), Eric Hobsbawm
brought a new rigour to G. D. H. Cole's arguments about the links
between working-class standards of living and the temper of popular politics.[19] Edward Thompson, in contrast, was one of the few Marxists of his
generation to challenge economic reductionism when studying the
popular politics of industrial, no less than pre-industrial, societies.[20] As a
result, whilst his choice of subject matter tended to reinforce the periodisation of the 'three-phase' model – notably in *William Morris* (1955),
'Homage to Tom Maguire' (1960), and *The making of the English working
class* (1963), his determination to rediscover and celebrate an unbroken
tradition of English popular radicalism tended to echo earlier arguments
about the continuity of democratic political struggles.[21] This was no acci-

[18] See Bill Schwarz, '"The people" in history: the Communist Party Historians' Group,
1946–56', in the Centre for Contemporary Cultural Studies' collection, *Making histories:
studies in history-writing and politics* (London, 1982), pp. 44–95; Samuel, 'British Marxist
historians'; Eric Hobsbawm, 'The Communist Party Historians' Group', in Maurice
Cornforth (ed.), *Rebels and their causes: essays in honour of A. L. Morton* (London, 1978);
Harvey J. Kaye, *The British Marxist historians: an introductory analysis* (Cambridge, 1984),
and *The education of desire: Marxists and the writing of history* (New York, 1992), esp. ch 5.
Though see Miles Taylor, 'The beginnings of modern British social history?', *History
Workshop Journal*, 43 (1997), pp. 155–76, which stresses the predominantly non-Marxist
origins of determinism in mainstream British social history.
[19] Eric Hobsbawm, *Labour's turning point, 1880–1900: extracts from contemporary sources*
(London, 1948); 'Trends in the British labour movement since 1850', *Science and Society*,
13 (1949); 'Economic fluctuations and some social movements since 1800', *Economic
History Review*, 5 (1952–53), pp. 1–25, and 'The labour aristocracy in nineteenth-century
Britain' in J. Saville (ed.), *Democracy and the labour movement: essays in honour of Dona Torr*
(London, 1954). The three essays were subsequently reprinted in Hobsbawm's *Labouring
men: studies in the history of labour* (London, 1964). Hobsbawm's later writing is often
more strongly sociological; see in particular the discussion of working-class culture and
residence in *Worlds of labour: further studies in the history of labour* (London, 1984).
[20] See Schwarz, '"The people" in history', pp. 66–92. Schwarz notes the contrast between
Hobsbawm's concerns in *Primitive rebels* (Manchester, 1959) and *Labouring men*
(London, 1964). Maurice Dobb's influential *Studies in the development of capitalism*
(London, 1946) set the tone for the study of 'modern' industrialised societies among
post-war Marxist scholars.
[21] E. P. Thompson, *William Morris: Romantic to revolutionary* (London, 1955); 'Homage to
Tom Maguire', in Asa Briggs and John Saville (eds.), *Essays in labour history in memory of
G. D. H. Cole*, vol. 1 (London, 1960); and *The making of the English working class* (London,
1963, subsequent references from Pelican edn., London, 1968).

dent. The Communist party historians, as a group, were acutely conscious of the common ground they shared with an earlier generation of
radical historians – hence their determination to defend historians such
as Tawney in their controversies with the new generation of Namierite
political historians.[22] Similarly, Thompson was far from alone in his
concern to champion the native radicalism and rebelliousness of the
English 'common people'.[23] But in the 1950s it was Thompson, more
than any of his contemporaries, who found these traditions alive among
the nineteenth-century industrial working class. In 'Homage to Tom
Maguire' Thompson recognised the deep-rooted political and cultural
traditions which set the context for, and profoundly influenced the character of, the vibrant socialist politics of the West Riding in the 1890s –
Chartism, radical non-conformity, independent labour organisation and
dialect writing all played their part in the emergent political culture. The
result is a rich, decidedly non-determinist, account of the genesis of independent labour politics which remains unrivalled within the historiography.[24] That said, Thompson had no doubt that popular political
traditions had been fundamentally transformed by rapid industrialisation
in the early nineteenth century. His influential work on the popular
defence of 'custom' in eighteenth-century England rests on the assumption that this is a politics of transition – that aspects of the market
economy have already been internalized (hence the determination of food
'rioters' to assert a customary price), but that the focus of popular politics
remains on consumption and the price of commodities, rather than on
production and the price of labour.[25] Recent work has reminded us that
customary notions of the 'fair wage' remained central to industrial bargaining throughout the nineteenth century, while one could argue that
the claim to subsistence at a 'fair' price was also widely upheld, not only
through co-operation but also in the popular response to crises such as
the cotton famine of the early 1860s, or the shortages of the two world
wars.[26] This is not to suggest some seamless continuity between the
popular politics of the mid eighteenth and mid twentieth centuries, but
only to caution against the tendency, present even in Thompson's work,
to exaggerate the disjuncture brought by industrialisation. The

---

[22] See Hobsbawm, 'Where are British historians going?', *Marxist Quarterly*, 2 (1955), pp.
14–26; Christopher Hill, 'R. H. Tawney: an appreciation', *History Today* (December,
1980), p. 47.
[23] See Samuel, 'British Marxist historians', and Schwarz, '"The People" in history'.
[24] Thompson, 'Homage to Tom Maguire'.
[25] For instance see E. P. Thompson, *Customs in common* (Penguin edn., London, 1993), pp.
252–8, 260–2.
[26] On wage bargaining see Patrick Joyce (ed.), *The historical meanings of work*, (Cambridge,
1987); and *Visions of the people: industrial England and the question of class, 1840–1914*,
(1991), chs. 4–6. On co-operation, see Stephen Yeo (ed.), *New views of co-operation*
(London, 1988).

Londoners who ambushed coal wagons during the harsh winter of 1916–17, only to insist on paying the official (controlled) price for their cargo, were responding to scarcity and profiteering much as Thompson's pre-industrial crowd might have done.[27]

Thompson's emphasis on the need 'to rescue the poor stockinger . . . from the enormous condescension of posterity' inspired a generation of historians to write 'history from below', and to proclaim the importance of understanding social, economic and political change from the perspective of previously marginalised social groups.[28] For many, Thompson's appeal was that he seemed to have thrown off the straitjacket of economic reductionism, without abandoning an emphasis on class and class struggle. However, perhaps because its agenda was to rediscover 'lost' histories, the new social history of the 1960s and 1970s produced relatively few studies of popular politics during the classic period of 'the rise of class politics' between 1880 and 1920. Most studies either followed Thompson's lead by examining the putative class struggles of the late eighteenth and early nineteenth centuries,[29] or sought instead to explain the alleged absence of class politics in the mid-Victorian period.[30] Studies of popular politics after 1880, either remained within the established traditions of labour history (which Henry Pelling had given a new authority during the 1950s and 1960s),[31] or belonged to

---

[27] The Times, 6 February 1917; for a discussion of popular responses to wartime scarcity, see Bernard Waites, "The government of the home front and the "moral economy" of the working class', in P. H. Liddle (ed.), Home fires and foreign fields (London, 1985); and Jonathan Manning, 'La guerre et la consommation civile à Londres, 1914–1918', Guerres Mondiales et Conflits Contemporains, 183 (1996), pp. 29–45, which draws heavily on Jon Lawrence, 'Coal and the metropolis: keeping the home fires burning' and 'Housing in London, 1914–1918' (unpublished papers).

[28] Thompson, Making, p. 12.

[29] For instance, Eric Hobsbawm and George Rudé, Captain Swing (London, 1969); Iorwerth Prothero, Artisans and politics: John Gast and his times (Folkestone, 1979); Patricia Hollis, Pressure from without in early Victorian England (London, 1974); Dorothy Thompson, The early Chartists (London, 1971); John Belchem, Orator Hunt: Henry Hunt and English working-class radicalism (Oxford, 1985). For a perceptive commentary, see Miles Taylor, 'Rethinking the Chartists: searching for synthesis in the historiography of Chartism', Historical Journal, 39 (1996), pp. 479–95.

[30] See especially Royden Harrison, Before the socialists: studies in labour and politics, 1861–1881 (London, 1965); Geoffrey Crossick, An artisan élite in Victorian society: Kentish London, 1840–1880 (London, 1978); Robert Gray, The Labour aristocracy in Victorian Edinburgh (Oxford, 1976); Patrick Joyce, Work, society and politics: the culture of the factory in later Victorian England (Brighton, 1980); Neville Kirk, The growth of working-class reformism in mid-Victorian England (London, 1985) – and from a different tradition, Trygve Tholfsen, Working-class radicalism in mid-Victorian Britain (London, 1976).

[31] For Henry Pelling, see especially The Origins of the Labour party (Oxford, 1954); America and the British Left: from Bright to Bevan (London, 1956); A short history of the Labour party (London, 1961); A history of British trade unionism (London, 1963) and Social geography of British elections, 1885–1910 (London, 1967). His collection of more speculative essays Popular politics and society in late Victorian Britain (London, 1968) fits less easily into the 'labour history' tradition.

the liberal, rather than the radical-socialist, historiographical tradition. Indeed, as we shall see, it was liberal historians such as Peter Clarke and John Vincent who gave a new theoretical rigour to the idea of 'the rise of class politics' during this period.[32] But before examining their work in greater detail, it will be useful to examine some of the assumptions about popular politics which informed the 'histories from below' written under the influence of E. P. Thompson during the 1960s and 1970s.

Almost from the outset Thompson and his followers were sharply criticised by others on the Left for taking the break with economic determinism too far. Their work, it was argued, placed exaggerated weight on the determining role of consciousness and agency, whilst failing to develop adequate analyses of (in their view) causally prior social and economic structures.[33] This whole debate can now seem rather dated. Not only has 'post-structuralism' posed a radical epistemological challenge to its basic tenets (see chapter 3), but even mainstream sociology has come to question the structure/agency dichotomy which underpinned earlier debates. Anthony Giddens' theory of 'structuration', and Pierre Bourdieu's concept of 'habitus' – perhaps the two most influential sociological theories of recent years – both seek to demonstrate the complex ways in which agency and structure are not just interdependent, but actually indivisible.[34] At the same time, a new generation of critics has found in Thompson not a hopeless idealism but a residual determinism[35] – though this can seem harsh in the light of Thompson's famous comments in the preface to *The making*:

The class experience is largely determined by the productive relations into which men are born – or enter involuntarily. Class-consciousness is the way in which these experiences are handled in cultural terms: embodied in traditions, value-systems, ideas, and institutional forms. If the experience appears as determined,

---

[32] See especially John Vincent, *Pollbooks: how Victorians voted* (Cambridge, 1967); Peter Clarke, *Lancashire and the New Liberalism* (Cambridge, 1971) and 'Electoral sociology of modern Britain', *History*, 57 (1972), pp. 31–55.

[33] See especially, Perry Anderson, 'Origins of the present crisis', *New Left Review*, 23 (1964), pp. 26–53, *Arguments within English Marxism* (London, 1980); Richard Johnson, 'Edward Thompson, Eugene Genovese and socialist humanist history', *History Workshop Journal*, 6 (1978), pp. 79–100, and the ill-tempered debate recorded in Raphael Samuel (ed.), *People's history and socialist theory* (London, 1981), pp. 375–408.

[34] See Anthony Giddens, *The constitution of society: outline of the theory of structuration* (Cambridge, 1986); Pierre Bourdieu, *Distinction: a social critique of the judgement of taste*, trans. Richard Nice (London, 1984), and *The logic of practice*, trans. Richard Nice (Cambridge, 1990). See also Philip Abrams, *Historical sociology* (Shepton Mallet, 1982), and Lynn Hunt (ed.), *The new cultural history* (Berkeley, Calif., 1989), esp. intro. and ch. 3, which highlights the prominence of similar themes in recent anthropological discourse.

[35] See especially William Sewell, 'How classes are made: critical reflections on E. P. Thompson's theory of working-class formation', in Harvey J. Kaye and K. McClelland (eds.), *E. P. Thompson: critical perspectives* (Cambridge, 1990).

class-consciousness does not. We can see a *logic* in the responses of similar occupational groups undergoing similar experiences, but we cannot predict any *law*.[36]

As this extract suggests, Thompson's analysis is organised largely around the concepts of 'experience' and 'consciousness'; for him 'class' should not be seen 'as a "structure", nor even as a "category", but as something which in fact happens (and can be shown to have happened) in human relationships'.[37] In other words, 'class' exists for Thompson only in action and in consciousness. Marx's distinction between 'class in-itself' and 'class for-itself', first outlined in *The poverty of philosophy* (1847), is thereby lost. Class is rooted, not in concrete 'relations of production', but in the 'experience' of those relations, and especially in collective responses to that experience. Class, in Thompson's hands, does appear to be an intensely subjective term – in essence it describes a specific form of cultural and political practice. There are strengths to this approach. In particular, it allows the historian to capture much of the fluidity of human relationships and of consciousness. But there are also weaknesses. The constraints on agency, the social forces outside an individual's control, play a backstage role in Thompson's histories. So too do those periods when the working class has *not* been engaged in dramatic forms of class struggle. And finally, so do all those workers who do not meet the required criteria of consciousness to be considered part of the 'class in action'. For by Thompson's definition class only 'happens' when 'some men, as a result of common experiences (inherited or shared), feel and articulate the identity of their interests as between themselves, and as against other men whose interests are different from (and usually opposed to) theirs'.[38] As this passage suggests, it is in his understanding of 'interests' that Thompson sometimes writes as a determinist. By positing the existence of objective interests, Thompson is able to make the connection between 'experience' and 'consciousness' appear unproblematic and more or less unmediated. The lessons learnt from 'experience' are dictated by objective interests rooted back in the relations of production, although Thompson is clear that cultural traditions will influence *how* these objective lessons are learnt.[39] Hence he insists that 'conscious-

---

[36] Thompson, *Making*, p. 9 (original emphasis).
[37] *Ibid.*, p. 8, the argument is reiterated in 'The peculiarities of the English', in E. P. Thompson, *The poverty of theory and other essays* (London, 1978), pp. 84–6.
[38] *Ibid.*, pp. 8–9; the argument was developed to its logical conclusion in E.P. Thompson, 'Eighteenth-century English society: class struggle without class?', *Social History*, 3 (1978), pp. 133–65.
[39] See Thompson, *The poverty of theory*, pp. 199–201. For critical assessments of this view of experience, see especially Suzanne Desan, 'Crowds, community and ritual in the work of E. P. Thompson and Natalie Davies', in Hunt (ed.), *New cultural history*, esp. pp. 54–5, and Joan Scott, 'The evidence of experience', *Critical Inquiry*, 17 (1991), pp. 773–97.

ness of class arises in the same way in different times and places, but never in just the same way'.[40]

In the 1970s historians attached to the Birmingham Centre for Contemporary Cultural Studies sought to chart a middle course between Thompson's 'culturalism' (as they described it) and the structuralism of his principal (Althusserian) Marxist critics.[41] Leaning heavily on Gramsci's later writings, the approach developed by the Birmingham School has much to recommend it – not least in its emphasis on the cultural heterogeneity to be found *within* different social classes. For instance, Richard Johnson argues:

> If there are features in the position of the 'labourer' that are common to a whole working class, there are a myriad of features which are not. These may always become objects of political practices seeking greater division or a unity. It follows that there can be no simple or 'expressive' relation between economic classes and cultural forms, and that we should start any such analysis by looking out for contradictions, taboos, displacements in a culture, as well as unities.[42]

However, the emphasis on 'displacement' and 'contradiction' here provide a clue to the limited nature of the Birmingham School's break with determinism. They may not wish to treat consciousness as an analogue of social being, but this does not mean abandoning the distinction between 'true' and 'false' consciousness derived from the Lenin/Lukacs tradition of Marxism. Following Gramsci, Richard Johnson argues that the 'lived impulse' of practical activity can be contradicted by 'verbal' conceptions from outside. In essence, the claim is that practical activity would necessarily produce 'true' class consciousness, were it not for the ability of ideologies to intercede between experience and consciousness – that is to operate within the very space that Thompson tends to deny given his approach to the relationship between popular culture and politics. Inherent in this Gramscian emphasis on 'ideological hegemony' is the danger that history will concentrate less on the reconstruction of past political cultures, than on explaining the non-development of 'true' or 'hegemonic' proletarian consciousness.[43]

---

[40] Thompson, *Making*, p. 9; see also Thompson, *The poverty of theory*, pp. 367–8, where Thompson does much to challenge the notion of 'objective interests' arguing that '[i]nterests are what interest people, including what interests them nearest to the heart'.

[41] On popular politics and culture, see especially Centre for Contemporary Cultural Studies, *Making histories*; Clarke et al., *Working-class culture*; and Mary Langan and Bill Schwarz (eds.), *Crises in the British state, 1880–1930* (London, 1985).

[42] Johnson, 'Three problematics', p. 235.

[43] For all its subtle qualifications and nuances this is ultimately the case in Robert Gray's 'Bourgeois hegemony in Victorian Britain', in Jon Bloomfield (ed.), *The Communist University of London: papers on class, hegemony and party* (London, 1977), pp. 73–93. For a more Stalinist treatment of these themes, see George Barnsby, 'Dictatorship of the bourgeoisie: social control in the nineteenth-century Black Country', *Our History*, pamphlet 55 (London, 1972).

IV

Turning now to the liberal historiography of the 1960s and 1970s, it is perhaps not surprising that, in seeking to explain the social bases of British politics, historians from this tradition turned, not to Marx or Gramsci, but to liberal social theorists such as Weber, Lipset and Dahrendorf, and to political scientists such as Butler, McKenzie and Rose who had pioneered the development of 'psephology'. Together these influences shaped what has become known as the 'electoral sociology' approach to British politics; an approach which, through the influential work of historians such as Peter Clarke, John Vincent, James Cornford and T. J. Nossiter, continues to inform much of our understanding of popular politics in Britain between 1832 and 1914.[44] In some respects this is surprising, since the theoretical assumptions underpinning 'electoral sociology' are no less reductionist than those underpinning most Marxist social histories. A reminder, perhaps, that much of the revisionism of the 1980s has been inspired more by political than theoretical shifts within academia.

Following the lead of post-war American theorists of political pluralism such as Berelson, Lazarsfeld and Lipset, the historians of 'electoral sociology' tend to portray party politics as an arena in which pre-existing interests are represented, and conflicts are reconciled.[45] The motivations of voters are therefore interpreted through a fairly simple model of rational self-interest which can be inferred from 'objective interests' and membership of discernible reference groups such as religious, occupational or ethnic communities. It is when trying to identify these voter interest-groups that liberal historians have generally turned to non-Marxist social theory. Perhaps the most influential and ambitious theoretical borrowings have been John Vincent's use of Dahrendorf, and his reconceptualisation of class in terms of group conflict over authority and power, and Peter

---

[44] For a fuller discussion of these themes see, Jon Lawrence and Miles Taylor, 'Electoral sociology and the historians', in their *Party, state and society*, and Jon Lawrence and Jane Elliott, 'Parliamentary election results reconsidered: an analysis of borough elections, 1885–1910', *Parliamentary History*, 16, 1 (1997), [E. H. H. Green (ed.), *An age of transition*], pp. 18–28. Key texts include: James Cornford, 'The transformation of Conservatism in the late nineteenth century', *Victorian Studies*, 7 (1963), pp. 35–66; Vincent, *Pollbooks*; Clarke, *Lancashire and the New Liberalism*; T. J. Nossiter, *Influence, opinion and political idioms in reformed England: case studies from the north-east* (Hassocks, 1975).

[45] Influential texts include Paul Lazarsfeld, Bernard Berelson and Hazel Gaudet, *The People's Choice: how the voter makes up his mind in a presidential campaign* (New York, 1944); Bernard Berelson, Paul Lazarsfeld and William McPhee, *Voting: a study of opinion formation in a presidential campaign* (Chicago, 1954); Seymour Lipset, *Political man: the social basis of politics* (London, 1960); Seymour Lipset and Stein Rokkan (eds.), *Party systems and voter alignments: cross-national perspectives* (New York, 1967), pp. 1–64 (introduction).

Clarke's use of the Weberian distinction between class, status and power. Significantly neither Vincent nor Clarke places theory at the heart of their major historical analyses. Instead, both produced separate theoretical essays which more or less coincided with the publication of their substantive political histories.[46] Following Dahrendorf in *Class and class conflict in industrial society* (1959), Vincent offers a radical reassessment of class analysis, arguing that 'classes are not primarily nor at all economic groupings'. Marxist and normative understandings of class are rejected in favour of an emphasis on class as, 'operational collectivities, acting at national level to achieve or prevent general changes in the structure of the political order (including the Church), and in a lesser degree, to change the kind of person in authority . . . an operational collectivity . . . corresponds to parts of various strata, themselves not operational units.'[47] The trouble with this brilliant analysis of participation in Victorian politics is that it is essentially an elaborately theorised description rather than an explanation. It is precisely the origins of Vincent's 'operational collectivities' that need to be explained. In effect, Vincent simply redefines 'class' so that it applies to groups with a shared political consciousness, and insists that consciousness is not derived primarily from economic interests. To be fair Vincent is conscious of this problem, but, by suggesting that economically constructed identities could give coherence to these collectivities, his solution to the problem threatens to make the theory itself seem redundant.[48] Similarly, his emphasis on the rise of materialist, class-based politics from the late nineteenth century might be thought to echo the traditional narratives of labour and social history – though for Vincent this development was largely fortuitous, rather than being the result of inevitable processes of social and economic change, and marked a *loss* of radicalism since, by his reading, questions about the distribution of power gave way to questions about the distribution of things.

Whereas Vincent sees the late nineteenth century as a period when economic definitions of class replaced more political ones, and equates this with the shift from Radical-Liberal to Labour politics, Clarke argues that the key shift occurred *within* Liberal politics as the 'status politics' of shared religious sentiment gave way to the 'class politics' of material interest. As Clarke explained in a letter to *History Workshop Journal* in

[46] John Vincent's essays in *Pollbooks* followed a year after *The formation of the Liberal Party, 1857–1868* (London, 1966). Peter Clarke's essay 'Electoral sociology of modern Britain' followed a year after *Lancashire and the New Liberalism*. For the theoretical claims of the latter study, see *ibid.*, pp. 14–19.

[47] Vincent, *Pollbooks*, pp. 28–9. It should be added that the argument here does not fit easily with the emphasis on the local genesis of popular Liberalism to be found in *The formation of the Liberal party* (see chapter 3).

[48] Vincent, *Pollbooks*, pp. 29–31; cf. Clarke, *Lancashire and the New Liberalism*, p. 16 (n4).

1978, his use of Weber was not intended to shift historical analysis from economic class to class as 'status strata'. On the contrary, he claimed, 'the shared values and style of life of status groups made them, on my reading, the basis of what I called communal politics or cultural politics, not of class politics'.[49] Indeed, the bed-rock of Clarke's analysis is this distinction between 'status politics' based on shared values and identities (of which religion is the prime example), and class politics based on objective material interests. As he explains in the article 'Electoral sociology of modern Britain', 'the old structure of status-based politics had been closely linked with the rivalries of local religious communities and had helped the Conservative party; whereas by 1910 Liberalism and Labour were working together within an essentially national framework to propagate a progressive programme with a class-based appeal.'[50] The assumption is clear: 'modern' politics are class politics, it was 'traditional' or 'pre-modern' politics which relied on Weberian 'status groups'. Indeed, in this influential discussion of the strengths of 'electoral sociology' Clarke observes that 'explanations in terms of class have a virtually universal application' in 'modern democracies'.[51] That said, in practice Clarke is less reductionist than most champions of 'electoral sociology', hence the central emphasis on the Liberal party's successful adaptation to forces of social and economic change in *Lancashire and the New Liberalism*. Clarke thus breaks with the narrowly 'expressive' view of parties characteristic of much political science literature in the 1960s, but still parties are credited only with the ability to respond to change, their creative role is narrowly circumscribed.[52] Indeed, an element of reductionism can also be identified in Clarke's treatment of 'pre-modern' or 'status' politics: we are told that 'the values which men hold – their normative beliefs – are, like the comparisons they make about their position, conditioned by the social structure'.[53] Clarke does make a gesture towards the complex, multidimensional nature of social identity when he acknowledges that 'one person might well have been a member, or at least a potential member, of more than one [reference] group', but he quickly dismisses this very real methodological difficulty by insisting that 'the extent to which a particular group is uppermost in a person's mind – the

---

[49] *History Workshop Journal*, 5 (Spring 1978), p. 220. Clarke was replying to Alun Howkins, 'Edwardian Liberalism and industrial unrest: a class view of the decline of Liberalism', *History Workshop Journal*, 4 (1977), pp. 143–61.

[50] Clarke, 'Electoral sociology', p. 51.   [51] *Ibid.*, p. 33.

[52] By the early 1980s Clarke was placing greater emphasis on ideology and the 'purchase' of political ideas over individuals and social groups, see Peter Clarke, 'Political history in the 1980s: ideas and interests', *Journal of Interdisciplinary History*, 12 (1981), pp. 45–8.

[53] Clarke, 'Electoral sociology', p. 41 – though undoubtedly 'conditioned' does not suggest strict determination.

salience of reference groups – is what is important'.[54] In effect we are asked to read the Victorian voter's mind in order to determine the vital factor of political motivation. This is a hopeless task, and underlines the explanatory weakness of electoral sociology as a tool of historical analysis.

Since the late 1970s social explanation has become increasingly unfashionable with historians of modern British politics. Among liberal scholars there has been a general shift of focus away from 'popular' to 'high' politics, probably reflecting in part criticism of the excessively society-centred perspective of 'electoral sociology' from within political science, as well as a more general reaction to apparent class de-alignment in contemporary politics.[55] At the same time the more radical advocates of 'history from below' have been moving away from traditional forms of class analysis under the combined influence of feminist theory, post-structuralism, and a diffuse, but all-pervasive, socialist-pessimism. And yet whilst the confidence in social explanation which characterised both 'electoral sociology' and 'history from below' in the 1960s has waned, the basic narrative of the 'rise of class politics' remains largely unchallenged within mainstream political historiography. For instance, John Turner's brief sketch of pre-war party politics at the beginning of *The Great War and British politics* (1992) relies heavily on traditional arguments about the relationship between structural and political change to sustain its conclusion that by 1914 British politics 'had gone a great deal of the way' to being 'completely assimilated to a class-based political structure'.[56] Perhaps more surprisingly, Patrick Joyce's major revisionist study of English popular politics, *Visions of the People* (1991), also retains most of the central elements of the traditional narrative of the 'rise of class politics', though Joyce shifts the chronology of change so that the breakthrough to 'class politics' only occurs after the First World War.[57]

---

[54] *Ibid.*, p. 42.
[55] Key works in the political and social sciences include, Bo Sarvlik and Ivor Crewe, *Decade of dealignment: the Conservative victory of 1979 and electoral trends in the 1970s* (Cambridge, 1983); A. Heath, R. Jowell and J. Curtice, *How Britain votes* (Oxford, 1985); P. Dunleavy and T. Husbands, *British democracy at the crossroads: voting and party competition in the 1980s* (London, 1985); and Patrick Dunleavy, *Democracy, bureaucracy and public choice: economic explanations in political science* (New York, 1991). In many respects though, the shift away from 'popular' politics among liberal historians predates these developments, see especially A. B. Cooke and John Vincent, *The governing passion: Cabinet Government and party politics in Britain, 1885–86* (Brighton, 1974) and Peter Clarke, *Liberals and social democrats* (Cambridge, 1978).
[56] Turner, *The Great War and British politics*, p. 36, and more generally pp. 25–37. Despite Turner's cryptic formulation that 'political outcomes seem to become intelligible only if the determining effect of long-term social change is interpreted in the light of short-term political and economic expedients' (p. 10) he is in fact heavily reliant on orthodox structural explanations throughout this section.
[57] For instance, Joyce, *Visions of the people*, pp. 4, 6, 9, 19, 140, 314, 329, 336, 342 (see below, chapter 3).

Thus whilst 'revisionist' historians such as Joyce may appear to play down, or even deny, the utility of 'class' for studies of nineteenth-century popular politics, they have done little to challenge the idea of 'the rise of class politics' between the 1880s and 1920s. Nor have 'revisionist' historians shown much inclination to challenge the empirical findings which underpin the argument that rapid economic and social change led to a major disjuncture in the development of British popular politics at the end of the nineteenth century. This reluctance to engage with debates about the nature of social and economic change is probably inevitable given the epistemological standpoint of 'revisionist' historians, but it is nonetheless unfortunate. Before moving on to consider the historiographical significance of recent 'revisionist' approaches in chapter 3, I therefore propose to take a detour by reopening the debate about the nature, and the political significance, of late Victorian and Edwardian social and cultural change. In particular I wish to explore the central question of whether, from the 1870s onwards, one can talk of the emergence of a new, more socially and culturally homogeneous urban working class.

2 Working-class homogeneity reconsidered

I

Historians have identified three main aspects of social change which contributed to making Britain a more class divided and class conscious society between 1870 and 1914: the erosion of artisanal independence in the workplace, the growth of residential segregation by class, and the growth of cultural homogeneity within the urban working class. These themes were systematically explored in a series of major studies of working-class Victorian society published during the 1970s.[1] Since then, though not uncriticised, the approach has been strongly defended and developed, first by Eric Hobsbawm in his influential collection of essays *Worlds of labour* (1984), and more recently by Mike Savage and Andrew Miles in *The remaking of the British working class*.[2] This emphasis on the structural transformation of the British working class after 1870 is examined at length in the present chapter because it remains central to the whole notion of 'the rise of class' in modern British politics. We need to ask both how strong *were* trends towards working-class homogenisation during this period, and, what were the political implications of any social changes that did occur?

II

There have been many attempts, not always complimentary, to link the decline of artisanal independence in the workplace to shifts in working-

---

[1] See especially, Gareth Stedman Jones, 'Working-class culture and working-class politics in London, 1870–1900: notes on the remaking of the working class', *Journal of Social History*, 7 (1974), pp. 460–508; Ross McKibbin, *The evolution of the Labour party, 1910–1924* (Oxford, 1974); Robert Gray, *The labour aristocracy in Victorian Edinburgh* (Oxford, 1976); Geoffrey Crossick, *An artisan élite in Victorian society: Kentish London, 1840–1880* (London, 1978); Crossick (ed.), *The lower middle class in Britain, 1870–1914* (London, 1977); Richard Price, *Masters, unions and men: workers' control in building and the rise of labour* (Cambridge, 1980).

[2] Eric Hobsbawm, *Worlds of labour: further studies in the history of labour* (London, 1984), esp. chs. 10–14; Mike Savage and Andrew Miles, *The remaking of the British working class, 1840–1940* (Historical Connections Series) (London, 1994). For criticism of Hobsbawm's approach, see Alastair Reid, 'Class and organization', *Historical Journal*, 30 (1987), pp. 225–38, and Andrew Davies, *Leisure, gender and poverty: working-class culture in Salford and Manchester, 1900–1939* (Buckingham, 1992), pp. 169–70.

class politics. In the 1970s Gareth Stedman Jones suggested that a shift from the 'formal' to the 'real' subordination of wage labour to capital may have been a key factor undermining the working-class militancy of the early nineteenth century, and that the decline of artisans' workplace culture may have had a similar effect in London at the end of the century.[3] In their studies of the so-called 'labour aristocracy' Crossick and Gray both portray the threat to craft skills as a major factor radicalising artisans as they were pushed back into the massed ranks of the manual working class, while according to Richard Price the erosion of workers' informal controls over the work process was equally radicalising in the later nineteenth century.[4] In recent years there has been a sustained critique of these arguments. Not only have historians challenged the value of the 'labour aristocracy' as a tool of analysis,[5] they have also increasingly questioned whether 'de-skilling' and the loss of job control were in fact significant features of British industry before the First World War. Historians such as Jonathan Zeitlin and Alastair Reid have argued that strong trade unions were often able to manage the introduction of new technologies in ways which preserved job control and even strengthened the position of skilled workers and their unions.[6]

In their recent restatement of the structuralist position Savage and Miles largely accept the force of empirical and theoretical criticism of the 'de-skilling' argument, and choose instead to place the weight of their

[3] Gareth Stedman Jones, 'Class struggle and the industrial revolution', *New Left Review*, 90 (1975), pp. 35–69; and 'Working class culture'; both essays are reproduced in his *Languages of class: studies in English working-class history, 1832–1982* (Cambridge, 1983), pp. 25–75 and 179–238.

[4] On the 'de-skilling' of craft-workers, see Gray, *Labour aristocracy*, pp. 165–83; Crossick, *An artisan elite*, pp. 248–9; Hobsbawm, *Labouring men*, pp. 324–5, and *Worlds of labour*, pp. 198, 206, 266–7. On job control, see Price, *Masters, union and men*.

[5] See especially H. F. Moorhouse, 'The Marxist theory of the labour aristocracy', *Social History*, 3 (1978), pp. 61–82; Alastair Reid, 'Politics and economics in the formation of the British working class: a response to Moorhouse', *Social History*, 3 (1978); and 'Intelligent artisans and aristocrats of labour: the essays of Thomas Wright', in Jay Winter (ed.), *The working class in modern British history: essays in honour of Henry Pelling* (Cambridge, 1983). Robert Gray, *The aristocracy of labour in nineteenth-century Britain, c. 1850–1914* (Basingstoke, 1981) registers many of the earlier criticisms.

[6] See Alastair Reid, 'Politics and the division of labour, 1880–1920', and Jonathan Zeitlin, 'Industrial structure, employer strategy and the diffusion of job control in Britain, 1850–1920' both in W. Mommsen and H. Husung (eds.), *The development of trade unionism in Britain and Germany* (London, 1985); Zeitlin, 'Craft control and the division of labour: engineers and compositors in Britain, 1880–1930', *Cambridge Journal of Economics*, 3 (1979), pp. 263–74; Royden Harrison and Jonathan Zeitlin (eds.), *Divisions of labour: skilled workers and technological change in nineteenth-century England* (Brighton, 1985), esp. chs. 5 & 6; and Reid, 'Employers' strategies and craft production: the British shipbuilding industry, 1870–1950', in Steven Tolliday and Jonathan Zeitlin (eds.), *The power to manage? Employers and industrial relations in comparative historical perspective* (London, 1991). Also Charles More, *Skill and the English working class, 1870–1914* (London, 1980), and Stephen Wood (ed.), *The degradation of work? Skill, deskilling and the labour process* (London, 1982), esp. chs by More and Penn.

argument on more general labour market changes which threatened working-class independence and led to the demand for independent political action to protect (male) workers' rights.[7] A key theme of their argument is the growing bureaucratisation of labour markets, which tended to weaken workers' control over both hiring and promotion. They also argue that from the 1880s employers in many sectors of industry became increasingly willing to employ women and boys in preference to adult males in order to force down unit labour costs.[8] There are, however, problems with this line of argument. Firstly, where the employment of women and boys did increase, this was not necessarily at the expense of skilled male labour, and was in any case often accompanied by an extension of trade unionism among the new workers, so that overall organisation may actually have improved.[9] Secondly, there is little reason to accept their argument that labour market changes worked to reduce the distinctions between skilled and unskilled labour. On the contrary, as a result of the experience of wartime 'dilution' policies, and the perceived injustice of both the Trade Card scheme and the Restoration of Pre-War Practices Act, British trade unions emerged from the First World War more bitterly divided than ever before.[10] In 1919, John Beard, president of the Workers' Union, was denouncing Labour for upholding 'the narrow outlook of craft unionism', which he argued amounted to telling the labourer 'get back to your place, dog'.[11] Finally, the great reluctance of private employers to introduce women workers on to new industrial processes throughout the First World War, despite the acute shortages of skilled male labour, suggests that customary ideas about gender roles may well have been more powerful than the urge for profit-maximisation.[12] In this

[7] Savage and Miles, *The remaking*, ch. 3.   [8] *Ibid.*, pp. 50–1.

[9] See Alan Fox, *A history of the National Union of Boot and Shoe Operatives, 1874–1957* (Oxford, 1958), pp. 306–21; for local examples of successful union incorporation of women and youths see, *[Wolverhampton] Express and Star*, 7 February 1896; *The Wolverhampton Chronicle*, 28 February 1906, 11 October and 6 December 1911.

[10] See Trevor Wilson, *The myriad faces of war: Britain and the Great War, 1914–1918* (Cambridge, 1986), pp. 526–7 on the divisiveness of union influence over conscription; Iain McLean, *The legend of red Clydeside* (Edinburgh, 1983); James Hinton, *The first shop stewards' movement* (London, 1973).

[11] *The Workers' Union Record*, October 1919; the union was later involved in a protracted and bitter dispute with the Ironfounders' society which had called a strike to prevent members of general unions from working on 'skilled' processes, see *ibid.*, December 1919, February and March 1920; *The Monthly Journal of Gas, Municipal and General Workers*, December 1919 and January and February 1920. For general context see Richard Hyman, *The Workers' Union* (Oxford, 1971), pp. 121–7.

[12] See especially Deborah Thom, 'Women's employment in wartime Britain', in Richard Wall and Jay Winter (eds.), *The upheaval of war: family, work and welfare in Europe, 1914–1918* (Cambridge, 1988); Alastair Reid, 'Dilution, trade unionism and the state', in S. Tolliday and J. Zeitlin (eds.), *Shop floor bargaining and the state* (Cambridge, 1985); Gail Braybon, *Women workers in the First World War* (Routledge reprint, London, 1989), pp. 82–90.

respect it is tempting to conclude that, despite their stated opposition to the 'linguistic turn' taken by many historians in recent years, Savage and Miles have themselves tended to misread the rhetorical strategies of some labour leaders for a faithful description of employer strategy. Or perhaps it is simply that their *a priori* model of employer behaviour (to 'reduce their insecurity by making profits, which they do by exploiting workers') stands in for any serious analysis of labour market strategies before, during and after the First World War.[13]

III

Historians keen to stress the growing homogeneity of the manual working class in the early twentieth century, have often placed particular emphasis on patterns of residence – arguing that from the 1880s the flight of the urban middle classes out to the new suburbs, meant that Britain's towns and cities became dominated by increasingly cohesive and homogeneous working-class communities. These communities, it is suggested, were no longer subject to the social and political influence of middle-class elites, and became instead the core areas for the growth of the new labour politics.[14] Again Savage and Miles have recently restated these arguments, arguing that the period 1880–1920 saw 'the rise of the working-class neighbourhood' as Britain's industrial cities became 'increasingly defined as working-class spaces'.[15] Savage and Miles offer a sophisticated account of urban change around the turn of the century, stressing in particular that it was during this period that Britain's cities began to become more stable social environments as migration slowed and households tended to move less frequently (especially after the introduction of controlled rents in 1915). In the end, however, they exaggerate the growth of social segregation before the First World War in a number of respects. Firstly, migration to the suburbs was by no means a uniquely middle-class phenomenon, either in London or in the provinces. Secondly, there is at least as much evidence of intra-class as inter-class residential segregation, with the poorest districts often denuded of better-paid manual workers whilst they still retained their small middle-class 'elite' of shopkeepers and publicans. Such areas might be termed 'working-class neighbourhoods' in the sense that they were populated overwhelmingly by manual workers, but this can easily obscure processes of residential segregation between different groups of manual workers. Finally, since non-residence had not proved an insuperable barrier to social and political influence in the nineteenth

---

[13] Savage and Miles, *The remaking*, p. 20.
[14] For instance, see Crossick (ed.), *The lower middle class*, pp. 48–51; Hobsbawm, *Worlds of Labour*, pp. 204–7; Gray, *The labour aristocracy*, pp. 18 and 169.
[15] Savage and Miles, *The remaking*, pp. 62–72.

century, either for the gentry or the new industrial and commercial elites,[16] it is hard to see why 'physical withdrawal' should be given such explanatory weight in the later period – here their argument needs a great deal more elaboration.

Clearly it is important to develop a strong understanding of the changing character of urban life in order to understand urban politics. It does matter that in the 1900s most politicians were mainly addressing second, third or fourth generation natives of their local communities, rather than recent migrants. It also matters that by the late nineteenth century subordinate urban groups had much greater scope for engaging in sustained and independent political activity than their forebears earlier in the century. Here, the growth of formal organisations, the spread of literacy, the extension of leisure time and the removal of some formal barriers to political activism (such as property qualifications for urban councils) were all important. Such changes necessarily altered the relationship between politicians and the public, even if population shifts were not simultaneously creating new single-class communities of working-class 'urbanites' and middle-class 'suburbanites'. Unfortunately, our knowledge of early twentieth-century patterns of residence is relatively weak, and is likely to remain so until the relevant census returns become available for historical analysis.[17] To fill this gap in our understanding historians have often turned to the detailed reports of the Board of Trade's 1908 inquiry into the cost of living of the working classes.[18] In all investigators reported on 131 urban communities, paying considerable attention to patterns of residence by house-type (number of rooms, facilities etc.)

[16] See Richard Trainor, *Black country élites: the exercise of authority in an industrialized area, 1830–1900* (Oxford, 1993); David Cannadine, *Lords and landlords: the aristocracy and the towns, 1774–1967* (Leicester, 1980); and John Garrard, *Leadership and power in Victorian industrial towns, 1830–80* (Manchester, 1983), pp. 86–90, 215–17 on the strong links between many wealthy Salford residents and Manchester politics. For a contemporary account of the social influence that an absentee employer's family could seek to wield, see Lady Florence Bell, *At the works: a study of a manufacturing town* (London, 1907). The Bells lived first at Redcar, and then yet further from their Middlesbrough steel plants at Northallerton.

[17] On the nineteenth-century census, see E. A. Wrigley (ed.), *Nineteenth-century society: essays in the use of quantitative methods for the study of social data* (Cambridge, 1972); R. Lawton (ed.), *The census and social structure: an interpretative guide to nineteenth-century censuses for England and Wales* (London, 1978); Edward Higgs, *Making sense of the census: the manuscript returns for England and Wales, 1801–1901* (HMSO, London, 1989). Also the analyses in chapter 6 below.

[18] Board of Trade, *Report of an Enquiry by the Board of Trade into Working-Class Rents, Housing and Retail Prices and Standard Rates of Wages in the United Kingdom* (PP1908, Cd.3864, vol. CVII) – hereafter cited as *Cost of Living*; cited in Crossick (ed.), *Lower middle class in Britain*, pp. 50–1; Hobsbawm, *Worlds of labour*, p. 205. For a discussion of the report's historical significance, see E. P. Hennock, 'The measurement of urban poverty: from the metropolis to the nation', *Economic History Review*, 2nd ser., 40 (1987), pp. 208–27.

and by district. There are, however, a number of problems with the report as a source for social historians. For one thing, the survey is by no means exhaustive – important towns such as West Bromwich, Brighton, the Rhondda and West Hartlepool were never visited, while smaller and less industrial towns such as Taunton and Chester were included.[19] More seriously, it is far from clear that investigators shared a common understanding of who 'the working classes' actually were. On the whole, reports tend to adopt the dominant normative usage, treating only manual workers as 'working class' – so that the residential patterns of foremen and clerks are discussed separately. However, some reports seem to adopt a much more inclusive definition, at least when assessing the overall social character of a community. For instance, the report says of East Ham that 'the whole of the borough is working class in general character', even though the 1901 census suggests that almost 30 per cent of the adult male population were employed in clerical, professional or commercial occupations.[20] Interestingly, the investigator's assessment of the 'character' of this district seems to be based on its low proportion of indoor servants – in other words, the reference point is the equation of servant-keeping with 'the middle class proper', a definition of social class that was also deployed in contemporary social surveys such as Rowntree's *Poverty: a study of town life*.[21]

For all its short-comings, the Board of Trade report none the less offers important insights into the residential patterns of Edwardian Britain. It suggests a great deal of variation between communities in terms both of the quality of housing and the patterns of occupancy. An analysis of the 115 reports on Welsh and English urban areas does not provide substantial support for the existence of monolithic one-class communities by the 1900s – except on the most local scale. Only in London and its immediate environs does social homogeneity appear to

[19] The Registrar General estimated the population of these boroughs in mid-1905 as Brighton 127,183; Rhondda 124,988; West Hartlepool 71,313; West Bromwich 67,823, compared with Chester 38,966 and Taunton 22,073 (General Register Office [Great Britain], *Quarterly Return for Marriages, Births and Deaths, 1905* (HMSO, London), part 2, pp. xiv–xxiv).

[20] Out of a male workforce of 27,926, 8,250 (29.5 per cent) were returned in professional and commercial categories – including 2,821 'dealers' – most would have been small traders, see *Census of England and Wales, 1901*, PP1902, Cd.1148, vol. CXVIII *(County of Essex)*, pp. 68–9.

[21] See B. Seebohm Rowntree, *Poverty: a study of town life* (London, 1901), pp. xi and 14. Also Charles Booth, *Labour and life of the people*, 2 vols. + App. (3rd edn., London, 1891), I, 'East London', p. 60 where servant-keeping defines Class H, the 'upper middle class'. It is interesting and important to note that of 38,468 people living in households headed by a clerk or 'company agent' Booth classified only 21.8 per cent as either lower or upper middle class (Classes G & H); he considered 8.2 per cent to be 'poor' or 'very poor' (Classes B, C & D) – and the remainder (70.1 per cent) to be part of Classes E & F – his regular and better-paid wage-earning class; *ibid.*, pp. 34–5 (table I).

have become the norm by this date, which is perhaps rather ironic given how weak Labour remained in the capital before the First World War.[22] In all, 22 of the 115 local reports (or 19 per cent) refer to some degree of clear physical segregation between manual and non-manual workers, either by street or by district. All but four of these districts are in Greater London – the exceptions being Halifax, Luton, Middlesbrough and Plymouth. In only three cases (Leyton, Luton and Middlesbrough) does a local report suggest that there is more than a *tendency* for manual and non-manual workers to live physically apart – in different parts of the town or borough. A further eight reports make no mention of manual/non-manual segregation, but suggest that the wealthy lived apart in exclusive residential areas.[23] On the other hand, fourteen reports (12 per cent) refer either to working-class housing being scattered through-out the borough, or to significant working-class migration to the new suburbs. There is no obvious pattern in this group – London boroughs, provincial cities and small county towns are all included. It is perhaps significant, however, that the eight examples citing significant working-class migration to the suburbs all come from the provinces (Birmingham, Bristol, Chester, Coventry, Manchester & Salford, Nottingham, Southampton and Worcester).[24] Finally, nineteen reports (16 per cent) refer to some degree of physical segregation between skilled and unskilled workers, or between artisans and 'the poor'. Again provincial towns and cities predominate, with local reports suggesting rigid residential segregation *within* the working class in nine urban areas including Cardiff, Coventry, Crewe, Newport, Wolverhampton and York. In contrast only two of the forty-three metropolitan reports suggest such intra-class segregation.[25]

[22] The ten Scottish towns and cities covered in the report have been excluded from the following analysis because of the very different character of the housing stock north of the border, and the distinctive patterns of residence. As the report comments, '[t]here is little in common between working-class houses in Scotland and those in England', *Cost of Living*, p. xx (see also pp. 509–10). The six reports on Irish towns and cities have also been excluded. On London politics, see John Davis, 'Radical clubs and London politics, 1870–1900', in David Feldman and Gareth Stedman Jones (eds.), *Metropolis: London histories and representations since 1800* (London, 1989); Stedman Jones, 'Working-class culture'; Paul Thompson, *Socialists, Liberals and Labour: the struggles for London, 1885–1914* (London, 1967).

[23] These are Paddington, East Ham, Keighley, Manchester & Salford, Sheffield, Stockton, Warrington and Wolverhampton – only one report (Enfield) makes explicit reference to wealthy residents being scattered across the urban area. This pattern must have been very unusual by the early twentieth century.

[24] In addition, eight local reports record working-class housing being scattered throughout the town or borough: Fulham, Lewisham, Wandsworth, Kidderminster, Macclesfield, Southampton, Wigan and Worcester.

[25] Bermondsey and Poplar – though in both cases the report suggests that intra-class segregation was the rule, rather than merely a general tendency.

More difficult to interpret is the information on the pattern of occupation by house-*type* (i.e. house size or style) rather than by geographical location (i.e. district or street). In all, the Board of Trade inquiry identifies twenty-eight urban areas (24 per cent of the total) where the best type of popular house (usually with five or six rooms) tended to be occupied exclusively or mainly by 'clerks, foremen, insurance agents, shop assistants &c'.[26] Although only two reports, those for Leyton and Luton, suggest rigid segregation by house-type. On the other hand, seventeen local reports (15 per cent) suggest that artisans and clerks occupied such houses indiscriminately. Nor was this true only in 'smaller industrial towns' as Crossick suggests; the reports for East Ham, Birkenhead, Manchester & Salford, Newcastle, Portsmouth and Sheffield all record this pattern of occupancy.[27] At the same time thirty-two reports (28 per cent) record that the skilled and the unskilled, or artisans and 'the poor', tended to occupy different types of houses, at different rents.[28] Again the sample is overwhelmingly provincial, with a strong bias towards industrial towns such as Coventry, Derby, Rochdale and Wolverhampton, rather than the large conurbations. Only seven reports talk explicitly of different sections of the working class occupying the same types of houses – although these examples (Walthamstow, Grimsby, Norwich, Nottingham, Portsmouth, Preston and Stockport) are widely dispersed and important.

Accounts of segregation by house-type present two main problems of interpretation. Firstly, houses of different types were often constructed in the same street or even side by side. In Stockton terraces consisted of alternate four- and five-bedroom houses, while on Tyneside, where the 'cottage flat' predominated, first-floor flats were often larger and more desirable than those on the ground floor.[29] In Gateshead first-floor flats with attic bedrooms were often rented by 'clerks, shop assistants and workers of similar social position' – who therefore lived quite literally on

---

[26] From the local report on Birmingham, *Cost of Living*, p. 85.

[27] Crossick (ed.), *The lower middle class in Britain*, p. 50. Crossick also suggests that 'the artisan areas of Wolverhampton spread to the east, while tradesmen and clerks followed the substantial middle classes to the western outskirts' (*ibid.*, p. 51). The report on Wolverhampton actually states that 'Wolverhampton has a "west end" and an "east end", and though the artisan population of the town *occupies houses in both districts*, the majority live in the east end' (emphasis added). Indeed, if anything the exclusivity of the 'west end' was declining in the 1900s as trams and buses opened up development in this previously exclusive middle-class enclave. On mid-century segregation in the town see Mark Shaw, 'The ecology of social change: Wolverhampton, 1851–1871', *Transactions of the Institute of British Geographers*, new ser., 2 (1977), pp. 332–48.

[28] In twelve cases, including Enfield, Cardiff, Derby, Stoke, Wolverhampton and Worcester this is presented as a rigid segregation within the working class.

[29] *Cost of Living*, p. 437 for Stockton. For other examples of mixed urban morphology see the local reports on Chester (p. 156), Halifax (p. 211) and Hanley (p. 218).

top of the manual working class.[30] Even new developments often included houses of different sizes – the reports for Hull, Nottingham and Taunton note that houses were still being built with four as well as six rooms, while the housing stock of suburban Birmingham is also described as very varied.[31] It is therefore difficult to accept Hobsbawm's argument that 'since the better housing was commonly the more recent housing, we may reasonably suppose that segregation was increasing' – especially since he himself acknowledges that nearly as many local reports record the better type of popular house 'being inhabited indifferently by "artisans, clerks, insurance agents, shopmen and the like"' as record a tendency for non-manual workers to predominate.[32] One might also mention that several local reports, including those for Croydon, Southampton and Tottenham, suggest that it was common for less affluent workers to become tenants of large six-room houses in order to sub-let part of the house to others.[33]

Secondly, when interpreting information about segregation by house-type we need to recognise that often differential patterns of occupancy may simply reflect differential incomes, since better houses usually commanded a higher rental (other things being equal).[34] Income is cited as the major factor determining choice of housing in many reports, and appears to have accounted for a large part of both intra-class and inter-class differentiation in patterns of occupancy. In Tottenham, six-room houses were occupied by clerks, 'or by artisans with families including supplemental earners', in Macclesfield new five-room houses were mainly occupied by families 'in which the children are old enough to become wage-earners'.[35] But, if differentiation by house-type frequently involved neither physical separation, nor a conscious desire to underscore class distinctions through symbols of status, it should be clear that it can hardly be mobilised as a major factor underpinning a thesis of social

[30] *Ibid.*, p. 192 (ground-floor flats had only three rooms) – this occupancy pattern also occurred in parts of Newcastle. In contrast Owen, in *The ragged-trousered philanthropists*, lives in the attic flat of an otherwise middle-class block – and is said to be ostracised by the other tenants, see the Panther edn. (1965), pp. 75–77.

[31] *Cost of Living*, pp. 85 (Birmingham), 231 (Hull), 352 (Nottingham), and 465 (Taunton).

[32] Hobsbawm, *Worlds of labour*, p. 205.

[33] *Cost of Living*, pp. 54–5 (Tottenham), 150 (Chatham & Gillingham), 172 (Croydon), 418 (Southampton).

[34] Although good central accommodation could often command a higher rental than larger properties in the suburbs – especially where there was great demand for proximity to employment in the central district, for instance see the local report on Halifax, *ibid.*, p. 211.

[35] *Ibid.*, pp. 54–5 (Tottenham), 290 (Macclesfield). See also the report on Preston, where relatively high female earnings helped to blur social differentiation in patterns of residence (pp. 382–3). Other reports explaining residence patterns explicitly in terms of income differentials include Northampton (p. 339), South Shields (p. 425), and Sunderland (p. 450).

segregation and increased residential homogeneity within the working class. Moreover, since only four out of seventy-two non-metropolitan reports identify even a *tendency* for manual and non-manual workers to live physically apart (either by street or by district), we must surely conclude that outside London there is very little to support arguments about 'the rise of the working-class neighbourhood' before the First World War. With at least as much evidence of intra-class as inter-class segregation (again outside London), one might even argue that processes of out-migration were denuding the older, central districts of their working-class 'elite' (including trade union officials, co-operators, political activists and the like) rather than their middle-class elite of shopkeepers and publicans (for whom mobility was often constrained by the need to maintain good relations with their local customers).[36] The study of the geography of labour activism in pre-war Wolverhampton (chapter 6) certainly supports this hypothesis – only 14 per cent of Labour and trade union leaders were found to live in the old, central wards of the town in the pre-war period.[37]

IV

Finally, proponents of socio-structural explanations of the rise of Labour have often stressed the growth of distinctive class cultures among manual and non-manual workers at the close of the nineteenth century. Once again it is argued that skilled artisans found themselves forced back into the working class – this time by the growing snobbishness and social exclusivity of the expanding 'salariat' on the one hand, and the growth of a mass leisure culture within the working class on the other.[38] Geoffrey Crossick has probably pushed speculation about the social and political significance of the growth of clerical employment further than most historians by arguing that

> the emergence of a distinctive white-collar stratum, earning little, if any more than the better-paid workers, but priding itself on its salaried and non-manual status, was an explicit threat to labour aristocrats ... rejection of these aristocrats by an increasingly numerous and self-conscious lower middle class may be seen as a factor pushing them back into the working class.[39]

[36] See Robert Roberts, *The classic slum: Salford life in the first quarter of the century* (Pelican edn, London, 1973), p. 15; and *A ragged schooling: growing up in the classic slum* (Fontana edn, London, 1978), pp. 11, 15–23, 188–9.

[37] For a discussion of the political consequences of plebeian activists abandoning over-crowded central districts for the suburbs, see Ernest Benn, *Happier days: recollections and reflections* (London, 1949), p. 38, where he notes that the Radical Association in St George's-in-the East and Wapping lost all its officials to migration within a single year.

[38] For examples, see Hobsbawm, *Worlds of labour*, pp. 184–5; 194–213; Gray, *The labour aristocracy*, pp. 116–18; Crossick, *An artisan elite*, pp. 248–9; and *Lower middle class*, pp. 12–13 and 48–53; and Stedman Jones, *Languages of class*, esp. p. 228n ('Working-class culture').

[39] Crossick, *An artisan elite*, p. 249.

But manual workers, including the so-called 'labour aristocrats', had long resented the social pretensions of sections of the lower middle class. In 1867 Thomas Wright, the 'journeyman engineer' from south-east London, was denouncing 'the snobby, genteel kind of person who, with the manners and education of an underbred counter-skipper, and an income less than a good mechanic, sacrifices comfort and honesty to keep up appearances.'[40] While a year later he was arguing that the idea of 'the Great Unwashed', as he called his second collection of essays on working-class life,

exactly embodies the working-class idea of themselves, excluding, as it does, not only the 'counter-skipper' class, whom the great unwashed regard (unjustly perhaps) as their inferiors, but also professional men, merchants, M.P.'s, and others who, though claiming to be, and in the literal sense really being, working men, are by the unwashed looked upon as 'swells'.[41]

Significantly Wright does not exclude the small master from his definition of 'the working classes', for in Victorian Britain it was generally the performance of manual labour, rather than selling one's labour power, which defined one's status as 'working class'.[42] That said, many unions certainly saw the divide between 'masters' and 'men' as decisive in labour matters – for instance Martin Haddow, the Glasgow socialist, recalls being rejected as the Electrical Union's delegate to the local Trades Council because he had recently set himself up as a 'wee cork' (a small employer).[43]

It would be wrong, therefore, to suggest, either that relations between manual and non-manual workers were free from social tensions in late Victorian Britain, or that such class antagonisms were of no political significance. However, we should be sceptical about attempts to assert a direct link between evidence of inter-class tension and the emergence of independent Labour politics in the late nineteenth century. Not only had social tensions long existed, but they could be as strong in areas where Labour politics were weak or non-existent, as where they were strong. Indeed, as historians are increasingly beginning to recognise, Liberal and Conservative politics, at least in their more populist variants, had been saturated with 'languages of class' more or less throughout the nineteenth

[40] A Journeyman Engineer [Thomas Wright], *Some habits and customs of the working classes* (London, 1867), p. vii – a tension acknowledged by Crossick in *The lower middle class*, p. 37. See also F. M. Leventhal, *Respectable Radical: George Howell and Victorian working-class politics* (London, 1971), p. 17.

[41] The Journeyman Engineer [Thomas Wright], *The Great Unwashed* (London, 1868), p. viii.

[42] See Paul de Rousiers, *The labour question in Britain*, trans. F. L. D. Herbertson (London 1896), pp. 4–10.

[43] William Martin Haddow, *My seventy years* (Glasgow, 1943), p. 29 – Haddow had been the founder of the Glasgow Electrical Union.

century. To be fair, these languages of class were highly gendered, focusing, as they did, on contested conceptions of the putative virtues of the independent working-*man*,[44] but they were also constructed around a whole series of assumptions about the meaning of manual labour – about the peculiar qualities of the newly-enfranchised 'horny-handed sons of toil', to use just one of the well-worn clichés of late nineteenth-century party politics.[45] On the other hand, evidence suggests that many early socialist and labour activists were either themselves lower middle class,[46] or were keen to emphasise the classless nature of their political programme. In good Gladstonian style, most saw themselves as engaged in the battle of the 'masses against the classes', rather than in the class war.[47]

Historians have also made much of the emergence of a more homogeneous and solidaristic working-class culture after 1880 – the corollary in part of the supposed growth of more homogeneous working-class communities. Gareth Stedman Jones and Ross McKibbin portray this culture as essentially conservative, defensive and inward-looking, and see its characteristics as reproduced in the politics of the emergent Labour party.[48] Others have been more cautious about assuming a direct relationship between popular culture and politics, and have preferred simply to stress the political consequences of a heightened sense of working-class social and cultural distinctiveness.[49] For instance Robert Gray argues that 'whereas the artisan leisure pursuits of the third quarter of the century

[44] See Jon Lawrence, 'Class and gender in the making of urban Toryism, 1880–1914', *English Historical Review*, 108 (1993), pp. 629–52, and Keith McClelland, 'Some thoughts on masculinity and the "representative artisan" in Britain, 1850–1880', *Gender & History*, 1 (1989), pp. 164–77.

[45] For an example of conservative hostility to this 'perilous superstition', see 'The programme of the Radicals', *Quarterly Review*, 135 (1873), pp. 543–4, which claims that after 1871 few would now question 'the dangers of implicitly trusting masses'.

[46] See below, chapter 6 for a discussion of the prominence of clerks, shopkeepers and even professional workers in pre-war Labour politics at Wolverhampton. See also J. Keir Hardie, *My confession of faith in the Labour Alliance* (London, nd [1909]), pp. 7–8; Alastair Reid, 'Glasgow socialism', *Social History*, 11 (1986), pp. 89–97; Deian Hopkin, 'The membership of the Independent Labour Party, 1904–10: a spatial and occupational analysis', *International Review of Social History*, 20 (1975), pp. 175–97; and Carl Levy, 'Education and self-education: staffing the early ILP', in Levy (ed.), *Socialism and the intelligentsia, 1880–1914* (London, 1987).

[47] For instance, see Ramsay MacDonald, *Socialism and government*, 2 vols. (London, 1909), I, p. xxviii. In his dispute with craft unionism after the war John Beard, the Workers' Union leader, argued that many Labour leaders were 'wedded . . . to class interests' while his union stood for 'the equal rights of men and women in industry', *The Workers' Union Record*, October 1919.

[48] Stedman Jones, 'Working-class culture'; McKibbin, *Evolution of the Labour party*. Both have since modified their views, see especially Stedman Jones, *Languages of class*, pp. 9–11, 22–4, 239–56, and Ross McKibbin, *The ideologies of class: social relations in Britain, 1880–1950* (Oxford, 1990), chs. 1 and 9.

[49] For instance, Hobsbawm, *Worlds of labour*, pp. 176–213; Gray, *The labour aristocracy*, pp. 115–20; Neville Kirk, '"Traditional" working-class culture and "the rise of labour": some preliminary questions and observations', *Social History*, 16 (1991), pp. 203–16.

tended to separate various strata of the working class, the development of football as a mass spectator sport made for a more homogeneous urban working-class culture'.[50] Such arguments are flawed at a number of levels. For one thing, they underestimate the extent to which popular culture had always provided contexts within which workers could mix irrespective of status or skill. Street markets, public holidays, fairs and of course parliamentary and municipal elections had always been arenas in which workers mixed regardless of their 'status' or 'skill' – although this is not to suggest that such social interaction was necessarily harmonious, either in the mid-Victorian period or later.[51] Nor should one imagine that more commercialised forms of leisure were automatically more divisive during the mid-Victorian period. In his 1867 essay 'Among the Gods', Thomas Wright stresses the mixing of working-class roughs and 'orderlies' at the theatre, and writes approvingly of 'the roughs' exuberant love of theatre and their effectiveness in silencing the interruptions of well-to-do drunks.[52]

Arguments which stress the growing cultural homogeneity of manual workers also tend to exaggerate both the inclusiveness of many aspects of popular culture, and their distinctively proletarian character. As Andrew Davies reminds us, not only was there great diversity in the forms of working-class leisure, but many leisure activities remained highly gendered.[53] Indeed, some leisure activities, notably spectator sports such as professional football, were becoming increasingly male-dominated during this period as they became more popular.[54] Others, such as the working-men's club movement, institutionalised exclusion based on gender from the outset.[55] At the same time, poverty also remained a

[50] Gray, *The labour aristocracy*, p. 117.

[51] On markets, see Andrew Davies, 'Saturday night markets in Manchester and Salford, 1840–1939' *Manchester Region History Review*, 1, 2 (1987), pp. 3–12; and more generally his *Leisure, gender and poverty*. See also Peter Bailey, *Leisure and class in Victorian England: rational recreation and the contest for control, 1830–1885* (London, 1978), pp. 86–91; and James Vernon, *Politics and the people: a study in English political culture, c. 1815–1867* (Cambridge, 1993), for discussion of election rituals; also Gissing's famous description of London's 'multitudes' at the Crystal Palace on August bank holiday Monday in *The Nether World* (1889), chapter 12 ('Io Saturnalia!').

[52] Wright, *Some habits*, pp. 152–67, see also his essay 'Easter with the unwashed' in his *The Great Unwashed*, pp. 234–45. For a wider discussion of Wright's social vision see Reid, 'Intelligent artisans'.

[53] Davies, *Leisure, gender and poverty*, esp. chs. 2 and 3; hence also Joanna Bourke's emphasis on the plurality of working-class cultures in her *Working-class cultures in Britain, 1890–1960: gender, class and ethnicity* (London, 1994).

[54] Tony Mason, *Association football and English society, 1863–1915* (Brighton, 1980), pp. 152–3; also Davies, *Leisure, gender and poverty*, p. 38.

[55] See George Tremlett, *Clubmen: history of the Working Men's Club and Institute Union* (London, 1987); and *The first century* (London, 1962). Few clubs excluded women completely, but the limits of women's participation in the clubs was defined by the male members and club officials.

barrier preventing many from enjoying full participation in popular associational cultures, hence the continued importance of non-commercial forms of leisure.[56] Finally, historians have recently begun to question whether it makes sense to describe aspects of urban popular culture such as music hall, mass spectator sport, or the fish & chip supper as distinctively 'working-class' at all. It is not always acknowledged that these were as much facets of urban as class culture, enjoyed as much by non-manual as manual workers in many communities. Weight of numbers might suggest otherwise, after all manual workers and their dependants may have made up as much as 80 per cent of the adult population in the Edwardian period, but it is not without reason that cultural conservatives decried the emergence of 'mass' rather than 'proletarian' culture in this period.[57] Although it has been suggested that in many urban communities class may have been so all-embracing that it required no special articulation,[58] this seems implausible as a description of conditions anywhere but in the most homogeneous single-industry town.[59] Even here we should surely expect that, given the growth of communication networks and the sharpening of class hostilities during and after the First World War (notably in the post-war 'middle-class reaction'), overt class meanings would have been inscribed upon such cultural practices if they were perceived as being relevant to these cornerstones of everyday life.[60]

V

There are, therefore, strong grounds for rejecting the idea that growing working-class homogeneity – be it economic, social or cultural homo-

---

[56] See Davies, *Leisure, gender and poverty*, esp. pp. 168–73; also McKibbin, *Ideologies of class*, chs. 4, 5 and 8. Many of the classic manifestations of the new 'working-class' or 'mass' leisure culture reached the peak of their popularity, not in the 1900s, nor even between the wars, but after 1945. For instance, 60 per cent of English and Welsh football clubs recorded their record gates after 1945, compared with only one club before 1914 – calculated from figures in Simon Inglis, *The football grounds of England and Wales* (London, 1983), pp. 16–17.

[57] Briggs, 'Language of "mass"'; John Carey, *The intellectuals and the masses: pride and prejudice among the literary intelligentsia, 1880–1939* (London, 1992). For pre-war discussions, see J. A. Hobson, *The psychology of jingoism*, (London, 1901); Graham Wallas, *The great society: a psychological analysis* (London, 1914).

[58] E.g. Savage and Miles, *The remaking*, p. 18.

[59] For a discussion of locality and class-consciousness along such lines, see Raymond Williams, 'The ragged-arsed philanthropists', in David Alfred (ed.), *The Robert Tressell Lectures, 1981–88* (WEA, Rochester, 1988), pp. 24–6.

[60] On the First World War and class, see C. F. G. Masterman, *England after war: a study*, (London, nd. [1922]); Bernard Waites, *A class society at war: England, 1914–18* (Leamington Spa, 1987); Tony Adams, 'The formation of the Co-operative party reconsidered', *International Review of Social History*, 32 (1987), pp. 48–68; and 'Labour and the First World War: economy, politics and the erosion of local peculiarity', *Journal of Local and Regional Studies*, 10 (1990), pp. 23–47.

geneity – provided the vital catalyst either for the emergence of independent Labour politics, or more generally for 'the rise of class politics'. But if the more mechanical forms socio-structural explanation serve poorly as models for understanding shifts in party politics and popular allegiance, it does not follow that social explanation as a whole should be abandoned. Despite the recent claims of some 'revisionist' historians of nineteenth-century Britain, no meaningful history of popular politics can be written which ignores the material factors which often shape both the terms upon which subordinate groups are able to act politically, and many of the fundamental concerns of the politics they embrace. The challenge, as many historians now recognise, is to develop truly non-reductionist and non-teleological ways of understanding this relationship between material life and popular politics.[61] The following chapter will begin by assessing the implications of the recent 'revisionist' treatment of popular politics and the rise of Labour, before outlining the approach which has been adopted in the present study.

[61] See Robert Gray, 'Class, politics and historical "revisionism"', *Social History*, 19, 2 (1994), pp. 209–20. Thompsonians would argue that this is already the essence of their practice; see Neville Kirk, 'History, language, ideas and post-modernism: a materialist view', *Social History*, 19, 2 (1994), pp. 221–40.

3   Relocating popular politics

Many of the historical certainties which once underpinned the notion of 'the rise of class politics' have come into question over the last decade. In particular, both liberal and radical-socialist historians have become highly suspicious of the application of sociological theories to problems of historical explanation – and especially to the explanation of political belief. But, as we have seen, the retreat from social explanation has by no means been as comprehensive as commentators sometimes suggest.[1] Among liberal historians the widespread shift to the study of 'high politics' and public policy has not been accompanied by any systematic critique either of 'electoral sociology' as a methodology, or of the major historical works written under its influence during the 1960s and 1970s.[2] Among historians who remain committed to the study of popular politics, there are inevitably some who have either unequivocally rejected or not registered recent challenges to traditional forms of social explanation and class analysis.[3] Rather more interesting, however, is the significant body of self-consciously 'revisionist' history which retains significant elements of the older historical paradigms. For instance, on the one hand, there are historians such as Alastair Reid and Eugenio Biagini, who stress the continuities of nineteenth-century radical politics, but who have by no

[1] E.g. Mike Savage and Andrew Miles, *The remaking of the British working class, 1840–1940* (London, 1994), pp. 10–17; Robert Gray, 'Class, politics and historical "revisionism"', *Social History*, 19, 2 (1994); pp. 209–20; Neville Kirk, 'History, language, ideas and postmodernism: a materialist view', *Social History*, 19, 2 (1994), pp. 221–40.

[2] See Jon Lawrence and Miles Taylor, 'Electoral sociology and the historians', in Jon Lawrence and Miles Taylor (eds.), *Party, state and society: electoral behaviour in Britain since 1820* (Aldershot, 1997); also Jon Lawrence and Jane Elliott, 'Parliamentary election results reconsidered: an analysis of borough elections, 1885–1910', *Parliamentary History*, 16, 1 (1997), [E. H. H. Green (ed.), *An age of transition*], pp. 18–28.

[3] See Neville Kirk, *Labour and society in Britain and the USA*, 2 vols. (Aldershot, 1994); Bryan D. Palmer, *Descent into discourse: the reification of language and the writing of social history* (Philadelphia, 1990); or Keith Laybourn, 'The rise of Labour and the decline of Liberalism: the state of the debate', *History*, 80 (1995), pp. 207–26.

means abandoned social explanation as a whole.[4] Whilst on the other hand, there are historians such as Patrick Joyce and James Vernon, who offer a much more sustained engagement with the 'post-modernist' critique of social explanation, but who none the less retain many elements of the 'traditional' narrative of nineteenth-century popular politics – including, at least in Joyce's case the broad outlines of the 'three-stage model' of nineteenth-century popular politics, with its emphasis on discontinuity.[5] As so often in historical controversy, 'revisionist' may not, therefore, be the most helpful label to attach to much of the new writing on nineteenth-century popular politics – but for want of a better alternative it will be retained in the discussion of recent historiography which follows.

II

Since the late 1980s there has undoubtedly been a great resurgence of interest in the dynamics of Victorian popular politics, much of it from an innovative and avowedly heterodox perspective. Taken together, this work has done much to re-establish the position of popular politics as a legitimate subject for historical investigation. Mindful that it is never wise to try to classify one's colleagues, I none the less want to suggest that this new writing can be divided into three broad approaches ('schools' would be too strong a term). For the sake of exposition I have termed these: sociological 'revisionism', empirical 'revisionism' and post-modernist 'revisionism'. I propose to examine each of these in turn before concluding (section VI) the chapter with an extended discussion of the principles which inform the study of popular politics in the present volume. Since it is in the nature of historiographical critique to seem detached and negative, however much one may strive to 'read generously', I should perhaps state at the outset that the works discussed in this chapter have strongly influenced my own approach to the study of popular politics – as should be amply clear from the tenor of the concluding discussion.

---

[4] See Eugenio Biagini and Alastair Reid, 'Currents of radicalism, 1850–1914', in their edited collection *Currents of Radicalism: popular radicalism, organised labour and party politics in Britain, 1850–1914* (Cambridge, 1991); Alastair Reid, *Social classes and social relations in Britain, 1850–1914* (Basingstoke, 1992), Eugenio Biagini, *Liberty, retrenchment and reform: popular Liberalism in the age of Gladstone, 1860–1880* (Cambridge, 1992); and Biagini (ed.), *Community and citizenship: Liberals, Radicals and collective identities in the British Isles, 1865–1931* (Cambridge, 1996).

[5] Patrick Joyce, *Visions of the people: industrial England and the question of class, 1840–1914* (Cambridge, 1991); though this is less true of his largely biographical study *Democratic subjects: the self and the social in nineteenth-century England* (Cambridge, 1994); James Vernon, *Politics and the people: a study in English political culture, c. 1815–1867* (Cambridge, 1993). These works are discussed more fully below.

Turning first to sociological 'revisionism', I am thinking here of the work of historians who, though still explicitly committed to the place of social explanation in the study of popular politics, have none the less been careful to distance themselves both from economic reductionism and from the narrow focus on radicalised minorities which has so often characterised 'history from below' in the past. The work of Mike Savage has been especially important here. A sociologist by training and temperament, Savage has sought to reassert the need for systematic social analysis as the bedrock of any adequate understanding of popular politics. Thus in *The dynamics of working-class politics* (1987) he argues that 'it is most useful to conceptualise working-class politics in terms of reducing working-class insecurity'.[6] Three types of working-class political strategy are identified: 'mutualist' (as in friendly societies and co-operatives); 'economistic' (notably trade union collective bargaining), and 'statist' (as in the state provision of social services). Savage argues that local circumstances, and particularly the nature of the local division of labour, will determine which of these strategies is considered the most viable form of 'working-class politics'.[7] The analytical rigour of this approach has proved attractive to a number of historians. For instance, its influence can be traced in Duncan Tanner's massive history of the early Labour party, especially in Tanner's discussion of the social and economic circumstances which shaped Labour politics on the ground in specific localities, and in his treatment of the rise of 'statist' policies within the party.[8]

Unlike some earlier social theorists turned historian, Savage is acutely aware of the pitfalls of social reductionism. As he and Andrew Miles put it in *The remaking of the British working class* (1994), 'there is, indeed, no automatic relationship between the social structure and political movements', rather, following Stedman Jones, they stress 'the complexity of the connections between, economic, social, cultural and political change'.[9] At a number of points the inherently contingent character of politics is acknowledged, as is the role politicians and political organisations can play in constructing alliances and mobilising support.[10] The authors recognise, however, that contingency and indeterminacy are not absolute. On the contrary, Savage and Miles distinguish between what

---

[6] Michael Savage, *The dynamics of working-class politics: the labour movement in Preston, 1880–1940* (Cambridge, 1987), p. 15.   [7] *Ibid.*, pp. 20–8, 39–61.

[8] Duncan Tanner, *Political change and the Labour party, 1900–1918* (Cambridge, 1990), esp. pp. 420–2, 424, 427, 431–2, 437. See also D. M. Tanner, 'Political alignment in England and Wales, c. 1906–22', unpublished PhD thesis, University College, London, 1985, which explores many similar themes but does not register the same sociological influences.   [9] Savage and Miles, *The remaking*, p.17.

[10] E.g. *ibid.*, pp. 19–20, 74; also Savage, *Dynamics*, pp. 62, 189–90.

they term, with strong echoes of Gramsci, 'practical' and 'formal' politics.[11] Social explanation, they suggest, remains vital to our understanding of 'practical' politics, rooted as these are in the material struggles and stratagems of every day life. In fact, 'practical politics' are defined more narrowly than this might suggest, since we are told that 'for labour, the reduction of insecurity is tied up with the need to undermine the commodity status of labour power, and it is this which must be seen as the class-based interest on which practical politics are based.'[12] The approach undoubtedly works best in areas dominated by a single industry (hence in *The dynamics of working-class politics* Savage focuses much attention on localities such as the coalmining communities of the south Wales valleys, Lancashire cotton towns, Sheffield steel-making districts or Scotland's 'Juteopolis' Dundee).[13] More socially and industrially mixed communities may well have been omitted because here, not only must politicians play a central role in the construction of alliances, they must also actively strive to create a sense of shared political interests, rather than simply tap into some pre-existing unity at the level of 'practical' politics. But even in single industry towns, such as those examined by Savage, the connections between the 'politics of every-day life' and the politics of party competition are surely more complex than his methodology would suggest. The practical strategies developed by members of subordinate groups in order to survive (if not prosper) within capitalist societies cannot be reduced to a formalistic logic based on the sociologist's perception of 'objective interests' and economic rationality. By denying this, Savage offers us a study, not of 'working-class politics' (in the descriptive sense of a study of the diverse political positions embraced by working people at any given time), but of political practices deemed to be 'working-class' because they conform to a set of *a priori* assumptions about what ends it would be rational for working people to pursue in politics. And for Savage, as we have seen, this means politics are 'working-class' only if they tend to reduce the insecurity of labour within a capitalist economy.

In many respects, therefore, far from abandoning social reductionism, Savage simply refines it by offering a new, more sophisticated typology of 'objective interests' sensitive to the varied social structures of different

---

[11] Savage and Miles, *The remaking*, p. 19; the distinction is also central to Savage's approach in *Dynamics*, see pp. 19 and 62.

[12] *Ibid.*, p. 17; cf. Savage and Miles, *The remaking*, p. 20.

[13] E.g. Savage, *Dynamics*, pp. 33–8, 48–56, though in his more recent work Savage has become increasingly critical of this emphasis on locality. See 'Space, networks and class formation', in Neville Kirk (ed.), *Social class and Marxism: defences and challenges* (Aldershot, 1996); and 'Some thoughts on space and locality in sociological theory and research', *CCSR Occasional Paper*, 12, (1997), pp. 18–28.

localities.[14] Indeed, we are explicitly told that recent attempts by historians to problematise consciousness are 'most unpromising', and that the historical interest in the relationship between culture and politics is, in general, misplaced.[15] This argument seems to reflect an underlying impatience with the inherent 'woolliness' of historical investigations into popular culture – and especially with their tendency to prefer 'reconstruction' (ie. description) over analysis and explanation. This critique of 'culturalist' approaches to the problem of understanding popular politics has some merit. However much they may wish to move beyond mere redescription, accounts of the culture of popular politics will never be able to claim the same analytical rigour as accounts which privilege sociostructural change and the logic of 'objective interests'. They can, however, offer insights into the genesis and the complexity of popular belief systems which undermine any attempt to 'model' the dynamics of political action from reasoning about 'objective interests'. The 'culturalists' are surely right to insist that, whilst popular belief systems may be shaped by the realities of material life, they are not *determined* by those realities, and so the influence they assert over how people act – both in 'the politics of every-day life' and in 'formal' party politics – must be studied in its own right. It is not adequate to argue that 'people's day-to-day practices are only weakly affected by any wider cultural values', since by doing so we deny people subjectivity itself – their hopes and aspirations, even their understanding of the meaning of their own lives, become of no consequence in understanding their politics.[16] One cannot argue that questions of culture and belief are irrelevant to people's everyday strategies – to do so is to suggest that 'practical' and 'formal' politics have nothing whatsoever in common – that they are wholly different realms of human activity. This is not spelled out in Savage's work, but it does probably explain why, despite the criticisms raised in the previous chapter against his recent restatement of the 'homogenisation' thesis, Savage's structural analysis of the *potential* for working-class political mobilisation in a particular time and place is often more convincing than his explanations of why one party rather than another should prove a successful force

---

[14] See Mike Savage, 'Understanding political alignments in contemporary Britain: do localities matter?', *Political Geography Quarterly*, 6 (1987), pp. 53–76; and 'Urban politics and the rise of the Labour party, 1919–1939', in L. Jamieson and H. Corr (eds.), *State, private life and political change*, Explorations in Sociology, No. 32 (Basingstoke, 1990); 'Urban history and social class: two paradigms', *Urban History*, 20 (1993), pp. 61–77.

[15] Savage, *Dynamics*, p. 5.

[16] *Ibid.*, p. 5 – though at other times Savage appears to be arguing only that we can never access this realm of past belief and aspiration, not that it is of no consequence (eg. *Dynamics*, p. 4).

for mobilisation. All too often, such questions, in many respects the key questions for political historians, are simply relegated to the status of the 'contingent' and hence unknowable.

III

As I have already suggested, my second category, the so-called 'empirical revisionists', are defined, not by their break with social explanation, which has been at best partial, but by their break with the established chronologies of nineteenth-century popular politics. As suggested, the work of Eugenio Biagini and Alastair Reid has perhaps been most important here.[17] Their work has done much to undermine the emphasis on discontinuity in accounts of nineteenth-century popular politics, both through its emphasis on the vitality of mid-Victorian popular radicalism, and through its insistence on seeing Labour politics as a movement within, rather than against, the radical tradition. There is much to commend in this restatement of the continuity thesis, assuming it is taken as a corrective to the notion that the 1840s and the 1880s represented major disjunctures in British political history, rather than as an argument about the essential immutability of British popular politics.[18] But this thesis, which is rapidly becoming a new orthodoxy, also has its problems. Not least of these is its largely unproblematic account of Radical/Liberal relations, and its apparent blindness, or at least indifference, to the failures, as well as the successes, of Liberalism as a mass movement. There is a real danger here of creating a new Whig history – a triumphalist account of the forward march of popular liberalism, no less mythical than earlier accounts of the forward march of labour.[19] Major Liberal reversals such as the election defeat of 1874 are too easily dismissed. Biagini argues that the Liberals won 'a majority of the popular vote in each of the kingdoms', and suggests they lost only because of 'the peculiar unfairness of the distribution of seats' and because 'the electors were left insufficient time to realize the full implications of the Liberal programme'.[20] This despite the

---

[17] See especially Biagini and Reid (eds.), *Currents of Radicalism*; Biagini, *Liberty, retrenchment and reform*.

[18] Jon Lawrence, 'Popular Radicalism and the socialist revival in Britain', *Journal of British Studies*, 31 (April, 1992), pp. 163–86 also offers a critique of the 'three-stage model' of nineteenth-century popular politics, but suggests that both Radicalism and socialism were broad ideological traditions in Victorian Britain. For a sophisticated discussion of the diversity and mutability of post-Chartist 'Radicalisms', see Miles Taylor, *The decline of British Radicalism, 1847–1860* (Oxford, 1995).

[19] For instance, see Biagini, *Liberty, retrenchment and reform*, ch. 7; cf. Martin Jacques and Francis Mulhearn (eds.), *The forward march of labour halted?* (London, 1981); though to be fair, Biagini is conscious of this danger, see *Liberty, retrenchment and reform*, p. 297.

[20] *Ibid.*, pp. 113 and 118.

fact that in his analysis of the 1874 defeat Gladstone himself dismissed such arguments as 'untenable', not least because 'the Tory party had a large majority of the uncontested seats'.[21] Nor is there any attempt to explain the growth of popular Toryism in many traditional Radical strongholds from the 1870s. Whilst there is also a sense in which the radical credentials of mainstream Liberalism seem overdrawn at the expense of the cautious, even conservative Liberalism which historians such as Jonathan Parry and Terry Jenkins have recently delineated with a new clarity.[22] Seen as a detailed study of the political culture which sustained popular Gladstonianism over more than three decades, Biagini's analysis has much to commend it. But it is difficult to resist the conclusion that it remains too partial and too partisan to have wider implications for the study of popular politics in Britain.

Turning now to the methodology of the 'empirical revisionists', it is important to acknowledge that their work does engage with historical and social theory. Thus Eugenio Biagini frequently acknowledges the influence of Weberian social science in *Liberty, retrenchment and reform*,[23] whilst Alastair Reid has from the outset made use of social theories as an aid to historical understanding,[24] and in recent years has gone further, developing his own six-point typology for analysing social relations in later nineteenth-century Britain, and suggesting a model of 'cycles in public life' which seems to resurrect the notion of 'discontinuity' in nineteenth-century popular politics.[25] Moreover, whilst theory may not be central to their 'revisionism', it is possible to identify certain common elements in their treatment of popular politics. Firstly, there is a strong emphasis on the political activist and on popular political organisations, but less interest in the broader question of understanding the relationship between popular belief systems and formal party politics. Either it is assumed that the ideas and aspirations of the non-activist majority can be

---

[21] W. E. Gladstone, 'Electoral facts', *Nineteenth Century*, 4 (1878), pp. 955–68, esp. p. 960.

[22] J. P. Parry, *Democracy and religion: Gladstone and the Liberal party, 1867–1875* (Cambridge, 1986), and *The rise and fall of Liberal Government in Victorian Britain* (New Haven, 1993); T. A. Jenkins, *Gladstone, Whiggery and the Liberal party, 1874–1886* (Oxford, 1988); and *The Liberal ascendancy, 1830–1886* (Basingstoke, 1994).

[23] For instance, Biagini, *Liberty, retrenchment and reform*, pp. 34, 251–2, 371, interestingly he also cites that other great influence on liberal scholarship in the 1960s and 1970s Ralf Dahrendorf (*ibid.*, p. 7).

[24] Alastair Reid, 'Politics and economics in the formation of the British working-class: a response to H. F. Moorhouse', *Social History*, 3 (1978), pp. 347–61, which makes use of Marx's *Capital, vol. III*; 'World War One and the working class in Britain', in Arthur Marwick (ed.), *Total war and social change* (Basingstoke, 1988), which makes use of Andrzewski's 'Military Participation Ratio' theory; 'The subject of labour history', *Labour History Review*, 55, 3 (1990), pp. 5–6, which argues for the affinities between Thompson and German Idealism, and Pelling and Smithian political economy.

[25] Reid, *Social classes*, pp. 39–40; 63.

read off from those of the activist minority, or the radical libertarianism of English popular opinion is simply taken as given – the constant backdrop against which politicians compete for popular allegiance and office.[26] This approach undoubtedly reflects a conscious attempt to rehabilitate the pragmatic labour history of Henry Pelling (and before him of the Webbs), and therefore to reassert the importance of studying political organisations and shifts in state policy.[27] But there is little evidence that Biagini and Reid endorse the full-blown critique of 'history from below' outlined in Jonathan Zeitlin's manifesto piece 'From labour history to the history of industrial relations'.[28] Rather, references to the strength of radical popular traditions frequently take the place of any more sustained engagement with 'history from below'. This is unfortunate, since, as Reid acknowledged in his earlier writing, it does not follow that, having over-turned reductionist assumptions about the connections between 'class experience' and popular politics, one is then absolved from having to ask difficult questions about the relationship between material life and polit-ical practice.[29] Hence the tendency to exaggerate the correspondence between the pronouncements of political activists and the beliefs and aspirations of the wider populace. In the process, their work too often fails to explore the tensions which must necessarily arise within a representa-tive democracy between popular movements and party organisations, and more fundamentally between all would-be political leaders and those they seek to represent.

IV

Finally we turn to the treatment of popular politics developed by what I've called (rather inelegantly) the 'post-modernist revisionists' to denote

---

[26] E.g. Biagini and Reid, 'Currents of radicalism', pp. 5, 12, 18–19; Reid, 'Old unionism reconsidered: the radicalism of Robert Knight, 1870–1900', in *Currents of radicalism*, pp. 214–43, esp. p. 238. See Gray, 'Class, politics and historical "revisionism"', pp. 217–20.

[27] The influence of Pelling is particularly strong in Alastair Reid's case, see 'Subject of labour history'; 'Old unionism reconsidered', p. 215 (n4); Henry Pelling and Alastair Reid, *A short history of the Labour party* (11th edn, Basingstoke, 1996), but it is also regis-tered in Biagini and Reid, 'Currents of radicalism', p. 16. Pelling himself frequently offers the same broad-brush approach to the study of popular opinion, see *Popular politics and society in late Victorian Britain* (2nd edn, Basingstoke, 1979), esp. chs 1, 2 and 10.

[28] Jonathan Zeitlin, 'From labour history to the history of industrial relations', *Economic History Review*, 2nd ser., 40 (1987) pp. 159–84. See also Jonathan Zeitlin, Richard Price and James E. Cronin, 'Debating "rank-and-filist" labour history', *International Review of Social History*, 34 (1989), pp. 42–102.

[29] See Reid, 'Politics and economics', esp. pp. 359–61, which offers a powerful reading of the constraints upon working-class political agency and the mediating role of trade unions and similar organisations. Also his essay, 'Intelligent artisans and aristocrats of labour: the essays of Thomas Wright', in Jay Winter (ed.), *The working class in modern British history: essays in honour of Henry Pelling* (Cambridge, 1983).

their greater interest in the so-called 'linguistic turn' and its critique of traditional forms of causal explanation in the social sciences. Of course post-modernism is itself a highly contested intellectual field, and it is perhaps not surprising that historians of nineteenth-century popular politics have woven very different histories out of their engagement with its controversies. In this discussion I want to look at the contrasting work of three historians: Gareth Stedman Jones, Patrick Joyce and James Vernon. In some respects, Stedman Jones's essay 'The language of Chartism' (1982) marked the first significant impact of post-structuralist thinking on the treatment of nineteenth-century politics.[30] In this essay Stedman Jones argues that 'the ideology of Chartism cannot be constructed in abstraction from its linguistic form', and that 'the growth and decline of Chartism was a function of its capacity to persuade its constituency to interpret their distress or discontent within the terms of its political language'.[31]

In *Languages of class*, published the following year, Stedman Jones developed this critique of social determinism further, signalling in the process his own waning faith in Marxism as a self-sufficient system of historical explanation. Discussing the genesis of his revisionist approach to social history Stedman Jones recalls that 'I became increasingly critical of the prevalent treatment of the "social" as something outside of, and logically – and often, though not necessarily, chronologically – prior to its articulation through language.'[32] In particular, Stedman Jones is critical of reductionist accounts of 'class politics', and declares his own intention to treat class 'as a discursive rather than as an ontological reality, the central effort being to explain languages of class from the nature of politics rather than the character of politics from the nature of class'.[33] In other words, Stedman Jones is arguing that political consciousness should be understood as the product, not of social or class position, nor even of social experience, but of the political and social discourses through which people interpret their experience and determine their 'interests'.[34] This point is amplified later in a discussion of E. P. Thompson's conception of class consciousness. Stedman Jones acknowledges the importance of

[30] Gareth Stedman Jones, "The language of Chartism", in James Epstein and Dorothy Thompson (eds.), *The Chartist experience: studies in working-class radicalism and culture, 1830–1860* (Basingstoke, 1982), pp. 3–58. A reworked and lengthened version appeared as 'Rethinking Chartism' in the author's *Languages of class: studies in English working class history, 1832–1982* (Cambridge, 1983), pp. 90–178.

[31] Stedman Jones, 'The language of Chartism', pp. 6 and 7. For a clear and balanced discussion of its substantive themes, see Miles Taylor, 'Rethinking the Chartists: searching for synthesis in the historiography of Chartism', *Historical Journal*, 39 (1996), pp. 479–95. Also, Jon Lawrence and Miles Taylor, 'The poverty of protest: Gareth Stedman Jones and the politics of language: a reply', *Social History*, 18 (1993), pp. 1–15.

[32] Stedman Jones, *Languages of class*, p. 7.   [33] *Ibid.*, p. 8.

[34] Here lies the core of Stedman Jones's difference with the Thompsonian position.

Thompson's break with reductionism, but argues that his approach still compresses 'social being' and 'social consciousness', leaving 'little independent space to the ideological context within which the coherence of a particular language of class can be reconstituted.'[35]

It is perhaps one of the weaknesses of *Languages of class* that Stedman Jones does not make more explicit the theoretical premises from which he is working. True, we are told that the social historian's common-sense view of the lessons of experience 'cannot acknowledge . . . all the criticism which has been levelled at it since the broader significance of Saussure's work was understood',[36] but this is no more than a vague gesture towards the highly contested terrain of post-structuralist theory. Just how completely Stedman Jones wishes us to make the 'linguistic turn' remains an issue of great contention, not least because he has declined to get involved in the sometimes bitter controversies about post-structuralism and social history which have raged since the mid 1980s.[37] There is no doubt that one *can* read the introduction to *Languages of class* as a definitive statement about the primacy of discourse – that in the parlance of current controversies one can read it as embodying a new 'linguistic determinism'. The claim to have 'applied a non-referential conception of language to the study of Chartist speeches and writings', appears to suggest a 'hard' version of the post-structuralist method, in which we are offered a close reading of discursive forms, unhindered by questions of authorial intention or broader context.[38] But this is not what Stedman Jones provides. Rather, his conception of a 'non-referential' analysis refers only to his refusal to flesh out his readings of texts by referring to a supposedly prior and determining social context. He is quite prepared to interpret texts by reference to their intellectual and political context, or even to assumptions about the changing character of the contemporary state.[39] In

[35] *Languages of class*, p. 101.   [36] *Ibid.*, p. 20.

[37] For instance, see Neville Kirk, 'In defence of class: a critique of recent revisionist writing upon the nineteenth-century English working class', *International Review of Social History*, 32 (1987), pp. 2–47; Palmer, *Descent into discourse*; the debate on 'History and post-modernism' involving Lawrence Stone, Patrick Joyce, Catriona Kelly and Gabrielle Spiegel in *Past & Present*, 131 (May, 1991), pp. 217–18; 133 (November, 1991), pp. 204–13; and 135 (May 1992), pp. 189–208. Also David Mayfield and Susan Thorne, 'Social history and its discontents: Gareth Stedman Jones and the politics of language', *Social History*, 17 (1992), pp. 165–88; Lawrence and Taylor, 'Poverty of protest'; James Vernon, 'Who's afraid of the "linguistic turn"? the politics of social history and its discontents', *Social History*, 10 (1994), pp. 82–97; Kirk, 'History, language, ideas'; Richard Price, 'Historiography, narrative and the nineteenth-century', *Journal of British Studies*, 35 (1996), pp. 220–56. Stedman Jones does offer some comments on the critical response to *Languages of class* in an interview with Peter Schöttler to be found in Gareth Stedman Jones, *Klassen, politik und sprache: für eine theorieorientierte sozialgeschicte* (Münster, 1988), pp. 277–318.

[38] Stedman Jones, *Languages of class*, p. 21.

[39] For instance 'Rethinking Chartism', pp. 173–8; and 'Why is the Labour party in a mess?', pp. 250–4 (both essays are in *Languages of class*).

Stedman Jones's work language-centred analysis appears to be embraced as an heuristic device – it is championed, not as a new universally applicable system of historical explanation, but as a specific means of overcoming the explanatory weaknesses of a narrowly materialist approach to the analysis of popular politics in general, and the Chartist movement in particular.[40]

It is this which explains many of the ambiguities of *Languages of class*. Rather than denying any role to material determinations, Stedman Jones is arguing that the historian will never be able satisfactorily to grasp the nature of such determinations. In defending his investigations into the 'languages of class', Stedman Jones argues that 'To peer straight through these languages into the structural changes to which they may be notionally referred is no substitute for such an investigation, not because there is not a relationship of some kind, *but because such connections can never be established with any satisfying degree of finality*' (emphasis added).[41] The more historical essays in *Languages of class*, such as 'Rethinking Chartism' and 'Why is the Labour party in a mess?', underline the qualified nature of Stedman Jones's break with social explanation. For instance, in the essay on the fortunes of the Labour party he acknowledges that

Changes in the social realm necessarily form a large part of the *raw material* out of which different political languages and practices may be forged and reforged. But such changes are not bearers of essential political meaning in themselves. They are only endowed with particular political meanings so far as they are effectively articulated through specific forms of political discourse and practice. There are no simple rules of translation from the social to the political.[42] (emphasis added)

Similarly in 'Rethinking Chartism' Stedman Jones rejects the view that 'the analysis of language can provide an exhaustive account of Chartism' and adds that '[i]t is not a question of replacing a social interpretation by a linguistic interpretation, but rather it is how the two relate, that must be rethought. Abstractly, the matter determines the possibility of the form, but the form conditions the development of the matter.'[43] In both cases we see Stedman Jones anxious to escape the charge of idealism, although it is perhaps significant that he appears prepared to grant only a passive, delimiting role to material factors. Despite arguing that the task for historians is to rethink the relationship between social change and discursive practice, rather than to replace the primacy of the social with the primacy of the political, one is left with the sense that Stedman Jones has turned his back on the analysis of social structure and popular cultures in *Languages of class*. Certainly this is the implicit message of the following passage:

---

[40] See Lawrence and Taylor, 'Poverty of protest', pp. 2–8, 12–13; Taylor, 'Rethinking the Chartists', esp. pp. 482–8.   [41] Stedman Jones, *Languages of class*, p. 22.
[42] *Ibid.*, p. 242.   [43] Stedman Jones, *Languages of class*, p. 95.

between the changing character of social life and the order of politics there is no simple, synchronous or directly transitive line of connection, either in one direction or the other. To begin *at the other end of the chain* does not obliterate the significance of the work of the social historian, but locates its significance in a different perspective.[44] (emphasis added)

Here the social historian, and social history, seem to occupy the place of a marginalised 'other' – a view reinforced by the observation that in any history of Labour politics written along the lines of *Languages of class* 'the place of the social would have to be . . . resituated within discursive relations'.[45]

These problems are compounded in *Languages of class* by the fact that Stedman Jones is working, as he himself admits, with a rather narrow definition of political discourse, which tends to exclude all but the formal, public discourses of political organisations such as the Chartist movement or the Labour party.[46] There is little recognition of the fact that to succeed party discourses must engage with, and in part echo, pre-existing popular beliefs and aspirations. Put simply, *Languages of class* underestimates the problem of reception for a language-based analysis of politics.[47] By excluding from study the informal, and often localised political discourses through which people articulate the struggles and aspirations of their every-day lives, Stedman Jones underestimates the extent to which the terms of popular politics could be contested and even overturned 'on the ground'. For instance, as critics of 'Rethinking Chartism' have pointed out, by embracing the language of 'the People's rights' Chartists were trying to appropriate and destabilize key assumptions of English political discourse which equated citizenship with the ownership of property.[48] Similarly, at the end of the century, populist Tories, many of them manual workers, extended the notion of 'fair trade' – the protection of industries facing 'unfair' competition in the market-place, to include the protection of the worker from 'unfair' competition in the labour market.[49] In other words, whilst *Languages of class* may be right to insist that we must open up the space between 'social being' and 'social con-

---

[44] *Ibid.*, p. 24.   [45] *Ibid.*, p. 23.

[46] For recognition of this problem, see *ibid.*, p. 95 (n10); and comments in *Klassen, Politik und Sprache*, pp. 312–13. The most acute criticism along these lines is offered by Robert Gray, 'The deconstructing of the English working class', *Social History*, 11 (1986), pp. 363–73.   [47] Lawrence and Taylor, 'The poverty of protest', p. 13.

[48] James Epstein, 'Rethinking the categories of working-class history', *Labour/Le Travail*, 18 (1986), pp. 195–208, esp. 200–01.

[49] See Jon Lawrence, 'Class and gender in the making of urban Toryism, 1880–1914', *English Historical Review*, 108 (1993), pp. 629–52, Richard Trainor, *Black country élites: the exercise of authority in an industrialized area, 1830–1900* (Oxford, 1993), p. 222; and David Feldman, 'The importance of being English: Jewish immigration and the decay of liberal England', in David Feldman and Gareth Stedman Jones (eds.), *Metropolis: London histories and representations since 1820* (London, 1989).

sciousness' in order to analyze the discourses through which people make sense of the social world, its definition of those discourses is ultimately too narrow for historians interested in understanding the dynamics of popular politics. Just as Biagini and Reid tend to privilege the politics of the activist minority, so Stedman Jones privileges formal party discourse – in neither case is there a sustained attempt to explain why, and on what terms, large numbers of people were mobilized behind particular political projects at particular historical moments.

On the other hand, *Languages of class* does offer a compelling analysis of how political parties attempt to define and mould their constituencies within democratic polities. Interestingly, Ellen Meiskins Wood acknowledges this point. Whilst lambasting Stedman Jones for his 'retreat from class', she none the less concedes that his approach

may be illuminating as a much more limited statement about the formation of electoral parties, the constitution of electoral constituencies, the construction of cross-class alliances, and the function of language and rhetoric in abstracting political perceptions from material conditions and antagonisms for the purpose of creating political identities.[50]

Concerned as she is with the political implications of Stedman Jones's waning belief in Marxism and class analysis, Meiskins Wood clearly considers such contributions to the understanding of popular politics to be of little consequence. From the historian's perspective this seems, to say the least, unreasonable. We may criticise Stedman Jones for focusing too exclusively on the creative, initiatory role of organisations and party politicians, but this should not prevent us from recognising that his approach offers real insights into political practice at this crucial level.

V

If the extent of Stedman Jones's commitment to the 'linguistic turn' remains open to question, the same cannot be said of the other two 'postmodernist revisionists' under consideration in this discussion: Patrick Joyce and James Vernon. Both have made strident interventions into the debate on the state and future of social history in which they unequivocally portray themselves as champions of post-modernism and the 'linguistic turn'.[51] According to Joyce 'the events, structures and processes of the past are indistinguishable from the forms of documentary representa-

---

[50] Ellen Meiskins Wood, *The retreat from class: a new 'true' socialism* (London, 1986), p. 114. There is more than a hint of the old 'false consciousness' argument in this extract.

[51] See Joyce, 'History and post-modernism'; 'The imaginary discontents of social history: a note of response', *Social History*, 18 (1993) pp. 81–5; *Democratic subjects*, pp. 4–13; and 'The end of social history?', *Social History*, 20 (1995), pp. 73–91. Vernon, *Politics and the people*; and 'Who's afraid?'

tion, the conceptual and political appropriations, and the historical discourses that construct them'.[52] Vernon's position is more ambiguous. He acknowledges that '[t]here will always be a place for social structural approaches', and denies any intention to argue 'that society or the real do not exist', but he offers few clues as to how one might apply his rather dogmatic reading of 'the linguistic turn' and its methodological imperatives to the historical analysis of social structures.[53] Interestingly, in their substantive historical analyses both Joyce and Vernon have tended to be pragmatic in their approach, deploying critical methodologies associated with post-structuralism to develop fresh interpretations of nineteenth-century popular politics, without troubling themselves overmuch about the epistemological basis of their claims to historical insight. Although there are many parallels in their work, not least the fact that neither poses a significant challenge to the traditional periodisation of nineteenth-century politics, their differences, both of approach and exposition, are sufficiently great to demand separate treatment. I will look first at the work of Patrick Joyce, and in particular at his major revisionist study *Visions of the people* (1991).

A rich, if dense, study of the interaction of popular cultures and politics in nineteenth-century Britain, *Visions of the people* has many strengths, not least, as one might expect, its treatment of popular Conservatism, its subtle analysis of the shifting place of custom in workplace cultures, and its exploration of dialect and oral culture in industrial England.[54] Equally convincing is the emphasis on popular strategies to 'civilise' capitalism. Joyce argues that ideas such as the 'good employer' were used prescriptively rather than descriptively by mid-Victorian trade union leaders. Their use was evidence, not of a craven acceptance of dominant values, but of a determined effort to influence those values 'from below'.[55] In sections such as these Joyce's reading of popular politics is clear and persuasive. Unfortunately, the same cannot be said for the book as a whole, which is marred by a confusing debate about the character of 'class' and 'populist' politics, and by a surprisingly uncritical acceptance of many orthodoxies of nineteenth-century political historiography. At one level *Visions of the people* can be read as an extended critique of the ways in which social historians have deployed the concept of 'class' as a tool of historical analysis. In most cases, suggests Joyce, they would capture the political and social vision of nineteenth-century plebeian activists much

---

[52] Joyce, 'History and post-modernism', p. 208.   [53] Vernon, 'Who's afraid?', p. 96.

[54] E.g. Joyce, *Visions of the people*, chs. 2–4; cf. Patrick Joyce, *Work, Society and politics: the culture of the factory in later Victorian England* (Brighton, 1980), and Joyce (ed.), *The historical meanings of work* (Cambridge, 1987).

[55] Joyce, *Visions of the people*, pp. 109–10.

better if they thought in terms of 'populism' rather than of 'class'. Much of the work is written as though 'class' and 'populist' are distinct and dichotomous analytical terms, and considerable space is devoted to judging whether a particular movement or political discourse is best designated as essentially 'class' or 'populist'.[56] The unhelpfulness of this exercise is merely compounded by Joyce's acknowledgment that 'what so often presents itself when conceptions of the social order are considered is not quite "populism" and not quite "class"'.[57] Unfortunately, rather than explore these ambiguities and tensions within popular conceptions of society, Joyce prefers to classify any social phenomenon into one camp or the other. Joyce defends himself against the charge that he is imposing artificial analytic categories upon the complexities of popular culture by arguing that

> it still seems to make sense to speak of these large generic categories simply because they seem quite clearly to have been there, part of historical experience, as well as elements in a definition. In themselves, individual aspects such as class, people and nation were fusions of different loyalties, but they do none the less seem each to have had recognisably distinct forms, and culture was not the incoherent, discordant thing it is sometimes taken to be.[58]

Besides underlining the limits to Joyce's endorsement of 'post-modernist' critical methodologies,[59] this quotation makes clear the depth of his commitment to classifying practices, and his belief in the essential coherence and internal rationality of popular belief systems. Yet, as most social theorists now acknowledge, social perception is highly context-specific – a dichotomous view of class relations in the workplace, need not translate into a dichotomous view of class relations in the neighbourhood, or in party politics.[60] More fundamentally, I would suggest that a close critical reading of any text or discursive practice is likely to reveal considerable ambiguities and even contradictions in perceptions of the social order. It is by no means uncommon to find the universal and consensual discourses Joyce terms 'populist' and the conflictual, anti-capitalist and socially exclusive discourses he calls 'class' used side-by-side within popular politics. For instance, in a critique of Joyce's analysis of the poli-

---

[56] See *ibid.*, pp. 10–15, 56–74, 78, 314–16, 333–36.   [57] *Ibid.*, p. 12.   [58] *Ibid.*, p. 12.

[59] Joyce acknowledges as much in his more recent work *Democratic subjects*, p. 11. He observes of *Visions of the people* 'I wanted still to write a grand, traditional narrative, and sought, uneasily, to find the subject for that narrative in "the people"'. See also James Epstein, 'The populist turn', *Journal of British Studies*, 32 (1993), pp. 177–89.

[60] For instance, Anthony Giddens, *The constitution of society: outline of the theory of structuration* (Cambridge, 1984); Howard Newby, *The deferential worker: a study of farm workers in East Anglia* (London, 1977). See also Peter Bailey, '"Will the real Bill Banks please stand up?": a role analysis of Victorian working-class respectability', *Journal of Social History*, 12 (1979), pp. 336–53.

tics of anti-slavery in Lancashire, Janet Toole has shown how local trade union activists combined the liberal, humanitarian critique of slavery as a moral evil, with a much more class-specific critique which emphasised the common bonds between the plantation worker/slave and the factory worker/slave: twin victims of the unscrupulous, profit-greedy Lancashire cotton magnates.[61] There is a similar tension in the political language of the burgeoning working-men's club movement of the 1890s. On the one hand, club leaders defended their movement from its many critics by appealing to the 'universal rights' of free association and freedom from arbitrary authority. On the other hand they insisted that all clubs should be controlled by 'bona fide working men', and warned against the danger of infiltration by the lower middle classes.[62]

Besides exaggerating both the coherence of popular belief systems, and their correspondence to the abstractions of social theory, Joyce's approach also depends on an unjustifiably narrow definition of what constitutes 'class consciousness'. At one point Joyce suggests that three elements need to be present before one can talk of a 'class' presence in popular politics: a sense of conflict or struggle, social exclusivity, and the primacy of economic interests divided along the capital/labour axis.[63] In itself this is an exacting definition, but Joyce later makes it clear that a 'true' class analysis must also contain a critique of the capitalist profit-motive.[64] Joyce wants to embrace 'an analytical definition of class' as a corrective to 'the infinite elasticity of class' characteristic of 'the Thompsonian view of the priority of class struggle'.[65] Although Joyce insists that he is not resurrecting the distinction between 'true' and 'false' consciousness, formulations such as: 'the consciousness of *a class* need not be the consciousness of *class*', presuppose reference to *a priori* criteria of what constitutes 'real' or 'full' class consciousness (and, of course, to the notion of social classes existing outside/prior to language).[66] Later Joyce acknowledges that the strong, but predominantly non-conflictual, forms of social identity characteristic of manual workers by the late nineteenth century might equally be understood, either as manifestations of a

---

[61] Janet Toole, 'Workers and slaves: class relations in south Lancashire in the time of the cotton famine', unpublished paper, read at the Economic and Social History Seminar, University of Liverpool, 1994.

[62] See *Club and Institute Journal*, 17 March 1894, March 1895, January 1896; also *The Wolverhampton Chronicle*, 6 September 1893, and J. Lawrence, 'Party politics and the people: continuity and change in the political history of Wolverhampton, 1815–1914', Unpublished PhD thesis, University of Cambridge, 1989, pp. 121–3.

[63] Joyce, *Visions*, p. 11 – to loosen this conception of class is, according to Joyce, to render one's analysis meaningless (*ibid.*, pp. 13–14).   [64] *Ibid.*, p. 78.   [65] *Ibid.*, pp. 14–15.

[66] *Ibid.*, p. 15 (original emphasis); variants of this argument can be found at pp. 97, 316, and 332. For Joyce's insistence that he is *not* working with 'platonic notions of class' see *ibid.*, p. 14, and his essay 'Imaginary discontents' (though see Joyce, *Democratic subjects*, p. 11).

deep-seated 'populism' (he talks of 'labourist populism'), or as 'the English (and British) case of class, in which class identity (but not class opposition) has been strong'.[67] Apart from underlining the 'infinite elasticity' of Joyce's conception of 'populism', this argument tends to conflate 'labour consciousness' and Labour politics. Here Joyce's argument bears a striking resemblance to the work of Ross McKibbin, or the early Stedman Jones – both of whom portray Labour politics as a natural outgrowth of the solid, but essentially conservative, sense of social class among English workers.[68] This may seem harsh – certainly *Visions of the people* is intended to take us far beyond the cultural reductionism of these earlier analyses of Labour politics. However, many of the potential strengths of its analysis of popular politics are ultimately obscured by the unhelpfulness of the dominant 'class'/'populist' paradigm.[69]

As I have already suggested, the historical 'revisionism' of Patrick Joyce and James Vernon is primarily concerned, not with overturning the familiar landmarks of nineteenth-century political history, but with challenging the conventions of historical analysis and the political assumptions built into traditional narratives. For instance, the basic contours of the 'three-stage' model of nineteenth-century popular politics are clearly recognisable in *Visions of the people*. We are told how ideas of 'independence' and 'conflict' present in early nineteenth-century forms of class identity were 'eclipsed' (though not altogether lost) during the mid-Victorian period; how, through the popular resonances of Palmerstonian foreign policy, 'class boundaries were still further dissolved'; and how 'bourgeois and workingmen's [contrasting] visions of Improvement' helped 'cement considerable common feeling' in towns such as Ashton.[70] Perhaps more surprisingly, Joyce also retains the idea of the 'rise of class politics' as a key factor determining the break up of this communitarian politics in the early twentieth century. The argument here is tentative, but Joyce suggests that we should push 'the rise of class' forward from the

[67] *Ibid.*, p. 334 – see also p. 316, where Joyce makes a similar point, before concluding that 'labour consciousness', or 'a new "labourist" manifestation of populism' might be a more helpful way of conceptualising the growing self-identity of manual workers.

[68] Ross McKibbin, *The evolution of the Labour party, 1910–1924* (Oxford, 1974), and Gareth Stedman Jones, 'Working-class culture and working-class politics in London, 1870–1900: notes on the remaking of the working class', *Journal of Social History*, 7 (1974), pp. 460–508.

[69] This difficulty is overcome in *Democratic subjects*, but here Joyce's conviction that '[t]here is no overarching coherence evident in either the polity, the economy or the social system' ('History and post-modernism', p. 208) produces a series of interesting biographical readings, but few substantive conclusions.

[70] Joyce, *Visions of the people*, pp. 58, 60, 61. Later Joyce pushes the argument for 'stabilization' further, arguing that the 'gospel of Improvement' was 'a major ground upon which social and class tensions were *resolved*' in mid-Victorian Britain, *ibid.*, p. 104 (emphasis added).

1890s to the 1910s and 1920s – understanding it less as an outcome of inevitable processes of social change, than of the political and social fall-out of 'total war'.[71] By stressing 'conjuncture', rather than 'structure', Joyce successfully escapes the pitfalls of social reductionism and class teleology. But his implicit emphasis on the 'modernisation' of British politics after 1867 (in arguments about the 'triumph of party', the rise and fall of local political elites, and the shift from communitarian to material-ist political agendas), leaves him no less dependent on a mechanism of 'transition', such as 'the rise of class' than the champions of 'electoral sociology' and traditional social history in the 1960s and 1970s.[72] As I will argue in chapter 7, it is only by re-examining this model of the 'moderni-sation' of party politics after 1867 that historians can free themselves from many of the misconceptions about the relationship between 'class' and popular politics.

The 'modernisation' of politics is also central to the recent work of James Vernon, although here it seen as an engine for the disempowerment and disinheritance of popular politics, rather than as an agent of recon-ciliation and integration.[73] In Vernon's *Politics and the people* the 'triumph of party' marks the final demise of the robust and independent political traditions of plebeian England – party politics, we are told, 'disciplined, regulated and disabled popular politics'.[74] Like Joyce, Vernon insists upon the autonomous development of both cultural politics and party organisation at the local level during the nineteenth century.[75] An argu-ment that is never fully reconciled with his claim that the 'most striking and interesting' feature of the constituencies he studies are the similarities between them – 'suggesting . . . the existence of a national political culture, albeit with strong local and regional mediations'.[76]

As with Joyce's *Visions of the people*, there is much to commend in Vernon's analysis of popular politics. The careful attention to the visual and oral, as well as the written, dimensions of popular politics is innova-tive and successful, as is the discussion of the symbolic politics of public space. There is no doubt that *Politics and the people* offers an unusually rich and subtle reading of the culture of nineteenth-century urban popular politics. At the same time, the argument that nominally 'progres-

---

[71] *Ibid.*, pp. 4, 6, 9, 140, 314, 329, 336 and 342.
[72] For emphasis on the integrative role of political parties, see *ibid.*, pp. 69, 72; on the central role of local political elites in the 'taming of class', see p. 59; on the subsequent decline of communitarian politics, see pp. 111–12.
[73] Vernon, *Politics and the people*; for a more extensive critique of this work, see Jon Lawrence, 'The decline of English popular politics?', *Parliamentary History*, 13 (1994) pp. 333–7.
[74] Vernon, *Politics and the people*, p. 337. See also pp. 103–4, 175, 182 and 249.
[75] E.g. *ibid.*, p. 181 where we are told that 'parties were invented at constituency level'.
[76] *Ibid.*, p. 11; see also p. 335.

sive' and 'democratic' reforms played a key role in limiting the scope for popular political participation is in many respects compelling.[77] For instance, Vernon argues that the Secret Ballot Act was concerned less with breaking the undue influence of local social elites, than with controlling the excesses of the new urban electors and excluding the non-elector altogether (by abolishing nomination day and the elaborate rituals of the hustings, 'improving' polling arrangements, and destroying the effectiveness of exclusive dealing as a means of influencing the poll).[78]

Despite these strengths, however, *Politics and the people* must be seen as a flawed attempt to reinterpret nineteenth-century popular politics. Ultimately the strengths of Vernon's new 'cultural history of politics' are ones of description, not explanation. Attention to the reconstruction of popular political cultures is necessary, but not sufficient, for an adequate understanding of popular politics as a whole. However, perhaps the greatest problem with Vernon's analysis is, as he more or less acknowledges in the book's closing pages, the fundamental tension between its claim to offer an open-ended reading of the 'indeterminacy and ambiguity' of popular politics, and the relentless, uni-linear logic of its account of the closure of the 'public political sphere'.[79] Here Vernon appears to be making heuristic use of Habermas' analysis in *The structural transformation of the public sphere*: transposing the account so that the closure of the public sphere as a forum for rational and critical debate, becomes its closure as an arena for genuinely inclusive and empowering forms of political participation.[80] This is a dangerous strategy. The strongly teleological nature of Habermas' theory virtually precludes an open-ended reading of popular politics. As a result, Vernon's analysis seriously underestimates the indeterminacy and ambiguity of the relationship between would-be party politicians and 'the people'. The relentless logic of Vernon's 'closure' narrative produces a narrow, and one-directional analysis of popular politics – where the 'triumph of party', and of the party politician, is considered to be absolute by the later nineteenth

---

[77] There are definite parallels here with David Vincent's work, especially his *Literacy and popular culture: England, 1750–1914* (Cambridge, 1989); see Vernon, *Politics and the people*, pp. 141–2.

[78] E.g. *ibid.*, pp. 157–8.

[79] For claims to embrace post-modernist critical readings of culture see *ibid.*, pp. 1, 5–11; for references to Habermas and the closure of the public political sphere, see pp. 7, 7n and 105n; for Vernon's recognition of the tension here see, pp. 338–9. See also Geoff Eley, 'Edward Thompson, social history and political culture: the making of a working-class public, 1780–1850', in Harvey J. Kaye and Keith McClelland (eds.), *E. P. Thompson: critical perspectives* (Cambridge, 1990).

[80] *Ibid.*, pp. 7, 7n and 105n. See Jürgen Habermas, *The structural transformation of the public sphere* (1962; Engl. trans. 1989); also C. Calhoun (ed.), *Habermas and the public sphere* (Cambridge, Mass., 1992).

century.[81] Vernon's discussion of the growth of 'ticketing' – the practice of controlling access to public meetings through the use of tickets – illustrates this point well. Ticketing is portrayed primarily as a means of constricting and controlling public political space – as one more step in the incremental 'rise of party'.[82] However, as Vernon acknowledges, 'ticketing' allowed politicians to exclude the disorderly, the hostile and the poor – suggesting that politicians who resorted to this device were often more mindful of the intractability of popular politics, than of its malleability. Ticketing, by this reading, would have to be seen (at least in part) as a defensive response to the persistence of the 'politics of disruption'. Moreover, because many politicians continued to insist that the popular acclaim of the crowd, and the ability to hold open meetings of one's constituents, were marks of political legitimacy – a public mandate – ticketing was often roundly denounced by opponents as an affront to the local populace and an admission of unpopularity (these themes are explored more fully in chapter 7).

Vernon's determination to eschew the analysis of 'high politics' and state policy also contributes to the attenuated nature of his analysis of popular politics. Apparently convinced that the revival of interest in state power, and the growing emphasis on its formative influence over many aspects of everyday life, are deeply pernicious, Vernon denies himself the analytical tools necessary adequately to analyse the origins and consequences of nineteenth-century 'reform' legislation.[83] As a result, whilst Vernon argues that government 'reforms' of electoral practice played a crucial role in the 'taming' of popular politics, the legislative process itself, like most aspects of what Vernon calls 'official' culture, is never analysed in any detail. In particular, we get little sense of the crucial paradox of electoral 'reforms': that the legislators who devised and enacted these measures were also the constituency MPs holding annual meetings of account and often sanctioning the 'politics of disruption'. In other words, they were legislating to change the practices which they themselves sustained; the traditions which, very often, they had upheld from the hustings. These complexities are missing from Vernon's story – we see only the consequences of constraining legislation passed down from 'on high' – the inter-related worlds of Westminster and the constituency remain artificially sundered by a very narrow interpretation of the brief to write 'history from below'.

---

[81] Vernon, *Politics and the people*, pp. 182, 248–9, 337–8.
[82] *Ibid.*, pp. 226–30 – though Vernon also stresses that ticketing was used to encourage female participation in politics – if only as the supportive dependants of male political subjects.
[83] See Vernon, *Politics and the people*, p. 8, and his comments in 'Who's afraid?', pp. 86–8.

Many of these themes are taken up in chapter 7, which focuses primarily on popular attitudes to party in Britain after the Second Reform Act. Here it is argued that we need to question not only the traditional emphasis on the inclusive and integrative role of the mass party after 1867, but also the very notion of the 'triumph of party'. The concept of the 'closure' of popular politics, with its overtones of a lost 'golden age' of plebeian liberties, is rejected. It is suggested that the most significant turning point for popular politics, was not the 'reform' legislation of the later nineteenth-century, nor the growth of party organisation in the constituencies, but, firstly, the emergence of the Labour party – with its strong commitment to the construction of a 'rational' democracy – and, secondly, the cultural and political legacy of the First World War. But before exploring these themes in greater detail, it would be useful to summarise the main conclusions that might be drawn from the preceding discussion of the historiography of popular politics. How should we relocate the study of popular politics?

VI

What follows is intended, not as a declaratory manifesto for historical 'best practice' but as a brief outline of the assumptions and influences which have helped shape the substantive study of English popular politics which follows. Put at its simplest, a principal argument of the book is that studies of popular politics must focus greater critical attention on the relationship between political activists, of whatever persuasion, and those they seek to represent politically. We must recognise that precisely because this relationship is one of 'representation' it must constantly be negotiated and renegotiated – the 'formal' politics of political organisations can never be a complete and faithful reflection of the interests (objectively *or* subjectively defined) of those who are represented. The 'organic' activist – indistinguishable in every respect from his or her fellow workers – is no more than a romantic illusion; 'representation' necessarily involves exclusion and denial, as well as inclusion and recognition. In studying popular politics, we are therefore studying the interaction between the worlds of 'formal' and 'informal' politics, conscious that the relationship between the two is never unmediated, and that our analysis must therefore always be sensitive to the tensions and ambiguities in the relationship between 'leaders' and 'led'.

Almost by definition, this approach to the study of popular politics demands, not only that we break with narrow conceptions of the remit to write 'history from below' but also that we reject the artificial and debilitating gulf which has developed between the study of 'high' and 'popular' politics. Many critics have noted the dangers inherent in an overly strict interpretation of the brief to write 'history from below'.[84] They have also noted the partiality of many histories written under its influence, and the tendency to focus on the social and political world of a radicalised minority, at the expense of understanding the lives of the vast majority. There is probably an in-built tendency for 'history from below', and the study of 'the popular' more generally, to exaggerate and romanticise evidence of plebeian resistance to 'authority', but working with a broad definition of 'the popular' does provide some corrective.[85] Though, as we shall see, the 'popular' itself is a problematic term since it can easily be misread as signifying either a dichotomous and oppositional relationship with an 'other' (such as 'elite', 'high', or 'educated') or a simple, internal unity, as in 'the common people' (when in fact definitions of 'the popular' were themselves highly contested and frequently exclusionary).[86] Although much of the criticism of 'history from below' has been well-founded, it does not follow that we should abandon attempts to study the 'politics of every-day life', and concentrate instead only on the world of formal (organisational) politics. Such an approach may make sense for the 'high politics' study, with its limited horizons and self-contained logic, but histories with a broader vision, and more substantial explanatory ambitions, cannot afford to adopt this approach. Rather, they must seek to incorporate the outlook and concerns of 'history from below' within an analytical framework which gives due recognition to the role of political organisations, formal political discourses and state policy.

The writing of political history has come to depend upon the deployment of a set of dichotomous analytical categories which mirror this basic bifurcation of the subject. So much so that even when historians argue that oppositional categories like 'élite'/'plebeian', 'official'/'popular', 'national'/'local' or 'centre'/'periphery' are 'artificial and ahistorical', they

[84] E.g. Tony Judt, 'A clown in regal purple: social history and the historians', *History Workshop Journal*, 7 (1979), pp. 66–94; Geoff Eley and Keith Nield, 'Why does social history ignore politics?', *Social History*, 5 (1980), pp. 249–71; Jim Sharpe, 'History from below', in Peter Burke (ed.), *New perspectives on historical writing* (Cambridge, 1991); Richard Lachmann and Nelson A. Pichardo, 'Making history from above and below', *Social Science History*, 18 (1994), pp. 497–504.

[85] Though see Raymond Williams, *Keywords: a vocabulary of culture and society* (Fontana edn, London, 1988), pp. 236–8; Stuart Hall, 'Notes on deconstructing the popular', in Raphael Samuel (ed.), *People's history and socialist theory* (London, 1981), pp. 227–40.

[86] For the modern period feminist scholars have done most to highlight this important point, see esp. Denise Riley, *Am I that name? Feminism and the category of women in history* (Basingstoke, 1988); Joan Scott, *Gender and the politics of history* (New York, 1988). For critical engagements with the notion of popular culture in the early modern period, see especially Bob Scribner, 'Is a history of popular culture possible?', *History of European Ideas*, 10 (1989), pp. 175–91, and Tim Harris, 'Problematising popular culture' in his edited collection *Popular culture in England, c. 1500–1850* (Basingstoke, 1995).

often find it very difficult to escape their use in practice.[87] Terms such as 'local politics' or 'popular politics' cannot now easily be stripped of connotations derived from this framework of discreet and dichotomous analytical categories. In discussing 'local politics' one may wish simply to refer to political developments within a specific locality – but only the most careful usage can prevent this from being (mis)read as denoting a form of politics separate from, and somehow beyond the influence of, 'national' or Westminster politics. In this study terms such as 'local' and 'popular' have been used in a purely descriptive sense: 'of the locality' and 'widely supported among the populace'. They are not intended to imply a distinctive *type* of politics, let alone an argument for the causal primacy of 'the local' or 'the popular' in political analysis. Rather, the assumption throughout this study is that the 'local' and the 'national', 'popular' and 'elite' are interdependent (and mutually determining) aspects of politics. The task for studies of popular politics is to trace and explain this inter-connectedness – to show how local identities feed into and help shape national identities (and vice versa),[88] or to analyse how MPs might resolve tensions between their role at Westminster and in the constituencies (as in the example of the Victorian legislative attack on election rituals). What we need is a much more integrated approach to the history of popular politics – only then can we transcend the conceptual polarisations which have been entrenched by the division between 'high' and 'low' politics. This is the aim of the detailed case-study of popular politics in Wolverhampton developed in part II. Not to generalise from the particular, but to study the mediation of local and national, formal and informal political practices within the context of a specific locality.

It might be objected that the opposition between 'formal' and 'informal' politics suggested here is itself artificial and ahistorical. But this would be unfair, since the purpose of this terminology is not to posit a fundamental opposition between two distinct *types* of politics, but rather to stress the need to analyze the interaction between two distinct *sites* of politics. The first, the politics of organisations and movements, are by definition more formalised, and are usually more programmatic and consistent; the latter, the political discourses which collect around the practices of everyday life (occupational or leisure cultures, for example, or the language of the law), tend to be less systematic, but they are no less political. Again the task of the historian is to trace and to explain the interconnections between these two sites of politics. For instance, to recognise that popular conceptions of rights and the law may be influenced by

---

[87] E.g. Vernon, *Politics and the people*, pp. 8, 49, 99–101, 159, 208, 281–9, 333.
[88] Benedict Anderson, *Imagined communities: reflections on the origin and spread of nationalism* (London, 1983).

changes in legislation or judicial practice,[89] but also to recognise that the success of a political movement will often depend upon its ability (intentional or otherwise) to articulate key aspects of 'informal' politics – one thinks of the connections between Gladstonian Liberalism and conceptions of independence and self-reliance among organised manual workers, or between late Victorian popular Conservatism and the defence of the working-man's right to enjoy his leisure time (and his beer) free from interference.[90]

Finally, I would like to end this discussion by suggesting what seem to me to be four key questions to be addressed in the historical analysis of popular politics. I do not claim that the present study has answers to them all, only that they are the sort of questions that need constantly to be asked if we are to develop a more adequate understanding of the relationship between politicians and the people they sought to represent. Firstly, we need to ask how social and economic factors shape the ability of 'subordinate' groups (those lacking access to social, economic and cultural capital)[91] to act politically, and even to be mobilised from outside. It is here that the recent reassertion of the need for social analysis by Savage and others is so important – we *do* need to know about patterns of residence, stability of population, hours of work, levels of poverty, employment practices, and a whole series of related factors if we are to understand the basic parameters of political activity within communities.[92] Focusing on the cultural, social and financial resources available for popular politics within a given locality, will not necessarily reveal much about the *content* of those politics, but it should reveal a great deal about their *form* – about the ability to sustain independent social and political organisation, or the strength and local 'rootedness' of any would-be popular leaders.

---

[89] Much valuable work has been done along such lines for pre nineteenth-century Britain. See especially John Brewer and John Styles (eds.), *An ungovernable people: the English and their law in the seventeenth and eighteenth centuries* (London, 1980), and Andy Wood, 'Social conflict and social change in the mining communities of north-west Derbyshire', *International Review of Social History*, 38 (1993), pp. 31–58; and 'Beyond post-revisionism? The Civil War allegiances of the miners of the Derbyshire "Peak Country"', *Historical Journal*, 40 (1997), pp. 23–40. Also Jennifer Davis, '"Jennings Buildings" and the Royal Borough: the construction of the underclass in mid-Victorian England', in Feldman and Stedman Jones (eds.), *Metropolis: London*.

[90] See Lawrence, 'Class and gender'; Keith McClelland, 'Some thoughts on masculinity and the "representative artisan" in Britain, 1850–1880', *Gender & History*, 1 (1989), pp. 164–77.

[91] Cf. Pierre Bourdieu, *Distinction: a social critique of the judgement of taste*, trans. Richard Nice (London, 1984), esp. ch. 2.

[92] These themes are explored more fully in Jon Lawrence, 'The dynamics of urban politics, 1867–1914', in Jon Lawrence and Miles Taylor (eds.), *Party, state and society: electoral behaviour in Britain since 1820* (Aldershot, 1997).

Crucial to any such analysis is a clear recognition of the limited scope for individual political 'resistance' enjoyed by those lacking economic, social and cultural resources within capitalist societies. Our analysis of popular politics needs to be sensitive to the factors which constrain political activity – it is no use categorising political behaviour in terms of a simple dichotomy between 'resistance' on the one hand and 'incorporation' on the other. Powerlessness alone makes 'pure' resistance all but impossible for most people most of the time, but it does not follow that they have therefore been 'incorporated' into a set of dominant norms and values (indeed one might question just how coherent such dominant norms and values have been historically – outside of Gramscian historiography that is).[93] By studying the interaction between 'formal' and 'informal' politics, that is by focusing on the space between organised politics and the beliefs and practices of everyday life, one is by definition recognising the incompleteness of 'incorporation'. For the space between 'formal' and 'informal' politics – between politicians and those they seek to represent – is one site where powerlessness can be transcended, if only in partial or symbolic ways. Here one does find scope for people to assert some degree of independence and self-identity, and even, on occasion, to challenge the authority and legitimacy of those socially and politically more powerful than themselves. In this sense we need to broaden our conception of 'resistance' so that it becomes sensitive to the political meanings embedded in the most mundane practices of everyday life.[94]

'Resistance', in this loose sense, might be found in the 'appropriation' of political events (for instance disrupting meetings, or over-turning their stated purpose) or in the carnival aspects of many election rituals, or simply in the 'appropriation' of formal political discourse (as in the case of the politics of 'fair trade'). There are, however, inherent dangers here. By calling for a greater sensitivity to the myriad forms of popular 'resistance' embedded in everyday political practice, it is all too easy to lapse into a new romantic populism – dedicated to celebrating the discovery of previously hidden radical, or even 'revolutionary', popular traditions. This would be profoundly unhelpful. Certainly, in the present study, analysis of such everyday 'practices of resistance' is intended only as a

---

[93] E.g. Robert Morris, *Class, sect and party: the making of the British middle class, 1820–50* (Manchester, 1990), for a more pragmatic approach see Trainor, *Black country élites*, or John Garrard, *Leadership and power in Victorian industrial towns, 1830–80* (Manchester, 1983) and 'Urban elites, 1850–1914: the rule and decline of a new squirearchy', *Albion*, 27 (1995), pp. 583–621.

[94] For recent, though theoretically quite distinct, explorations of such themes, see Michel de Certeau, *The practice of everyday life*, trans. Steven F. Rendall (Berkeley, Calif., 1984), and James C. Scott, *Domination and the arts of resistance: hidden transcripts* (New Haven, Conn., 1990).

corrective to exaggerated accounts of the 'incorporation' of popular politics, and the 'triumph of party'. It should be stressed that such 'practices of resistance' could be at least as exclusionary as formal party politics – as the machismo surrounding the 'politics of disruption' amply illustrates (see chapter 7). They could also be distinctly reactionary.[95]

The second big question is how we understand the role of organisation in the shaping of popular politics. It is clear that through organisation those lacking social, economic and cultural resources have been able to transcend their relative powerlessness and exert significant influence in the arena of formal politics. As we have already noted, a strong associational culture can enable even the poorest to become involved in sustained political self-activity. Organisations can provide collective resources to mirror those of wealthy elites: a large membership represents a form of social capital (albeit very different from the capital amassed in the social networks of the well-to-do); an organisation's financial reserves and its ability to call on the contributions of members represent forms of economic capital; while cultural capital comes from the ability to tap members' unrecognised talents – here the 'autodidact' worker, frustrated by structural inequalities from using his or her acquired cultural capital, is especially important. Moreover, organisations can provide more than collective resources – they can also provide the bases for a collective politics. Or rather, they can play a key role in the construction of a collective politics. As Alastair Reid argues, such organisations have often played a key role in constructing political unity among fragmented groups of workers through 'conscious manoeuvre, choice, negotiation and compromise'.[96] There is much to recommend this 'realist' perspective of the constraints upon spontaneous popular politics in a capitalist society. We must none the less remain attentive to the processes of exclusion and misrepresentation inherent in any such attempt to construct a vision of the 'popular interest' within the arena of formal party politics. Unmediated (or 'organic') forms of representation *may* be possible within an organisation, but once that organisation seeks to speak for a wider constituency than its own membership – once it seeks to be a 'party' not an interest group – representation necessarily becomes much more problematic. Almost by definition the world-view of the activist is not the same as that of the non-activist – especially when the activist is also an 'autodidact', whose cultural points of reference may be very different from those of most

[95] As for instance the 'Church & King' riots of the 1790s, the British Brothers' League actions against 'Jewish aliens', or anti-black riots in the 1950s; see respectively R. B. Rose, 'The Priestley riots of 1791', *Past & Present*, 18 (1960), pp. 68–88; Feldman, 'Importance of being English'; and Edward Pilkington, *Beyond the mother country: West Indians and the Notting Hill white riots* (London, 1988), or David Taylor, 'The Middlesbrough riots of 1961: a comment', *Social History*, 18 (1993), pp. 73–9.

[96] Reid, 'Politics and economics', p. 360.

citizens.[97] As the case-study of Wolverhampton in part II makes clear, the Labour activist, no less than the Liberal or Conservative activist, had to transcend the gulf between the world of political activism – of party politics – and the everyday lives of potential voters. Indeed, this study suggests that before the First World War Labour activists were often less adept at bridging the gulf than their rivals in the established political parties. Here lies one of the great ironies of organisational politics. Labour politics developed, at least in part, as a response to the relative powerlessness of workers within the existing party political system. And yet, by assuming responsibility for constructing their own 'authentic' voice of popular politics, Labour politicians may have further reduced the scope for independent self-activity among working people. Implicit in Labour's claim to 'authenticity' was the denial of 'authenticity' to other political voices that claimed to represent 'the people' (see chapter 9). Some may argue that this was simply inevitable – that misrepresentation, exclusion and partisanship sprang, not from Labour's peculiar failings, but from the realities of political conflict, and the weakness of 'independent' forms of popular politics.[98] This may be so, but to understand the Labour politics of a particular period we must still understand how these processes of misrepresentation and exclusion operated.

The third question we need constantly to ask of any popular politics concerns the relationship between the construction and the reception of political discourse. It is relatively straightforward to analyse the construction of formal discourses through the political press, party literature and other written sources, but analysing the public's *reception* of these politics presents many problems. Conventional written sources can again prove useful – especially for recovering the more systematic attempts to adapt or extend the languages of formal politics to serve unintended ends, and for suggesting the ways in which politicians felt obliged to tailor their message to meet the expectations (or demands) of a popular audience. Such sources can also tell us a lot about more dramatic forms of 'reception' – about disrupted meetings, robust electoral rituals, and other forms of political 'disturbance'. But inevitably much will be left to inference – to the critical and interpretative skills of the historian – and much will simply remain unknown. It is undoubtedly the incompleteness of any history of

---

[97] See Chris Waters, *British socialists and the politics of popular culture, 1884–1914* (Manchester, 1990). Also Stephen Yeo, 'A new life: the religion of socialism in Britain, 1883–1896', *History Workshop Journal*, 4 (1977); Logie Barrow, 'Determinism and environmentalism in socialist thought', in Raphael Samuel and Gareth Stedman Jones (eds.), *Culture, ideology and politics: essays for Eric Hobsbawm* (London, 1982).

[98] E.g. Steven Fielding, 'What did "the People" want? The General Election of 1945', *Historical Journal*, 35 (1992), pp. 623–39; Steven Fielding, Peter Thompson and Nick Tiratsoo, *England arise! The Labour party and popular politics in 1940s Britain* (Manchester, 1995).

the reception of politics which makes those of a more scientific disposition shun the whole question of 'consciousness' and 'subjectivity' in favour of an emphasis on more tangible entities such as 'structures' and 'interests'. However, as has already been argued, this is a false solution. We cannot escape the need to develop a much more sensitive understanding of *subjective* interests. In particular, we need to recognise that conceptions of 'interest', like many of the practices of popular politics, often predominate less because they reflect the immediate 'objective' interests of a social group, than because they are legitimated by past discourses and practices. This should not be read as suggesting that popular politics are irredeemably anachronistic (or worse 'inappropriate'). Past discourses and practices represent a vital political resource – one to be drawn upon, and used creatively, by individuals and groups locked in contemporary political struggles.[99] It does, however, imply that 'structuralist' accounts of popular politics cannot but be incomplete.

Fourthly, and finally, studies of popular politics also need to ask what factors determine the ability of 'informal' discourses to influence wider political developments. Here, Michael Sonenscher's work on the interaction of political change and workplace discourses in the eighteenth-century French trades has been particularly influential.[100] For Britain the work of Robert Gray on the languages of factory reform and Keith McClelland on artisan notions of 'masculinity' probably comes closest to replicating these concerns.[101] Such work emphasises the complex and impartial nature of translations between the worlds of 'informal' and 'formal' politics. But as Sonenscher demonstrates, major historical disjunctures may transform the significance of pre-existing, but apparently marginal popular discourses, giving them a new political salience and power. Indeed as Carol Smith-Rosenberg has argued, when analysing discourses we must recognise both their historicity, and the fact that they are invariably the product of past conflicts over meaning, past struggles to define and order the social world.[102] As chapter 7 on the limitations of

---

[99] See Wood, 'Social conflict and social change'; 'Beyond post-revisionism?'; and 'The place of custom in plebeian political culture, 1550–1800', *Social History*, 22 (1997), pp. 46–60.

[100] Michael Sonenscher, 'The *sans culottes* of Year II: rethinking the language of labour in revolutionary France', *Social History*, 9 (1984), pp. 301–28, and *Work and wages: natural law, politics and the eighteenth-century French trades* (Cambridge, 1989), esp. ch. 10.

[101] Robert Gray, 'The languages of factory reform in Britain, *c.* 1830–1860', in Joyce (ed.), *Historical meanings of work*; McClelland, 'Masculinity and the "representative artisan"'. See also, Geoffrey Crossick, 'From gentlemen to the residuum: languages of social description in Victorian Britain', in Penny J. Cornfield (ed.), *Language, history and class* (Oxford, 1991).

[102] Carol Smith-Rosenberg, 'The body politic', in Elizabeth Weed (ed.), *Coming to terms: feminism, theory, politics* (London, 1989), p. 102.

party makes clear, 'closure', discursive or otherwise, is never complete. At particular moments, such as during elections, major industrial disputes or times of war, the idea of 'elite control' (still so popular with social historians) often visibly breaks down, but it is doubtful whether it is ever a helpful paradigm through which to understand social relations or political discourse.

Part II

A local study: Wolverhampton, *c.* 1860–1914

4   Liberal hegemony and its critics

I

Created with the passing of the First Reform Act in 1832, the Parliamentary borough of Wolverhampton was a double-member constituency until its sub-division into three single-member seats by the Redistribution Act of 1885. Throughout this period it was one of the largest, and most influential industrial seats in England – in 1851 it ranked seventh by population among the English boroughs.[1] The town of Wolverhampton formed the core of the Parliamentary borough, but it stretched far beyond the boundaries conferred on the town at its incorporation in 1848. In 1851 the new municipality claimed a population of 49,985, whereas the Parliamentary constituency boasted a population of 119,748.[2] In the east the constituency embraced the townships of Wednesfield and Willenhall, and in the south it included Bilston, Coseley and Sedgley. There were also a host of smaller communities including Heath Town, Short Heath, Little London, Ettingshall and Moseley Village. In 1881 these outlying communities provided 54 per cent of the population of the Wolverhampton constituency – a preponderance that was reflected at redistribution four years later.[3] Of the three seats created in 1885, one (Wolverhampton South) drew none of its electorate from the municipality of Wolverhampton, and another (Wolverhampton East) drew less than two-fifths. In fact over 70 per cent of the *town's* population was concentrated in just one of the new constituencies – Wolverhampton West.[4] Moreover, as we shall see, the three constituencies created in 1885 displayed very different patterns of partisanship between 1885 and 1914.

---

[1] After Liverpool, Manchester, Birmingham, Leeds, Bristol and Sheffield, *Census of Great Britain, 1851*, vol. I, 'Population tables' (*Parl. Papers*, 1852–53, vol. LXXXIII, Pt I), 'Summary tables', pp. cciv-ccvii.   [2] *Ibid.*, 'Division VI', pp. 110 and 112.

[3] *Census of England and Wales, 1881*, vol. I, 'Counties' (*Parl. Papers*, 1883, vol. LXXVIII), pp. 343 and 345.

[4] See *Midland Evening News*, 24 November 1885; *Wolverhampton Chronicle*, 25 November 1885 and 7 July 1886; and *Census of England and Wales, 1891*, vol. I (*Parl. Papers*, 1893–94, CIV), p. 320.

Wolverhampton East remained solidly Liberal (though the Tories came close to victory at a by-election in 1908), Wolverhampton West was Conservative at six out of eight pre-war elections, while Wolverhampton South was not contested until Villiers' death in 1898, and then proved highly marginal, with three Unionist and two Liberal victories before the war (see table 4.1). Given this degree of divergence after 1885, we should be very cautious in making generalisations about the political temperament of the old two-member borough. Indeed, as we shall see below, by the mid 1870s there were already strong signs of a divergence between the politics of Wolverhampton and those of the outlying townships.

II

The bulk of this chapter is concerned with the mid-Victorian popular politics of Wolverhampton, and especially with the relationship between plebeian Radicalism and the town's powerful Liberal elite. However, it will be useful to begin with a brief sketch of popular politics in the town before the 1860s. In places this necessarily touches upon events already discussed in the work of the Black Country historian George Barnsby, but the intention here is not to present a systematic critique of his Marxist account of local working-class politics, but rather to provide a vital background for the discussion of later nineteenth-century popular politics which follows.[5]

It is not until the 1830s that we can begin to talk with some certainty about the extent of popular radicalism in Wolverhampton.[6] In the Autumn of 1831, when the House of Lords threw out the Whig Reform Bill, working-class Radical activists were quick to ally themselves with wealthy Radicals, such as the ironmaster and banker Richard Fryer, who planned to establish a branch of Attwood's Political Union in the town. At first many moderate reformers held aloof from this agitation, apparently distrustful of Fryer's populist style, but by May 1832 most had thrown their lot in with the Radicals, however reluctantly.[7] Even so, there remained deep divisions between the two wings of the reform movement: the 'moderates' and their 'Whig' allies on the one hand, and the Radicals

---

[5] George Barnsby, *The working-class movement in the Black Country, 1750–1867* (Wolverhampton, 1977); based on his thesis 'The working class movement in the Black Country, 1815–1867', MA thesis, University of Birmingham, 1966. See also V. Tunsiri, 'The party politics of the Black Country and neighbourhood, 1832–1867', MA thesis University of Birmingham, 1964, and G. B. Kent, 'Party politics in the county of Staffordshire during the years 1830 to 1847', MA thesis, University of Birmingham, 1959.

[6] For a discussion of earlier, fleeting, attempts to establish popular Radical organisations in the town, see Barnsby, *Working-class movement*, pp. 21–3.

[7] *Wolverhampton Chronicle*, 19 October 1831; Tunsiri, 'Party politics', pp. 7–9.

Table 4.1 *Winning party and percentage majority at Wolverhampton Parliamentary elections, 1885–1910*

Year	Wolverhampton East	Wolverhampton South	Wolverhampton West
1885	Liberal 19.6	Liberal Unopp.	Conservative 2.0
1886	Liberal 17.6	Liberal Unionist Unopp.	Liberal 1.6
1892	Liberal Unopp.	Liberal Unionist Unopp.	Conservative 13.2
1895	Liberal 14.8	Liberal Unionist Unopp.	Conservative 9.4
1898[a]	—	Liberal Unionist 1.4	—
1900	Liberal Unopp.	Liberal 2.4	Conservative Unopp.
1906	Liberal 34.2	Liberal 7.6	Labour 1.6
1908[a]	Liberal 0.0	—	—
1910(J)	Liberal 8.4	Conservative 3.8	Conservative 4.8
1910(D)	Liberal 13.4	Conservative 3.8	Conservative 2.6

Note:
[a] denotes Parliamentary by-election.
Source: F. W. S. Craig, *British Parliamentary election results, 1885–1910.*

and their plebeian supporters on the other. By June 1832, six months before the first General Election under the new franchise, both sides had nominated their candidate for the new double-member Wolverhampton constituency: Fryer himself would stand in the Radical interest, while the Whigs and moderates would be represented by William Whitmore, a Shropshire landowner whose support for reform of the Corn Laws placed his present Bridgnorth seat in some jeopardy. Although there is no evidence of a formal agreement to divide the representation of the borough, both sides observed a political truce in public, offering no support to those who sought to run a second Whig or Radical candidate. During the election campaign the two camps continued to avoid public controversy, although there was widespread suspicion that behind the scenes the

'Fryerites' were supporting John Nicholson, a London ultra-Radical, who had come forward as an anti-Whig/pro-Fryer candidate. On nomination day supporters of the two Radicals made it impossible for either Whitmore, or George Holyoake, the Tory candidate, even to reach the hustings. On polling day there was again considerable disorder, with widespread attacks on prominent Whig and Tory sympathisers.[8]

Interestingly Whitmore topped the poll, thanks to strong support in the south of the constituency where landlord influence was most pronounced, but Fryer had won most support in Wolverhampton, Willenhall and Wednesfield – where a significant proportion of electors had voted for the straight Radical ticket.[9] Moderate reformers such as the ironmaster John Barker were appalled by Fryer's flirtation with 'the mob', but they continued to fear the consequences of an outright break with the Radicals. Fryer's public attacks on the Melbourne Government did nothing to smooth relations, nor did Whitmore's sudden decision to stand down (or 'run away' – as some of his supporters saw it) on the eve of the 1835 election.[10] A complete split between 'moderate' and Radical reformers seemed inevitable until Fryer suddenly announced that he too would stand down – ostensibly on the grounds of ill-health. Though evidence is inconclusive, it seems likely that a deal had been hatched to bring forward two candidates from outside the borough who would be more or less acceptable to both sides. As a result, Thomas Thornely, a Liverpool merchant and Unitarian, and Charles Pelham Villiers, third son of the Whig Earl of Clarendon, were persuaded to come forward as Liberal candidates. Interestingly, with his son Richard acting as the intermediary, Fryer seems to have played an important part in persuading Villiers to stand – underlining the extent to which bringing in non-local candidates helped to blur the partisan divisions among the town's reformers.[11]

As in 1832 the ultra-Radicals brought forward John Nicholson as their champion – this time in direct opposition to both Thornely and Villiers. The Radicals reserved their special enmity for Villiers, whom they argued had been foisted on the borough by the secret machinations of Barker, Fryer and the emergent Liberal elite. During the campaign Villiers was fiercely attacked for his Whig ancestry, his flirtation with liberal Toryism in the 1820s and because he was suspected of being a Government 'placeman' seeking a safe borough. On the other hand, Thornely, as a Unitarian, received little support from the district's landowners who still

---

[8] *Wolverhampton Chronicle*, 5, 12 and 19 December; Tunsiri, 'Party politics', pp. 153–8.
[9] *Wolverhampton Chronicle*, 19 December 1832.
[10] Tunsiri, 'Party politics', p. 159 – citing the Rev. Leigh of St Leonards, Bilston.
[11] See *Wolverhampton Chronicle*, 7 January 1835, and *ibid.*, 1 March 1882 (obituary of Fryer jnr). Also *The Times*, 10 June 1879 (letter from Fryer's daughter on the origins of Villiers' candidacy).

exerted considerable influence in the south of the borough.[12] It was therefore simply a coincidence that the two 'official' Liberals polled the same
number of votes (776) – just over 70 per cent of their vote was made up of
straight Liberal 'splits', Villiers received 155 votes split with the Tory,
while Thornely received 131 split with Nicholson.[13] It is clear, however,
that there was already considerable identification with Liberalism as a
cohesive political movement by the mid 1830s. This was to intensify over
the next few years. In May 1835 a by-election for the county seat of South
Staffordshire sparked major political disturbances in Wolverhampton
after it had become clear that the Tory landowner, Sir F. H. L. Goodricke,
had won the seat. The Riot Act was read and the military called in to
restore order to the town.[14] Immediately after these disturbances Liberal
leaders determined to set up more formal party organisation in the town,
founding the Wolverhampton Reform Association in June 1835 at a
meeting attended by 200 local supporters. Finally the General Election of
1837 produced Wolverhampton's first straight two-party contest, with
Villiers and Thornely opposed by two Tory candidates: John Benbow and
Captain J. R. Burton.[15] Before the contest Thornely reported that
Nicholson's ultra-Radical supporters had gone over to Villiers, and this
seemed to be confirmed during the election. Not only did the Radicals
fail to run an independent candidate for the first time, but when the
Tories tried to disrupt the sitting MPs' nomination their plans were
thwarted by the intervention of Radical workers from the tin-plate and
japanning trades.[16]

It is clear that, despite his retirement, Richard Fryer continued to exert
a great influence over Wolverhampton politics throughout this period. It
was Fryer who persuaded Villiers to introduce an annual Parliamentary
resolution for the repeal of the Corn Laws, and he also organised the

---

[12] *Wolverhampton Chronicle*, 7 and 14 January; *The Times*, 1, 3 and 5 January 1835; Tunsiri,
'Party politics', pp. 159–63; Villiers to Clarendon, 10 January 1835 in Sir Robert Maxwell,
The life and letters of George William Frederick, Fourth Earl of Clarendon, 2 vols. (London,
1913), p. 85.

[13] See Henry Stooks Smith, *The Parliaments of England from 1715 to 1847* (2nd edn,
Chichester, 1973), p. 306.

[14] *Wolverhampton Chronicle*, 27 May and 3 June 1835 – the Liberal leaders on Anson's election committee claimed that the military exacerbated the situation by their use of exces-
sive force. Also *Parl. Papers*, 1835, vol. XLVI, p. 245f (*Minutes of Evidence taken at
Wolverhampton on Inquiry into Proceedings, May 1835*).

[15] Tunsiri, 'Party politics', pp. 193–202 and 352; *Wolverhampton Chronicle*, 3 and 10 June
1835 and 26 July 1837.

[16] Thornely to Villiers, nd [Easter 1837], folio 18 – quoting the opinion of Henry Walker, the
prominent Wolverhampton Liberal (Thornely–Villiers Correspondence, SR 1094,
BLPES); W. H. Jones, *The story of the japan, tin-plate working and iron-braziers trades,
bicycle and galvanizing trades and enamelware manufacture in Wolverhampton and district*
(London, 1900), pp. 16–20; *Wolverhampton Chronicle*, 26 July 1837, unlike in 1832 the two
'official' reform candidates polled almost equally in each of the six polling districts.

public meeting in support of Villiers' first motion in 1838. Similarly, in 1839 Fryer appears to have been the key figure in a campaign among Wolverhampton Liberals threatening to unseat Villiers and Thornely unless they became more critical of the Whig ministry.[17] But whilst Fryer remained content to push Radical causes from within the Liberal establishment, others, lacking his wealth and power, chose to organise independently. Thus, when a group of local Radicals set up a new branch of the Wolverhampton Political Union in November 1838, in order to support the Chartist National Convention, they shunned the patronage of Wolverhampton's established Radical political leaders.[18] Subsequent Chartist organisations continued this tradition drawing their strength predominantly from among male manual workers, with a smattering of clerks, shopkeepers and small masters, but no large-scale employers.[19] Convinced, as the leaders of the Wolverhampton Political Union put it, that 'only after changing Parliament itself' would other reforms become possible, these plebeian Radicals were deeply alienated from the Whig Governments of the 1830s, and deeply suspicious of local Liberal leaders associated with those Governments.[20] However, by 1842, with the Whigs out of office and Chartism at the height of its influence, the different strands of Radical opinion in the town did briefly find common cause behind a programme of Corn Law Repeal and universal male suffrage jointly endorsed by the leaders of the town's Chartist and Anti-Corn Law movements. Announced before a crowd of 5,000 in St James's Square, many Wolverhampton Liberals were from the outset suspicious of this alliance with Chartist democracy – their hostility intensified after the great strike movement of August and September 1842. That said, as late as December 1843, prosperous local reformers such as Thomas Simkiss were still calling on Villiers and Thornely to link free trade to the campaign for universal suffrage.[21] Both MPs considered this a dangerous and unhelpful tactic, and lamented that their Liberal friends at

[17] Thornely to Villiers, 20 May 1839 (folio 36); Thornely to Villiers, nd [December 1839?] – folio 192, *Thornely–Villiers correspondence* (BLPES); W. O. Henderson, *Charles Pelham Villiers and the Repeal of the Corn Laws* (Oxford, 1975), p. 8. For Villiers' attempts to learn about the question in 1838, see Richard Cobden to Villiers, 17 February 1838 (BL Add MS 43 662, Cobden Papers, XVI, folios 1–6).

[18] Barnsby, *Working-class movement*, p. 61; Tunsiri, 'Party politics', pp. 231–2; *Wolverhampton Chronicle*, 21 November 1838; *The Charter*, 24 March 1839.

[19] See Lawrence, 'Party politics and the people', pp. 4–5 (and figure 1) for a detailed occupational analysis of Black Country nominees to the Chartist General Council in 1842 – 80 per cent of Wolverhampton delegates appear to have been manual workers, though this figure was higher still in nearby Wednesbury, Bilston and Walsall.

[20] Cited in Barnsby, *Working-class movement*, p. 63.

[21] *The Northern Star*, 26 February and 5 March 1842; Thornely to Villiers, 15 December 1843, and Villiers to Thornely, 16 December 1843 (Thornely–Villiers Correspondence, folios 79 and 80). Also Tunsiri, 'Party politics', pp. 232–5.

Wolverhampton had 'lost weight a great deal with the people' since the 1830s – with the activist minority turning to ultra-radicalism, and the remainder lapsing into political indifference.[22] In fact the Chartists too were losing influence by the mid 1840s, as was underlined by Joseph Linney's failed bid to stand at Wolverhampton in the 1847 General Election – support was so weak that he could not even afford to sustain his candidacy long enough to force a nomination day (open) vote.[23] Even the Chartist revival of 1848 had little impact in Wolverhampton, where local energies seem to have been devoted almost exclusively to developing a powerful branch of the National Land Company, rather than to political agitation.[24]

Organised Radicalism remained weak in Wolverhampton throughout the 1850s. Despite frequent overtures from the strong Chartist Associations which survived in Bilston and Dudley, plebeian radical leaders showed little inclination to re-establish independent political organisation until 1857, when Ernest Jones launched his cross-class Political Reform League. A series of meetings called to support the new campaign met with a strong response, and by early 1858 a Wolverhampton Reform Committee had been established. This flurry of activity was soon dissipated by the collapse of Jones's movement nationally, but it proved that there remained a significant, if largely untapped, Radical constituency in the town. One reason for the relative quiescence of Wolverhampton radicalism was undoubtedly the absence of contested Parliamentary elections during this period. After their resounding defeat in 1837, the Tories did not contest the seat again at a General Election until 1874 – though, as we shall see, they did bring forward a candidate at the by-election of 1861, apparently encouraged by the appearance of rival Liberal candidates. Indeed according to Villiers, by the late 1840s all the Wolverhampton Tories were Peelite free traders, who were more or less reconciled to the political status quo.[25] Villiers himself was already emerging as a popular 'tribune of the people' thanks to his part in overcoming aristocratic resistance to repealing the 'bread tax', while the elderly Thornely also enjoyed widespread respect in Wolverhampton. On

---

[22] Villiers to Thornely, 16 December 1843 – folio 80 (Thornely–Villiers Correspondence, BLPES).
[23] *The Northern Star*, 10 July 1847 – lamenting the apathy shown throughout the Black Country; *Wolverhampton Chronicle*, 4 August 1847.
[24] *The Northern Star*, 8 January and 15 April 1848; Barnsby, *Working-class movement*, pp. 120 and 149; David Phillips, 'Riots and public order in the Black Country', in R. Quinault and J. Stevenson (eds.), *Popular protest and public order: six studies in British history, 1790–1920* (London, 1974), p. 158.
[25] Villiers to Thornely, 15 January 1849 – folio 120 (Thornely–Villiers Correspondence, BLPES).

the other hand, the local Liberal establishment was certainly not beyond criticism. There was widespread suspicion that Wolverhampton's 'inner circle' of Liberal leaders used their influence to gain lucrative appointments in local government, and to dominate both the magistracy and the newly created municipal Corporation. Significantly correspondence between Thornely and Villiers suggests a shared resentment at the demands of local Liberals for preferment, and considerable concern at the unpopularity of the new Corporation and its councillors.[26] When Thornely's failing health forced him to stand down in 1859 it is clear that both he and Villiers expected there to be a contested election. That his successor was chosen by just thirty local Liberals meeting in private at the Ironmasters' Rooms of the Exchange appeared designed to make a contest more likely. Especially when Wolverhampton's Liberal leaders subsequently failed to invite supporters from the outlying towns to a 'public' meeting called to endorse the choice of Sir Richard Bethell as the new Liberal candidate. In the end a contest was avoided, mainly, Thornely felt, because they had been 'lucky' that Sir Richard 'took with the people'.[27]

When, two years later, Sir Richard was obliged to vacate his seat on his appointment as Lord Chancellor, local Liberal leaders were unable to repeat the coup of 1859. This time 100 local Liberals were invited to a private selection meeting at the Star and Garter Hotel in Wolverhampton, choosing T. M. Weguelin, the former Governor of the Bank of England, from a panel of five suggested candidates. As in 1859 there was an immediate outcry against the 'self-constituted leaders' of the Liberal party, but unlike in 1859 the cause of 'independence' found a local champion – in the unlikely guise of 'Baron Sam' Griffiths, a wealthy local ironmaster. Griffiths ran an unashamedly populist campaign as the 'independent' Liberal – recalling his prominent part in defence of the town's tin-plate workers during a bitter trade dispute, and backing substantial Parliamentary reform and vote by ballot. But at the heart of Griffiths' appeal lay the claim to be a local man who would promote the interests of the whole town, rather than just those of a narrow, self-seeking elite. Griffiths promised to 'smash this great oligarchy which has bound

[26] See Thornely to Villiers, 22 August 1856 – folio 146; and Thornely to Villiers, nd – folio 192 (Thornely–Villiers Correspondence, BLPES). See also Roger Swift, 'The English urban magistracy and the administration of justice during the early nineteenth century: Wolverhampton, 1815–1860', *Midland History*, 17 (1992), pp. 75–92.

[27] Thornely to Villiers, 10 December 1856 – folio 150; and Thornely to Villiers, nd [May 1859?] – folio 180 (Thornely–Villiers Correspondence, BLPES); *Wolverhampton Chronicle*, 13 April 1859; Tunsiri, 'Party politics', p. 363. The 'inner circle's' first choice had been Ralph Bernal Osborne, suggesting that the flame of radicalism was not entirely extinguished at Wolverhampton – Sir Richard Bethell had been Attorney-General in the last Liberal Government.

the borough and beaten down and trampled on [its] rights for the last five and twenty years'. He denounced the Liberal leaders' cosy relationship with London's political wire-pullers, suggesting that they had repeatedly sold the representation of Wolverhampton in return for the spoils of mag- istracies or government office for themselves.[28] Griffiths appeal was explicitly anti-party: he told the towns-folk that he 'wished to put down this party feeling. They, the electors, the inhabitants of Wolverhampton, were the party.'[29] If the *Wolverhampton Chronicle* is to be trusted Weguelin did little to blunt Griffiths' criticisms when, in his first major speech in the borough, he made a major slip by suggesting that he thought he was fighting Sheffield rather than Wolverhampton.[30]

Even so the electorate kept faith with the official Liberal leadership – returning Weguelin with a comfortable majority of 591 over Griffiths; although thanks to a relatively low turnout (68 per cent), and the inter- vention of Alexander Staveley Hill, a popular local Tory, Weguelin's vote represented only a third of the borough's registered electors.[31] In Bilston, where resentment at exclusion from the Wolverhampton clique was most pronounced, Griffiths topped the poll with 247 votes to 154 for Weguelin, and 130 for Staveley Hill.[32] There can also be little doubt that Griffiths would have triumphed if the election had been fought on a wider fran- chise. At the show of hands on nomination day Griffiths won easily, while after the polls had closed between 15,000 and 20,000 of his supporters filled the town centre – cheering their champion and harassing anyone thought to be connected with his defeat.[33] More so than Nicholson in 1835, Sam Griffiths had been able to mobilize considerable popular feeling against the traditional leaders of Wolverhampton Liberalism. One factor in his success may have been that local Liberal leaders could no longer rely on the public's violent hatred of Toryism to bolster their own popularity. In fact, when Griffiths addressed his massed supporters after the poll he was able to draw a massive cheer from the crowd by praising the honest campaign fought by Staveley Hill.

III

Although Griffiths portrayed himself during the campaign as 'a Liberal of the extreme school', most Wolverhampton Radicals were uncomfortable

---

[28] *Wolverhampton Chronicle*, 3 July 1861 – on the 'spoils of the game', see J. Vincent, *The formation of the British Liberal party, 1857–68* (2nd edn, Hassock, 1976), pp. 126–38.

[29] *Staffordshire Advertiser*, 29 June 1861, cited in Tunsiri, 'Party politics', p. 365.

[30] *Wolverhampton Chronicle*, 3 July 1861.

[31] Calculated from F. W. S. Craig, *British Parliamentary election results, 1832–1885* (2nd edn, Aldershot, 1989), p. 338.   [32] Tunsiri, 'Party politics', p. 271.

[33] *Wolverhampton Chronicle*, 3 July 1861, and *The Times*, 2 and 3 July 1861; also Tunsiri, 'Party politics', pp. 268–71 and 365.

with his candidature, not least because of his blatant manipulation of his large workforce throughout the campaign. They might join in the popular outcry against the secretive Liberal elite (the cry of 'We gull 'em again' was apparently best favoured in Radical circles), but they could hardly enthuse about Griffiths usurpation of the popular mantle.[34] Radicals could, however, take some heart from the fact that popular opinion (especially among their natural constituency: the non-electors) now shared their dissatisfaction with the narrow base and increasingly conservative character of local Liberalism. In 1861 they had no organisational basis from which to influence the course of local politics – five years later, when a measure of Parliamentary Reform seemed imminent, things were very different. National factors played their part in this revival of Radical fortunes, but perhaps more important, in the case of Wolverhampton, was the rapid growth and the unparalleled politicisation of the local trade union movement between 1860 and 1865. Besides a proliferation of new trade societies, these years also saw the emergence of a new generation of trade union leaders who believed that many of the grievances of working people could best be redressed by political rather than industrial means.[35] Though our main source is his own newspaper, there are strong grounds for believing that these Wolverhampton trade unionists were greatly influenced by George Potter, leader of the London building workers' nine hour struggles between 1859 and 1861, and a strong critic of attempts to maintain a rigid separation between political and industrial activity. By April 1864 Potter's *Bee-Hive* appears to have enjoyed a wide readership among Wolverhampton labour leaders, and in 1865 the paper consolidated its influence with local trade unionists by offering solid support to Midland building workers and Staffordshire ironworkers involved in bitter disputes with their employers.[36]

The Wolverhampton Trades Council, founded in August 1865, quickly emerged as a fierce partisan both of the new more political style of trade unionism, and of Potter in his growing conflicts with the national trade

[34] See *The Times*, 2 and 3 July 1861; Jones, *Story of trades*, p. 104. Also *Wolverhampton Chronicle*, 4 April and 27 June 1866 for retrospective accounts of the Radicals' bitterness over the 1861 campaign.

[35] New trade societies included the Amalgamated Carpenters, the Operative Bricklayers, the Builders' Labourers, the Co-operative Plate-lock Makers, the Rivetters and Finishers, the Ironworkers Association and the Locomotive Enginemen – many of these were purely local societies rather than branches of national unions.

[36] *The Bee-Hive*, 2 April 1864 and for the two disputes *ibid.*, 17 December to 18 February 1865 and 1 April 1865. See also S. Coltham, '*The Bee-Hive* newspaper: its origin and early struggles', in A. Briggs and J. Saville (eds.), *Essays in labour history* (London, 1960), I, pp. 174–204; and 'English working-class newspapers in 1867', *Victorian Studies*, 13 (1969), pp. 159–80;; and Thomas Wright, *Our new masters* (London, 1873), pp. 333–53. Ironically it was Potter's intervention in these two Midland disputes that did most to alienate him form the leaders of the new model unions in London – the so-called 'Junta'.

union leaders known collectively as 'the Junta'.[37] Formed out of a 'standing conference' of local trade societies organised to defend the town's cooperative plate-locksmiths against employer hostility, the Wolverhampton Trades Council was a strong advocate of labour solidarity and trade union federalism.[38] Within months of its inaugural meeting it was at the centre of plans to organise a national trades conference which marked a vital step in the formation of the Trades Union Congress in 1868.[39] The Council also campaigned both locally and nationally for reform of the trade union laws, and for the abolition of the iniquitous Master and Servants Acts, widely used by Wolverhampton employers to instill workplace discipline (between 1858 and 1867 more workers were sued for breach of contract under the Acts in Wolverhampton than in any other borough).[40]

The Council's campaigns for trade solidarity and the legal emancipation of labour were elements within a broader politico-industrial strategy. And yet, while these policies have generally been judged 'radical', or even 'class conscious' by historians, other policies, equally part of this broader strategy, have been dismissed as conservative or elitist. In particular, support for industrial arbitration and Parliamentary reform among mid-Victorian labour leaders has been seen in these terms. This is mistaken. In Wolverhampton, as elsewhere, arbitration was supported, not in recognition of the fundamental harmony of interests between employers and workers, but as a strategy for ending the arbitrariness and anarchy of contemporary industrial relations by reforming the conduct of both employers and (non-union) labour. Wolverhampton's labour leaders were united over the desirability of these goals, but they were divided over whether arbitration could in fact be made to work. The carpenters, tinsmiths and the Trades Council leaders were convinced that it could, while the bricklayers and house painters remained openly hostile rather than just sceptical. And yet the two groups co-operated fully on all other issues, and shared a common acceptance, both that strikes were

---

[37] For the formation of the Council in August 1865 see *The Bee-Hive*, 23 September 1865 and 15 September 1866, and Lawrence, 'Party politics and the people', p. 12n. For the Council's strong backing of Potter against 'the Junta', see *The Bee-Hive*, 28 October 1865.

[38] See *The Bee-Hive*, 15 and 22 April, 24 June, 23 September and 14 October 1865; but also B. Jones, *Co-operative production*, 2 vols. (Oxford, 1894), II, pp. 437–44. Some important groups, including the ironworkers, engineers and miners, supported the cooperative workers but declined to join the Trades Council.

[39] *The Bee-Hive*, 14 April 1866; A. E. Musson, *Trade union and social history* (London, 1974) p. 40.

[40] See *The Bee-Hive*, 24 October and 25 November 1865, 13 January and 15 September 1866, and 9 March 1867. Also D. Simon, 'Master and servant', in J. Saville (ed.), *Democracy and the labour movement* (London, 1954), and D. C. Woods, 'The operation of the master and Servant Acts in the Black Country, 1858–1875', *Midland History*, 7 (1982), pp. 93–115.

inevitable, and that it was the duty of trade unionists to support workers involved in disputes. Indeed, since trade union leaders were still frequently victimised in Wolverhampton, especially after local trade disputes, it is hardly surprising that this 'realist' view of industrial relations should prevail.[41]

Wolverhampton's trade unionists formed only one element in the vociferous campaign for Parliamentary reform which flourished in Wolverhampton during 1866 and 1867. The reform agitation in Wolverhampton grew directly out of suspicions that the town's Liberal leaders intended to oppose Gladstone's modest proposals for Parliamentary reform. An *ad hoc* Working Men's Reform Committee was established in March 1866, with a central committee dominated by trade unionists and other plebeian radicals. There was little support for calls to confine the agitation to the non-electors – from the outset the aim seems to have been to rally support for reform among the town's established Liberal leadership. At the first mass reform meeting, held in early April, the members of the committee persuaded more than twenty local Liberal leaders, including Henry Walker and Thomas Simkiss (veterans of the 1832 agitation), to sit alongside them on the platform.[42] Some on the committee were clearly unhappy with Gladstone's cautious Bill, retaining as it did the principle of property-based qualification, but they appear to have accepted the need for pragmatism in order to defeat the powerfully entrenched opponents of reform, both locally and at Westminster. Certainly ultra-Radicals such as the newsagent Adam Taylor and the former Chartist leader Joseph Linney made it clear that their personal commitment to universal suffrage remained undiminished.[43]

In the end, of course, this strategy of compromise was thwarted by the Parliamentary alliance of the 'Adullamite' Liberals with the Conservative Opposition. In Wolverhampton Radical frustration at yet another failed attempt to revise the 1832 settlement was compounded by anger at the role wealthy local Liberals were believed to have played in persuading

---

[41] On arbitration and its opponents, see *The Bee-Hive*, 13 May to 12 August 1865 *passim*, 2 December 1865, and 12 and 19 May and 27 October 1866. See also V. L. Allen, 'The origins of industrial conciliation and arbitration', *International Review of Social History*, 9 (1964), esp. pp. 240 and 245–6; R. Price, *Masters, unions and men: work control in building and the rise of labour, 1830–1914* (Cambridge, 1980), pp. 105–6 and 109, and J. H. Porter, 'Wage bargaining under conciliation agreements', *Economic History Review*, 2nd series, 23 (1970), pp. 460–75. On victimization and support for strikes, see *Wolverhampton Chronicle*, 24 January 1866; *The Bee-Hive*, 1 December 1866; *The Miner and Workmen's Examiner*, 12 June 1875.

[42] *Wolverhampton Chronicle*, 4 and 11 April 1866 – the paint and varnish manufacturer Sam Mander, and the publisher Alfred Hinde appear to have acted as intermediaries between the committee and members of the Liberal party.

[43] *Wolverhampton Chronicle*, 11 April and 27 June 1866.

H. J. W. J. Foley and W. O. Foster, the Liberal MPs for the county seat of South Staffordshire, to join the 'Adullamites'. It was known that thirty 'influential Liberal electors' had met in secret at the Swan Hotel early in June in order to plan how to 'prevent the evil which must result from the extension of the franchise among the operatives'. Most Radicals felt sure that this conspiracy had been decisive in the defeat of reform, and memory of the meeting continued to poison Liberal/Radical relations for many months.[44] Indeed a mass meeting of the Working Men's Reform Committee held at the end of June, ostensibly to protest at the defeat of reform, developed into a full-scale challenge to the local Liberal elite. Adam Taylor declared that 'cliquism should be no more in Wolverhampton' and that, 'the thirty or a hundred who had been in the habit of selecting candidates for the representation should do it no longer'. Others recalled the grievances of the 1861 by-election more directly. The Committee's direct challenge to official Liberalism was underlined by its decision to reconstitute itself as the Working Men's Liberal Association, with Adam Taylor as its secretary.[45] However, once again there was a strong desire to retain the support of reform-minded Liberal leaders – Sam Mander was one of three Liberal leaders invited to serve on the committee of the new association, while other leading figures were appointed honorary vice-presidents. The new Association took the agitation for reform directly into the workshops and factories of Wolverhampton, and it appears that this agitation did much to convince activists of the need to make a formal commitment to full manhood suffrage by affiliating to the London-based Reform League.[46] When the Association's leaders proposed this move in October, it was the solicitor Henry Fowler, the future MP and cabinet minister, who led the opposition. Fowler's arguments, which centred around the need to restrict the franchise to 'respectable' and 'intelligent' workers, were defeated by a margin of more than two to one. At the meeting Fowler had argued that working men needed the support of the town's influential Liberal leaders – this support was now swiftly withdrawn. Only one of the middle-class vice presidents of the old Working Men's Liberal Association agreed to serve in the same capacity on the Wolverhampton Reform League.[47] Despite this exodus, or perhaps because of it, the new Reform League flourished. By December it had developed an extensive ward-based organisation throughout the town, and could claim more registered branches (six) than any town other than London and Birmingham.

[44] See *Wolverhampton Chronicle*, 6 and 27 June and 28 November 1866, 8 May 1867.
[45] *Ibid.*, 27 June 1866.   [46] *Ibid.*, 4 July and 8 August 1866.
[47] *Wolverhampton Chronicle*, 3 October and 28 November 1866; E. H. Fowler, *The life story of Henry Hartley Fowler, First Viscount Wolverhampton* (London, 1912), pp. 67–77.

Membership is less certain, but by April 1867 this was estimated at 600 by the local press.[48]

The Reform League established strong relations with local trade societies, indeed two, the General Carpenters and the Upholsterers, set up special branches for their members. This relationship was reinforced when the League asked George Potter to address a mass reform meeting in January 1867. In planning for Potter's visit the League's 'Democratisation Committee' worked closely with the Trades Council and other local trade societies.[49] Potter himself appears to have been a great success, judging from the *local* press – though his message to the Wolverhampton reformers was undoubtedly more intemperate than most of the Reform League leadership in London would have sanctioned. According to Potter, a democratic franchise would allow working people to purge Parliament of 'hostile class interests', and to ensure that reform would be passed forthwith he claimed (somewhat inventively) that

The London reformers meant to call on the men in the provinces to make a march on the metropolis and to take possession of it entirely (loud cheers). They meant to ask the labouring, honest working men of Wolverhampton to join the men of Birmingham and to start on a certain day for London . . . That policy settled the question in 1832[50]

These echoes of an earlier phase of working-class protest clearly went down well with Potter's Wolverhampton audience, but this should not lead us to overlook the altered temperament of the reform movement of the 1860s from that of the 1830s or 1840s. Mid-century Radicals undoubtedly embraced a less conflictual model of society and polity than their early nineteenth-century counter-parts, but this had much to do with the fact that they no longer faced a state as openly repressive, as corrupt or as closed to reform as earlier Radicals.[51] We should not, therefore, be surprised that the Working Men's Liberal Association concluded

---

[48] *George Howell Collection* (Bishopsgate Institute), *Reform League Archive*, 'List of departments and branches', nd [January 1867]; *Wolverhampton Chronicle*, 24 April 1867.

[49] *George Howell Collection*, 'List of departments and branches'; *Wolverhampton Chronicle*, 19 December 1866, 16 and 23 January 1867; *The Bee-Hive*, 2 February and 9 March 1867.

[50] *Wolverhampton Chronicle*, 30 January 1867. See also *The Commonwealth*, 2 February 1867, which comments dismissively that the question of such a march 'has never been canvassed'. Potter had in fact been voted off the Executive Committee of the Reform League in December and was generally out of favour, see F. M. Leventhal, *Respectable Radical: George Howell and Victorian working-class politics* (London, 1971), p. 61.

[51] See Philip Harling and Peter Mandler, 'From "fiscal-military" state to laissez faire state, 1760–1850', *Journal of British Studies*, 32 (1993), pp. 44–70; Philip Harling, 'Rethinking Old Corruption', *Past and Present*, 147 (1995), pp. 127–58; and *The waning of Old Corruption: the politics of economical reform in Britain, 1779–1846* (Oxford, 1996); Gareth Stedman Jones, *Languages of class: studies in English working-class history, 1832–1982* (Cambridge, 1983), pp. 173–8; Jon Lawrence, 'Popular Radicalism and the socialist revival in Britain', *Journal of British Studies*, 31 (1992), pp. 163–86, esp. pp. 166–70.

its meetings by singing 'God Save the Queen', or that Reform League officials presented a loyal address to Queen Victoria when she visited Wolverhampton late in 1866, and marched behind a banner proclaiming 'Our Queen, Our Country and Our Rights' – working-class Radicals might still be deeply suspicious of privilege and authority, might still rail against 'class government' and slave-driving employers, but they did not feel as fundamentally alienated from the state or the political system as their political forebears.[52]

IV

As we have seen, however, there are signs that many Wolverhampton Radicals did feel alienated from Liberalism, or rather from the local Liberal party (it is clear that national leaders such as Gladstone, Bright, and of course Villiers, were widely revered, even by former Chartist firebrands such as Joseph Linney). If anything relations with the local Liberal establishment deteriorated as the reform agitation came to a head in 1867. In April 1867 Sam Mander publicly acknowledged that the attitude of the Wolverhampton Liberal Party to the reform question 'might well excite grave doubts'. In fact, it did much more. When not one member of the town's sixty-man Liberal Committee supported a motion proposed by Linney and the local Reform League president George Griffiths in favour of *household* suffrage and the ballot, there was a general outcry. The Reform League called a special meeting to denounce the attitude of the town's 'so-called Liberal Party', at which Linney observed that even apparently sympathetic Liberals such as Mander and Bantock dropped all pretence to be 'true Liberals' once they were amongst their own kind.[53]

At this point a clash between the plebeian Radicals of the Reform League and the small group of wealthy men who controlled the Wolverhampton Liberal Committee seemed inevitable. In fact no such clash materialised – Wolverhampton avoided an election on the new householder franchise in 1868, and the Liberal elite were subsequently able to 'democratise' their political organisation on their own terms (and at their own pace). Clearly this needs some explanation. Firstly, it is likely that things would have been very different if the Conservatives had shown signs of forcing an election in 1868, but it was well known that they possessed neither the organisation nor the money to do so. Once the Liberal Committee had dropped its rather rash plans to create a vacancy for Henry Fowler at Wolverhampton by persuading Villiers to fight the

---

[52] *Wolverhampton Chronicle*, 27 June and 28 November 1866, 24 April 1867.
[53] *Ibid.*, 24 April and 7 May 1867.

county seat of South Staffordshire, there seemed even less prospect of a contest.[54] This also squared the Radicals' pitch. Having spent the past two years or more contrasting Villiers and Weguelin's unequivocal stance on reform with the half-hearted attitude of local Liberal leaders, Wolverhampton Radicals could hardly now propose to unseat either of them. However, the Radicals' problems ran much deeper than this – for the unity, political purpose, and above all the organisational strength that had characterised the movement during 1866–67 had all but disappeared eighteen months later when a General Election was finally called. As in so many districts, the once-powerful branches of the Reform League appear to have quietly disappeared once Parliament accepted the household suffrage.[55] After 1867 the town's more independent-minded Radicals channelled their energies into a wide range of advanced political causes, notably secularism and republicanism, but these had little appeal, or relevance, for the majority of workers who had been drawn into the reform agitation of the mid 1860s. Moreover, the organisations they developed to promote these causes generally proved to be short-lived, small-scale and riven by internecine disputes.[56]

At the same time the local trade union movement, which had done so much to nurture the more assertive political culture of the 1860s, contracted dramatically in the economic slump at the end of the decade.[57] Many trade societies simply folded in these years, others facing the desperate battle for survival had little time for politics. Most damaging of all was the collapse of the Trades Council itself at the end of 1868.[58] It was five years before local trade unionists felt strong enough to found a new Council, by which time Wolverhampton's Liberal leaders had already introduced a new 'democratic' organisation which gave little scope for genuine popular involvement, trade union or otherwise. In May 1871 the Wolverhampton Liberal Committee announced that it intended to

---

54 For rumours of this plan, see *Wolverhampton Chronicle*, 8 May 1867. In fact J. W. Hall came forward at the last-minute as a Conservative candidate only to withdraw on nomination day, *ibid.*, 18 November 1868.
55 This pre-dates the Howell–Glynn pact which is often seen as completing the process of decline, see Leventhal, *Respectable Radical*, pp. 103–11; R. Harrison, 'The British working class and the General Election of 1868', *International Review of Social History*, 7 (1962) pp. 351–99; and A. F. Thompson, 'Gladstone's whips and the General Election of 1868', *English Historical Review*, 63 (1948), pp. 189–200.
56 For details of the various secularist and republican organisations established in Wolverhampton after 1867, see: *The National Reformer*, 10 March 1867, 23 August 1868, 4 and 11 April and 28 November 1869, 6 March 1870, 31 August 1873 to 24 May 1874 *passim*, and 16 December 1882 to 29 June 1883 *passim*; *The Republican*, 15 May 1871.
57 See G. C. Allen, *The industrial development of Birmingham and the Black Country, 1860–1927* (London, 1929), pp. 175–6. The slump developed in the wake of the financial crisis of 1866.
58 For details of the Council's decline, see Lawrence, 'Party politics and the people', p. 27.

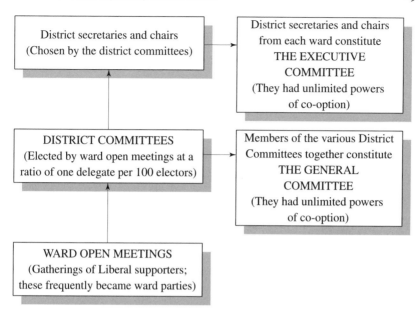

Figure 4.1 The three-tier structure of the 1871 Wolverhampton Liberal Association.

disband itself in favour of a new, more democratic form of organisation based on ward meetings. It therefore appointed Henry Walker, the veteran Liberal leader, chairman of a Provisional Committee charged with drawing up a formal constitution for the proposed Wolverhampton Liberal Association. Walker did his work well, creating an organisation which appeared, on the surface, to be genuinely open and democratic, but which in reality retained power securely in the hands of the narrow elite that had dominated Wolverhampton Liberalism since the 1830s. The first thing to note is that the new Association did not formally sanction the creation of ward parties with individual party members. Rather, open meetings of Liberal supporters were called in each ward in order to elect a district Liberal Committee on the basis of one committee delegate for every 100 electors (see figure 4.1). This not only limited popular involvement to a single meeting, it also favoured districts with above average levels of enfranchisement – generally the more prosperous districts. Together, the delegates to these district committees constituted the General Committee of the Liberal Association, while the secretaries and chairmen chosen by each District Committee together constituted its Executive Committee. In turn, both these central committees were given unlimited powers to co-opt additional members.[59] In itself this dramatically limited the scope for direct accountability, but the Provisional Committee also drew up lists of prominent men deemed to be 'entitled to election on the ward committees', and then sought to ensure that ward meetings simply ratified these lists.[60] Finally, the new constitution left not only day-to-day affairs, but most matters of any importance, solely in the hands of the fifty men who made up the new Executive Committee – the 'inner circle' of the old Liberal Committee had simply recreated itself in a new guise.

Reports in the local press suggest that the ward open meetings held in the early summer excited little interest from the general public. Some prominent members of the old Working Men's Liberal Association and Reform League organisations, such as Markland, McConnell and Fullwood, took part, but most appear to have remained aloof.[61] Few trade union leaders appear to have participated in the new Association, reflecting a widespread sense in the 1870s that industrial politics and *party* politics should not become entangled. Indeed when the Wolverhampton Trades Council was reconstituted in the early 1870s it was written into its constitution that it should be a 'non-political' body. Although, as a bitter controversy on the Council in 1875 made clear, for most trade unionists 'non-political' meant 'non-party', not 'unpolitical'. When a group of delegates to the Council proposed to move a resolution supporting Samuel Plimsoll's tactics in the campaign against over-laden ships, a member of the genuinely unpolitical Steam Engine Makers' Society objected to 'the introduction of political matters into their proceedings'. In reply Oliver, of the tailors union, argued that 'if they were to exclude this subject, and were not in any way to interfere in so-called politics, then for ever more they must hold their peace with relation to the labour laws, and all other obnoxious Acts which might affect the operative classes'. But it was Marshall, like Oliver a survivor from the first Trades Council, who summed up the mood of Wolverhampton trade unionism in the 1870s when he pointed out that, 'of course it was not for them to meddle in the differences as between Liberals and Conservatives, but they were fully allowed to interfere as to any legislation affecting labour in any shape or form'.[62] Far from being a sign of creeping 'reformism', 'non-political' trade unionism therefore reflected the determination of local labour

---

[59] *Wolverhampton Chronicle*, 26 April and 10 May 1871.   [60] *Ibid.*, 14 June 1871.
[61] *Ibid.*, 24 May and 14 June 1871.
[62] *The Miner and Workmen's Examiner*, 7 August 1875 – Plimsoll had been expelled from the Commons for refusing to exempt members of the House from his scathing attack on British shipowners. The Steam Engine makers subsequently withdrew from the Council, *ibid.*, 25 September 1875.

leaders to preserve the independence of their organisations. It should be seen as further evidence that the influence of party was often much less pronounced 'on the ground' than historians have allowed. One might also add, at this point, that these mid-Victorian labour leaders continued to embrace a very strong sense of social class. George Paddey, the Trades Council president, attacked sectarian and elitist attitudes among some union members, and demanded sympathy for fellow workers too weak to sustain a union.[63] Even Richard Juggins, the moderate nut and bolt makers' leader, denounced the Liberals' trade union reforms of 1871 as 'unjustifiable class legislation'.[64] Nor should we be surprised that class feeling was so strong in labour circles at this time – perhaps stronger than during the classic period of the 'rise of class politics' later in the century. After all, by the 1890s trade unionism was beginning to spread among non-manual workers such as railway clerks, insurance workers, shop assistants and teachers, whereas in the 1860s and 1870s it remained the preserve of manual workers. True a Wolverhampton Clerks Association existed during the later 1870s, but this was essentially a social club established with employer patronage, rather than a trade union.[65] Indeed, social barriers between manual and non-manual workers were very strong in mid-Victorian Wolverhampton, as was testified by the early history of the working-men's club movement in the town. The first working-men's club, established in 1864, apparently failed because local working men resented the large numbers of clerks and shop assistants who had joined. In 1866 the Trades Council approached the movement's founder, the Reverend Henry Solly, with plans to establish a rival club which would be confined strictly to the working classes, and which would show greater sympathy to trade unionism. These plans came to nothing, and by the following year the club was said to consist almost solely of clerks, shop-workers and tradesmen.[66]

But if suspicion of party ran deep in the 1870s, especially in trade union circles, it should not be imagined that popular Liberalism had wholly lost its resonance. On the contrary, in 1874 the first contested General Election at Wolverhampton for almost forty years saw Villiers and Weguelin returned with massive majorities over their lone Conservative challenger, despite the Liberal party's poor performance nationally. The result was Villiers 10,358; Weguelin 10,036; Williams (Conservative) 3,628. Partisanship proved very strong – just one in every fifty voters split their votes between the parties. On the other hand, turnout, at 60 per

---

[63] *The Bee-Hive*, 2 October 1875.   [64] *Wolverhampton Chronicle*, 6 August 1873.
[65] *Wolverhampton Chronicle*, 9 January 1878.
[66] *Wolverhampton Chronicle*, 31 January 1866, and 30 January 1867; *The Commonwealth*, 24 November 1866.

cent, was low, though this owed much to widespread intimidation and disorder.[67] The Liberals' success owed much to the fact that local Liberal leaders had persuaded the town's sitting MPs to disassociate themselves from much Liberal Government policy, including the clauses of the recent Education Act which angered non-conformist opinion, and the deficiencies in the Master and Servant Act and Criminal Law Amendment Act which angered trade unionists. When Villiers addressed a crowd of over 1,500 workers outside the G. W. R. locomotive works he attacked both pieces of legislation vociferously, to the great delight of his audience.[68] Villiers' ability to gain a sympathetic, even enthusiastic, hearing from such a large open air meeting outside the town's largest factory conveyed a powerful symbolic message of popular legitimacy, as the Conservative candidate Walter Williams seems to have recognised, for he quickly tried to emulate Villiers's success. He too concentrated on attacking the outgoing Government's poor record on trade union and labour law reform, but he was met only by a barrage of abuse and cat-calls, and was eventually forced to abandon his meeting.[69]

On election day itself there were early signs of the strength of Liberal feeling in the borough when a crowd of over 1,000 miners and local youths gathered outside the polling station at Wednesfield, to the east of Wolverhampton, and began jeering and jostling known Conservatives as they came up to vote. When the police tried to clear the area the crowd became more violent, and it became impossible for Conservatives to vote at all. At Heath Town, a township between Wednesfield and Wolverhampton, local miners and ironworkers again disrupted polling, though with less violence. While at Willenhall, where there had been a number of bloody exchanges between gangs of Liberals and Tories armed with make-shift weapons in the run-up to the election, polling day itself saw the town over-run by thousands of locksmiths, ironworkers and miners chanting Liberal election songs and determined to keep the Conservatives off the streets. Armed, as before, with an array of impromptu weapons, they forced the Tories to close their committee rooms and lie low all day.[70]

Events in Wolverhampton, however, followed a quite different course, with much popular violence directed at the Liberals, rather than at their opponents. One factor behind this was undoubtedly the considerable ill-feeling which had developed between leaders of the town's sizeable Irish

---

[67] Turnout and 'splits' calculated from figures in Craig, *Parliamentary results, 1832–1885*, pp. 339 and 669.

[68] *Wolverhampton Chronicle*, 4 February 1874. This election appears to have been the last time that Villiers visited Wolverhampton, though he continued to represent the town until his death in 1897.   [69] *Ibid.*

[70] *Wolverhampton Chronicle*, 11 February 1874; also *The Times*, 5 February 1874.

population and the local Liberal party over the fate of Catholic voluntary schools.[71] This antagonism lay behind the concerted heckling at Liberal meetings late in the campaign, and an attack on the Liberal committee rooms on the night before the poll. However, the town was quiet on election day itself until rumours began to circulate of Liberal rioting at Wednesfield, Willenhall and Sedgley. A crowd of two or three thousand youths quickly formed, and began a series of bloody assaults on anyone sporting Liberal colours. For an hour or so the crowd seems to have been a purely anti-Liberal one, but later in the afternoon the violence and intimidation became much less discriminating. New gangs formed – including one from the Stafford Street district which paraded the town chanting for Irish Home Rule and wearing both Nationalist and Liberal party colours. With the police unable to regain control, and the riot spreading to the prosperous western suburbs, the poll was closed early and the declaration delayed until the following day.[72]

Undoubtedly the significance of these disturbances transcends the narrow world of party politics. In particular they reflect the deep-seated frustrations of Wolverhampton's impoverished and stigmatised Irish minority, and a more general resentment towards the wealth and privilege of the town's prosperous 'west end'.[73] But it is still significant that so much of this popular resentment should have been directed against the Liberal party, when elsewhere in the borough the party was clearly still perceived as the champion of the dispossessed and the marginalised. Wolverhampton Liberalism had long formed the 'political establishment' of the town, but it was now becoming increasingly possible to question the popular legitimacy of its power. Indeed on the eve of the 1874 poll *The Wolverhampton Chronicle* had in fact predicted that if the election were to exclude Wolverhampton's industrial hinterland, and be confined just to the municipality itself, the Conservatives might well emerge victorious.[74]

V

Four years later Wolverhampton witnessed popular political disturbances which for the first time assumed an unambiguously pro-Conservative

[71] *Wolverhampton Chronicle*, 4 February 1874. The 1871 census shows 3.4 per cent of the town's population had been born in Ireland, though it is estimated that over 17 per cent of the population were of Irish descent at this time, R. Swift, 'Anti-Catholicism and Irish disturbances: public order in mid-Victorian Wolverhampton', *Midland History*, 9 (1984), p. 88.   [72] *Wolverhampton Chronicle*, 11 February 1874.

[73] On the emergence of this prosperous district, see M. Shaw, 'The ecology of social change: Wolverhampton, 1851–71', *Transactions of the Institute of British Geographers* (new series) 2 (1977), pp. 332–48. It was also widely felt that wealthy Councillors ensured that the 'west end' was specially favoured for municipal improvements.

[74] *Wolverhampton Chronicle*, 4 February 1874.

form. The immediate cause was the decision of local Liberal leaders to organise a mass meeting at the Agricultural Hall to demonstrate Wolverhampton's opposition to the Conservative Government's bellicose foreign policy which seemed to threaten war with Russia in the Near East. When the Liberals refused to allow a platform to the Government's supporters, and made it clear that amendments from the floor would not be accepted, local Conservatives laid plans to disrupt the meeting so that it could not pass any resolutions. The Conservatives clearly feared that the Liberals might carry off a coup – presenting a tightly controlled Liberal party meeting as the voice of public opinion in Wolverhampton. Tory Councillors therefore called on supporters of the Government to pack the meeting, and to demonstrate outside if they were denied entry. They also hired a brass band to play patriotic songs outside the hall. Clearly the Wolverhampton's 'Jingo' demonstrations were not spontaneous outpourings of popular patriotic feeling, rather they represented a bold bid by Conservative politicians to turn the 'politics of disruption' against their Liberal foes after years of being the victims of similar tactics. Their strategy proved a great success. Inside the hall hundreds of 'Jingoes' waved red flags and handkerchiefs (red was the Tory colour locally) and disrupted proceedings with renditions of 'Rule Britannia', 'Britons never shall be slaves', and their anthem of the moment, MacDermott's 'Jingo' song. Outside the hall a crowd of perhaps 2,000 joined in the singing and general mayhem, until eventually Fowler and his fellow Liberal leaders were forced to abandon the meeting.[75] The following night the Tories sought to capitalise on their success by organising their own 'town's meeting' to voice Wolverhampton's support for Disraeli's anti-Russian policies. Estimates suggest that their colourful open-air meeting may have attracted as many as 10,000 people. Besides denouncing the 'autocratic Russian bear', Tory councillors also played the anti-party card: attacking the town's 'Liberal faction' for trying to 'dictate and rule the borough autocratically', and for placing party above nation at a time of national crisis.[76]

Once the excitement of these demonstrations had begun to fade many local Liberals began to suggest that they were of little long-term significance. 'The real working class', they suggested, had not been involved, the jingoes inside the Agricultural Hall had been a hired mob, and the massive crowd at the Tories' own meeting simply reflected the love of spectacle among working people, rather than any deep-felt polit-

---

[75] *The Wolverhampton Evening Express,* 31 January and 1 February 1878; *Wolverhampton Chronicle,* 6 February 1878.

[76] *Wolverhampton Chronicle,* 6 February 1878; *The Wolverhampton Evening Express,* 2 February 1878; *The Midland Examiner and Wolverhampton Times,* 9 February 1878.

ical convictions.[77] Interestingly these explanations of the phenomenon have been largely reproduced by subsequent historians, but they are difficult to reconcile with the Liberals' more spontaneous reactions at the height of the disturbances. For instance J. Dewes, the manager of the plate-lock co-operative, tried to quell the opposition in the Agricultural Hall by appealing to the jingoes as 'fellow working men'. While the Radical-leaning *Midland Examiner*'s immediate reaction had been to lament that Disraeli's Reform Act had 'plunged English politics into the whirlpool of a politically uneducated class'.[78]

Even when the immediate crisis had passed more thoughtful Liberal leaders recognised that the jingo demonstrations reflected a growing gulf between themselves and the Wolverhampton people. Alderman John Jones noted that in the past 'liberalism had always been treated with respect by the working classes of Wolverhampton', and he concluded that the events of the previous week therefore made it essential that Liberals should ensure the working classes truly understood their message.[79] Perhaps most revealing of all, however, was the sudden announcement that the Wolverhampton Liberal Association would now be thoroughly democratised. The possibility of reform had been muted during 1877, and had long been demanded by Radical activists, but there is little doubt that it was the shock of the jingo demonstrations that spurred Liberal leaders to action.[80] Significantly, Henry Walker acknowledged that adopting the new scheme would involve the party abandoning the practice of selection in favour of genuine democratic election. Ward parties were given a full place in the party structure, and became directly responsible for electing delegates to the General and Executive Committees. These in turn were stripped of their powers of co-option. The practice of drawing up slates of 'approved' candidates was also dropped. The ward meetings held over the following weeks to elect the new committees drew an unprecedented response, and for the first time included a significant number of local labour leaders. These meetings were not, however, without some demonstration of ill-feeling towards the local Liberal hier-

---

[77] *The Midland Examiner and Wolverhampton Times*, 9 February 1878.
[78] *The Midland Examiner and Wolverhampton Times*, 2 February 1878, for details of the paper see *The newspaper press directory*, (London, 1877). For a historical treatment of jingoism echoing more complacent Liberal voices, see H. Cunningham, 'Jingoism and the working classes, 1877–78', *Bulletin of the Society for the Study of Labour History*, 19 (1969), pp. 6–9.
[79] *The Midland Examiner and Wolverhampton Times*, 9 February 1878.
[80] Affiliation to the National Liberal Federation put some pressure on the Association to reform itself. Francis Schnadhorst may have given advice on the subject when he visited Wolverhampton in late 1877 – *National Liberal Federation Records*, 'Proceedings attending the formation of the National Federation of Liberal Associations' (Harvester microfilm). For an earlier call to by-pass the undemocratic Liberal Association by creating a new, more Radical, organisation, see *The Miner and Workman's Examiner*, 29 December 1876.

archy. At Whitmore Reans one Radical complained that 'the working classes were ignored' until there was a political crisis to sort out. W. M. Fuller reassured him that now 'power would really be in the hands of the working classes', and went on to suggest that, whereas previous attempts to organise working men had been unsuccessful, the new democratic organisation would prove genuinely popular.[81] Similarly the tube manufacturer John Brotherton admitted that in the past Liberal leaders had been 'too isolated', and hoped that by opening up the party they would win 'the co-operation of the leading, sensible working men, who would try to instil into the minds of their fellow working men right and proper views'.[82] Interestingly, when the new arrangements were put to the test the following year by Weguelin's announcement that he would stand down at the next election, it soon became clear that the Executive Committee remained determined to exert full control. They sought to circumvent, rather than challenge, the constitutional right of the General Committee (or Liberal Four Hundred) to select parliamentary candidates – and did so by authorizing themselves to draw up a short-list for the Four Hundred to consider. It seems fairly certain that the Executive was determined to honour a long-standing commitment to Henry Fowler, and the short-list they drew up seemed calculated to ensure there would be no contest. When one young hopeful, the Speaker's son A. G. Brand, showed no sign of withdrawing he was bluntly told that 'feeling in the Borough was strongly in favour of a local man'. Significantly, when he finally did stand down the Executive praised his 'generous self-sacrifice' even though it left only Fowler in the field. Presented with this *fait accompli* only one brave soul on the Liberal Four Hundred was prepared to vote against Fowler's adoption.[83]

In the wake of the jingo demonstrations Wolverhampton Conservatives also began to develop more permanent, and broad-based, forms of organisation. In early 1878 the only formal Conservative party institution in the town had been the gentleman's club established at the old Deanery the previous summer.[84] By the end of 1878 Wolverhampton possessed a fully developed Conservative Association, with ward and workplace branches open to a general membership. The inner industrial ward of St John's

[81] *The Miner*, 23 February 1878; see also *The Midland Examiner and Wolverhampton Times*, 9 and 23 February 1878.
[82] *The Midland Examiner and Wolverhampton Times*, 9 February 1878.
[83] *Wolverhampton Chronicle*, 14 May, 11 and 18 June; also Fowler, *Life of Henry Fowler*, p. 494 (*sic*). Analysed in greater detail in Lawrence, 'Party politics and the people', pp. 81–2.
[84] *The Miner and Workman's Examiner*, 29 December 1896; also *Wolverhampton Chronicle*, 1 April 1896, and F. Mason, *The book of Wolverhampton: the story of an industrial town* (Buckingham, 1979) p. 92.

claimed over 250 members by May 1879, and overall it is clear that the new organisation was a considerable success.[85] Even so, the Conservative's still failed to make any significant inroads into the Liberals' political ascendency at the 1880 General Election. Alfred Hickman, the prominent local ironmaster and colliery owner, polled 5,874 votes compared with 12,197 for Villiers and 11,606 for Henry Fowler (who therefore became the first local man to represent the town since Richard Fryer's retirement in 1835).[86] However, if we turn to local press reports of how the parties were believed to have fared in different parts of the borough the story becomes a little more complicated. There seems no doubt that in the towns and villages which lay between Wolverhampton and Walsall to the east, the Liberal party remained completely dominant. Though even here the Conservative party could perhaps take some comfort from the fact that the intimidation of its supporters was much less pronounced than in 1874. The Liberals were also said to be dominant in the east end wards of Wolverhampton, which were dominated by iron-making and related heavy industries, and in Stafford Street, with its mixed population of radical artisans and Irish. But the Tories seem to have polled much better elsewhere in the town. In the affluent suburbs to the west, as one might expect, but also in more plebeian districts such as Whitmore Reans, Blakenhall and the old central wards of St John's and St Paul's the Tories more than held their own.[87] Significantly, in 1885 the Boundary Commissioners placed all these districts into a single constituency: Wolverhampton West, which therefore became a much more attractive prospect for the Conservatives than the old double-member constituency, where Wolverhampton's radical hinterland had always predominated.[88] Indeed, at the first election for the new seat the Conservatives did triumph – with Alfred Hickman, the ironmaster who had come a poor third in 1880, returned ahead of Sir William Plowden by 153 votes. This decision was reversed at the 1886 election, with Plowden securing the majority by 123 votes, apparently thanks to the tactical shifts among Irish voters. However in the elections of 1892 and 1895 Hickman transformed Wolverhampton West into a strong-hold of Conservatism, securing majorities of 1,116 and 823 at successive

[85] *The Midland Examiner and Wolverhampton Times*, 23 February and 30 March 1878; *Wolverhampton Evening Express*, 29 March and 23 October 1878; *Wolverhampton Chronicle*, 28 May 1879.
[86] Fowler was born at Sunderland, and came to Wolverhampton in 1855, aged twenty-five, because his widowed mother had moved there, *Dictionary of national biography, supplement, 1901–1911* (Oxford edn, 1920), pp. 49–50.
[87] *The Wolverhampton Evening Express*, 31 March 1880.
[88] Wolverhampton West also included districts still renowned for their Radicalism in 1880, including St George's and St Matthew's in the 'east end'.

elections. In 1900 his return was not even opposed by a demoralized and largely defunct Liberal party. In the next chapter we will examine the causes, and the consequences, of this upsurge in popular Toryism in greater detail.

5 Popular Toryism and the origins of Labour politics

I

According to Henry Pelling the political gulf between the east and west divisions of Wolverhampton after 1885 requires little explanation. Wolverhampton East was 'more uniformly working-class' than other Black Country seats and therefore more anti-Conservative; Wolverhampton West was 'rather middle-class' in character and therefore leant strongly towards the Conservatives.[1] There is, of course, something in this argument: Wolverhampton's 'west end' included large tracts of substantial suburban housing, while the 'east end' was dominated by heavy industry and considerable poverty. However, Pelling overlooks the fact that only one of the classic 'east end' wards (St James's) was actually in Wolverhampton East – St George's and St Matthew's were both part of the western division.[2] St Peter's and St Mary's, the other two Wolverhampton wards in the eastern division were not dominated by the iron and coal industries of the 'east end'. The town centre ward of St Peter's was now largely depopulated, and its electorate included a sizeable business vote which the Tories had tried to persuade the boundary commissioners to graft on to the marginal western division. St Mary's was largely a working-class ward, but the strength of the brewing interest (and of Catholicism) meant that it was far from hopeless territory for the Conservatives. In any case, as we have seen, nearly two-thirds of the electorate for Wolverhampton East came from the industrial villages and townships which had grown up between the two towns of Wolverhampton and Walsall. There seems little reason to believe that these communities were in fact more monolithically working class than other parts of the Black Country, such as Wednesbury or Dudley where Conservatism became a powerful force in the late nineteenth century.

[1] Henry Pelling, *Social geography of British elections, 1885–1910* (London, 1967), pp. 184 and 186–7.
[2] Hence, health reports, and other surveys, emphasising distinctions between conditions in the east and west of the town should not be read as descriptions of conditions in the two constituencies, Pelling, *Social geography*, p. 187n.

It also seems doubtful whether Wolverhampton West was really as strongly middle-class in character as has been suggested. Pelling supports this claim by noting that Fowler declined to fight the seat in 1885 because it had 'sprung up only in recent years by the extension of suburbia'. However, we should perhaps be sceptical about this argument. Fowler himself sat as an Alderman for the west-end, and largely suburban ward of St Mark's until early 1885. Perhaps more significantly, in January 1885 he told the boundary commissioners that all of Wolverhampton was socially mixed, and that even in the most prosperous west-end wards houses rated at under £10 per annum out-numbered the houses of the wealthy by more than two-to-one.[3]

Clearly we cannot explain Hickman's four election victories at Wolverhampton West, and especially the two clear-cut victories of 1892 and 1895, simply in terms of the town's large middle class. For one thing non-conformity continued to bind a significant section of the town's middle-class population to Liberalism, with the Wesleyan and Congregational churches providing many of the party's leading figures.[4] Nor can Hickman's victories be explained simply in terms of working-class abstentions during the 1890s. Only the General Election of January 1910 (itself a Conservative victory) recorded a higher poll than that of 1892 when Hickman unseated the Liberal Sir William Plowden by 1,116 votes on an 89.4 per cent poll. And just as there is no evidence that Wolverhampton Tories relied for their success on keeping the turnout low, so there is no evidence that they relied on keeping the electorate small either.[5] In fact the electorate grew as a proportion of the male population during the 1890s, albeit very slowly.[6]

[3] *Wolverhampton Chronicle*, 21 January 1885. Fowler's argument (which defined the wealthy as those occupying houses rated at over £50 per annum) ignored the fact that *within* the large west-end wards there was considerable social segregation. See M. Shaw, 'The ecology of social change: Wolverhampton, 1851–1871', *Transactions of the Institute of British Geographers*, (new series) 2 (1977), pp. 332–48, and below, chapter 6, pp. 133–8.

[4] W. H. Jones, *The Congregational churches of Wolverhampton, 1664–1894* (London, 1894), pp. 147–8; G. W. Jones, *Borough politics: a study of Wolverhampton Town Council, 1888–1964* (London, 1969), pp. 36–7.

[5] For an emphasis on the Conservative's anti-democratic strategies nationally, see E. H. H. Green, 'Radical Conservatism: the electoral genesis of tariff reform', *Historical Journal*, 28 (1985), pp. 667–92; for claims of their importance 'on the ground', see J. P. Cornford, 'The transformation of Conservatism in the late nineteenth century', *Victorian Studies*, 7 (1963), pp. 35–66; and Paul Thompson, 'Liberals, Radicals and Labour in London, 1885–1914', *Past and Present*, 27 (1964), p. 79. The argument is questioned in Jon Lawrence and Jane Elliott, 'Parliamentary election results reconsidered: an analysis of borough elections, 1885–1910', *Parliamentary History*, 16, 1 (1997) [E. H. H. Green (ed.), *An age of transition*], pp. 18–28.

[6] In 1891 the electorate of Wolverhampton West stood at 9,099, equivalent to 29.4 per cent of the male population; in 1901 this figure had risen to 31.5 per cent. By 1911 it had climbed sharply, to 37.2, mainly because of more generous interpretations of the lodger franchise, which rose ten-fold between 1886 and 1910; see *Census of England and Wales*

If class factors alone cannot explain the upsurge of popular Toryism in Wolverhampton, perhaps religion was the key. The strong links between the dissenting churches and the town's Liberal leadership have already been noted, and there were also strong links between Anglicanism and Conservatism, especially in support of state-funded voluntary education. Prominent Anglican Liberals in the town had been defecting to the Conservatives since at least the 1850s – and this trend seems to have become more pronounced after 1870. Indeed, in 1876 Liberal Churchmen held a meeting to protest that their party had been taken over by the non-conformists and their pressure groups.[7] If Anglicanism was much stronger in Wolverhampton West than in other parts of the Black Country it might be that such defections were not just confined to the wealthy elite, and that they therefore played a part in the eclipse of Liberalism in the town. Fortunately the religious censuses of 1851 and 1881 provide the basis for a rough comparison of the strength of different denominations even though the first survey covered the whole of the old Parliamentary borough of Wolverhampton, while the later survey was confined to the town itself. Methodological differences between the two surveys, combined with the effects of three decades of rapid social change prevent any *systematic* comparison being made, but a number of general conclusions can be drawn. Firstly, the surveys suggest that overall church attendance was considerably higher in 1851 than in 1881 – attendance rates fell from 38 per cent of the total population across the Parliamentary borough in 1851, to just 26 per cent in the municipality thirty years later.[8] Secondly, the Anglican Church accounted for a larger proportion of churchgoers in Wolverhampton in 1881 than in the district as a whole in 1851 (40.1 per cent, compared with 34.1 per cent in the earlier survey). Thirdly, the more plebeian branches of dissent, notably the Primitive and United Methodists, were much weaker in Wolverhampton in 1881 than

1891, vol. I (*Parl. Papers*, 1893–94, CIV), p. 320; *Census of England and Wales, 1901*, 'County of Stafford' (*Parl. Papers*, 1902 Cd. 1125 CXXI), p. 4; *Census of England and Wales, 1911*, vol. 3 (*Parl. Papers*, 1912–13, Cd. 6343, CXII), p. 15; *Return Relating to Electors*, 1886 (*Parl. Papers*, 1886, LII); 1891 (*Parl. Papers*, 1890–91, LXII); 1901 (*Parl. Papers*, 1901, LIX); and 1911 (*Parl. Papers*, 1911, LXII). The above calculations make no allowance for plural voters.

[7] *The Miner and Workmen's Examiner*, 29 December 1876. See also *The Midland Examiner and Wolverhampton Times*, 6 and 13 April 1878 on the defection of prominent Churchmen such as Robert Walker.

[8] Calculated from figures in *Parl. Papers*, 1852–53, vol. XXXIX, p. 73 (*Religious Worship in England and Wales*); Horace Mann, *Religious worship in England and Wales* (London, 1854); and Andrew Mearns, *The statistics of attendance at public worship* (London, 1882). I have calculated attendance using the two-thirds method, and have made an estimate for the five churches left unvisited in 1851; see Lawrence, 'Party politics', pp. 55–8, and D. M. Thompsom, 'The 1851 religious census: problems and possibilities', *Victorian Studies*, 11 (1967–68), pp. 87–97. The same sources and method are used for the remainder of this discussion.

they had been in the constituency as a whole in 1851 (just 4.3 per cent of churchgoers compared with 13.2 per cent in the larger area in 1851). This finding is supported by an analysis of the membership records of local non-conformist churches which shows that on the eve of the war the Primitive and United Methodists between them claimed only 500 members in Wolverhampton, compared with 1,116 Congregationalists and 1,050 Wesleyan Methodists.[9] Moreover, during the nineteenth century both the Congregationalist and Wesleyan churches gravitated to prosperous western districts and, according to contemporaries, became much less plebeian in the process.[10]

There are, therefore, strong grounds for believing that non-conformity was weaker in Wolverhampton than in surrounding districts, and that its influence may have been especially weak in working-class districts. As a result of this relative weakness, the Anglican Church appears to have been more dominant in Wolverhampton than in adjacent Black Country towns. Certainly Anglicanism had a strong influence over the provision of education in the town – nearly 42 per cent of pupils attended Church schools in the mid 1890s.[11] Moreover, these schools were strongest in the west of the town, in areas such as St John's, St Paul's and Whitmore Reans, where popular Toryism was most pronounced.[12] However, we should still be wary of treating religious identities as a self-sufficient explanation for late nineteenth-century popular Toryism in Wolverhampton. Firstly, Wolverhampton's Church schools had been even more dominant before the passing of the 1870 Education Act, but Conservatism had remained extremely weak in the town.[13] Secondly, measured by indicators such as denominational schooling the Anglican establishment was much more deeply entrenched in neighbouring townships such as Wednesfield, but these often remained politically Radical.[14]

[9] See Lawrence, 'Party politics', pp. 55–7, which provides a fuller discussion of the denominational breakdown and social characteristics of church membership in Wolverhampton. Details of local Methodist circuits are held in the *Wolverhampton Methodist Archive* (WRL), also *Congregational Yearbook 1914*, p. 310.

[10] See Jones, *Congregational churches*, p. 147; A. C. Pratt, *Black Country churches* (London, 1891), pp. 114–15; *The Congregational Yearbook, 1914* (London, 1914), p. 310; *Wolverhampton Methodist Archive*, (WRL) circuit membership records, 1907–1914. On the social basis of Wesleyanism nationally, see C. D. Field, 'The social structure of English Methodism', *British Journal of Sociology*, 28 (1977), pp. 199–225.

[11] *Wolverhampton Chronicle*, 20 September 1893 – the remainder divided as follows: Board Schools, 38.6 per cent; Catholic, 15.0 per cent; Wesleyan, 4.6 per cent. For an argument stressing the strong links between high-levels of Anglican schooling and urban Conservatism, see F. Bealey and H. Pelling, *Labour and politics: a history of the Labour Representation Committee* (London, 1958), pp. 5–6 (they define high as over 40 per cent).

[12] Lawrence, 'Party politics', pp. 58–9 and figures 9 and 10; and *Parl. Papers*, 1875, vol. LIX, pp. 294–7 (*Return relating to school fees*).

[13] See *Parl. Papers*, 1852–53, vol. LXXIX, p. 142 (*Schools aided by Parliamentary grants*).

[14] In 1885, 57 per cent of Wednesfield pupils attended Church schools, *Wolverhampton Chronicle*, 7 October 1885.

Finally, and perhaps most importantly, one has to acknowledge that throughout the 1880s, when popular Conservatism was growing rapidly, there appears to have been little sectarian conflict in Wolverhampton, even in the field of education policy. In 1885 the various parties agreed to co-operate to avoid the expense and inconvenience of School Board elections, while in 1888, when negotiations broke down largely because of the intervention of two independent Labour candidates, the resulting election stimulated little public interest and a turnout of barely 30 per cent.[15]

It seems likely, therefore, that Anglicanism was only one element, and perhaps not the most important, in the construction of late nineteenth-century popular Toryism in Wolverhampton. It seems doubtful whether, on its own, the influence of Established religion would have been strong enough to undermine Liberal hegemony in the town. Most historians would accept this argument, since the principal explanation for Black Country Conservatism at the turn of the century has been economic rather than religious: the decline of the district's staple heavy industries and the consequent attraction of Tory protectionism (this is often combined with the claim that the Black Country was simply absorbed into Chamberlain's Unionist fiefdom).[16] There can be no doubt that Wolverhampton was hit hard by trade depression in the late 1870s and early 1880s. Many of the town's largest and most prestigious employers, including the Shrubbery and Chillington ironworks, Old Hall tinplate factory and the Chubb lock works, closed down.[17] These economic difficulties are reflected in demographic statistics for the town: population growth slowed – falling from 12.2 per cent in the 1860s to 9.1 per cent in the 1880s – and large numbers of workers migrated from the town. During these years many local employers did come to support protectionist trade policies. In 1878 a local 'Fair Trade' society was formed, and the following year a group of employers formed a Protectionist Society intending to make a concerted bid for working-class support.[18] By the early 1890s few employers in the iron and coal industries of the 'east end'

---

[15] *Express and Star*, 17 November 1888; the success of Labour's non-sectarian populist programme at School Board elections in the 1890s tends to reinforce this argument, see below, pp. 000–00.

[16] For example, see Pelling, *Social geography*, pp. 186–7; and 'Working-class Conservatives', *Historical Journal*, 13 (1970), pp. 341–3; M. C. Hurst, 'Joseph Chamberlain and west Midlands politics, 1886–1895', *Dugdal Society Occasional Papers*, 15 (Oxford, 1962).

[17] A. Hinde, *A handy history of Wolverhampton and guide to the district* (Wolverhampton, 1884), pp. 13–17; J. T. Jeffcock, *Original Wolverhampton guide and visitor's handbook* (2nd edn, Wolverhampton, 1884) p. 103; *Reports of the Royal Commission on the Depression of Trade and Industry*, Parl. Papers, 1886, vol. XXI Cd. 4621, p. 112; Parl. Papers, 1886, vol. XXII Cd. 4715, I, pp. 41, 51 and 92, and Parl. Papers, 1886, vol. XXIII Cd. 4797, pp. 213–15; Allen, *Industrial development of Birmingham*, pp. 146, 205 and 226.

[18] B. H. Brown, *The Tariff reform movement in Great Britain, 1881–1895* (New York, 1943), pp. 11, 16–17.

remained loyal to the Liberals, even prominent Wesleyans such as the hurdle and agricultural tools manufacturer Samuel Bayliss had gone over to the Conservatives.[19] On the other hand, it is less clear that the workers in these depressed industries followed their employers' example and broke with Liberalism. The 'east end' wards of St Matthew's, St George's and St James's (in the eastern division), like the ironworkers' union leaders, remained strongly Liberal throughout the period.[20] There are also problems matching the chronology of trade depression to the growth of popular Conservatism. Whereas the local economy was most depressed from the late 1870s to the mid 1880s, the revival of Conservative fortunes might be said to have begun much earlier, and not reached its peak until the 1890s. By this time the Wolverhampton economy had recovered much of its old dynamism, with rapid employment growth in industries such as electrical engineering, bicycle manufacture, the brass and tubes trades, and (until the turn of the century) galvanised and corrugated iron manufacture.[21] As we have seen, in 1880, when the trade depression was at its height, and the calls for protection from local employers were most vociferous, the Conservatives polled very poorly indeed. Similarly, in 1906, when the Wolverhampton economy was suffering acutely from the migration of its great iron-sheeting industries to coastal sites, the Conservatives again fared badly at the polls – receiving only 43 per cent of the popular vote across the Parliamentary borough, and losing all three seats.[22]

II

Wolverhampton Tories found their most vocal working-class supporters, not among the impoverished ironworkers and toolmakers of the 'east

---

[19] *Express and Star*, 5 July 1892 and 9 April 1907. Prominent exceptions to the trend included John and Joseph Jones, J. B. Hayward and George Miller. It should be noted that local iron masters traditionally had strong ties with local Tory landowners because of their interest in mining rights; see Tunsiri, 'Party politics', pp. 160–1, 195–6, 202.

[20] *Express and Star*, 29 October 1891 and 28 October 1897; *Wolverhampton Chronicle*, 7 July 1886; *The Midland Counties Express*, 23 May 1896. Tory victories at municipal elections in the early 1890s were very much 'against the grain', and were achieved because of intensive campaigning on the drink issue, see below, p. 107.

[21] Jones, *Japan, tinplate and iron braziers trades*, pp. 138–78; Allen, *Industrial development of Birmingham*, pp. 216–18, 227–31, 260–2, 293–9 and 308. Population growth stood at 13.9 per cent for the 1890s.

[22] On the removal of the galvanized and corrugated iron industries to sites at Ellesmere Port and Newport, and its consequences for the local economy, see Jones, *Japan, tinplate and iron braziers trades*, pp. 177–8; Allen, *Industrial development of Birmingham*, pp. 289–9; *Express and Star*, 19 March 1903, 22 January 1904 and 23 September 1907. The Wolverhampton population increased by only 1.2 per cent between 1901 and 1911, and emigration was again considerable. By 1911 only 51.5 per cent of people born in Wolverhampton were still resident there, compared with 76 per cent in Leicester, *Census of England and Wales, 1911*, IX, 'Birthplaces', pp. 39–41, 81–3.

end', but among skilled workers in more prosperous trades such as engineering and brass-ware. It was representatives from these trades who challenged the Lib–Lab tendencies of many Trades Council leaders in the late 1880s, and who played the most prominent part in the working men's Tory clubs that flourished in Wolverhampton at this time. It is not easy to find convincing economic explanations for this. For one thing, the engineering industry produced as many Radical and Socialist activists, as Tory ones – even within a single factory such as the GWR works on Stafford Road.[23] The brassworkers were more uniformly Conservative, at least in Wolverhampton, but plausible economic explanations for this are hard to find. The industry grew continuously in the later nineteenth century, apparently oblivious to the economic cycles effecting other trades, and employment more than doubled between 1871 and 1901.[24] Moreover, the industry experienced very little foreign competition thanks to the idiosyncrasies of English tastes (it produced primarily for *civilian* consumption at home so economic links to Tory militarism and imperialism also seem unlikely).[25]

To understand brassworker Toryism, or popular Toryism more generally for that matter, we must pay much more careful attention to the language and practice of those Tory politicians who consciously sought to appeal to a 'mass' constituency. Only then can we begin to assess the relative significance of religious loyalties, economic insecurities and other factors in the construction of a viable popular Tory tradition in Wolverhampton at the end of the nineteenth century. First of all, it will be useful to identify the Tory populists as individuals, since it is clear that many Conservatives shunned both the hurly-burly of mass politics, and the concessions to popular feeling they inevitably demanded. There were, of course, the working-class Tory activists themselves, men such as the brassworkers' leaders William Roughley and James Scott, or Jabez Howard and A. L. Greenall of the ASE. There were also non-unionists such as Abiathar Weaver, a shoemaker, who became Wolverhampton's first working-class councillor in 1891. The second group of Tory populists

---

[23] Jon Lawrence, 'Class and gender in the making of urban Toryism, 1880–1914', *English Historical Review*, 108 (1993), pp. 629–52 (pp. 641–2).

[24] The number of male brassworkers recorded by the census increased from 471 in 1871 to 979 in 1901, *Census of England and Wales, 1871*, vol. III, 'Population abstracts' (*Parl. Papers*, 1873, LXXII pt I,), p. 335, and *Census of England and Wales, 1901*, County of Stafford (*Parl. Papers*, 1902, Cd. 1125 CXXI,), p. 86 notes b & c; also Allen, *Industrial development of Birmingham*, pp. 216–17. Nationally the brassworkers union was strongly Gladstonian, expelling S. W. Maddocks, its Conservative-leaning president, in 1885 for intervening against the Lib–Lab Henry Broadhurst at Birmingham, Bordesley in the General Election – *Webb Trade Union Collection* (BLPES), E, A, vol. XIX, f. 41; Brown, *Tariff Reform movement*, pp. 31–7.

[25] Allen, *Industrial development of Birmingham*, p. 217; *Webb Trade Union Collection*, (BLPES), E, A, vol. XIX, f. 10.

were the publican-politicians such as Levi Johnson, Jeremiah Mason, Joseph Lawrence and John Griffiths, all of whom ran substantial public houses in working-class parts of town. Besides these two core groups, there were a number of individuals who consistently espoused populist causes in the 1880s and 1890s, including J. W. Hamp, a local doctor, and Arthur Hollingsworth, the chairman of Wolverhampton Wanderers football club. Apart from their politics, these men shared an important common characteristic, a proximity to working-class life that was not based on a relationship of dependence – despite Hickman, employers were surprisingly rare among the Tory populists in Wolverhampton, suggesting that deference was not an essential feature of Tory success.

It would be wrong to suggest that the Tory populists constituted a party within a party, but there were a number of political themes which distinguished them from other, more mainstream, Conservative politicians in the town. As we shall see, the Tory populists were still passionate in defence of Church and Queen, and in their celebration of national power at home and abroad, but they also made more explicitly class-based appeals for the working-man's vote. For instance, they frequently made forthright attacks on the way local politicians, Conservative as well as Liberal, had neglected the poorer parts of the town whilst financing extravagant schemes for 'improving' more prosperous central and western neighbourhoods. That said, it was undoubtedly the 'Liberal Junta', and especially Henry Fowler, mayor of Wolverhampton in 1863, who were most closely associated with such policies in Tory rhetoric. Tory politicians argued that it was time Council revenues were directed towards the drab, unhealthy working-class districts of the 'east end' (and elsewhere), and they called for the provision of public wash-houses, swimming baths, and parks, as well as better maintained streets and court yards.[26] Wolverhampton's Tory populists also played a prominent part in the campaign for 'fair wage' clauses to be written into all council contracts. Indeed, whilst the issue had long been advocated by the local Trades Council, and had the support of some Liberal councillors, it was in fact the Tory publican Levi Johnson who successfully introduced the policy in 1891.[27] This reflected a long-established theme of Tory populism: that Liberal subservience to *laissez-faire* meant that only the Tories were prepared to pass legislation which would be of direct benefit to working men. Jabez Howard and other working-class Tory activists had consistently attacked the Liberals for their poor record on factory reform,

---

[26] For instance, see *Express and Star*, 28 July 1890; 16 April and 2 November 1891. On Fowler as architect of grand improvement schemes, see Jones, *Borough politics*, p. 26; Hinde, *Handy history*, p. 13.

[27] *Express and Star*, 13 March and 10 April 1889, 27 and 31 October 1891; Jones, *Borough politics*, p. 44.

shorter hours and trade union recognition, and the 'fair wage' issue rein-forced their image of Toryism as more humane and paternal.[28]

As I have discussed elsewhere, a central element of popular Toryism in Wolverhampton, as in many towns, was the claim to stand for the defence of 'the pleasures of the people' and especially of the working-man's right to enjoy a quiet drink free from interference.[29] Certainly it was only when the drink issue came to the fore that Conservatives were able to win significant support from voters in the depressed and impoverished wards of the 'east end'. Hence it was two Tory publicans, Joseph Lawrence and John Griffiths, who came forward in November 1891 to unseat the Liberal councillors, and prominent temperance advocates, George Thorne and S. Larkinson in St Matthew's and St James's respectively. Fighting almost solely on the issue of 'free trade' in drink, and celebrating the special virtues of the working-man's 'sparkling warm ale', both candidates were returned after campaigns which drew unparalleled interest from press and public alike (the turnout in St Matthew's was 89.3 per cent – higher than in most General Elections).[30] Reacting to the growing influence of nonconformism over local Liberal politics, and the increasing interest in securing moral rather than political reforms, the populist Tories were able to develop a powerful, if essentially negative political appeal, in which they presented themselves as the champions of a traditional – not to say mythical – popular culture of 'cakes and ale', manly sports and living for the moment. Here Tory paternalism on (some) social questions, com-bined with residual elements of an older paternalism which looked indul-gently on the 'pleasures of the people', to create a powerful challenge to an increasingly uncertain and demoralized local Liberal party.[31] Tories claimed (not wholly accurately) to have led the resistance to the abolition of the town's historic race meeting and fair. Indeed their own 'summer festival', developed in the 1880s, was actively promoted as an attempt to recreate the old festivities of the races for townsfolk regardless of party affiliation.[32] The strong connections between Wolverhampton Toryism

[28] For instance, *Midland Examiner and Wolverhampton Times*, 30 March 1878; *Express and Star*, 21 April 1884. On the attitudes of Black Country elites, including employers, see Richard Trainor, *Black Country elites: the exercise of authority in an industrialized area, 1830–1900* (Oxford, 1993), pp. 217–22; Sheila Blackburn, 'Employers and social policy: the Black Country chainmakers, the minimum wage, and the Cradley Heath strike of 1910', *Midland History*, 12 (1987), pp. 85–101.

[29] Lawrence, 'Gender and class', pp. 638–44.

[30] See *ibid.*, pp. 639–40; and *Express and Star*, 2 and 3 November 1891.

[31] For an example of earlier Tory populism, see *Wolverhampton Chronicle*, 26 July 1837 – local Tories apparently called for the restoration of cock-fighting and bull-baiting, and denounced the inhumanity of the Whig Poor Law.

[32] *Express and Star*, 30 June 1884; on the old race meeting and the campaign against it see, F. W. Hackwood, *Staffordshire customs, superstitions and folklore* (East Ardsley, 1974 – first published, Lichfield, 1924), p. 106; Pratt, *Black Country Methodism*, pp. 103–4.

and professional sports carried similar overtones, and culminated in the Tory stranglehold over the affairs of Wolverhampton Wanderers football club in the 1890s, and the high-profile manipulation of the team (and its players) in the Tory cause at Parliamentary elections.[33]

As this brief treatment suggests, the defence of the customary 'pleasures of the people' was intimately bound up with the critique of nonconformity as a political force seeking to legislate for the moral improvement of the working classes. When Wolverhampton Tories alleged that local Liberalism had been taken over a clique of 'radical, nonconforming political dissenters' this was not simply a sectarian remark designed to inflame Anglican passions, but rather part of a systematic critique of the interventionist political agenda of late Victorian nonconformity.[34] In a community such as Wolverhampton, where nonconformity was relatively weak, especially in working-class districts, it was a strategy likely to have considerable impact so long as Liberal notions of social reform continued to revolve around reforming the personal habits of individuals, rather than the social and economic circumstances of their lives.

Finally, late Victorian popular Toryism was, of course, also concerned with the politics of Empire and national assertiveness. Although given that Hickman was unseated at Wolverhampton West in the Home Rule election of 1886, and that the Conservatives' combined vote in the divisions contested at both elections fell from 46 per cent in 1885 to 45 per cent in 1886, we should perhaps be cautious about assuming that patriotism was necessarily such an unqualified asset to Wolverhampton Conservatives.[35] That said, there can be no doubt that at General Elections in the 1890s the connections between the Conservative party, the Union and national prestige were both unquestioned and widely celebrated in many of the poorest parts of Wolverhampton. For instance at the 1892 election the pro-Liberal *Express and Star* noted that West Wolverhampton's 'courts, alleys and backyards seemed to have gone mad in the Tory interest', being everywhere festooned in Union Jacks and red flags (still the Tory colour in Wolverhampton). Off Salop Street, near the town centre, the entrance to a poor court was emblazoned with a large

---

[33]   See Lawrence, 'Party politics', pp. 72–3, and 'Gender and class', pp. 640–1. The extent of this connection between the Tory party and the Wolves seems to have been unusual (and unusually profitable for the politicians involved – including the MP Alfred Hickman who was club president).

[34]   *The Midland Examiner and Wolverhampton Times*, 30 March 1878; on the extent to which Wolverhampton Borough Council was divided along sectarian lines by the turn of the century, see Jones, *Borough politics*, pp. 137–40.

[35]   Villiers was returned unopposed for Wolverhampton South at both elections, though from 1886 he was returned as a Liberal Unionist.

flag depicting a group of British soldiers and sailors, above the motto 'Union is Strength: Britons to the rescue! Vote for the Unionist candidate and defend the flag'. To underline this strong partisanship women in the courts apparently sported large red shawls though it was mid summer.[36] Given the crushing poverty suffered by most of the residents of this part of Wolverhampton there must obviously be some suspicion that Tory landlords played a part in organising this display of patriotic fervour on behalf of Hickman and Conservatism, though despite its partisanship the *Express and Star* does not suggest this. What cannot be denied is that in this part of town the working-class electors enthusiastically supported a Tory version of patriotism. It should also be noted that the patriotism espoused appealed to British, rather than English, national identities, perhaps suggesting that Tory patriotism was a more innovative and adaptive force than is sometimes claimed.[37]

During the South African War of 1899–1902, Wolverhampton witnessed further strong expressions of working-class patriotism, contrary to Richard Price's claim that working people had little interest in the conflict.[38] Since Price's case is based largely on a survey of the wartime mood of metropolitan working-men's clubs, it is perhaps especially significant that in Wolverhampton the club movement responded very differently to the war. The fact that most local working-men's clubs organised subscription funds to support the dependants of reservists sent to war does not in itself undermine Price's argument (he recognises that there was concern for the well-being of fellow workers forced to risk their lives in a distant and hostile country). However, when the members of Heath Town working men's club decided to set up a support fund we are told that they first listened with enthusiasm to a 'warlike oration' from a former soldier. Since Heath Town was a radical stronghold in Fowler's Wolverhampton East constituency, it is perhaps hardly surprising that Wolverhampton clubs such as the 'West End' should prove equally receptive to nationalist, and even militarist politics during the war. Since these clubs were avowedly non-party, having been set up by working-men who resented the politicisation of the drink issue by both Liberals *and*

---

[36] *Express and Star*, 5 July 1892.
[37] For instance see H. Cunningham, 'The Conservative party and patriotism', in R. Colls and P. Dodd (eds.), *Englishness: politics and culture, 1880–1920* (London, 1986), esp. pp. 192–6. On the social characteristics of the Brook Street/Salop Street district, and especially the notorious slum area 'Besom Yard' – see *The Evening Express*, 17 January 1884 ('The poor of Wolverhampton'), and *Express and Star*, 16 July 1895 – the district's significant Italian and Romany community may have ruled out a narrow appeal to 'Englishness'.
[38] R. Price, *An imperial war and the British working class: working-class attitudes and reactions to the Boer War, 1899–1902* (London, 1972), pp. 94–6 and 239–42.

Conservatives (many went so far as to ban political discussion on their premises), the fact that they took such an unequivocal stance on the war seems particularly significant.[39] Perhaps inevitably the town's Conservative working men's clubs took their patriotism even further. Indeed, on Mafeking night celebrations at the Whitmore Reans Constitutional Club appear to have got badly out of hand to the annoyance of many local residents.[40]

III

The growth of popular Toryism in Wolverhampton posed serious problems, both for the official leaders of the Liberal party and for the predominantly Radical-leaning leaders of the town's trade union movement. If the jingo demonstration of 1878 had led to widespread political anxiety in Liberal circles, the steady Conservative advance in Wolverhampton West during the 1880s and 1890s caused much more profound difficulties. One problem was that the Conservatives had become much more assiduous in their fêting of potential voters, especially between elections when the scope for 'treating' remained considerable even after the Corrupt Practices Act of 1883. The Tories' great 'summer festivals' of the 1880s were denounced by some Liberals as debasing politics by offering the masses vulgar spectacles such as 'greasy pole' routines and negro comic-singers, rather than seeking to improve and educate them.[41] However, such scruples did not prevent Wolverhampton Liberals from organising their own party 'fêtes' on a grand-scale from the late 1880s, and in June 1890 over 5,000 people were accommodated at the Molineux sports ground for a Liberal 'fête and demonstration' which included professional cycle races, fireworks, and acrobatics, but not much politics.[42] The Primrose League, which grew rapidly in Wolverhampton between 1885 and the early 1890s, posed a more unremitting challenge to Wolverhampton Liberals, since from the outset the League's local 'habitations' put a great deal of effort into organising social events such as concerts, 'meat teas' and special feasts in the poorer districts of town to

---

[39] *The Club and Institute Journal*, December 1899; Price, *Imperial war*, pp. 46–96 and 233–42. One problem with Price's method is that he focuses on metropolitan working-men's clubs, many of which had been established explicitly as radical clubs in the 1870s and 1880s, the Wolverhampton clubs in contrast were not only non-party, but also non-political, see *The Midland Counties Express*, 7 March and 25 April 1896, also *Express and Star*, 6 October 1893.   [40] *Express and Star*, 21 and 22 May 1900.
[41] *Wolverhampton Chronicle*, 31 October 1888, charges made by Phillip Stanhope, the MP for Wednesbury, in an address to the Wolverhampton Women's Liberal Association.
[42] *Express and Star*, 1 July 1890; also *Wolverhampton Chronicle*, 27 June 1888 – for details of a smaller Liberal fête which included the re-enactment by local school-children of the British capture of a Chinese fort in 1857.

commemorate royal birthdays, military victories and the like.[43] The formation of the Women's Central Liberal Association appears to have been a direct response to the success of the Primrose League in harnessing women's political enthusiasm for propagandist purposes. For almost a decade after Plowden's resounding defeat at the 1892 election the association was virtually the only Liberal organisation active in Wolverhampton West, but it was always plagued by problems of inadequate resources, and was not immune from the charge of seeking to 'improve' its working-class clients as well as feed and amuse them.[44]

Wolverhampton Liberals also had great difficulties knowing how far they should imitate the Tories' successful development of working-men's social clubs during the 1880s. By 1886 there were four working-men's Conservative clubs in Wolverhampton West alone, including the North Street club which may have had as many as a thousand members at this time.[45] The intention behind the creation of this network of political clubs was to provide local Conservative candidates with a body of willing volunteers at election time given that the 1883 Corrupt Practices Act had outlawed the payment of election workers such as canvassers, tellers and the like.[46] Historians have usually followed A. L. Lowell by arguing that, whilst the clubs may have reinforced members' party allegiances, they were of limited practical value.[47] As we shall see, Wolverhampton offers only limited support for this thesis. The working-men's Conservative clubs played a prominent part in Hickman's election campaigns of the mid 1880s and 1890s, as well as providing a focal point for the victory celebrations in 1885, 1892 and 1895. On the other hand, the clubs were

---

[43] E.g. *The Primrose League Gazette*, 2 June 1888; *Wolverhampton Chronicle*, 15 July 1885. The Churchill Habitation had over 1,000 members by 1888, while by 1891 there were three 'Habitations' based in or adjacent to the town – though the Staveley-Hill Habitation at Bushbury did its political work in the county seat of Kingswinford; *Wolverhampton Chronicle*, 22 April 1885; *The Primrose League Gazette*, 20 October 188 and 20 June 1891; *The Midland Evening News*, 29 April 1891.

[44] For details of the Association, see *The Liberal and Radical Yearbook, 1887* (Harvester reprint, Brighton, 1974); *Wolverhampton Chronicle*, 31 October 1888; *Midland Counties Express*, 23 May 1896. Also R. A. Wright, 'Liberal party organisation and politics in Birmingham, Coventry and Wolverhampton – with special reference to the development of independent Labour politics', Unpubl. PhD thesis, Univ. of Birmingham, 1978, p. 150.

[45] For details of the North Street club, see *The Evening Express*, 31 December 1883, 19 January and 21 April 1884 (when one Tory claimed the North Street club already had 1,200 members). On other clubs, see *The Midland Evening News*, 6 and 17 July 1886.

[46] See *[Wolverhampton] Evening Express*, 19 Jan. 1884; also 'The condition of the Conservative Party in the Midland Counties' published as part of *The Seventeenth Annual Conference Report of the National Union of Conservative and Constitutional Associations*, 1883 (Micro Methods Microfilm edition), and below, chapter 7, pp. 178–80.

[47] A. L. Lowell, *The Government of England*, 2 vols. (1908; London, 1921), II, pp. 6–8; also M. Ostrogorski, *Democracy and the organization of political parties*, 2 vols (London, 1902), I, pp. 424–32.

never quite the compliant tools that Wolverhampton's Conservative leaders had hoped to create. For instance, in 1890 representatives from the North Street club began negotiations with the Radical-dominated Trades Council about running a joint slate of non-party 'Labour' candidates at future local elections. When this scheme eventually foundered, the North Street club proceeded to select and run its own 'Labour' candidate, the shoemaker Abiathar Weaver, with very little support from the local Conservative establishment.[48] Once elected Weaver was embraced by local Conservatives as a symbol of their new-found rapport with the Tory working-man, but his campaign had relied almost exclusively on the resources of the working-men's clubs (hence his total lack of vehicles on election day), and had placed considerable emphasis on the themes of independence from party, and social justice for working-men. In his victory address, Weaver was still insistent that he was 'independent of any party – political or otherwise (Applause). He was a working man's representative'. Far from being a stooge of anti-union Tory leaders, as some have suggested, Weaver went out of his way to stress his full support for trade unionism, insisting that he was a non-unionist only because there was no branch of his union in Wolverhampton.[49]

Liberal efforts to develop a rival network of popular social clubs were beset by two fundamental problems. Firstly, the deeply ingrained reluctance of many Liberal leaders to be associated with organisations which encouraged working-class drinking habits (hence the troubled history of the teetotal Willenhall Working-men's Liberal club, which was eventually forced to allow drink as the only means of securing its survival).[50] Secondly, Liberals often objected in principle to the promotion of single-class organisations, especially where social exclusivity was written explicitly into the club's constitution (as it was with many working-men's social clubs), rather than simply being a consequence of 'market' forces (high membership tariffs). When the North Street Liberal club was established in 1881 it maintained its exclusivity in just this way – intended to rival the Old Deanery Conservative club, it was modelled on a traditional gentlemen's club and levied an annual subscription of four guineas (two

---

[48] *Express and Star*, 7 and 28 November 1890; 16 and 25 April 1891; *Wolverhampton Chronicle*, 29 October and 7 November 1890.

[49] *Express and Star*, 2 May 1891. For confirmation of the Conservative party's general lack of support, see *ibid.*, 16 and 29 April, 1 May 1891; *The Midland Evening News*, 30 April and 1 May 1891. For claims Weaver's campaign was a Tory conspiracy to promote anti-unionism, see Wright, 'Liberal party organisation', pp. 135–6; also Jones, *Borough politics*, pp. 84–5, who wrongly suggests Weaver was elected for suburban Merridale. His victory was in fact achieved in St Paul's, which had a large working-class population near the town centre, Merridale was created in 1896.

[50] See the history of the club in *The Wolverhampton Chronicle*, 6 May 1896.

month's wages for many Black Country workers).[51] In 1883 (again coin-
ciding with the passing of the Corrupt Practices Act), Wolverhampton
Liberals opened an alternative, more 'popular' club, the 'Villiers Reform'.
At first it was not a great success, according to Villiers because local
Liberal leaders had failed to allow it the autonomy, and the genuine plebeian control, which characterised the dynamic Radical clubs of the
metropolis. Interestingly, Villiers continued to support the club, and to
press for its reform even after his break with Gladstone over Home Rule
in 1886, and in 1887 the constitution was finally altered to give the club
greater autonomy.[52] By this time a second popular club, the 'Fowler
Reform', had been established, though it too was not at first strictly self-
governing, and like its sister organisation always remained dependent on
financial subsidies for its survival.[53] Both clubs appear briefly to have
flourished after asserting their independence in the late 1880s. For
instance, the Fowler club led the local campaign in support of the London
dockers during the great strike of 1889, while the Villiers club played a
prominent part in the 'Labour revival' which gripped Wolverhampton in
1890 and 1891, hosting numerous meetings addressed by national leaders
of the new Labour and socialist politics, as well as providing the venue for
a series of socialist lectures organised by the local Fabian Society. By the
mid 1890s, however, the club was little more than a working-men's social
club, thanks to the mass defection of its activist element to the newly
established Independent Labour Club, while the Fowler club had long
since been wound up.[54]

The problems for Wolverhampton Liberals seeking to adapt to the new
tenor of popular politics in their town were greatly accentuated by more
fundamental political difficulties during the 1880s and 1890s. Relations
between local party leaders and the radical rank and file remained uneasy.

[51] For details of the club's history, see *The Wolverhampton Chronicle*, 15 April 1896, on the
Old Deanery Conservative club, see *ibid.*, 1 April 1896. The North Street club was
effectively under Liberal-Unionist control from 1886 until August 1890 after the defection of many of its leading members over the Home Rule issue, *ibid.*, and *The Midland
Evening News*, 2 July 1886.
[52] See *The Evening Express*, 16 February 1884; and the Villiers–McIllwraith correspondence
(WRL) V to M, 25 February and 5 March 1885, 24 June 1887.
[53] *Wolverhampton Chronicle*, 4 February 1885, which suggests the club was formed in late
1884, ie. before the division of Wolverhampton Parliamentary Borough into three constituencies. Also Villiers–McIllwraith correspondence (WRL), V to M, 16 September
1887; *Express and Star*, 7 September 1889.
[54] On the Fowler club's support for the London dock strike see *Express and Star*, 30 August
and 7 and 10 September 1889; on the Villiers club's involvement in the Labour revival of
1890–91, see *The Workman's Times*, 5 September 1890; *Fabian News*, March and April
1891; *Express and Star*, 22 January and 5 and 20 February, and 6 July 1891. On the apolit-
ical atmosphere at the Villiers club by the mid-1890s, see *Wolverhampton Chronicle*, 26
February 1896.

When the newly established Wolverhampton West Liberal Association came to select a candidate in 1885 it soon became clear that the Executive would not be able to manipulate proceedings as completely as its predecessor had done in 1880. This time, ward parties were asked to nominate potential candidates for selection, though of the twenty-four names brought forward the Executive chose to pursue only nine. Again there was no general ballot, nor even an election among the members of the constituency's newly created Liberal Two-Hundred. The Executive alone was responsible for selecting the retired civil servant William Plowden, though there are indications that, before endorsing the 'recommendation', the Two-Hundred insisted that Plowden should publicly commit himself to a strong Radical programme including disestablishment and disendowment of the Church of England, abolition of the State pension list, Indian Home Rule and Bradlaugh's right to sit in Parliament.[55]

There seems to have been a strong sense of political malaise among Wolverhampton Liberals in 1885, apparently induced primarily by disillusionment with the outgoing Gladstone government. During the campaign even Fowler readily acknowledged that the Government had made serious mistakes, especially in foreign policy, while in private Villiers, who at eighty-three no longer played an active part in Wolverhampton politics, was deeply critical both of the Irish coercion policy and the annexation of Egypt. Wolverhampton Radicals seem to have shared these sentiments: William McConnell had deep misgivings about many Government policies, while William McIllwraith, a secularist and a key figure at the Villiers club, lamented the 'political suspension in the opinion of the popular party' at Wolverhampton.[56] Indeed early in the campaign Liberal leaders felt obliged to call on party members to 'sink their differences' and rally round Plowden to avoid his defeat.[57]

Radical trade union leaders appear to have shared the general sense of political uncertainty and anxiety at the continuing growth of popular Toryism in once radical districts such as St John's and Whitmore Reans. On the eve of the 1885 General Election the carpenters' leader and Trades Council official Fred Mee, a stalwart of the Fowler Reform Club, began secret negotiations with James Adams, secretary of the Wolverhampton Liberal Association, aimed at securing Liberal party funding for a number of Lib–Lab candidates to be run against Tory councillors.

[55] *Wolverhampton Chronicle*, 8 July 1885; on the re-organisation of the local Liberal party after the Redistribution Act of 1885 see, *ibid.*, 28 January and 15 and 22 April 1885.
[56] For the opinions of Villiers and McIllwraith, see the Villiers–McIllwraith correspondence (WRL), V to M, 25 March, 28 March, and 9 November 1885. For McConnell see, *Wolverhampton Chronicle*, 15 April 1885; for Fowler, *Times*, 9 November 1885.
[57] *Wolverhampton Chronicle*, 7 October 1885.

Reaction from Mee's colleagues on the Council was overwhelmingly hostile, the Tory-leaning engineers and brassworkers immediately withdrew their delegates (including the Council's president and secretary), as did the boilermakers and tailors, while even staunchly Radical unions such as the tinplate workers and the Typographical Association passed motions of censure.[58] Clearly chastened by this experience, Trades Council leaders agreed that henceforth they would rely on less partisan methods such as petitioning candidates to endorse their political programme. However, the ambition to secure municipal office, which had been stimulated by the removal of property qualifications for local office in 1882, remained undiminished for men like Mee. In 1887, the Council came close to running the insurance agents' leader Charles Cole in the affluent ward of St Mark's, and in November 1888 it did agree to run an independent Labour slate in the School Board elections – selecting Mee and Isaac Page, also an insurance agent, as its candidates. The campaign itself was a dismal failure – despite the cumulative voting system (an elector could cast all eleven votes for the same candidate) neither Labour man came close to election (the two candidates polled 5 per cent of the total vote).[59] But on the other hand the election did allow Council leaders to begin developing a distinctive political voice by presenting themselves as champions of working-class parents against the ignorance and indifference of mainstream party politicians who would never dream of sending their own children to the Board schools they administered. They demanded the equalisation of school fees (as a prelude to their total abolition), greater sympathy for parents forced to keep their children from school by poverty, and the restoration of the Grammar school and other educational charities to genuine popular control.[60] In these years the Trades Council was developing a political programme with unmistakeable class overtones. Just as they defended poor parents from prosecution, so they defended the Council's 'scavengers' or the unemployed when they were criticised by well-to-do local politicians. As we have seen, the Trades Council of the 1860s and 1870s had been no less strident in its defence of local working-class interests. Indeed, if anything there had been a blurring of the distinctions between manual and non-manual

---

[58] *The Midland Evening News*, 8 July 1885.
[59] *Express and Star*, 6 July 1887, 16 November 1888. On the cumulative voting system, see D. R. Pugh, 'A note on School Board elections: some north-western contests in the nineties', *History of Education*, 6 (1977), pp. 115–20. Conservative engineers secured the permanent secession of the Wolverhampton ASE between these two bids for municipal office by Trades Council Radicals, see *Express and Star*, 20 February 1888 – thereafter a group of Radical engineers supported their own delegation to the Council by voluntary subscription, until the scheme collapsed after the debacle of the 1892 election, see *Wolverhampton Chronicle*, 28 September 1892.   [60] *Express and Star*, 26 September 1888.

labour on the Council. Whereas in the 1860s Council leaders had railed against shopkeepers and clerks over-running the town's working men's club movement, now many of the champions of the new Labour politics were themselves non-manual workers such as Cole and Page (or Mee by some definitions since he was actually a foreman carpenter). In Wolverhampton, mid-Victorian trade unionism had in contrast been confined exclusively to the world of manual labour.[61]

Having struggled to survive during the difficult trade conditions between 1878 and 1885, the Trades Council was now growing rapidly, despite the secession of some Tory dominated unions. Unions established in the town's 'boom' industries, such as the toolmakers, the galvanizers and tinners and the electricians, joined the Council, but so too did a number of unions organizing among the traditionally difficult metal-working industries of the 'east end', including edge-tool workers and agricultural implement makers. In 1889 the Wolverhampton branch of the Knights of Labour, a general union recruiting heavily in previously unorganized trades, affiliated to the Council further strengthening the position of the 'advanced' wing of the local labour movement.[62] Even so, most Council delegates remained profoundly wary of any intervention into formal party politics, conscious both that the union movement was politically divided, and that the claim to 'independence' would be jealously defended by ordinary union members.[63] This resistance to a more assertive political strategy appears to have been broken during the winter of 1889–90, partly by the rapid growth in Wolverhampton of the new general unions, but perhaps more importantly by the political lessons that many union leaders drew from the success of the London dock strike of August/September 1889. With the exception of Mee's carpenters, Wolverhampton trade societies had played little part in the movement to support the London dockers organised by the *Express and Star* newspaper and the Fowler club, but afterwards the strikes' leaders were heralded as

[61] For example, see *Express and Star*, 23 September 1885, 13 March and 10 April 1889; *Wolverhampton Chronicle*, 17 January and 14 March 1890.

[62] *Wolverhampton Chronicle*, 21 October 1885; *Webb Trade Union collection* (BLPES), E, A, vol. IV f. 299 and vol. XX f. 72; *Express and Star*, 2 April 1906 (toolmakers' anniversary). On the Knights of Labour, see *ibid.*, 26 September 1888, 30 August and 27 September 1889, *Wolverhampton Chronicle*, 2 April and 6 June 1890 – the Knights' 'assembly' was established in 1887 and claimed 240 members a year later. For a discussion of this American-based labour organisation, see H. Pelling, 'The Knights of Labour in Britain, 1880–1901', *Economic History Review*, 2nd ser., 9 (1956), pp. 313–31. For information on the Midland Counties Trade Federation, which pioneered unionism in many of the 'east end' trades, see E. Taylor, 'The working-class movement in the Black Country, 1863–1914', Unpubl. PhD, University of Keele, 1974, pp. 276–99.

[63] For example, *Express and Star*, 29 September 1886, 6 July 1887, 30 August and 27 September 1889.

champions of an invigorated labour movement, perhaps in part because they had demonstrated the ability of skilled workers such as Mann and Burns to organise and lead a mass movement of the poor and dispossessed.[64] Almost overnight the Trades Council embraced a comprehensive 'Labour programme' including the legal eight day, a policy previously shunned as unrealistic and divisive.[65]

The most important sign of the Council's new political assertiveness was the decision, taken in September 1890, to form a Labour Representation Committee (LRC) for the specific purpose of supporting trade union representatives on the town council, School Board and other local government bodies. It was agreed to levy ½d per member per quarter from affiliated societies, although this was increased to 2d per member in 1892 in order to improve the compensation paid to Labour representatives for lost earnings. The new LRC immediately selected Fred Mee as its prospective candidate for the town council, and resolved, significantly, that he should fight the next seat to come vacant on the council (thereby underlining that this was not another cosy deal with Wolverhampton's beleaguered Liberals aimed at opposing Tory candidates in working-class wards).[66] The Trades Council annual report published at this time noted, rather cryptically, that 'although your council have had offers from outside sources, we feel it would neither add to our dignity nor independence to receive such aid'. The aid in question was almost certainly offered by prominent Liberals, anxious both to keep radical trade union leaders 'within the fold', and to resurrect the Mee/Adams strategy of 1885 for countering the advance of popular Toryism. Significantly when Mee came forward as Labour candidate for the affluent ward of St Mark's in November 1890, his candidature was proposed and seconded by Liberal stalwarts George Thorne and T. G. Baker, while his meetings were addressed by most of the town's leading middle-class Radicals. In the end Mee lost to his Tory opponent, the iron-monger Colonel McBean, by the convincing margin of 347 votes.[67] The following May, when a vacancy occurred in the 'east end' ward of St

---

[64] On reactions to the strike, see *Express and Star*, 30 August, 7, 10 and 13 September 1889; on the growth of 'New Unions' locally, see *ibid.*, 17 October 1892; *The Workman's Times*, 16 July, 22 August and 10 October 1890; *Wolverhampton Chronicle*, 11 January 1893; *Webb Trade Union collection*, (BLPES), E, A, vol. IV, f. 299.

[65] For details of this volte-face, see *Express and Star*, 5 June 1889; *Wolverhampton Chronicle*, 12 February 1890.

[66] *Express and Star*, 19 September 1890. For details of the scheme, see *The Birmingham Workman's Times*, 12 September 1890; *Express and Star*, 31 July and 24 September 1891; *Webb Trade Union collection*, (BLPES), E. A. vol. IV, f. 299.

[67] See *The Birmingham Workman's Times*, 12 September 1890; *Wolverhampton Chronicle*, 29 October 1890, 5 November 1890; *The Workman's Times*, 31 October 1890.

George's, the Trades Council selected the shoemaker James Stevenson as its champion. Like Mee, Stevenson was a prominent working-class Liberal, actively involved in his ward Liberal party, the local Reform clubs, and the Wolverhampton West Liberal Three Hundred. Also like Mee he was proposed by a leading middle-class Radical, and received the active support of his ward Liberal party. Moreover, when Stevenson's unopposed return looked likely to be annulled because of irregularities in his nomination papers, it was the local Liberal party, rather than the impoverished Trades Council, which helped him to fight the case in the courts.[68]

It can be seen, therefore, that there is little substance to the argument that the formation of the LRC, and the Labour campaigns of November 1890 and May 1891 represented a break with Lib–Lab traditions born of frustration with the Liberal party's hostility to working-class representation.[69] On the contrary, Wolverhampton in the early 1890s was witnessing the emergence of a new generation of Liberal leaders, such as George Thorne, Price Lewis, T. G. Baker and Stephen Craddock who actively encouraged both trade unionism and working-class representation. Indeed, when Abiathar Weaver stood as a Tory 'labour' candidate in April 1891, George Thorne insisted on supporting him, despite the shoemaker's well-known Tory connections, arguing that Wolverhampton needed more working-class councillors, whatever their party politics might be.[70] As we have seen, the Trades Council had initially taken the same view (hence the negotiations with Weaver's North Street club), but by the spring of 1891 this spirit of co-operation had completely evaporated. Perhaps resentful that the North Street club had chosen to run Weaver, a non-unionist, as its candidate, the Council immediately resolved to oppose him. Unable to find a candidate willing to stand from their own ranks they ended up nominating a local publican, Patrick Connolly. Connolly's Labour credentials appeared at best flimsy, especially once the Weaver camp began denouncing him as an employer of sweated labour. The Council's extraordinary stance drew widespread criticism, and resulted in Mee being howled down when he tried to address the inaugural meeting of a new branch of the coopers' union at the Springfield brewery.[71]

---

[68] *Express and Star*, 8 and 12 May; 12, 13 and 15 July 1891; *Wolverhampton Chronicle*, 31 July 1891. Up for re-election in November, Stevenson was again proposed by his Liberal employer Stephen Craddock, *Express and Star*, 26 October 1891. For details of Mee's Liberal credentials, see *ibid.*, 22 January and 5 December 1891, 1 February 1892.

[69] See Wright, 'Liberal party organization', pp. 31–3, 135–6.

[70] *Express and Star*, 24 April 1891.

[71] *Express and Star*, 31 March and 21 and 22 April 1891; *The Midland Evening News*, 28 April 1891. Connolly eventually polled 600 votes, 82 fewer than Weaver.

Like Thorne, the newly established Wolverhampton Fabian Society took a much more sympathetic line towards Weaver, continuing to refer to him as a Labour representative even after his election. Throughout 1891 the Fabian society persistently campaigned for the Trades Council to embrace a more genuinely independent political stance, though initially with little success.[72] At the School Board elections in November the Council again put forward its own Labour slate, but the open meeting which agreed to run the two Labour candidates was chaired by T. G. Baker (a Liberal shoe manufacturer), while at a second meeting a motion to avoid a contest by running a joint slate of five with the Liberals was defeated by only one vote. In the end Labour did extremely well, returning both candidates on an aggregate poll of 11,439, compared with only 10,719 for the four 'School Board' (ie. Liberal) candidates.[73] Perhaps encouraged by this result, or worn down by the criticisms of its growing socialist minority, the Council finally issued a manifesto in December 1891 which included a formal commitment to strict political independence: henceforth, it declared, 'all Labour candidates should be independent of any party or faction'.[74] During the first half of 1892 a number of prominent Radical trade unionists, including Councillor Stevenson, joined either the Fabians or the proto-'Independent Labour party' being organised through the pages of Burgess's *Workman's Times*. Stevenson, in particular, made it clear that his decision was prompted by 'the vacillating and selfish spirit of the Liberal leaders' – by which he appears to have meant the party's national leaders, since his relations with Craddock, Thorne and the other Wolverhampton Radicals remained close and cordial.[75]

At the beginning of the 1892 General Election campaign Trades Council leaders confirmed their commitment to strict independence, but as the likelihood of Hickman securing a resounding Tory victory loomed larger this resolve quickly evaporated. Even the local Fabian Society, which had recently been campaigning for the formation of an Independent Labour party, agreed to call on its supporters to back Plowden in preference to his Tory opponent. The Trades Council leaders went further, campaigning wholeheartedly for Plowden on the days

---

[72] On the origins and early politics of the Wolverhampton Fabian society, see *Fabian News*, March and April 1891; *Express and Star*, 22 January, 5 and 20 February, 30 March, 10, 17 and 23 April, 6 July 1891. For a detailed discussion of the campaign to win Radical trade unionists to socialism and political independence, see Lawrence, 'Party politics', pp. 92–7.

[73] *Express and Star*, 24 September and 4 November 1891; *Wolverhampton Chronicle*, 18 November 1891.   [74] *Express and Star*, 19 December 1891.

[75] *The Workman's Times*, 25 June 1892; *Fabian News*, June 1892 – Stevenson claimed to have been 'converted' to socialism at a Fabian lecture given by Enid Stacy.

immediately before the poll. Once again Tory trade unionists were incensed by this open display of partisanship. Roughley and Scott of the brassworkers organised a petition which continued to circulate around the pubs and workshops of Wolverhampton long after Hickman had been returned with a massive 1,116 vote majority.[76] This episode marked a turning-point in Wolverhampton Labour politics. Henceforth the dominant voices on the Trades Council were men like William Day (Typographical Association), Harry Moreton (NUBSO), and James Stevenson who had long argued that Labour must break all ties with the established political parties. In this objective they were undoubtedly assisted by the near-total collapse of Liberal organisation in Wolverhampton after the 1892 defeat. Certainly the decision to bar Radical sympathisers such as Thorne and Price Lewis from attending the May Day celebrations suggested a profound rift with Liberalism – especially since local socialist celebrities and representatives of the recently formed ILP *were* invited to address the crowd (estimated at between ten and twelve thousand by the local press).[77] Within months of this meeting, having organised a series of lectures on the theme 'Why an Independent Labour Party?', the local Fabian Society finally succeeded in launching a Wolverhampton branch of the ILP.[78] Interestingly, at the inaugural meeting, would-be members of the new party were asked to declare their former party allegiances – apparently because some feared accusations of 'jobbery by the party hacks' (underlining once more the widespread suspicion of the 'party wire-puller' in popular politics). It turned out that the members were divided almost equally between former Liberals, and those who claimed to be new to party politics – there were only two former Tories present.[79]

For perhaps four or five years the ILP was extremely influential in Wolverhampton. In large measure this was because the young activists who flocked to the propaganda work of the local Labour Church and Clarion cyclists also threw themselves into practical work such as trade union organisation and electoral campaigning under the new 'Independent Labour' banner. It was this practical activity which allowed

[76] *Express and Star*, 29 June, 4, 5 and 6 July, 3 August 1892; *Wolverhampton Chronicle*, 6 July 1892; *The Workman's Times*, 16 July 1892. For the Fabians' more cautious endorsement of Plowden (which repeated the call for a Wolverhampton ILP), see *Local Fabian Society Collection* (BLPES), Coll. Misc. 375, vol. 5, f. 89; also *The Workman's Times*, 25 June and 2 July 1892.

[77] *Wolverhampton Chronicle*, 19 April and 10 May 1893; on the decline of organised Liberalism, *ibid.*, 7 August 1895.

[78] *Wolverhampton Chronicle*, 30 August 1893; *Local Fabian Society collection* (BLPES), vol. 5 f. 97; *The Workman's Times*, 2 and 16 September 1893. The Fabian society subsequently declined as its members' energies were directed towards the new organisation, see *Fabian News*, February 1894 and Lawrence, 'Party politics', p. 96.

[79] *The Workman's Times*, 16 September 1893.

socialists to build strong relations with the town's wider trade union movement.[80] In Wolverhampton, and one suspects in many other districts, there was little evidence of a fundamental tension between 'the religion of socialism' and the more mundane, pragmatic world of electoral or trade union politics.[81] There is no doubt that the ideals of the new socialism, and especially its emphasis on living a 'new life', inspired a generation of (predominantly) young men to become active in many different fields of local political life. However, no less important to the growing influence of the new Wolverhampton ILP was the success of its Independent Labour Club established in John's Lane in 1894. Initially confined to party members, the club quickly threw its doors open to anyone not working for a rival political party – as a result membership rose sharply from 200 in the autumn, to nearly 900 by the following July. As the *Wolverhampton Chronicle* was obliged to recognise in its special report on the club in 1896, though run by the socialists, it 'satisfied, to a large extent, those who, whilst agreeing that labour interests should be "independent", were not prepared to become members of the Independent Labour Party.'[82] As the new 'Labour Club' flourished, so the Radical clubs established in the 1880s went into terminal decline. The Fowler Club appears to have gone under in the wake of the 1892 election defeat, while as we have seen the Villiers club survived only as a non-political social organisation. By the mid 1890s its ethos was said to be '"a plague on both political parties", or rather all political parties.'[83]

The success of this broad-church 'Labour Coalition' in Wolverhampton may well have been unusual. Certainly when John Trevor, the Labour Church leader, visited the town in late 1894, he reported that 'so far as I could judge, there does not appear to be in Wolverhampton that clear-cut division in Labour ranks that exists in most industrial centres'.[84] There were also soon signs of a rapprochement between Labour leaders and the radical wing of the Liberal

---

[80] For references to the Labour Church and Clarion movement in Wolverhampton see Lawrence, 'Party politics', p. 102n; young socialist activists involved in trade union organisation included Harry Gibson (general railway workers), J. H. Smith (gasworkers), George Parslow (bakers) and Tom Wilson (postmen). Seven 'ILPers' stood for the town council in the 1890s, two (Tom Frost and James Whittaker) subsequently sat on the borough council for a total of nearly seventy years.

[81] Contra S. Yeo, 'A new life: the religion of socialism in Britain, 1883–1896', *History Workshop Journal*, 4 (1977), pp. 5–56, esp. pp. 31, 43–4. For a very different perspective see Howell, *British workers and the ILP, passim.*

[82] *Wolverhampton Chronicle*, 4 March 1896. On the formation of the club, see *Express and Star*, 28 September 1894; on its altered membership rules, see *ibid.*, 30 November 1894 and 3 July 1895; and *The Midland Counties Express*, 29 February 1896.

[83] *Wolverhampton Chronicle*, 26 February 1896.

[84] *The Labour Prophet*, November 1894; for a discussion of declining socialist sectarianism elsewhere in Britain after 1895, see David Howell, *British workers and the Independent Labour party, 1888–1906* (Manchester, 1983), pp. 193–9, 202–3, and 277–82.

establishment. In 1894 the Trades Council rescinded its ban on Liberal speakers by inviting Price Lewis and George Thorne to address the May Day rally, and, perhaps more controversially, in November it agreed to support Fred Evans, a fishmonger and well-known local Radical, in a straight fight with a Tory solicitor at Dunstall. On the other hand, the Trades Council had no qualms about supporting ILP attempts to unseat right-wing Liberal Councillors such as B. E. Williams and William Hodgson, it ran a completely independent slate of five candidates at the 1894 School Board elections, and it refused to endorse the last-minute Liberal challenge to Hickman at the 1895 General Election, even though the Liberals had put up their old friend and supporter George Thorne.[85] Wolverhampton's trade union leaders also stood aloof when, in the wake of Thorne's decisive defeat, local Liberal politicians sought to re-establish a Wolverhampton West Liberal Association. Remarkably, on announcing their plans to consolidate the limited Liberal revival seen in 1895, the party's leaders published a list of eminent local Liberals they deemed worthy of office in the new organisation, including Thorne as President, Graham as chairman, Baker as vice-chairman, and Haslam as secretary. Dictation remained deeply ingrained in the ethos of local Liberalism, very much to its disadvantage in this instance as the scheme failed dismally.[86] Liberal revival would have to wait until after 1900, when the enthusiasm generated by the campaign against the Conservative Education Act finally rejuvenated Liberal activism in the town.

IV

If, as the preceding account suggests, independent Labour politics in Wolverhampton were based on a coalition between ethical socialists and more pragmatic trade union leaders – men who recognised that the rise of popular Toryism in the town meant that there was little scope for an old-style 'Lib-Lab' political strategy – it remains to be asked whether the new politics did in fact make any significant inroads into working-class Tory support.[87] Inevitably this is not an easy issue to resolve, especially since contested elections remained infrequent, and three-cornered contests

---

[85] *Express and Star*, 4 April, 7 May, 22 September, 5, 16, 29 and 31 October and 2 and 17 November 1894, 15 July 1895; *Wolverhampton Chronicle*, 24 February 1897.
[86] *Wolverhampton Chronicle*, 7 August 1895.
[87] It should be noted that the relationship was not without its strains even in the 1890s. In 1895 the Labour Representation Committee refused to endorse Will Sharrocks as ILP candidate for St Mary's, while in 1897 the Trades Council rebuked ILP activists for suggesting that Labour should stake a claim on Wolverhampton South given the state of Villiers' health; *Wolverhampton Chronicle*, 24 April 1895 and 21 July 1897.

were rarer still. However, in 1897 the *Express and Star* undertook a detailed survey of political feeling at the November School Board election. This was made possible by the complexities of the cumulative voting system, which obliged each party to maintain committee rooms adjacent to every polling booth in order to advise supporters on how to cast their thirteen votes in order to maximize the chance of returning the party's full slate of candidates. The *Express and Star* reporters simply recorded how many electors visited each party's committee rooms throughout the day. Of course, many electors simply voted according to their own preferences, without consulting the party representatives, while one also has to acknowledge that party identities were somewhat blurred by the denominational dimension of School Board politics. In 1897 there were four slates, not three, and only Labour fought under its own name. This time the Liberals fought under the label of 'Progressives'; the Conservatives fought as 'Denominationalists' (i.e. supporters of voluntary church schools); while there was also a separate Catholic slate which shared much of the Denominationalists' agenda, but drew its support from a very different constituency.[88]

The *Express and Star* survey suggests that, outside the 'East End' (where its candidates fared poorly), Labour was more than able to hold its own in working-class districts (predictably it made little impact in the prosperous western suburbs). In traditionally radical districts such as Stafford Road/Dunstall Hill Labour had a commanding lead over all other parties. In suburban Blakenhall, and in the densely populated district around Merridale Street and Great Brickkiln Street (where Weaver had won so much support as a working-class Tory candidate in 1891), Labour ran the traditionally dominant Church (i.e. Conservative) party neck-and-neck. In St John's, long established as a stronghold of working-class Toryism, Labour apparently provided the only serious challenge to the Anglican ascendency, without ever threatening its overthrow. Labour's greatest success, however, was to emerge as the dominant political force in the north-western suburb of Whitmore Reans, which had leant strongly towards Conservatism since the early 1880s. Finally, in the strongly Irish ward of St Mary's, Labour emerged as the dominant force in the recently developed Springfield district, with its large numbers of brewery, building and transport workers, but made little impression in the older, and more poverty-stricken parts of the ward around Stafford Street, where the Catholic party predominated. Significantly, Labour's campaign in Springfield was spearheaded by Peter Lalley, the local

[88] *Express and Star*, 17 and 18 November 1897 – Labour could not afford to run committee rooms at each polling station, but it did always have a representative present to ensure that supporters divided their votes so as to maximise each candidate's vote.

leader of the builders' labourers' union and himself of Irish-Catholic descent.[89]

This was Labour's best performance at a School Board election, its four candidates received 27,597 votes (25.9 per cent of the total), and all but one was elected. Had it not performed so poorly in the 'east end' it could easily have emerged as the dominant force on the Board. Labour's appeal was based on consciously rejecting traditional nonconformist/Anglican controversies over education. For Labour candidates the crucial question was not the appropriate form for religious instruction, but who should control the education of working-class children.[90] From the outset Labour stressed that it would run both Anglican and non-conformist candidates. As in 1894 efforts were made (unsuccessfully) to persuade William Roughley, the Tory brassworkers' leader, to join the Labour slate in order to underline its non-sectarian credentials.[91] As J. H. Smith, the Anglican gasworkers' leader and 'ILPer' put it in 1897, 'they did not say anything in their programme about religion. They were Labour men and it was their job to look after the education of the children and their physical condition'.[92]

Although the Church party had remained dominant in St John's in 1897, this ward subsequently emerged as Labour's great municipal success story. Between 1898 and 1913, Labour contested the ward on twelve separate occasions (St Matthew's, the next most contested ward, was fought on seven occasions during the same period). Nine of these campaigns ended in the return of a Labour councillor, including six contested elections.[93] One reason for this success was that Labour sought, at least officially, to distance itself from controversies over drink as much as over religion. Although many Labour leaders shared the nonconformist faith and temperance views of their Liberal opponents, these were rarely allowed to impinge on electoral politics. Instead, Liberal temperance fanatics and Tory publicans were denounced with equal venom, as Labour skilfully allied itself with the aspirations of the town's burgeoning working-men's club movement. During the 1890s, the local club movement was virulently anti-party, determined as it was to remove popular

---

[89] For details of the survey, see *Express and Star*, 18 November 1897; for the campaign generally see, *ibid.*, 17 and 18 November 1897. Whitmore Reans was a predominantly working-class district with an unusually high-level of home-ownership, for its recent Conservative traditions see, *The Midland Counties Evening Express*, 31 March 1880; *The Midland Evening News*, 5 July 1892; *Express and Star*, 16 July 1895.

[90] E.g. see *Express and Star*, 5 October 1894 and 16 November 1897; and *Wolverhampton Chronicle*, 22 October 1902.   [91] *Express and Star*, 8 May 1891; 22 September 1894.

[92] *Express and Star*, 16 November 1897.

[93] These figures exclude James Walsh's victory of 1908, since although he was endorsed by the Labour Representation Committee, this prominent Irish Nationalist leader subsequently chose to sit as an Independent.

leisure from the terrain of political controversy. As we shall see, the great success of the CIU-affiliated Central Labour Club helped consolidate this political alliance between Labour and the clubs.[94]

By adopting an essentially agnostic position on religious and temperance controversies the Labour party gave itself some chance of succeeding in predominantly working-class districts such as St John's and Whitmore Reans where pub and Church retained strong claims on voter allegiance. The strategy worked best when Labour found itself up against an orthodox representative of the local Conservative establishment. On such occasions the party was often able to win significant support from Tory trade union leaders, and even local publicans might sport its colours. But when Labour found itself facing a more populist opponent such support generally evaporated, and the party's touch often faltered. For instance in 1898 Tom Wilson, the postmen's leader, lost Dunstall ward by fifty-nine votes to James Steward, a popular local publican, though Labour had polled very well there at the 1897 School Board election. Steward ran a classic populist campaign: endorsing the municipalisation of the local gas, tram and cemetery companies, calling for a more rigorous interpretation of the Council's 'Fair Wages' policy, and billing himself as 'the trade unionists' candidate' on his election literature. Running a pub close to the large GWR locomotive works Steward apparently had no difficulties finding twenty trade unionists to sign his nomination papers. To cap his credentials as a populist Tory candidate he could also boast to have been a leading figure in the early history of the Stafford Road Football Club, for many years the premier football side in Wolverhampton, until eventually overshadowed by the Wanderers.[95] Interestingly, just weeks later Wilson won Dunstall in a three-cornered by-election which saw him push the Tory brassworkers' leader William Roughley into a poor third place. Roughley's political programme was very similar to that advocated by Steward in the earlier contest, but with few brassworkers in the ward Roughley presumably lacked the publican's personal popularity and influence.[96]

[94] *The Midland Counties Express*, 29 February 1896. Very little 'temperance business' appears to have been done at the Labour club, see *The Labour Prophet*, November 1894. For examples of Labour hostility to temperance politics, see *The Workman's Times*, 23 July 1892; *Wolverhampton Chronicle*, 27 November 1907 – and also a much earlier debate along these lines on Wolverhampton Trades Council, *The Miner and Workmen's Examiner*, 7 August 1875. This theme is explored more fully below, chapter 6, pp. 139–42.

[95] *Express and Star*, 27 October, 1 and 2 November 1898. On the Stafford Road Football Club, see P. M. Young, *Centenary Wolves, 1877–1977*, (Wolverhampton, 1976), pp. 3, 5, 9 and 17–19. The result in the first Dunstall contest was: Steward (Conservative), 475; Wilson (Labour), 416.

[96] The result in the second Dunstall contest was: Wilson (Labour), 417; Larkinson (Liberal) 290; Roughley (Conservative) 239, *Express and Star*, 17 and 25 November 1898.

Tom Frost, the carpenters' leader, suffered a similar fate in 1901 when he contested St John's ward against local publican Arthur Lamsdale. He lost the seat (which Labour had held since 1898) by 466 votes to 375. As with Wilson in Dunstall ward, within weeks of this defeat Frost had been returned by the same electors in a by-election against a Tory lock manufacturer. Nor, apparently, was this turn-around in political fortunes unexpected. As a Labour supporter explained, Lamsdale had won because he had strong working-class support: he had 'risen from among them [the workers] to become a popular local publican', whereas the new Tory candidate enjoyed no such claims on popular allegiance. In the second contest Frost made much of his Anglican background, which included singing with the choir of St John's Church as a boy, and highlighted the support of prominent publicans, trade unionists and Catholic leaders in the ward. In the end Frost won fairly comfortably, polling 132 votes more than at the previous contest.[97]

Interestingly, despite its nine successes in St John's ward in just fifteen years before the Great War, Labour always remained vulnerable to a genuinely popular Tory candidate. In 1908 Tom Frost again lost heavily in the ward, this time to J. F Myatt, the popular local brewer.[98] Similarly, when James Whittaker, the Labour party agent and a strong temperance advocate, fought the seat in 1912 he too was heavily defeated, this time by the furniture dealer Robert Clarkson, even though Whittaker had represented the ward continuously between 1903 and 1911.[99] In fact, as we shall see in the following chapter, there was no such thing as a 'safe' Labour ward in pre-war Wolverhampton. William Sharrocks, the boilermakers' leader, won a series of victories in the 'east end' ward of St Matthew's between 1901 and 1913, but his success was largely personal; other Labour candidates continued to fare poorly whenever they stood in the ward. Labour's difficulties reflected more than just the restrictive nature of the local government franchise (which was in effect a ratepayer franchise), they reflected fundamental tensions and ambiguities in the relationship between the emergent Labour party and the working people they sought to represent. The following chapter will explore this relationship as it developed between the early 1890s, when the ideals of a distinct 'Labour programme' were first championed by a coalition of ILP and Trades Council activists, down to the First World War. A central issue

[97] *Express and Star*, 16, 22, 23 and 26 November 1901 – Frost's supporters included James Scott, the influential Tory brassworkers' leader. The result in this second contest was Frost (Labour), 507; Gibbons (Conservative), 434.

[98] The result was Myatt (Conservative), 542; Frost (Labour), 403; *Wolverhampton Chronicle*, 4 November 1908.

[99] The result was Clarkson (Conservative), 523; Whittaker (Labour), 297; Roberts (Independent), 54; *Wolverhampton Chronicle*, 6 November 1912.

here will be the need to understand why the Labour party was (with the noteworthy exception of Sharrocks) so spectacularly unsuccessful in the poor, 'east end' of the town throughout this period, even though the population of this district was almost monolithically working class, and the local economy was dominated by large-scale, heavy industry.

6   Labour and the working class, 1890–1914

I

Labour's failure to establish strong political roots in the industrial districts of east Wolverhampton was not born simply of neglect. On the contrary, in the early 1890s the leaders of town's fledgling independent Labour movement concentrated much of their propaganda work and electoral campaigning in the poor 'east end' wards. Between July 1891 and January 1896 Labour candidates contested eight municipal seats; every one was in the 'east end'.[1] Still buoyed by the heady optimism of 1889–90, Labour activists believed, not only that the poor had most to gain from the new 'labour programme', but that the success of the 'New Unionism' suggested that they could definitely be mobilised to support such a programme. They were wrong. Labour candidates averaged just 34.8 per cent of the vote in contested elections in the 'east end' between 1891 and 1896. Worse still, the Labour vote fell steadily during the mid 1890s, from a high-point of 46.9 per cent in St Mary's in November 1894, to just 24.9 per cent in the same ward in January 1896, and 24.1 per cent in St Matthew's in November 1895.[2] On the propaganda front, socialist organisations such as the ILP and especially the Wolverhampton Labour Church put a great deal of effort into proselytising the east end poor. Again with precious little success. Reports suggest that their efforts were usually met with incredulity or indifference by local residents, and that occasionally this turned to outright hostility, as when an open-air Fabian meeting in the poor district of Monmore Green was broken up by a gang of 'drunken rowdies'.[3] In 1895 the ILP tried to reinforce its electoral efforts in the east by establishing a second Independent Labour club on

---

[1] Labour candidates contested St George's four times, St Mary's three times and St Matthew's once.

[2] These figures exclude a contested election at St George's in 1895 since this was a double member ward where each elector had two votes. Labour polled 541 votes, compared with 764 for the Conservative and 836 for the Liberal.

[3] *The Workman's Times*, 20 August 1892. For the difficulties experienced by the Labour Church activists in the East End see *The Labour Prophet*, July and October 1893.

Cannock Road (St Mary's). Named the Springfield Labour club it was intended as a base for the newly established ILP No. 2 branch. However, neither the branch nor the club flourished, propaganda work was largely ignored and the club soon became extremely insular; a socialist island quite divorced from the community within which it had been established.[4]

In November 1896 the ILP finally abandoned this strategy of concentrating on the east end by standing the greengrocer (and former shoemaker) Evan Evans in the newly created suburban ward of Graiseley. At the same time James Stevenson gave up his seat at St George's (an 'east end' seat he had never had to contest), and chose to sit for Graiseley in the west.[5] The new strategy met with immediate success: Evans defeated his Conservative opponent by 428 votes to 357. Wolverhampton now had two Labour councillors, both representing the south-western, and essentially suburban, ward of Graiseley.[6] After February 1897, when the ILP again suffered a heavy defeat at a by-election in St Mary's, the party increasingly concentrated on fighting seats in the south and west of the town.[7] Henceforth Labour all but ignored the three wards belonging to the Wolverhampton East parliamentary division (i.e. St Peter's, St Mary's and St James's). St Mary's was not fought again until 1919, and St Peter's and St James's were each contested just once down to 1914. St George's and St Matthew's, which lay in the Western Division, were contested more frequently: St George's was won in both 1910 and 1913, while St Matthew's, as we have already seen, was won on five occasions between 1901 and 1913 by the maverick boilermakers' leader Will Sharrocks (but lost decisively in 1903 and 1912 by James Whittaker). Sharrocks's success in the east end was unique, and owed little to the efforts of the wider Labour party in Wolverhampton. Precisely how Sharrocks managed to bridge the political gulf between Labour and the poor working class will be considered more fully later, but for now the important point to establish is that, if one excludes Sharrocks's elections from the calculations, Labour contested the five 'east end' wards on seven occasions between the ward reorganisation of 1896 and the First World War (winning twice); while it contested the four western wards of Blakenhall, Dunstall,

---

[4] On the formation of the club see *Express and Star*, 4 July 1895; there is a detailed report on the club in *The Midland Counties Express*, 16 May 1896.

[5] There was a general reorganisation of ward boundaries in 1896: the town now had twelve instead of eight wards, although the municipality itself was not enlarged. The new wards of Blakenhall, Graiseley, Park, Merridale and Dunstall were created by dividing St Mark's, St John's and St Paul's, the last of which ceased to exist.

[6] *Express and Star*, 3 November 1896.

[7] The 1897 contest in St Mary's was a low key affair with a poor turnout – Labour's vote slumped to 254, an all-time low, *Wolverhampton Chronicle*, 24 February 1897.

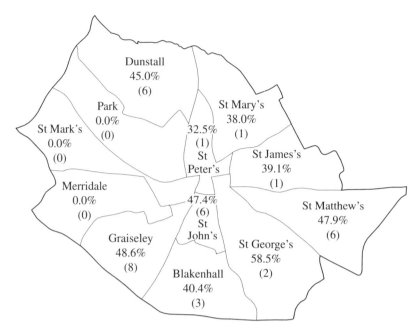

Figure 6.1 Average Labour vote at municipal elections, 1896-1914 (by ward) (figures in parentheses represent the number of *contested* elections involving Labour candidates).

Graiseley, and St John's on thirty three occasions (winning nineteen times): the remaining three wards: Park, Merridale and St Mark's, comprising the prestigious 'west end', were never contested by Labour during this period.

Results suggest that the decision to concentrate on the western wards was not an unqualified success (see figure 6.1). Despite sustained campaigning, Labour's hold on these seats remained distinctly tenuous before the First World War. In none of these wards did Labour candidates average 50 per cent of the vote (as they did in St George's), and only in one case did a Labour councillor manage to hold office continuously for more than a couple of terms (Evan Evans represented Graiseley from 1896 until his defeat by a Conservative in 1908). Given Sharrocks's victories in St Matthew's from 1901, and the two victories in St George's just before the war, one has to ask whether the bulk of the Wolverhampton Labour movement simply gave up on the 'east end' after the initial disappointments of the early 1890s. If they did, one reason may be that hardly any pre-war labour activists actually lived in the eastern half of town. Instead, the overwhelming majority resided on the northern and

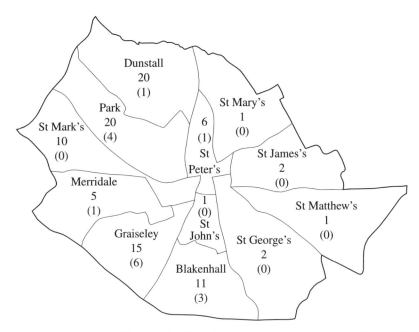

Figure 6.2 The distribution of recorded pre-war Labour addresses (by ward) (figures in parentheses indicate the number of 'secondary' addresses included in each total).

southern outskirts of the town in mixed residential districts such as Blakenhall, Dunstall Hill and Whitmore Reans. It has proved possible to trace the addresses of seventy-seven pre-war Labour leaders: including ILP members, Labour councillors and Poor Law Guardians, Trades Council leaders and other trades unionists actively involved in Labour politics. These addresses offer a valuable insight into the social geography of early Labour activism. In all, ninety-four separate addresses were recorded for these labour activists (removals were commonplace even among this activist minority).[8] Figure 6.2 shows the distribution of the ninety-four addresses by ward. Remarkably, over 85 per cent of the Labour activists traced were found to live in one of the six largely sub-urban wards which arched west from Dunstall in the north to Blakenhall in the south (figure 6.2). Only thirteen activists (14 per cent of the total) were traced to the six wards of central and eastern Wolverhampton, and half of these lived in a few streets of terraced houses at the northern edge

---

[8] Second and subsequent addresses were recorded separately to avoid confusion. The addresses were mainly culled from the local press, commercial directories and the *Wolverhampton Red Books* – civic guides published annually from 1892.

of St Peter's (bordering Dunstall and Park). What this tells us is that, whether they were fighting in a central ward like St John's or in eastern wards such as St James's and St Matthew's, pre-war Labour politicians were fighting in 'foreign' territory. They could no more claim to be rooted in these communities, to understand them from the inside, than could a wealthy 'west end' solicitor or company manager. Indeed Labour's claims to understand the needs and aspirations of these poor communities might well be considered weaker than those of local Tory publicans or Liberal shopkeepers, and even of other non-resident politicians such as the employer with a local factory, the doctor with a local surgery, or the minister from the local church or chapel. On the other hand, when Labour fought in Graiseley, Dunstall or Blakenhall things were very different – not only was this where most Labour activists lived, it was also where many of them worked, where they prayed, and where they socialised: here they were amongst their own, which may explain why these seats saw so many Labour challenges, despite the fact that these socially mixed communities were never safe Labour territory.[9]

Less easy to explain is why so few Labour activists lived in the older, more solidly working-class parts of the town in the first place. The decline of the iron trades, and the consequent heavy emigration of skilled workers from the district, may have been one factor. As we have seen, by 1911 nearly half the people born in Wolverhampton now lived elsewhere.[10] In addition, trade unions were relatively weak in the eastern districts, though this was not the case in central districts like St John's or St Paul's/St Mark's, where light-metal working was important, nor in St Mary's, with its railway, brewing and transport workers. Indeed even in the 'east end' unions were not wholly absent, some trades such as galvanized hollow-ware manufacture claimed almost 100 per cent unionization by the Edwardian period – it is just that the unions that did exist here tended to stand aloof from the Trades Council and its political ambitions. Down to the First World War unions here were as likely to support the pro-Liberal East End Progressive Association as to support the Labour party.[11] In other words, even allowing for the uneven geography of trade unionism in

---

[9] Labour candidates were involved in seventeen contested elections in the three suburban wards of Dunstall, Graiseley and Blakenhall between 1896 and 1913 – eleven of these contests ended in defeat. Interestingly, although twenty Labour activists were traced to Park ward (mainly living in Whitmore Reans), the seat was never contested by Labour, perhaps because overall it was much wealthier than the other three wards.

[10] See above, chapter 5, pp. 103 and 104n – the figure refers *only* to people still resident in Great Britain. The consequences of such demographic instability for the development of Labour politics are discussed more fully in chapter 9, pp. 240–46.

[11] On the hollowware trade, see *Express and Star*, 27 October 1911; for low levels of trade unionism among ironworkers, see *ibid.*, 3 October 1892, and 20 February 1903, where it is used as an important reason for Labour not to challenge Fowler in the East.

Figure 6.3 Wolverhampton districts used in the analysis of sampled 1881 census enumerators' returns.

Wolverhampton, Labour politicians were under-represented in the more solidly working-class parts of town. It is almost as though the same impulses which drove these activists to embrace socialism, or at least labour politics, also drove them to become suburbanites – as though the political rejection of poverty and industrial exploitation presupposed its physical rejection.

II

Because the map of Labour activism in Wolverhampton generated by the preceding analysis seemed so extreme, it was felt necessary to analyse the social character of the different districts with greater accuracy than the subjective accounts found in contemporary sources would allow. Besides checking the general accuracy of such sources, it was felt that a detailed analysis of census enumerators' returns would shed important light on patterns of residence in the 'Labour suburbs': did manual and non-manual workers live side-by-side, or were these areas internally differentiated by social class and status? Since so many labour historians have seen the growth of independent Labour politics as a product of increasingly homogeneous working-class communities and/or of growing conflict between manual and non-manual workers these were clearly important points to clarify. The analysis was undertaken on enumerators' returns for the 1881 population census, using a random sample of eighty streets drawn from across the town. In all the analysis covered 3,583 separate households, representing 26.7 per cent of the total households in Wolverhampton.[12] The data collected were then analysed by districts. Inevitably, more households were analysed in some districts than others; from a low of 235 households in Graiseley, to 426 in North Wolverhampton and 435 in Whitmore Reans.[13] Ranking the districts according to the percentage of male workers engaged in manual occupations confirmed the overwhelmingly proletarian character of the eastern districts, but it also showed that manual workers were in a majority (just) even in the 'west end', and that in the other suburban districts manual workers were clearly predominant (table 6.1). Indeed Graiseley, where Labour made its breakthrough in the mid 1890s, turned out to have a higher proportion of manual workers than either Springfield/Causeway Lake in the east, or St John's/St George's West on the southern edge of the town centre.

The structure of the male workforce was then further analysed using a relatively simple six-category classification system: manual workers were ascribed to one of three trade-based categories: light-metal working; iron and steel trades; and non-metal working. In turn, non-manual workers were ascribed to one of two categories: the 'lower middle class' and the 'substantial middle class'.[14] It may seem odd to divide manual workers by type of industry, rather than by skill, but it was felt both that this would more accurately reflect spatial divisions within the Wolverhampton working class, and that conventional schemes for dividing occupations into skilled, semi-skilled and unskilled strata were unhelpful given the

[12] Streets which traversed district boundaries were then sub-divided, and their returns analysed separately. No street was included from the small central ward of St Peter's, but since this was largely non-residential by 1881 this should not greatly distort the analysis; see *Wolverhampton Chronicle*, 21 January 1885. For full details of the survey see, Jon Lawrence, 'Party politics and the people: continuity and change in the political history of Wolverhampton, 1815–1914', unpubl. PhD thesis, University of Cambridge, 1989, pp. 119–22, and appendices A to C.

[13] For an explanation of the choice of these district boundaries see Lawrence, 'Party politics', p. 120n and Appendix A; for more details of the sample see *ibid.*, chapter 4, tables 5 and 6; for a map of the districts, see figure 6.3.

[14] The precise definitions used for each category are discussed in Lawrence, 'Party politics', Appendix B, which also gives details of the small residual category used to classify otherwise ambiguous cases. The occupational structure of the female workforce was analysed separately because of the special constraints which shaped the pattern of female employment in Wolverhampton as elsewhere, see *ibid.*, Appendix C.

Table 6.1 *The distribution of the 1881 census sample and proportion of male manual workers by district*

District	Sampled households	Employed males	Manual wkrs as % of all male wkrs	Rank order % male manual wkrs
Whitmore Reans	435	570	70	10
West End	305	416	51	11
North Wolverhampton	426	666	74	9
Old St Mary's	250	388	89	3
Springfield/Causeway Lake	236	382	81	6
Horseley Fields	270	445	96	1
St Matthew's/St George's East	373	538	92	2
St John's/St George's West	374	525	79	7
Blakenhall	324	476	75	8
Old St Paul's/St Mark's	355	543	86	4
Graiseley	235	370	83	5

Source: Database constructed from a random sample of census enumerators' returns for 1881 held at Wolverhampton Reference Library.

large numbers of (often unapprenticed) workers who gravitated to many of the town's depressed 'craft' industries. The results of this analysis are presented in table 6.2.[15] The strong geographic concentration of the iron and steel trades in the east (Horseley Fields and St Matthew's/St George's East) is confirmed (column B); in both districts over half the male workforce was engaged in these trades. Also confirmed is the concentration of light-metal working (including the brass and tin-plate trades) in the west, and especially the south-west where the adjacent districts of Graiseley, Old St Paul's/St Mark's, Blakenhall and St John's/St George's West account for four of the five highest concentrations of workers in this sector (column A). Perhaps not surprisingly workers in 'other manual occupations' tended to be distributed more evenly across the town, but the four highest concentrations occurred in adjacent northern districts (Old St Mary's, Whitmore Reans, Springfield/Causeway Lake and North Wolverhampton), reflecting the location of the town's principal railway stations, goods yards and sidings (column C). Turning to the 'lower middle class' category (clerks, salesmen, company agents, shopworkers, retailers and the like), the highest concentration, by some margin, was found in the prestigious 'west end' district (38 per cent), but

[15] The data are presented in five density-shaded maps in Lawrence, 'Party politics', chapter 4, figures 15–19.

Table 6.2 *An analysis of employment patterns among Wolverhampton male workers, by district (1881) (expressed as a percentage of each district's male workforce)*

District	A light metal	B iron trades	C other manual	D lower m-class	E substantial m-class
Whitmore Reans	25	5	**40**	25	3
West End	18	6	27	**38**	**11**
North Wolverhampton	**30**	9	**35**	20	**4**
Old St Mary's	24	19	**47**	10	0
Springfield/Causeway Lake	16	**27**	**38**	18	1
Horseley Fields	9	**57**	31	4	0
St Matthew's/St George's East	7	**54**	31	6	0
St John's/St George's West	**29**	16	34	15	**4**
Blakenhall	**31**	15	29	**21**	3
Old St Paul's/St Mark's	**37**	16	34	13	1
Graiseley	**45**	12	25	14	2

Notes:
Percentages do not always sum to 100 horizontally because of rounding.
Figures in bold denote above average concentration
Source: Database constructed from a random sample of census enumerators' returns for 1881 held at Wolverhampton Reference Library.

there were also above average concentrations in Whitmore Reans (25 per cent), Blakenhall (21 per cent), North Wolverhampton (20 per cent) and in the east at Springfield/Causeway Lake (18 per cent; see column D). Finally, the analysis confirms the overwhelming concentration of the 'substantial middle class' in the 'west end', a pattern of residential segregation established in the first half of the nineteenth century.[16] However it also suggests lesser concentrations of these groups (professionals, merchants, large employers, clergy and the like) in Blakenhall, Whitmore Reans, North Wolverhampton and, perhaps most interestingly, in the central district of St John's/St George's West, where a significant number of wealthy individuals, including the boot and shoe manufacturer Stephen Craddock, appear to have long resisted the 'flight to the suburbs', preferring still to reside in the substantial town houses of St John's Square and Snow Hill (column E).[17]

[16] On the earlier period, see M. Shaw, 'The ecology of social change: Wolverhampton, 1851–1871', *Trans. of the Institute of British Geographers*, new series 2 (1977) pp. 322–48, and 'Residential segregation in nineteenth-century cities: reply to Carter and Wheatley', *Area*, 12 (1980) pp. 318–20.

[17] Parts of these districts remained socially exclusive into the twentieth century, they were eventually absorbed into the expanding central business district.

There can therefore be little doubt that there was a strong tendency for the middle classes to gravitate to the western suburbs during the nineteenth century, but it is also clear that only in the east can one talk of communities that were monolithically working-class (and even here the Springfield/Causeway Lake district was something of an exception). In most of the town manual workers, though clearly in the majority, lived alongside significant numbers of lower-middle-class workers, while even the substantial middle class generally had some presence. What the preceding analysis does not tell us, however, is whether, in these more heterogeneous communities manual and non-manual workers were generally living side-by-side, or segregated – in separate streets or even separate neighbourhoods. Unfortunately, a random analysis based on the selection of streets (rather than of households) is not well-suited to investigating the question of segregation by sub-district (there are too few streets in each district), but it does still allow us to analyse the degree of manual/non-manual co-habitation *within* individual households: ie. the proportion of households that were internally 'mixed', with both manual and non-manual male workers sharing a roof and (given census definitions of a household) sharing a common dinner table. An analysis along these lines showed that in four districts between 8 and 10 per cent of all households were 'mixed' (ie. contained both manual and non-manual male workers); these were Blakenhall, Springfield/Causeway Lake, North Wolverhampton and Whitmore Reans (table 6.3, column A). These figures are inevitably rather low since in none of these districts did households with one or more non-manual workers constitute more than 30 per cent of all households (column B). In order to produce a more meaningful indication of the (minimum) level of manual/non-manual integration in each district it was therefore necessary to express the number of 'mixed' households as a percentage of all households with one or more non-manual male worker (column C).[18] The results of this exercise proved extremely interesting. It can be seen that, measured in this way, integration was low both in central districts such as Old St Mary's, Old St Paul's/St Mark's and Horseley Fields, and in the 'west end'. In four districts (Graiseley, St John's/St George's West, St Matthew's/St George's East and Whitmore Reans) approximately one quarter of all non-manual households were socially 'mixed'. Three districts recorded figures of over 30 per cent: Blakenhall and North Wolverhampton (both 32 per cent), and Springfield/Causeway Lake (39 per cent). The first two were key centres of Labour activism throughout the pre-war period, the last proved more problematic for Labour. As we have seen, both the Springfield

[18] Minimum level since this figure refers only to integration within single households: it takes no account either of kinship ties outside the immediate home, or of the fact that manual and non-manual workers may have been next-door neighbours, lifelong friends etc.

Table 6.3 *Mixed manual/non-manual households by district, Wolverhampton 1881*

District	Column A	Column B	Column C	Rank Order Column C
Whitmore Reans	8	30	27	4
West End	7	49	14	10
North Wolverhampton	9	27	33	2=
Old St Mary's	2	13	15	9
Springfield/Causeway Lake	9	23	39	1
Horseley Fields	1	6	17	8
St Matthew's/St George's East	2	8	25	5
St John's/St George's West	5	22	23	7
Blakenhall	10	30	33	2=
Old St Paul's/St Mark's	1	18	6	11
Graiseley	6	25	24	6

Notes:
Column A: Mixed manual/non-manual households as a percentage of *all* households in each district.
Column B: Households with one or more non-manual male workers as a percentage of all households in each district.
Column C: Mixed manual/non-manual households as a percentage of all households with non-manual workers in each district.
Source: Database constructed from a random sample of census enumerators' returns for 1881 held at Wolverhampton Reference Library.

Labour Club and the ILP No. 2 branch failed to prosper in this district, as did a string of Labour candidates for the town council – although Labour's triumph here in the 1897 School Board elections suggests that it probably should not have proved such difficult terrain.[19] Springfield reminds us that we should be careful not to argue that Labour politics necessarily flourished in newer, more socially heterogeneous communities, but overall the analysis does demonstrate both that Labour politics were weakest in the most proletarian districts such as Horseley Fields and Old St Mary's, and that there is a strong correlation between the social geography of Labour activism presented in figure 6.2, and high levels of 'social integration' as measured in table 6.3. One needs to be careful here since the districts are of unequal size, and we cannot express the data on Labour activism in percentage terms, but the match is none the less close. Three of the top five districts for Labour activists also appear in the top five for 'social integration': North Wolverhampton, Whitmore Reans and Blakenhall. Of the exceptions, the 'west end' partly ranks so high for

[19] See *Express and Star*, 18 November 1897, and above, chapter 5, pp. 123–5.

Labour activism because its so big, while Graiseley does at least rank sixth in terms of 'social integration'.

III

Though interesting as far as it goes, this analysis leaves unanswered the question of *why* Labour politics were so strong in the socially mixed suburban districts which had grown up in Wolverhampton since the mid-nineteenth century. 'Social integration' might not, after all, mean social harmony. On the contrary, one might argue that it was precisely in such mixed communities, where manual and non-manual workers frequently lived side-by-side, that social tensions and 'status conflict' would have been most intense, sowing the seeds for a new and distinctly proletarian politics.[20] Certainly there is evidence of considerable social tension in the more suburban parts of Wolverhampton, and this tension did often carry strong class overtones. Perhaps more interestingly, there are also indications that Labour politicians may have benefited directly from these class antagonisms when they first shifted the focus of their municipal campaigning from the 'east end' to the suburbs. As in the 1860s, the question of who controlled working men's clubs, and how they should be run, provided a focal point for the expression of social tensions between manual and non-manual workers.[21] The 1890s, as we have seen, saw a rapid growth of the club movement in Wolverhampton, largely in response to the growing politicisation of the drink issue by the temperance lobby and their political adversaries, the Tory publicans. In a few years in the early 1890s massive new clubs grew up in precisely those districts which also provided the backbone of the emerging Labour leadership.[22] Here, in the working-men's club movement, the voice of manual labour was expressed with clarity, and with a strong degree of class consciousness. Clubs such as the North Wolverhampton and the West End had constitutions which decreed that at least two-thirds of the management committee must be 'bona fide working men', while press reports strongly suggest the clubs' clientele was confined almost entirely to manual workers.[23] When the clubs came into conflict with 'respectable opinion' (as they often did given the widespread

---

[20] For example, Geoffrey Crossick (ed.), *The lower middle class in Britain, 1870–1914* (London, 1977), pp. 50–1.

[21] See above, chapter 4, p. 191 for a discussion of the Trades Council's attempts to reconstitute the town's working men's club as a social centre specifically for manual workers in the mid 1860s.

[22] Hence their names: the North Wolverhampton, the West End, and the Blakenhall Non-Political.

[23] On club constitutions see *The Midland Counties Express*, 7 March and 25 April 1896; for claims that the clientele at the West End club 'was a purely working class one', and that many came still dressed in their heavy work clothes see, *ibid.*, 25 April 1896.

suspicion that they were simply unregulated drinking dens), the club leadership presented themselves as fierce champions of working-class dignity and independence. For instance, in 1893 officials at the Lime Street club (later renamed the West End) called an 'indignation meeting' to denounce criticism of their club for its poor organisation and uncontrolled growth – the message was simple: their club, like the wider club movement, was a glorious example of 'the cooperation of working men'.[24]

The close relations between the club movement and Labour politicians in the later 1890s can be traced back to the formation of the ILP's Independent Labour Club in the Autumn of 1894. The Labour club was quick to affiliate to the Club and Institute Union, the national body which coordinated the working-men's club movement, and provided it with a political voice on the national stage.[25] From the outset the ILP body played a prominent part in the local club movement, helping to organise a borough-wide network of sports and games leagues (significantly called the 'Social and Labour Club' leagues).[26] Nor was co-operation confined to club matters. As early as February 1895 the West End and North Wolverhampton clubs had established a joint committee with the Central Labour Club to co-ordinate relief work among the unemployed of central and east Wolverhampton.[27] By 1897 it was generally agreed that at election time Labour candidates could rely on the strong support of the Wolverhampton clubs. During the School Board elections of 1897 the *Express and Star* spoke of Labour's highly successful campaign resting on the stalwart support of the town's social clubs, while Harry Gibson's important victory at Blakenhall in the same year was widely attributed to the unstinting support he had received from the Blakenhall Non-Political Working Men's Club.[28] Indeed after his election Gibson held his victory celebrations at the club, during which both he, and his Labour colleague James Stevenson, who had just successfully fought off a Conservative challenge in the adjacent ward of Graiseley, paid tribute 'to the power of the social clubs in the labour movement'.[29]

It would be wrong to suggest, however, that an unbreakable bond of class identity tied the working-men's club movement to the town's emergent Labour party. On the contrary, the alliance was essentially pragmatic: rooted in a shared determination to resist the politicisation of

[24] *Wolverhampton Chronicle*, 6 September 1893.
[25] See *The Club and Institute Journal*, March and December 1895; also *The 34th Annual Report of the Working Men's Club and Institute Union*, (CIU, London). For histories of the CIU see B.T. Hall, *Our sixty years: the story of the Working Men's Club and Institute Union* (London, 1922). Hall had himself been an active socialist in the 1890s.
[26] On the local sports leagues, see *Wolverhampton Chronicle*, 7 September 1897; and *The Club and Institute Journal*, February 1899 and February 1900.
[27] *The Club and Institute Journal*, March 1895.
[28] *Express and Star*, 2 and 15 November 1897.   [29] *Ibid.*, 2 November 1897.

popular leisure and religion by the established political parties. In the mid 1890s, when relations with Labour were at their most intimate, club leaders in Wolverhampton were convinced that temperance extremists had formed an 'unholy alliance' with the chairman of the Licensed Victuallers Association, and the officials of a local Conservative club, to secure the closure of the town's social clubs.[30] From the outset the club movement had been intensely hostile to party politics: hence the decision to call the Blakenhall club a 'Non-Political Working Men's Club', or the fact that above the main bar at the West End club hung a notice which declared that 'members are not allowed to introduce policemen, political agents and characters of that sort into the club'. As this notice suggests, there was also a general suspicion of authority in the clubs, a belief that 'the powers that be' would close them on the slightest pretext. The use of under-cover police to infiltrate the clubs was widely resented, and in one case led to the doorman at the West End club being charged with assault on an ex-policeman whom he believed to be a 'police spy'.[31]

In the mid-1890s Labour politicians echoed the hostility to party politics voiced by club leaders. A recurrent theme of Labour election campaigns was that it was time for people to 'dispose of party politics' and rally round the banner of labour.[32] Over time however, Labour itself inevitably developed more and more the characteristics of a traditional political party. The relative looseness of the Labour coalition of the 1890s, with its informal, if at times rather strained, alliance of socialist organisations and trade union officials, gave way to a party tightly controlled by the Trades Council leadership. In itself the evolution of Labour into a centralised, and rather authoritarian political party would probably have strained relations with the local club movement, but there were other, more fundamental tensions within the alliance of the 1890s. Firstly, as we saw in the discussion of patriotism and the Tory populists, the ethos of the clubs was genuinely non-political: hence the notice over the main bar at the West End club reminding members that 'no political arguments are permitted on the premises'.[33] The contrast with the Independent Labour club, where political controversy was apparently the main theme of conversation for all members, could hardly be greater.[34] Secondly,

[30] See *The Club and Institute Journal*, January 1896, it was this controversy over the organisation of the town's social clubs which prompted the *Midland Counties Express* to carry out its detailed investigations of local clubs during the first half of 1896.

[31] See *The Midland Counties Express*, 25 April, *Wolverhampton Chronicle*, 27 May 1896 and *The Club and Institute Journal*, February 1897.

[32] *Wolverhampton Chronicle*, 3 August 1892. In this speech Stevenson called on workers henceforth to recognise 'labour, and labour exclusively, as their motto'. See also, *Express and Star*, 14 May 1892 and 22 September 1894.

[33] *Midland Counties Express*, 25 April 1896.

[34] On the West End club, see *The Midland Counties Express*, 25 April 1896, for the atmosphere at the Labour club, see *ibid.*, 29 February 1896.

Labour nationally did little to defend the working-men's club movement against hostile state legislation, especially during the 1900s.[35] And thirdly, Labour politicians rarely echoed the robustly class-conscious language used by the club leaders when defending their movement from outside criticism. Far from employing the langauge of class solidarity, or class conflict, Labour politicians frequently assured local electors that they would uphold the interests of 'all classes'. During Labour's successful School Board campaign of 1897, the brassworkers' leader Thomas Moore went out of his way to stress that 'small property owners might safely leave their interests in the hands of labour candidates'.[36] To a certain extent electoral considerations shaped this cautious, cross-class approach – especially in straight fights with the Conservatives, when there was an understandable reluctance to alienate potential supporters from the Liberal middle class. There was also the fact that the municipal franchise under-represented manual workers, though probably not significantly more so than the Parliamentary franchise, since the exclusion of male lodger voters in municipal elections probably counter-balanced the class bias towards the well-to-do introduced by the inclusion of female house-holders. Indeed, since the lodger vote was quite limited at Wolverhampton there were more municipal than parliamentary electors. In 1885 Wolverhampton had 11,210 Parliamentary electors, including the three wards in the eastern division, but there were 12,210 municipal electors (1,400 of whom were women).[37] Even if all non-manual male workers possessed the municipal franchise (which they undoubtedly did not), this would still mean that almost two-thirds of male electors were manual workers, and that manual workers formed a clear majority in most wards (with the probable exception of Park, Merridale and St Mark's).

More important factors shaping Labour's rejection of sectarian class politics were its own heterogeneous social basis, and the powerful legacy of Radical political traditions on the early Labour movement. Down to the First World War few labour politicians had rejected the old Radical

---

[35] See S. Yeo, 'Working-class association, private capital, welfare and the state in the late nineteenth and twentieth centuries', in N. Parry, M. Rustin and C. Satyamurti (eds.), *Social work, welfare and the state* (London, 1979), esp. pp. 56–64; also 'Socialism, the state and some oppositional Englishness', in R. Colls and P. Dodd (eds.), *Englishness, politics and culture, 1880–1920* (London, 1986), pp. 329–44.

[36] *Express and Star*, 12 November 1897.

[37] Calculated from *Parl. Papers*, 1884–85, vol. LXVII, p. 30 (*Return of Municipal Boroughs, Part I: England and Wales*), and for the Parliamentary franchise of each ward, *Wolverhampton Chronicle*, 25 November 1885 and 7 July 1886, and *The Midland Evening Express*, 24 November 1885, no allowance is made for plural votes. M. G. Shepherd, 'The effects of the franchise on the social and sex composition of the municipal electorate', *Bulletin of the Society for the Study of Labour History*, 45 (1982), pp. 19–26, takes a more negative view of the impact of the municipal franchise on Labour nationally; but Tanner, *Political change and the Labour party*, pp. 125–8, largely supports the interpretation of the present study.

shibboleth that their's was a struggle of the 'industrious' sections of the community against the 'idle' and spendthrift. From the outset non-manual workers had played a prominent part in the growth of socialist and Labour politics in Wolverhampton. In the 1880s the insurance agents Isaac Page and Charles Cole had been key figures in the Trades Council's early flirtations with labour representation, while Joseph Whittaker and A. W. Buttery were also key figures in the town's early socialist movement. Wolverhampton socialist organisations continued to have a strong middle-class element in later years, and it was these middle-class socialists who did most to spread the cause of trade unionism among non-manual workers. Alf Fellows, secretary of the Wolverhampton ILP in the late 1890s, established a branch of the Shop Assistants' Union in 1899, while a few years later another ILP activist, Robert Millard, helped found a branch of the Postal Clerks' Union.[38] Perhaps most dramatic of all, however, was the formation, in late 1913, of a branch of the National Union of Clerks (NUC) by a group of local socialists including F. H. Fern. The union grew quickly, and by the following spring it was strong enough to call a strike over the issue of union recognition at the engineering firm of Rees Roturbo. This was the first dispute called by the NUC, and it drew nationwide attention. The fact that the strikers stayed out until the Autumn did much to enhance the reputation of non-manual trade unionism locally.[39]

By the 1900s the labour movement, and Labour politics, already represented far more than just the voice of organised manual workers. In Wolverhampton the Labour leadership included a large number of non-manual workers including shop assistants (Fellows and W. Lockett), clerks (Fern, Millard, A. Boden, A. J. Weaver and Charles Hill), insurance agents and commercial travellers (Charles Crosland, George Cook, H. J. Payne and J. H. Smith), shopkeepers (Evan Evans and F. Sproson), employers (Fred Barker, George Ling, George Lawley and Frank Tustin), and a smattering of men from the professions including the solicitor Randle Evans, and the optician James Steward. Nor do white-collar workers appear to have been marginalised within the labour movement. Alf Fellows was made Trades Council vice-president in 1903, while in 1913 the railway clerks Charles Hill and A. J. Weaver were respectively elected secretary and chairman of the Wolverhampton Labour party –

[38] *Wolverhampton Chronicle*, 21 June 1899 and 25 January 1905. Both unions affiliated to the local Trades Council within months of their foundation.

[39] See *The Wolverhampton Worker*, October 1913 and April 1914. Also D. Lockwood, *The black-coated worker: a study in class consciousness* (London, 1958), p. 164; F. Hughes, *By hand and by brain: the story of the Clerical and Administrative Workers' Union* (London, 1953), p. 40, and A. Marsh and V. Ryan (eds.), *Historical directory of trade unions*, 4 vols (Farnborough, 1980), I, pp. 34–5.

Hill held the post continuously until 1952.[40] By this time Labour's prospective parliamentary candidate for Wolverhampton West was himself a member of the Railway Clerks' Association – A. G. Walkden, the union's parliamentary secretary. Clearly there was little prejudice against non-manual workers – at least not when they were also good trade unionists.

This message was reinforced by the language of early Labour politics in Wolverhampton, which it would be difficult to classify as representing a 'politics of class'. Until recently there has been an almost unwritten assumption that labour politics meant 'working-class politics', and that in turn this meant the politics of manual labour.[41] These are not assumptions that stand up well to a systematic analysis of the political langauge actually articulated by early Labour leaders. For one thing, Labour politicians embraced a very broad conception of 'the working class' (or 'working classes' – an implicitly differentiated term still preferred by many Labour leaders down to the First World War). According to customary usage in Labour circles the term 'working class' included most non-manual employees, but it did not necessarily include all of those at the margins of capitalist society: as we shall see, a moral test was frequently employed to determine whether the poor and dispossessed merited inclusion within the 'working class proper'. Examples of Labour stressing the inclusiveness of its conception of 'the working class(es)' are not difficult to find. For instance, when Keir Hardie came to Wolverhampton in 1914 to lend his support to the clerical workers in their conflict with the Rees Roturbo management he welcomed the dispute as evidence that '[t]he very aristocracy of the working classes – the clerks and the teachers – were beginning to realise that they had one common aim with their brother the road sweeper'.[42] Similarly, when the Wolverhampton Labour party and local unions took up the cause of poorly paid clerks employed by the town council they laid great stress on their status as 'fellow workers', whilst simultaneously acknowledging their distinctiveness – their status as somehow slightly apart from other workers. As the Labour party's recently established free paper *The Wolverhampton Worker* put it, '[h]ere we have a municipality paying sweated wages to a body of men who, to say the least, are required to be a little better educated than the average worker. They are required to dress better than the ordinary workers, to keep up a respectable appearance,

---

[40] See *Wolverhampton Labour party minutes*, 2 January 1913 (Hill), and 2 October 1913 (Weaver); and see John Rowley, *Wolverhampton Labour party, 1907–51* (Wolverhampton, 1983), p. 3.

[41] Though see Patrick Joyce, *Visions of the people: industrial England and the question of class, 1840–1914* (Cambridge, 1991).   [42] *The Wolverhampton Workers*, March 1914.

and yet seven are employed at a starvation wage'.[43] There is no doubt that Labour politicians were acutely conscious of the ambiguous position white-collar workers occupied in late-Victorian and Edwardian labour markets. Indeed, it was precisely because they occupied an ill-defined position between management and workforce that Labour leaders were so keen to incorporate them within 'the working class': they were engaged in active political manoeuvring, not passive social description. This is the spirit in which one must read the article on 'the nondescript clerk' published by *The Wolverhampton Worker* during the Rees Roturbo strike. The article is worth reproducing at some length because it neatly captures, both the tensions within Labour's strategy of 'incorporating' the white collar worker, and many of the underlying assumptions which determined Labour's conception of the class structure as a whole.

'The Nondescript Clerk'. This seems rather discourteous to a really deserving section of the community. But I really don't know what to call them. They are certainly not millionaires; people like the Rees Roturbo see to that. They are rarely landlords; their wages will hardly pay the rent let alone buy property. They do not come from the House of Lords for they work for their living; if they work for their living they must be -ah, not so fast; the Town Clerk says 'No, they are not workmen!' And he should know, for is he not a clerk himself? I have been trying to classify the clerks, but I am afraid I must give up. If a clerk works for his living he is a – No try again! If a clerk steps out of the office, puts on overalls and takes his collar off, he is a workman. If a workman pushes a pen across a ledger at fifty miles an hour he ceases to be a workman and becomes a clerk. But what the d___ *is* a clerk? . . . [With Rees Roturbo] the Wolverhampton clerks have proved they are men. Ah! I have it at last! A clerk – if he is a member of the N.U.C. – is a *man*. I hope he will soon be a 'workman'.[44]

Clearly there is a great deal going on in this passage. For one thing we see that being a worker – or rather a work*man* – is defined as someone who is not a millionaire, not a landlord, and not an idle aristocrat. The essentially Radical pedigree of this social analysis is further underlined by singling out the House of Lords to symbolise the pernicious 'idle classes'. Only two positive qualities are used to define a 'real' worker: displaying manliness – for instance, by striking for one's rights or belonging to a union – and working for one's living. The two elements of the definition are by no means equally inclusive. All clerks presumably worked for their living – they belonged to the 'industrious', not the 'idle', classes. But very few had ever been involved in a strike, and still only a small minority

---

[43] *The Wolverhampton Worker*, August 1914. It had recently been established that seven adult clerks (over twenty-one) were employed by the Council on a salary below the recently introduced minimum wage of 24 shillings per week; the town clerk argued that clerical workers were not covered by the agreement.

[44] *The Wolverhampton Worker*, April 1914 (original emphasis).

belonged to a trade union. Moreover, the whole emphasis on 'manliness' – which was a common theme of Labour discourse during this period – strongly echoes a strand of popular culture, and old-style popular politics, which celebrated the peculiar virtues of the 'horny-handed sons of toil' and despised non-manual labour of any sort as somehow effete. As we have seen, these prejudices had been particularly strong in the mid-Victorian period, when trade unionism was still synonymous with manual labour, but they remained important well beyond the First World War.[45] But if Labour politics sometimes echoed this strong, almost caste like sense of class identity among manual workers, it did so half-heartedly and tangentially – as in *The Wolverhampton Worker*'s discussion of the 'nondescript clerk'. Rarely did a Labour politician seek to play on this narrower, more sectarian conception of class – though since it was essentially a social, rather than a political conception of class this may not have been a great strategic mistake. In any case the dominant definition of class in Labour discourse was undoubtedly inclusive – that the Labour party stood, as the first issue of *The Wolverhampton Worker* put it, for 'all who earn their living, whether by hand or by brain'.[46]

IV

In pre-war Labour discourse concepts such as 'the working class', 'the workers' and 'the people' were frequently used interchangeably to describe the party's chosen constituency. Again *The Wolverhampton Worker* provides excellent examples of this facet of pre-war Labour politics. Fiercely committed both to political independence and to socialism (this was no mouthpiece of Edwardian Progressivism), the newspaper's contributors none the less expressed themselves through a political language that remained steeped in the Radical tradition. For instance, in June 1913 the newspaper attempted to explain Labour's political philosophy in the following terms:

The people have a powerful weapon in the vote. Up to now they have allowed *vested interests* to use it as a stick to beat them with . . . There is no earthly reason why the *workers' interests* should not be represented equally strongly in the next Parliament as the vested interests are in the present one . . . the material sources of wealth, land and capital, are now owned and controlled by a small class of rich people in their own interests and against the interests of the great *mass of the people*. The Labour party is out to fight this *monopoly power* to the bitter end, and to *win back for the whole people* the common ownership of the means whereby the people must live. (emphasis added) [47]

---

[45] See Robert Roberts, *The classic slum: Salford life in the first quarter of this century* (Pelican edn, London, 1973), p. 19; S. Reynolds, R. Wooley and T. Wooley, *Seems so! A working class view of politics* (London, 1911), pp. 181–93, and above, chapter 2, pp. 35–9.

[46] *The Wolverhampton Worker*, May 1913.   [47] *Ibid.*, June 1913.

When Philip Snowden visited Wolverhampton in 1911 he was even more explicit in his denial that Labour stood for the politics of class. Addressing a mass meeting at the Wolverhampton Empire he apparently won a spontaneous round of applause for declaring that 'Labour was not a class, Labour was the nation'. He then went on to justify the introduction of punitive taxes against all forms of *unearned* income by observing that 'they were in politics to get for the people every penny of wealth created by them'.[48] It is also a mistake to imagine that Labour had abandoned the Radicals' traditional concern to uphold civic and democratic rights, in favour of an emphasis solely on social and economic rights.[49] According to *The Wolverhampton Worker* the Labour party existed to secure the workers' 'civic and economic rights as citizens of a free country', while A. G. Walkden, Labour's parliamentary candidate for Wolverhampton West, responded to the mounting political crisis in Ulster on the eve of the First World War by declaring that Labour would not allow '*the classes* to plot against the *rights of the people*'.[50]

That said, Labour politicians did articulate policies designed specifically to address the perceived grievances of manual workers. The so-called Labour Programme of the early 1890s, with its emphasis on the legal eight-hour day, minimum wages and later the right to work, was at heart a programme to transform the lives of poor manual workers. But Labour spoke for the poor and disadvantaged in the name of social justice, rather than class interest. Indeed some Labour politicians went further, articulating their concern for the poor in the language of national efficiency or even enlightened self interest. Although Labour politics have sometimes been presented as a source of reformist enthusiasm uncontaminated by intellectual fashions such as eugenism and national efficiency, it is noticeable that such discourses were enthusiastically seized upon by labour politicians embroiled in the controversies of local popular politics.[51] For instance when the railway guard Albert Bent stood in the poor 'east end' ward of St George's in 1913 his election address argued that '[p]eople underpaid, underfed, improperly clothed and housed are not likely to produce the perfect offspring which are desired for the welfare of the race, so that it cannot be denied that sweating wages are a

---

[48] *Express and Star*, 27 February 1911. This line of reasoning is acknowledged by Bernard Barker in, 'The anatomy of reformism: the social and political ideas of the Labour leadership in Yorkshire', *International Review of Social History*, 18 (1973), pp. 1–27. However, Barker concludes that in the final analysis Labour did stand for the 'representation of class interests', and that it was essentially a 'working-class party', although he then reproduces the linguistic slippage so characteristic of Labour politicians themselves by arguing that Labour stood for the 'conquest of power by the common people'.
[49] Cf. Hobsbawm, *Worlds of labour*, p. 211.
[50] *The Wolverhampton Worker*, June 1913; *Express and Star*, 4 May 1914 – emphasis added.
[51] Cf. E. P. Hennock, 'Poverty and social reforms', in Paul Johnson (ed.), *20th century Britain: economic, social and cultural change* (Harlow, 1994), esp. pp. 90–2.

bad business proposition for any nation'.[52] Perhaps more common was the explanation of Labour's social programme advanced by *The Wolverhampton Worker* in April 1914: 'The Labour movement appeals to all classes of the community . . . That the conditions of life of the working class stand in most need of improvement, however, is a fact about which there can be no argument.' As Walkden's outburst over the Ulster crisis suggests, for Labour politicians it was the rich and powerful who resorted to 'class politics', while they stood as the disinterested champions of 'the community'.[53]

This emphasis on the interests of the community had important implications. It could leave Labour appearing to champion action on behalf of the poor, not because they were the least fortunate stratum of the working class, but because they were a threat to the political, economic and social fabric of society. There was, it is true, a tendency to idealise the 'virtuous' and 'respectable' poor – portraying them as the hapless victims of an unjust economic system, but this carried echoes of philanthropic discourses about the 'deserving' and the 'undeserving' poor. Often the corollary of Labour's idealisation of the 'honest' poor was a tendency to advocate harsh, even coercive, measures against those workers who did not live such blameless lives. It is noticeable that, again like many mid-Victorian Radicals, Labour leaders frequently bracketed the idle rich and idle poor together as the common enemies of the industrious majority. For instance at a Wolverhampton Fabian rally in the early 1890s Harold Cox argued that '[i]t was right that those who did not work should be dragged down to the workhouse. But it was only fair that they should apply the argument all round.'[54] In the Edwardian period Labour leaders repeatedly made it clear that although workers had a right to work, this right brought with it the *obligation* to work: their advocacy of state support for the unemployed presupposed that the 'malingerer' who proved unwilling (or *unable*) to work would be dealt with severely. A contribution from Will Crooks to a Parliamentary debate on unemployment captures this outlook well. Having told the House that 'a man unwilling to work should be made to work' he responded to the cries of 'How?' from fellow MPs with the observation that 'by keeping him without food for a time he would work all right'.[55] In Wolverhampton, Tom Jones, a Labour Guardian, took a similar line during a debate on the evils of tramping (he was clearly unswayed by the fact that until recently it

[52] *The Wolverhampton Worker*, November 1913.
[53] *The Wolverhampton Worker*, April 1914. Emphasis on the politics of community, rather than of class was a recurrent theme of the Labour leader Ramsay MacDonald; see Bernard Barker (ed.), *Ramsay MacDonald's political writings* (London, 1972), especially pp. 44–8.   [54] *Express and Star*, 10 April 1891.
[55] *Parliamentary Debates*, 4th series, vol. 194, col. 1661.

had been a common practice even among skilled workers).[56] Jones argued that anyone found on the road should be sent to a special 'labour colony' for two years, and that during this time they should be kept from seeing their family as a deterrent against returning to the open road on release. Perhaps fearful of the likely expense of this policy Jones added that the colony regime would have to observe the principles of strict economy – he particularly recommended substituting dripping for butter in the inmates' diet.[57] Nor was Jones a lone voice in the Wolverhampton Labour movement. For instance in 1899 William Price, Trades Council president and another Labour Guardian, drew up a resolution on pensions for approval by the Wolverhampton Board. It called for a state pension of 5 shillings per week to paid from the age of 65; but only 'on condition that they [the recipients] had insured against sickness and funeral expenses for a certain period in a friendly or trade union society'. A Conservative Guardian, Thomas Norbury, moved an amendment which would drop the 'character test', and commit the Board to supporting the principle of universal state pensions for the elderly. In the ensuing vote Price and his colleague William Dilke (an 'ILPer'), found themselves in a minority of three in favour of imposing a character test.[58]

It is clear that many labour politicians saw the poor, or rather the 'undeserving' poor, as a canker upon society that needed to be swiftly removed before it corrupted and destroyed, first the 'deserving' poor, and then society as a whole. Again one finds the same arguments advanced by Labour politicians at Westminster and in the localities. In the Commons George Barnes, Labour MP for Glasgow Blackfriars, argued that the scourge of unemployment forced an artisan 'to sink down into the meaner streets of the town, where his children came into contact with the children of a class which was already pauperized and they became pauperized themselves'.[59] In Wolverhampton one finds Labour activists proposing to 'deal with the forlorn slummites in a scientific manner'.[60]

[56] See Eric Hobsbawm, 'The tramping artisan' in his *Labouring men: studies in the history of labour* (London, 1964); and the classic autobiographical account by Henry Broadhurst, *Henry Broadhurst: the story of his life from a stonemason's bench to the Treasury Bench* (London, 1901), pp. 20–33.

[57] *Wolverhampton Chronicle*, 26 July 1905. On the campaign for labour colonies before the war, see J. Harris, *Unemployment and politics: a study in English social policy* (2nd edn, Oxford, 1984), pp. 115–44 and 187–99. As is well-known many Labour leaders, including Lansbury, strongly supported such initiatives; see *The Poor Law Minority Report: a debate between George Lansbury and H. Quelch* (London, nd [1910]), pp. 6–7.

[58] *Wolverhampton Chronicle*, 15 May 1899.

[59] *Parliamentary Debates*, 4th series, vol. 194, cols. 1752–3. Barnes has been described as a Labour MP who offered a 'passionate, reiterated defence of the exploited and low paid'; P. Thane, 'The Labour party and state welfare', in K. D. Brown (ed.), *The first Labour party, 1906–14* (London, 1985), p. 191. He did offer such a defence, but concern for the plight of the poor did not preclude a morbid fear of the contagion of 'pauperism'.

[60] *The Wolverhampton Worker*, January 1914.

Frequently Labour leaders assumed that almost by definition the inhabitants of the town's impoverished courts and alleys must be so demoralised that they were beyond self help – the only hope was to impose acceptable standards of behaviour upon them. Thus in 1901 Frank Tustin, the secretary of the Trade Council Housing Committee, welcomed the fact that Wolverhampton town council had decided to introduce strict clauses into its agreements with municipal tenants by observing that his colleagues 'must remember that the people had sometimes to be saved from their own bad habits'.[61]

Labour's programme was simple: once saved from themselves, the 'forlorn slummites' would be transformed in the image of the respectable trade unionist or Labour activist. In the early days socialists had stressed the need to convert individuals to a new way of life through the 'gospel of socialism', but by the Edwardian period many were becoming sceptical about the scope for reason to flourish amidst the degradation of the slums. Instead, there was a growing emphasis on transformation through structural reform – either of the labour market (by eradicating casualized labour, and ending low pay), or of the slums themselves (through comprehensive clearance programmes). Whatever approach was favoured, few questioned that Labour leaders were the right people to oversee this transformation of the lives (and the habits) of the poor and disadvantaged. As the boot and shoe workers' leader Henry Moreton put it in 1894, 'Whose duty was it to look after the welfare of the workers but the trade unionists of the country? They had every right to the title of the Labour party. It was to the Labour party that the workers had to look for the improvement of their conditions'.[62] Through a colourful language of 'rights' and 'duties' Moreton was outlining an essentially imperious project; a small group of trade union leaders linked to the Trades Council were, in effect, to be the self-appointed leaders of Wolverhampton workers, responsible for deciding the terms on which their lives might be improved. There is of course little exceptional in this – the claim to leadership is always imperious, always implies speaking in the name of others, constructing a politics based on an external (and highly partial) perception of other peoples' needs and interests. What's interesting is that down to the First World War the labour movement in Wolverhampton claimed to be the natural leaders of workers it hardly knew, let alone understood. Geographically remote, and culturally distinct, from the great majority of the town's working population, the Labour leaders were in a profoundly ambiguous position. At times, to be fair, they perceived this difficulty and sought to overcome it, more usually they responded to political reverses by denouncing the workers themselves for their ignorance and weakness of character.

[61] *Wolverhampton Chronicle*, 26 January 1901.   [62] *Express and Star*, 15 November 1894.

Time and again one finds Wolverhampton's Labour leaders explaining the resistance to socialism or trade unionism among the poor in terms of the failings of the poor themselves. If Labour failed to prosper this could not be because its message was flawed, or its political style alienating, it could only be because 'the people' were not yet sufficiently well-educated to perceive the truth of the message before them. As one Wolverhampton Labour activist put it, 'the lack of education was at the root of every evil which affected the people'.[63] Liberal or Tory working men were generally portrayed as dullards, too slow to think for themselves, and therefore easy victims of the dreaded 'party wire-pullers'. In 1901, during Tom Frost's second campaign in St John's ward, Labour published an election pamphlet purporting to be the record of an exchange between two workers – Jim, the socialist autodidact, and Jack, his simple Tory workmate. Jack, we learn, is convinced that most of the town councillors are already workers, until Jim explains that in fact the vast majority are employers. To this Jack responds that at least this means they have a stake in the country. Jim replies: 'Jack, my boy, don't you think a working man aint got a stake in the country?'. The pamphlet is so contrived, and so numbing in its condescension, that one has to assume that Frost won despite, rather than because of, his publicity campaign.[64]

During the 1890s many Wolverhampton Labour leaders had continued to insist that the idle, the drunken and the ignorant were personally responsible for their condition, but by the eve of the 1914–18 war such attitudes were rare. Instead, the consensus in labour circles was that bad housing, poor diet, overcrowding and parental negligence (ie. environmental factors) were primarily to blame for the failings of the poor. Unfortunately, this new orthodoxy did not herald a more liberal approach to the poor themselves. Rather, crude moral individualism gave way to a new tyranny – environmental determinism – which decreed that the appalling conditions of the slums inevitably bred an appalling parody of humanity: the 'slummite'.[65] As *The Wolverhampton Worker* explained in 1913, 'it is undoubtedly true, that environment and the social conditions under which people live have much to do with deciding the moral well-being of a community'.[66] In a later article it argued that those brought up in a bad environment would turn out 'in the main, degenerate, immoral

[63] *Wolverhampton Chronicle*, 21 December 1904; see also below, chapter 9, pp. 257–63.
[64] *Express and Star*, 22 November 1901. See also S. MacIntyre, 'British labour, Marxism and working-class apathy in the nineteen-twenties', *Historical Journal*, 20 (1977), pp. 483–7, which discusses the inter-war socialist movement's similarly dismissive attitude towards 'Henry Dubb' – symbol of the uneducated, trusting British worker.
[65] See L. Barrow, 'Determinism and environmentalism in socialist thought', in R. Samuel and G. S. Jones (eds.), *Culture, ideology and politics: essays for Eric Hobsbawm* (London, 1982).   [66] *The Wolverhampton Worker*, May 1913.

and vicious'.[67] While in January 1914 the paper was arguing that the denizens of 'slumland' were like plants left to wither in a dank cellar. But all was not lost, the *Worker* reassured its readers. 'Deal with the forlorn slum-mites in a scientific manner, and they will revive and flourish too. Remove them to more habitable, pleasanter and *judiciously restricted* quarters and the wonderful change will take effect . . . perpetual poverty leads to hope-lessness and destruction.'[68] Although *The Wolverhampton Worker* was a free newspaper delivered door-to-door in poor districts such as St Matthew's, the sense here is of the poor, and the world they lived in, as both alien, and distinctly threatening. Just as the call for 'judiciously restricted quarters' carries echoes of Octavia Hill and the model dwellings movement of the later nineteenth century, so other labour newspapers tended to mimic the sensationalist 'social exploration' literature of the same period. For instance, a feature on 'slumland shadows' in *The Metal Worker* describes the experiences of a correspondent venturing into the slums to be con-fronted by brutal matrimonial fights watched by a 'nerve-deadened crowd' of 'coarse, vulgar-mouthed women' and brutalized men.[69]

Such harsh, unsympathetic visions of the slums and their inhabitants were largely born of ignorance and physical remoteness, but it should be recognised that Labour politicians did have access to more sensitive representations of the poor. For one thing, just as many were aware of debates about national efficiency and racial health, so many were also aware of the investigations into poverty carried out by Booth, Rowntree and others since the early 1890s. These studies were themselves not free from moral judgements about the causes of poverty, but they were widely held to have established both that a great deal of poverty was structural in origin, and that the bulk of the poor were engaged in a noble struggle to maintain a decent, respectable family life.[70] In Wolverhampton, the journalist Tom Fletcher had undertaken a series of careful, unsensation-alised investigations into 'local slums' in 1908. They were published in serial form under the title 'Our black stains'. Fletcher certainly found much squalor and dereliction, a great deal of which he attributed to neglectful landlords, but he also highlighted many examples of people determinedly struggling to overcome the disadvantages of their poverty. In Court 5, Pipers Row, Fletcher described how the residents, most of whom were ironfounders, had adorned their tiny, if well-kept, houses with elaborate hand-cast plaques, while in Court 4, Bell Street everything

[67] *Ibid.*, May 1914.   [68] *Ibid.*, January 1914.   [69] *The Metal Worker*, November 1908.
[70] See E. P. Hennock, 'The measurement of urban poverty: from the metropolis to the nation, 1880–1920', *Economic History Review*, 2nd ser., 40 (1987), pp. 208–27, and J. H. Veit-Wilson, 'Paradigms of poverty: a rehabilitation of B. S. Rowntree', *Journal of Social Policy*, 15 (1986), pp. 69–99.

was so clean and well-presented that Fletcher felt moved to call it 'picturesque'.[71]

The great strike movement which swept the Black Country in 1913 brought further evidence that most of the town's slum-dwellers cherished the virtues of cleanliness and respectability just as much as any Labour activist. When the Workers' Union organised a march through the town centre to publicise the strikers' cause the *Wolverhampton Chronicle* gave them sympathetic coverage, commenting that 'the girls all seemed small, as if they belonged to a small race. They bore the stamp of Monmore Green, where they had come from; but there was no raggedness or wildness. For strikers they were certainly good humoured.'[72] To be fair the Wolverhampton labour movement gave strong support to the strikers, or 'bottom dogs', as they became known. Regular collections were made at local engineering firms such as the Sunbeam motor works, and nearly twenty trade societies made donations.[73] As we shall see, these strikes did much to break down the isolation between Labour leaders and workers from the 'east end', but they did not bring about a wholesale transformation in Labour's belief that the poor, as much as the poverty they suffered from, represented a serious threat to the social and political order. *The Wolverhampton Worker* continued to focus, not on the concrete grievances and aspirations of 'east end' workers, but on the need to uproot them – they still wished to transform their lifestyle and culture by destroying their debased communities. In February 1914, just months after the great enthusiasm of the 'bottom dog' strikes, the paper was again informing its readers that workers in the 'east end' lived in a different world, a world of

back-to-back houses . . . in long, tedious, dreary rows; often unhealthily close to a factory, close to the drink shop, with nothing to induce a healthy state of mind or to develop strength of character . . . Consider the chance of a child born in such surroundings . . . It sees dirt, disease, drunkenness and ugliness in all its worst forms around it. Its moral outlook is blighted, its conscience is stunted, its intellect dwarfed in its infancy. Can we be surprised at its failings, then, compared to the child of the West End? . . . I do not expect roses out of cellars, nor do I expect a healthy working class out of slums.[74]

Again this commentary has to be read in the context of the near total absence of Labour activists from the 'east end': the children doomed to be intellectually and morally stunted were not their children. A report from a *Worker* correspondent exploring Monmore Green captures this remoteness especially well. He tells of coming across an old man and

[71] See Tom Fletcher, *Local slums: our black stains* (WRL, press cuttings). There are similar descriptions of slum districts around North Street, and of Court 1, Pipers Row.
[72] *Wolverhampton Chronicle*, 7 May 1913.
[73] *The Wolverhampton Worker*, June, July and August 1913.   [74] *Ibid.*, February 1914.

asking him 'if he suffered with rheumatism'. To the reply that the man did suffer from the complaint a little, the reporter tells us that, 'I assured him it would become chronic if he remained there'.[75] Not, one suspects, especially welcome or useful advice.

V

These attitudes towards poverty and the poor did not, however, go unchallenged in the pre-war Wolverhampton labour movement. On the contrary, both the populist councillor Will Sharrocks, and local women's organisations broke with the attitudes of mainstream Labour leaders – though as we shall see, they themselves had conflicting views on *how* the poor should be represented in politics. Sharrocks' success in the poor east end ward of St Matthew's has already been noted, as has the conspicuous failure of other, more orthodox, Labour leaders who stood there. But how did he do it? According to one authority, Sharrocks' success can simply be attributed to the proximity of the John Thompson boilerworks at Ettingshall – St Matthew's, it is suggested, was home to many loyal members of Sharrocks' union.[76] This seems unlikely. For one thing, it makes it hard to understand why Sharrocks went down to a heavy defeat in the same ward in 1895. It also ignores the fact that the John Thompson works were weakly organised, especially after the defeat of a strike over meal breaks in 1904.[77] In any case, skilled boilermakers at the factory would almost certainly have chosen to live in Ettingshall itself, or some other part of Bilston, rather than in the more distant and deprived district of St Matthew's. Indeed the 1891 census records only 115 boilermakers in the whole of Wolverhampton, whilst Staffordshire as a whole could claim 1,648.[78]

Rather than attribute Sharrocks' success in St Matthew's to 'the presence of the trade union tradition among the working class',[79] we need to explain how Sharrocks, and only Sharrocks, was able to overcome the fact that, until the 'bottom dog' strikes of 1913, workers here were for the most part unorganized.[80] One answer seems to be that, from the outset,

---

[75] *Ibid.*, January 1914.   [76] Jones, *Borough politics*, p. 88.

[77] *Express and Star*, 17 and 21 November 1904. See also PP 1908 vol. XXXIV, Cd. 4423, Q4281 (*Minutes of evidence taken before the Fair Wages Committee*) where Sharrocks acknowledges his union's weakness throughout the Black Country, and *Webb Trade Union Collection*, E, A, vol. IV, f. 299, for its weakness in Wolverhampton in the early 1890s.

[78] *Census of England and Wales, 1891*, vol. III (*Parl. Papers*, 1893–94, vol. CVI, pp. 250 and 258. Later censuses did not record boilermakers separately. Significantly during a long strike at John Thompson's in 1913, relief efforts among strikers' families were organised in Ettingshall itself, not in St Matthew's; see *Express and Star*, 21 and 23 June 1913.

[79] Jones, *Borough politics*, p. 89.

[80] Not withstanding the success of the galvanized hollowware workers' union.

Sharrocks adopted a populist style quite alien to mainstream labour traditions in Wolverhampton. Whereas most Labour leaders despised the vulgarity of contemporary popular politics, believing that the 'monster fêtes', street parades and organised disruption of mainstream party politics tended to debase the people, Sharrocks had no such reservations. During his first successful campaign, in November 1901, he took his message to the back streets and courts of St Matthew's on the back of a decorated lorry, accompanied by supporters ringing bells and carrying bright lanterns.[81] The message itself was no less populist: according to Sharrocks, Shepherd, the incumbent Conservative, had neglected the ward in favour of grandiose improvement schemes for the affluent and leafy 'west end'. Only he, Sharrocks, understood that the east too needed immediate improvements such as public baths, proper street lighting and branch libraries. Sharrocks had already established his populist credentials as a Labour member of the School Board from 1897 to 1900. Much to the annoyance of some of his Labour colleagues, Sharrocks had proved an unfailing champion of poor parents prosecuted because of their children's non-attendance at school. While later, as a member of the town's Education Committee, he campaigned for local school holidays to be reorganised so that they coincided with the local hop-picking season, and argued that poor mothers should be allowed to keep their children from school whenever there was sickness at home.[82]

Sharrocks relied on more than populism, however, to gain a political foothold in the poor 'east end'. Controversially, he also relied on tapping into the networks of influence and patronage built up by many of the district's prominent Liberal and Conservative politicians. When he fought against Shepherd in 1901 Sharrocks appears to have struck a secret deal with another prominent local Conservative, William Fellows, the owner of a stamping factory on Bilston Road. In return for promises of support should he himself stand in the ward at a later date, Fellows endorsed Sharrocks and worked hard to secure his return.[83] Sharrocks also maintained close relations with the East End Progressive Association – a left-leaning Liberal organisation that emerged as a powerful political force in the district during the Liberal revival of the early 1900s. In itself this was not unusual, Labour as a whole enjoyed warm relations with the association at this time, but Sharrocks went further. Unlike mainstream leaders, who were careful to work only with sympathetic Radicals such as James

---

[81] *Express and Star*, 31 October 1901.

[82] See *ibid.*, 12 November 1897; and *The Wolverhampton Worker*, November 1913. For his 1901 campaign, see *Wolverhampton Chronicle*, 25 September 1901; *Express and Star*, 31 October 1901.

[83] For speculation about the deal, see *Wolverhampton Chronicle*, 25 May 1903. Sharrocks had failed to support the prominent Labour leader James Whittaker when he stood against Fellows at a by-election in St Matthew's.

Crowe, and Peter Jones, a number of whom were themselves trade unionists, Sharrocks was also happy to support right-wing Liberal leaders such
as Henry Fowler, MP for Wolverhampton East, or Councillor A. B.
Bantock.[84]

Over the years Sharrocks' dependence on Liberal and Tory politicians
diminished. No pre-war Labour politician represented the same ward for
as long as Sharrocks, and none appears to have made more effort to use
his office to political advantage. When first elected to the council
Sharrocks concentrated on tightening up the operation of the 'fair wages'
policy introduced by Tory populists a decade earlier.[85] In later years he
emerged as the special champion of council manual workers, campaigning for improved conditions of service and a minimum wage of 6d per
hour.[86] There are even suggestions that Sharrocks may have exerted more
direct influence over the corporation workforce. In 1909 the Trades
Council discussed what to do about men who had left their union after
securing 'snug jobs under the Corporation'. Sharrocks' reaction was to
ask for their names so that he could repay them when they next asked for
any concessions – a response which says much about his attitude to the
rights and obligations of holding municipal power. There is even a
suggestion that Sharrocks' influence may have gone further – that these
men had only found work in the first place because, as good union men,
they had won his favour. It would be difficult to corroborate this interpretation, but it should be noted that such systems of patronage were frequently operated by Labour councillors between the wars, especially
where they represented areas, like Wolverhampton's 'east end', dominated by poor, unskilled workers.[87]

Undoubtedly, Sharrocks' greatest political triumph came with the
'bottom dog' strikes of 1913. Making full use of his contacts with local
political and social leaders, Sharrocks persuaded retailers, church groups
and even some employers to provide food, clothing and other aid for the
strikers' hard-pressed families. In co-operation with the Workers' Union
and the Women's Labour League, Sharrocks helped organise the distrib-

---

[84] In 1903 the East End Progressives stood down in St Matthew's to give Whittaker a
straight fight against Fellows, *Express and Star*, 30 April 1903 and *Wolverhampton
Chronicle*, 27 May 1903. On Sharrocks' support of right-wing Liberals, and his censure by
Labour, see *Express and Star*, 16 October 1903 and 5 January 1906; and *Wolverhampton
Labour party minutes*, 5 August 1909, and 3 November 1910.

[85] For details of the new regulations he introduced, see Sharrocks' evidence to the government's Fair Wages Committee, *Parl. Papers*, 1908, vol. xxxiv, Cd. 4423, Q4283–5.

[86] See *Express and Star*, 22 October 1904 and 23 October 1913.

[87] For instance, see Alan McKinlay, 'Labour and locality: Labour politics on Clydeside,
1900–1939', *Journal of Regional and Local Studies*, 10 (1990), pp. 48–59, and Alastair Reid,
'Glasgow socialism', *Social History*, 11 (1986), pp. 82–97; also John Marriott, *The culture of
labourism: the East End between the wars* (Edinburgh, 1991).

ution of relief throughout the 'east end' – much of it through local public houses such as the British Oak, on Bilston Road.[88] When Sharrocks came up for re-election a few months later his prestige had never been higher. Voters across the ward displayed his picture in their windows, and the general union branches, many of them newly established, campaigned tirelessly for his return. There was no longer any question of relying on the support and influence of the established parties. Sharrocks achieved his highest poll to date, defeating his Conservative opponent by 159 votes.[89]

Sharrocks' politics, though more attuned to the aspirations of poor voters than mainstream Labour leaders, none the less presupposed a dependent working class, wholly reliant on its political representatives to secure improved conditions of life. In contrast, the town's nascent women's organisations and their allies sought to break down such patterns of dependence, and to encourage the poor to emancipate themselves from their harsh conditions. Although there had long been critics of the party's harsh attitude towards the urban poor, it was the rapid growth of trade unionism among poor workers, and especially the 'bottom dog' strikes during the summer of 1913, which helped bring coherence and force to such oppositional voices. Like the London dock strike a quarter of a century earlier, this strike movement appeared to demonstrate that even the poorest, most down-trodden and disadvantaged workers were capable of self-emancipation. The Women's Labour League and the Cooperative Women's Guild both played a prominent part in support of the 1913 strike movement, helping to distribute food aid, and organising rudimentary health clinics to treat women and children weakened by hunger.[90] League members reported being shocked by the harsh conditions these women and their families had to endure. But whilst they lamented the 'degrading' and 'soul-destroying' effects of such unrelenting poverty, League members also claimed to be inspired by the 'quiet fortitude and courage displayed by the women-folk' themselves.[91]

In the wake of the strikes, Wolverhampton's Labour women's groups intensified their campaigning on issues such as free school meals for all, free children's health clinics and 'mother and baby' clinics, as well as calling for the state to support all widowed, deserted and unmarried

[88] See *Express and Star*, 16 and 22 May 1913; *The Wolverhampton Worker*, June and August 1913. George Lawley, the boot manufacturer and ILP activist, and James Whittaker also played a prominent part in the relief effort. The British Oak was adopted as the club house for the Monmore Green branch of the Workers' Union.

[89] See *Express and Star*, 27 and 31 October 1913; *The Wolverhampton Worker*, November 1913.

[90] See *Express and Star*, 8 July 1913 and *Wolverhampton Worker*, June and August 1913.

[91] *Ibid.*, June and August 1913.

mothers.[92] In advocating these policies they also showed themselves sensitive to the feelings of the poor themselves. Time and again women activists stressed that service must be offered to women, not imposed upon them, and that professionals must at all times respect the privacy and 'sanctity' of the working-class home.[93] They also recognised that welfare policies would remain widely unpopular so long as they remained associated with the stigma of charity (as they frequently did in pre-war labour circles). Whereas many Labour politicians still portrayed welfare measures as gifts bestowed by benevolent politicians, women's organisations insisted that they were no more than the recognition of basic human rights. Justifying their call for the state endowment of motherhood, the Co-operative Women's Guild insisted that 'every woman [has] a right to conditions under which she could bear and rear a healthy child. It was not a question of patronage or charity, it was the right of the woman.'[94] Significantly the women's groups drew strong support for their campaigns from general unions such as the gasworkers and especially the Workers' Union. For instance in July 1914 a meeting called to demand the introduction of free baby clinics in poor districts was jointly organised by the Workers' Union, the Women's Labour League, The Co-operative Women's Guild and the Railway Women's Guild.[95]

Undoubtedly one factor encouraging Labour women to challenge party orthodoxies was that, like the 'east end' poor, they were marginalised by the dominant assumptions of pre-war Labour politics. It was only on the eve of the First World War that women activists began to find a voice in the local labour movement, and even then it was only through auxiliary organisations: the official leadership remained all-male. As we have seen, the language of Labour politics was overtly 'masculinist' – bound up, as it was, with ideas of manly virtue – of what it meant to 'be a man'. Time and again local Labour politicians appealed to an explicitly male audience – an audience of 'breadwinners', of respectable family men, who were determined to assert their rights and proclaim their independence.[96] In part this may reflect the fact that, in Parliamentary elec-

---

[92] *Ibid.*, June and September 1913, January 1915.
[93] E.g. *ibid.*, August 1913 and August 1914. This growing sensitivity was very much a national phenomenon in Labour women's circles. The Fabian Women's group in London was making the same points, see Maud Pember Reeves, *Round about a pound a week* (1930; Virago edn, London, 1979), esp. pp. 5–7, 13–16; also Gillian Scott, '"The working-class women's most active and democratic movement": the Women's Co-operative Guild from 1883 to 195c', unpublished PhD thesis, University of Sussex, 1988.
[94] *The Wolverhampton Worker*, January 1915.
[95] *Ibid.*, August 1914. For support for the idea on the Trades Council, see *Express and Star*, 27 July 1914.
[96] For examples, see *Express and Star*, 28 September and 3 October 1892; *The Wolverhampton Worker*, March 1914; for fuller discussion, see Lawrence, 'Party politics', pp. 137–8.

tions at least, Labour *was* effectively addressing a male audience, although women certainly still attended its meetings and in local elections they already held 11.5 per cent of the vote by the mid 1880s.[97] In truth, the gender-bias of early Labour politics ran much deeper. In 1902 local Labour leaders underlined their hostility to female suffrage by insisting that, rather than support the campaign for an equal franchise (i.e. giving women the vote on the basis of the 1867/1884 settlements), Labour should concentrate on securing universal *male* suffrage. Not for them the half-way house of advocating adult suffrage.[98] Two years later they ignored an appeal for help from the Women's Local Government Society amidst jocular comments about the likelihood that women councillors would come into conflict with Wolverhampton's Labour members; no one raised the prospect that ending the sex bar might allow the return of women as Labour councillors.[99]

As women came to find a political voice, first through independent groups such as the Co-operative Women's Guild and the Railway Women's Guild, and then through the Women's Labour League itself, it was perhaps natural that they should seek to redefine Labour politics to make them less exclusory. Party records suggest that Wolverhampton's male leadership saw the new organisation (which they had planned to call the *Ladies'* Labour League) as a means both of mobilising women for party work (canvassing, registration and fundraising), and of dealing with awkward 'women's issues' such as child-care and maternal welfare.[100] In fact, the Labour women embraced a much more radical agenda which challenged labour orthodoxy on two fronts: firstly, by stressing the movement's historic neglect of women industrial workers, and secondly by stressing that the housewife was as much a worker as the miner or the furnaceman.[101] In so doing they not only challenged the male-centredness of early Labour politics, but began to redefine Labour's basic conception of 'the working class' in order to make it more explicitly inclu-

---

[97] *Parl. Papers*, 1884–85, LXVII, p. 30 (*Return Relating to Municipal Boroughs*).
[98] See *Wolverhampton Chronicle*, 27 August 1902. For the national picture, see M. Pugh, 'Labour and women's suffrage', in Brown (ed.), *The first Labour party*, pp. 233–51; and S. Holton, *Feminism and democracy: women's suffrage and reform politics in Britain, 1900–1918* (Cambridge, 1986), pp. 53–4, 61–2, 69–74 and 76–115.
[99] *Wolverhampton Chronicle*, 27 January 1904; for details of the national campaign, see P. Hollis, *Ladies elect: women in English local government, 1865–1914* (Oxford, 1987).
[100] See *Wolverhampton Labour party minutes*, 5 March 1912; *The Wolverhampton Worker*, September 1913. There was always a strong assumption that the Women's Labour League would provide refreshments at party functions, e.g. see *Wolverhampton Labour party minutes*, 27 May 1913.
[101] The Women's Labour League worked closely both with the Federation of Women Workers and with the Workers' Union; see *The Wolverhampton Worker*, January and August 1914.

sive. For instance, in 1914, the Women's Labour League voiced complaints about the poor design of recent council houses by noting that 'the "house" is not only a "home" to the woman it is her workshop, where the greater part of her life is spent'.[102]

As this discussion underlines, pre-war Labour politics were far from monolithic. And if the informal workings of the Labour coalition in the 1890s later gave way to a more disciplined party organisation dominated by the leaders of local unions affiliated to the Trades Council, this did not mean that alternative, dissentient voices were simply silenced. Rather, the years before the First World War saw vigorous debate, both on policy questions, and, perhaps more fundamentally, on what Labour should stand for, and whom it should represent. These issues, still unresolved at the outbreak of war in 1914, remind us that Labour politics were not simply the natural outgrowth of a more mature, assertive and homogeneous working class. By the very nature of their political activism, of their claim to lead, Labour politicians were of necessity set apart from the majority of working people, but as this detailed study of the party in Wolverhampton has demonstrated, they were also socially, and in large measure culturally 'apart'.[103] Fearful of popular Toryism, disillusioned by the failings of Liberalism, Labour politicians sought consciously to construct a new mass politics – construct here is the crucial word – the new politics did not come pre-packaged. As this chapter has shown, this was not an easy process, Labour politics were frequently greeted with indifference, if not outright hostility, by the very people whose interests they claimed to embody.

---

[102] *The Wolverhampton Worker*, February 1914; on more general attempts to raise the status of housewifery in this period, see J. Bourke, 'Housewifery in working-class England, 1860–1914', *Past and Present*, 143 (1994), pp. 167–97.
[103] For a useful discussion of socialist attitudes to popular culture in this period, see Chris Waters, *British socialists and the politics of popular culture, 1884–1914* (Manchester, 1990).

Part III

Party games, 1885–1914

7   Popular politics and the limitations of party

I

As we saw in part I, historians are generally agreed that the late nineteenth century witnessed the triumph of party organisation in British politics, and the integration of popular political forces into the ethos, if not the actual machinery, of the new mass parties in the constituencies.[1] There is almost general agreement, even in more recent 'revisionist' accounts of nineteenth-century politics, that, in the wake of the Second Reform Act of 1867, not only did political parties become firmly established as permanent organisations of mass mobilisation, but they exerted increasing control over the forms of popular political expression. Political parties, we are told, were the primary institutions 'socialising' the new mass electorate into the norms of the *pre-existing* political system.[2]

At the heart of most accounts of the transformation of popular politics between 1880 and 1920 is the belief that new social and economic forces began to undermine the equilibrium of popular politics established during the 1860s and 1870s. This equilibrium, it is argued, had been rooted in the strength of non-class, and essentially local political loyalties. Denominational loyalties were perhaps pre-eminent, but partisanship was also cemented by broader civic loyalties – including loyalty to the powerful new provincial urban elites which had done so much to stamp their identities on the emerging industrial communities of provincial

---

[1] See H. J. Hanham, *Elections and party management: politics in the time of Disraeli and Gladstone* (London, 1959); John Vincent, *The formation of the Liberal party, 1857–1868* (London, 1966); D. A. Hamer, *Liberal politics in the age of Gladstone and Rosebery: a study in leadership and policy* (Oxford, 1972); and *The politics of electoral pressure: a study in the history of Victorian reform agitations* (Hassocks, 1977); John Garrard, 'Parties, members and voters after 1867: a local study', *Historical Journal*, 20 (1977), pp. 145–63, a revised version of which appears in T. R. Gourvish and Alan O' Day (eds.), *Later Victorian Britain, 1867–1900*, Problems in Focus (Basingstoke, 1988). See chapter 3 for a discussion of the retention of this orthodoxy in much recent 'revisionist' writing.

[2] In some accounts the origins of the 'triumph of party' are traced back well before 1867, e.g. James Vernon, *Politics and the people: a study in English political culture, c. 1815–1867* (Cambridge, 1993).

England. After 1867, it is suggested, these powerful elites were able to use their wealth and social prestige to establish political structures capable of integrating the new voters into established patterns of partisanship – plebeian politics were 'tamed' and a narrow partisanship instilled. Political parties came to 'manage' popular politics as never before, and continued to do so, it is suggested, long after the decline of the local elites which had created them.[3] Parties evolved into primarily national organisations, dominated by professional politicians, and united around programmatic politics rooted in material (and at heart class) interests. The present chapter questions this orthodox account of the 'triumph of party'. It suggests that the relationship between 'party' and 'public' remained highly ambiguous down to 1914, and that partly in consequence democracy remained widely mistrusted and even feared. Indeed uncertainty about the likely course of democratic politics probably did more than anything else to shape the increasingly programmatic and materialist character of English politics before the First World War.

The chapter begins by exploring constraints on the 'politics of place' in late Victorian and Edwardian England, including the generally contested nature of claims to represent a locality, and the problematic nature of 'influence' in an urban, industrial setting. It argues that local parties were often divided by bitter conflicts which, more often than not, ran along political rather than social fault-lines. Many Radicals were never wholly reconciled to the Liberal coalition, and they were often highly suspicious of attempts to control local politics through the machinery of 'the caucus'. Indeed, resistance to party was more general, and it is argued that the late nineteenth-century 'triumph of party' was qualified firstly by electoral logic (which dictated that 'improving' voters must take a backseat to the more pressing need to win their allegiance), and secondly by the widespread belief that political legitimacy still rested, at least in part, in the open public meeting. This belief placed a premium on the political occupation of public space, and helped sustain a continued role for disruption and physical force in English electoral politics. Connivance in the orchestration of popular disturbances inevitably involved some loss of 'elite' control over the political process, but it also legitimated a set of practices which 'subaltern' groups, such as the Radical and Irish activists of London's East End, could appropriate for their own purposes. The clampdown on 'unauthorised' forms of political protest in the 1880s, and the fierce resistance to suffragette attempts to deploy the 'politics of disruption' at public meetings in the 1900s, demonstrates that such strate-

---

[3] E.g. Garrard, 'Parties, members and voters'; Patrick Joyce, *Work, society and politics: the culture of the factory in later Victorian England* (Brighton, 1980); Trygve Tholfsen, 'The origins of the Birmingham Caucus', *Historical Journal*, 2 (1959), pp. 161–84.

gies did not go uncontested. But if this is indisputable, so too is the fact that late Victorian and Edwardian political traditions placed significant limits on the power and influence of party machines.

II

By suggesting that we need to re-examine the role of local elites in the creation of political identities I do not wish to imply that the 'politics of place' were unimportant in late Victorian elections, only that they were rarely transparent or uncontested. Candidates did frequently argue that their local connections gave them special claim on the representation of a borough, but such claims were usually fiercely challenged by their political opponents. For instance, at South Shields in 1900 local Tories made much of their candidate's position as a major local employer, and denounced William Robson, the sitting Liberal MP (and future Attorney General), as an ambitious lawyer unconnected with the vital industries of the town.[4] Local Liberals directly challenged this attempt to reduce the election simply to 'a question of locality', but they also went to great lengths to establish rival local claims of their own.[5] Robson, it was pointed out, had been a willing advocate for local mining unions, and had turned down a safe seat at Leicester to stay loyal to the borough. Robson himself complained of being treated as 'an Outlander' in his own country, and in doing so he reminded locals that he might not be a Shieldsman, but he was 'a Tynesider born and bred on the banks of the river . . . He was a Northumbrian, a Tynesider, one of themselves.'[6] At the same time Robson pointed out that his opponent might be a powerful local employer, but he had nothing to say on local issues of importance to the people of South Shields. Robson, defending a majority of just 133 in 1895, won by over 3,000 votes – a rare triumph in the context of this 'Khaki' election, 'Outlander' or not.[7]

Sir Charles Palmer, who represented Jarrow, the Tyneside seat next to South Shields, from 1874 until his death in 1907, was one of only a small number of candidates who could claim to embody the 'politics of place'

---

[4] *Shields Daily Gazette*, 27 September and 1 October 1900.

[5] For instance, the Liberal *Shields Daily Gazette* frequently used inverted commas when referring to Redhead as the local candidate, see *ibid.*, 1 and 2 October 1900.

[6] *Ibid.*, 2 October 1900. Similarly, when Morley fought a by-election at Newcastle in 1883 he tried to claim local connections by noting that his mother had been born on Tyneside, see E. I. Waitt, 'John Morley, Joseph Cowen and Robert Spence Watson: Liberal divisions in Newcastle politics, 1873–1895', unpublished PhD thesis, University of Manchester, 1972, p. 184.

[7] On Robson's consolidation of his position at South Shields, see George W. Keeton, *A Liberal Attorney-General: being the life of Lord Robson of Jesmond, (1852–1918)* (London, 1949), pp. 79–82.

almost unchallenged.[8] Indeed the Conservatives declined to oppose him after 1880, and though he did face independent Labour challenges in 1885, 1892 and 1906, these were all defeated with great ease. In 1900, when it briefly looked as though the Tories might bring out a candidate because of Palmer's criticisms of the war in South Africa, the *Shields Daily Gazette*, which was to be so vociferous in its opposition to the 'politics of locality' at South Shields, reminded readers that Palmer, through the development of his great shipbuilding enterprise, was 'the only Shieldsman who has brought a town into being, and has lived to see it develop into a great industrial centre'.[9] In fact most candidates, including powerful employers, had to work hard to ensure that their local connections were an asset rather than a liability. Blatant attempts to exert political influence could easily backfire. For instance, in the 1900s Black Country Liberals made great capital out of the fact that the Unionist owners of the Patent-Axle Box works at Wednesfield chose to march their employees en masse to the poll.[10] More subtle forms of influence might be less resented, but they might also be less effective. It was widely assumed that aspiring Parliamentary candidates, local or 'Outlander', would make generous donations to local charities, sporting groups and other 'good causes' in their chosen constituency (indeed this could prove awkward for Labour, if, as apparently happened in Hardie's Merthyr, rumours began to circulate that their candidate was a man of wealth).[11] From the candidate's point of view, the problem was that because the 'nursing' of a constituency had become such a widespread custom, it could easily be understood by the electors, not as a gift enshrining unspoken assumptions of reciprocity on the part of recipients, but as a form of popular taxation exacted on the politically ambitious.[12] In the more 'corrupt' boroughs this conception of politics was quite explicit – as Trollope records in his famous indictment of his experience fighting at Beverley in 1868, '[i]t was a matter for study to see how at Beverley politics were appreciated because they might subserve electoral purposes,

---

[8] Before 1885 he sat for the county seat of North Durham which included the town of Jarrow.   [9] *Shields Daily Gazette*, 25 September 1900.

[10] See, *Wolverhampton Express and Star*, 7 May 1908. The paper claimed that most of the voters who were marched 'like a flock of sheep to the polling booth' were in fact 'importations from Birmingham'. Black Countrymen, it was suggested, could not be so easily bought. For a Tory perspective on the incident, see L. S. Amery, *My political life, vol. I: England before the storm, 1896–1914* (London, 1953), p. 332.

[11] It was apparently believed that Hardie owned a large estate in Scotland, see William Stewart, *J. Keir Hardie: a biography* (2nd edn, London, 1925), pp. 305–6; also Emrys Hughes, *Keir Hardie* (London, 1956), pp. 204–5.

[12] See William B. Gwyn, *Democracy and the cost of politics in Britain* (London, 1962), pp. 56–60, 127; also Peter Clarke, *Lancashire and the New Liberalism* (Cambridge, 1971), pp. 224–45.

and how little it was understood that electoral purposes, which are in themselves a nuisance, should be endured in order that they may subserve politics'.[13] As Willy Gladstone found at Whitby, declining to 'play the game' of cultivating a local presence could involve a candidate in endless conflicts both with his local party, and with the wider electorate.[14]

Of course, where the expectation of 'nursing' was deeply entrenched representation was likely to remain the preserve of the wealthy. But since the cost of election more or less guaranteed this anyway in most constituencies, the 'taxing' of candidates can perhaps be seen as a perfectly comprehensible strategy *in its own right* – certainly it was a strategy which need not depend upon (though it might coincide with) genuine allegiance towards a benefactor-candidate. Indeed, since all candidates were expected to act as benefactors, it is far from clear that such displays of paternalism did much to influence party allegiance at elections – as John Garrard has recently observed 'urban squires were honored [*sic*] if of the right party' – if not, they were simply fleeced.[15]

The ambiguities of the 'politics of place' are further underlined by the fact that 'outsider' candidates often augmented the nursing of a constituency by taking a house in the district so that they could qualify as local burgesses with full voting rights – essential for any credible appeal to 'local' credentials, but a painfully slow process under Victorian voter registration laws. Thus Ernest Benn recalls his father renting a villa in Cable Street when he was nursing the East End seat of St George's-in-the-East (he called it Gladstone House). Defeated by eleven votes at the 1895 election, he transferred his interest to the Bermondsey division of Southwark, taking a house in Thorburn Square so that again he 'might qualify as the resident candidate'.[16] Throughout this time the family home was Hoppea Hall at Upminster in Essex.

III

But if, as Benn's exploits would suggest, the continued popular resonances of the 'localist' appeal are not in doubt, it does not follow that we should accept in its entirety the traditional emphasis on the role of local

---

[13] Anthony Trollope, *An autobiography* (Williams and Norgate edn, London, 1946), p. 267. See also William Albery, *A parliamentary history of the ancient borough of Horsham, 1295–1885* (London, 1927), esp. pp. 339–44, 353–56, 434–40, 465.

[14] See Michael Bentley, 'Gladstonian Liberals and provincial notables: Whitby politics, 1868–80', *Historical Research*, 154 (1991), pp. 172–85.

[15] John Garrard, 'Urban elites, 1850–1914: the rule and decline of a new squirearchy?', *Albion*, 27 (1995), p. 597.

[16] Ernest Benn, *Happier days: recollections and reflections* (London, 1949), pp. 31–2; see also Hilaire Belloc, *Mr Clutterbuck's election* (London, 1908).

elites in the development of popular partisanship in later Victorian England. There are two main problems with approaches which emphasise the integrative role of local elites. Firstly, they tend to underestimate the antagonism that often existed *within* local Liberal and Tory organisations between factions with very different political agendas (and very different conceptions of how the locality should be represented politically). And secondly, they tend to underestimate the extent to which, even in the nineteenth century, popular partisanship was shaped by national rather than local political struggles, and was rooted in a well-developed sense of both Toryism and especially Liberalism as national political *movements*. As we will see, these two objections to the orthodox approach are inextricably linked.

When acknowledged, divisions within local parties are often presented as the product of underlying social divisions – most notably between established landed families and the new industrial and commercial elites of urban Britain, or between these urban elites and plebeian political groupings. This is of course too simple; local alliances were shaped primarily by political affinity, not social affinity. Whig or Tory landowners had few qualms about making common cause with like-minded industrialists and merchants,[17] just as Radicals defined themselves, first and foremost, by their programme, not their social position – hence the recurrent, if by no means unchanging, tradition of the 'gentleman leader' as a people's tribune.[18] As we saw with Wolverhampton in the 1830s, on occasion political conflict could become so intense that local political leaders would turn to politicians from outside their community to diffuse, and to a certain extent confuse, bitter local rivalries. Hence the choice of Villiers as a compromise candidate in 1835, and his eventual emergence as the unlikely embodiment (because of his defiant 'outsider' status) of the town's political identity and civic pride thanks to his part in the Repeal of the Corn Laws.[19]

In some highly politicised constituencies it seems likely that popular

[17] This is brought out well in Richard Trainor, *Black Country elites: the exercise of authority in an urban area, 1830–1900* (Oxford, 1993).

[18] See Miles Taylor, *The decline of British Radicalism, 1847–1860* (Oxford, 1995); also 'Interests, parties and the state: the urban electorate in England, c. 1820–72'; and David Eastwood, 'Contesting the politics of deference: the rural electorate, 1820–1860' both in Jon Lawrence and Miles Taylor (eds.), *Party, state and society: electoral behaviour in Britain since 1820* (Aldershot, 1997); also John Belchem and James Epstein, 'The nineteenth-century gentleman leader revisited', *Social History*, 22 (1997), pp. 174–93.

[19] Villiers made little attempt to 'nurse' Wolverhampton. On his election expenses, see the letter to George Villiers, 10 January 1835 in Herbert Maxwell (ed.), *The life and letters of George William Frederick, Fourth Earl of Clarendon*, (2 vols. (London, 1913), I, p. 85. Villiers notes that 'I did not give a glass of brandy and water to a human being, would not retain any agent, or treat, or allow ribbons, flags or music'. He was an infrequent visitor to the town even in his youth and paid no visits at all after 1874, though he sat for the borough until his death in 1898.

political allegiance was offered in spite of a candidate's local power and influence, rather than because of it. Although there were many constituencies in which internecine conflicts generated rival candidacies, especially on the Liberal side,[20] there were also many in which long-term conflict over control of local representation was briefly put aside in order to keep out the opposition at the election. For instance, the profound tensions between the 'moderate' and 'radical' wings of London Liberalism are well documented.[21] But whereas between 1868 and 1885 nearly 29 per cent of Parliamentary elections in the capital involved rival Liberal candidacies, between 1885 and 1914 this figure had fallen to just 2.4 per cent, despite the fact that the introduction of single-member constituencies in 1885 had, if anything, increased tensions over local representation.[22] In other words, we cannot take the incidence of rival Liberal candidacies as an accurate measure of the extent of division within local Liberal parties in late-Victorian Britain.

Even after 1867, Radical activists often remained equivocal in their attitude towards organised Liberalism. Many felt a profound loyalty towards Liberalism as a national movement of reform, without overcoming their deep suspicion of its local representatives – both on ideological grounds, and because of their undemocratic dominance of local public life. Here the recent work of historians such as Eugenio Biagini, Miles Taylor and Colin Matthew is important, underlining the extent to which nineteenth-century popular politics were preoccupied with questions of state policy, rather than just with the resolution of local status conflicts.[23] Fiscal policy, trade policy, foreign policy, the franchise and labour legislation all loomed large in Victorian popular politics – and to a considerable degree it was the Liberals' success in tackling these questions of national policy

[20] For instance see the analysis of the 1874 defeat offered in W. E. Gladstone, 'Electoral facts', *Nineteenth Century*, 4 (1878), pp. 955–68.

[21] See Paul Thompson, 'Liberals, Radicals and Labour in London, 1880–1900', *Past and Present*, 27 (1964), pp. 73–101; and *Socialists, Liberals and Labour: the struggle for London, 1885–1914* (London, 1967); John Davis, 'Radical clubs and London politics, 1870–1900', in David Feldman and Gareth Stedman Jones (eds.), *Metropolis: London histories and representations since 1800* (London, 1989).

[22] Figures calculated from the returns in F. W. S. Craig, *British Parliamentary election results, 1832–1885* (2nd edn, Aldershot, 1989), and *British Parliamentary election results, 1885–1918* (2nd edn, Aldershot, 1989). One factor here may have been the lesson of 'Progressive' cooperation on the LCC and local councils from the 1890s; see Pat Thane, 'Labour and local politics: radicalism, democracy and social reform, 1880–1914' in Eugenio Biagini and Alastair Reid (eds.), *Currents of radicalism: popular radicalism, organised labour and party politics in Britain, 1850–1914* (Cambridge, 1991), esp. pp. 245–53.

[23] See H. C. G. Matthew, 'Disraeli, Gladstone and the policy of mid-Victorian budgets', *Historical Journal*, 22 (1979), pp. 615–43; Eugenio Biagini, 'British trade unions and popular political economy, 1860–1880', *Historical Journal*, 30 (1987), pp. 811–40; Taylor, *Decline of British Radicalism*. The most compelling account of popular politics in terms of the working out of local status conflicts remains John Vincent's *Pollbooks: how Victorians voted* (Cambridge, 1967).

that secured their great period of ascendency between 1846 and 1886.[24] In particular this period witnessed the resolution of many historic Radical grievances as Liberal politicians sought, more or less consciously, to forge a new 'laissez-faire' state.[25] Though Radical incorporation into the new political order was by no means complete in 1867, it is apparent that the continued reduction of taxation on items of working-class consumption, the abolition of the stamp and paper duties which constrained the 'free press', and the championing of nationalist aspirations in Europe all helped to cement a strong identification with Liberalism among radical activists and ex-Chartists. Liberalism was thus at heart a national political movement – a broad and heterogeneous coalition of 'reformers' – rather than, as is sometimes suggested, a social movement of those who had been excluded from the polity under the *ancien regime* constitution.[26]

That said, I would not wish to dismiss the importance of the irrational and symbolic in Victorian popular politics. Local status conflicts, like local identities, undoubtedly played their part in *cementing* political partisanship – but we cannot hope to understand the *genesis* of political allegiance by focusing on such factors in isolation. In doing so we seriously underestimate the tensions which characterised party politics, and especially the politics of the Liberal coalition, throughout the nineteenth century.[27] Even during the 'golden age' of popular Liberalism in the 1860s and 1870s, the Radical press frequently sounded a sceptical, if not downright hostile note in its treatment of mainstream Liberalism. For instance in September 1867 one finds *The Bee-Hive*, which John Vincent suggests 'never put forward generalities about property and wealth',[28] lamenting the recent failure to secure full manhood suffrage in the Reform Act, and insisting that 'the legislation of the past has been essen-

---

[24] See Jonathan Parry, *The rise and fall of Liberal government in Victorian Britain* (New Haven, Conn., 1993); T. A. Jenkins, *The Liberal ascendancy, 1830–1886* (Basingstoke, 1994). Also Gareth Stedman Jones, 'Some notes on Karl Marx and the English labour movement', *History Workshop Journal*, 18 (1984), pp. 130–6.

[25] Philip Harling and Peter Mandler, 'From "fiscal-military" to "laissez-faire" state, 1760–1850', *Journal of British Studies*, 32 (1993), pp. 44–70.

[26] Eugenio Biagini, *Liberty, retrenchment and reform: popular Liberalism in the age of Gladstone, 1860–1880* (Cambridge, 1992); though see Taylor, *Decline of British Radicalism*, for a sense of the difficulties which beset this process throughout the 1850s; and, from a different (essentially class-based) perspective, Margot C. Finn, *After Chartism: class and nation in English radical politics, 1848–1874* (Cambridge, 1993).

[27] Though ironically this can also be said of Biagini's strongly 'rationalist' account of popular Liberalism, Biagini, *Liberty, retrenchment and reform*, p. 5; Biagini and Reid, 'Currents of radicalism', pp. 6–7.

[28] Vincent, *Formation of the Liberal party* (Pelican edn, 1972), p. 115. On *The Bee-Hive*, see Stephen Coltham, '*The Bee-Hive* newspaper: its origins and early struggles', in Asa Briggs and John Saville (eds.), *Essays in labour history*, 1 (London, 1960); and 'George Potter, the Junta and *The Bee-Hive*', *International Review of Social History*, 9 (1964), pp. 390–432, and 10 (1965), pp. 23–65; and 'English working-class newspapers in 1867', *Victorian Studies*, 13 (1969), pp. 159–80; also Biagini, *Liberty, retrenchment and reform*, p. 25.

tially the legislation of capital' and that 'the great cause of the down-
trodden and degraded position of so many thousands of the working
classes of our country is *the robbery which capital has perpetrated on labour
through legislation*'.[29] Indeed in 1876 the same journal took its critique
further, arguing that despite all the 'fussy talk' about Church education,
the army and navy, or the Eastern Question, only '[t]wo great thoughts, as
master thoughts, occupy the middle class in England . . . [t]he first is how
to get labour as cheaply as possible, and the next is how to provide for the
vice and misery necessarily attending such a state of things by the lowest
possible charge'.[30] Given such an analysis it is perhaps not surprising that
The Bee-Hive, like many of the radical activists who bought it, remained
strongly committed to the goal of independent political representation,
advocating that the working classes should select representatives 'wher-
ever practicable *from the ranks of labour*, from men who acknowledge
adherence to no mere party'.[31]

The mass circulation *Reynolds's Newspaper* argued along similar lines to
The Bee-Hive, though its choice of language was noticeably less temper-
ate. *Reynolds's* represented the unreconstructed voice of 'old-style' militant Radicalism – though by the mid-1870s it was already spicing its
Jacobin rhetoric with allusions to the more sanguinary aspects of
Continental socialism.[32] Far from displaying a 'desire to transcend class
in the name of broader social unities', as Patrick Joyce has suggested,[33]
Reynolds's embraced a highly polarised model of society, portraying itself
as the champion of 'the working class' (not 'classes', note) in its battle
against arbitrary authority and class government (at times it even claimed
to be the champion of 'the proletariat').[34] Rather than welcome Liberal
attempts to distinguish between the respectable working classes and the

---

[29] *The Bee-Hive*, 14 September 1867 (original emphasis).   [30] *Ibid.*, 11 November 1876.

[31] *Ibid.*, 14 September 1867 (original emphasis). See also *ibid.*, 12 October 1867 for the
paper's specific appeal to trade unionists 'to procure a direct Representation of Labour'
in Parliament. For a similar argument see *The Republican*, 1 October 1870, which calls for
the break up of the old political parties and the creation of a 'broad labour platform'.

[32] For discussion of *Reynolds's*, see Thomas Wright, *Our new masters* (1873), pp. 334–5 and
346; *The Dictionary of Labour Biography*, III, (London, 1976), p. 149; V. Berridge, 'Popular
sunday papers and mid-Victorian society', in G. Boyce, J. Curran and P. Wingates (eds.),
Newspaper history from the seventeenth century to the present day (1978), and A. Humpherys,
'Popular narrative and political discourse in *Reynolds's Weekly Newspaper*', in L. Blake, A.
Jones and L. Madden (eds.), *Investigating Victorian journalism* (Basingstoke, 1990).
Biagini, *Liberty, retrenchment and reform*, pp. 20–8 discusses both *Reynolds's* and many of
the provincial Radical papers of this period; for a discussion of radical papers in the
Midlands, see Aled Jones, 'Workmen's advocates: ideology and class in a mid-Victorian
newspaper system', in J. Shattock and M. Wolff (eds.), *The Victorian periodical press:
soundings and samplings* (Leicester, 1982).

[33] Joyce, *Visions of the people* p. 62 – an argument he elaborates at pp. 67–9.

[34] *Reynolds's Newspaper*, 2 September 1866, 13 October and 15 December 1867 and 21
March 1875 (where it attacks the fact that such a large proportion of 'the proletariat'
should end up in the workhouse).

'residuum' in the reform debate of 1866,[35] *Reynolds's* denounced the policy as an attempt to enfranchise 'working men who are most under the control of the middle classes'. Somewhat in the spirit of later proponents of the labour aristocracy thesis, *Reynolds's* argued that

the workmen whose ambitions and interests are more intimately bound up with the class of masters and capitalists, than with the great body of the labouring class – will be admitted partners, on a small scale, with the present monopolists of political and legislative power ... it will be admitting another batch of dependent voters.[36]

Like *The Bee-Hive*, *Reynolds's* believed that it was essential to secure Parliamentary representation independent of the two main parties, though its deep-seated suspicion of the sectarianism of the trade union movement led it to stress the representation of 'working men', rather than of 'labour'.[37] For the most part, therefore, *Reynolds's* maintained an essentially semi-detached attitude towards mainstream Liberalism. The main exception to this appears to have been the General Election of 1886, when the paper not only sided wholeheartedly with Gladstone and the Home Rulers, but also adopted a cross-class populist language in which Gladstone was portrayed as the working man's 'champion against class pride and class prejudice'.[38] By the time of the 1892 election, however, *Reynolds's* was again deeply disillusioned with Liberalism, and was placing its political hopes on the possible emergence of a new grouping of independent Labour and socialist MPs.[39]

If, as this admittedly brief analysis of the press would suggest, Radical inclusion within the Liberal coalition was always partial and conditional, then it becomes easier to understand the strong Radical contribution to late Victorian Labour politics without resorting to models of class polarisation. Indeed, it should be apparent from the preceding discussion that, far from representing an unproblematic politics of class union and harmony, mid-Victorian Radicalism could be at least as class-conscious and stubbornly independent as later Labour politics. So far the emphasis

[35] As argued by R. Harrison, *Beyond the socialists: studies in labour and politics* (London, 1965), p. 116; see also Trygve Tholfsen, *Working-class Radicalism in mid-Victorian Britain* (London, 1976), p. 320.

[36] *Reynolds's Newspaper*, 28 January 1866; for discussion of contemporary usage see M. A. Shepherd, 'The origins and incidence of the term "labour aristocracy"', *Bulletin of the Society for the Study of Labour History*, 37 (1978), pp. 51–67, and the reply by Joseph Melling, 'Aristocrats and artisans', *ibid.*, 39 (1979), pp. 16–22.

[37] For hostility to official trade unionism see *Reynolds's Newspaper*, 3 October 1886; for an emphasis on class representation see *ibid.*, 17 January 1886.

[38] *Ibid.*, 20 June 1886. Two weeks later the paper observed that 'working men owe a debt to Mr Gladstone because he has recognised their order' (*ibid.*, 4 July 1886). In contrast in 1875 *Reynolds's* can be found denouncing 'the defunct Whig Administration of Mr Gladstone' – i.e. his 1868–74 Liberal Government (*ibid.*, 17 October 1875).

[39] *Ibid.*, 17 July and 28 August 1892.

has been predominantly on the ideological tensions between Radicalism and mainstream Liberalism, but in many respects more fundamental was the antagonism towards local Liberal politicians believed to have usurped the representation of 'natural' Radical constituencies through their misuse of influence and organisation. The Radical press of the 1870s and 1880s repeatedly attacked local Liberal parties for conspiring to block Radical and Labour candidates, usually accusing them of being dominated by undemocratic cliques of lawyers, businessmen and shopkeepers. For instance, in 1875, frustration at the doctrinaire opposition of many Liberals to Cross's Artizan's Dwellings Bill led *The Bee-Hive* to observe that if Bright could display such narrow-minded 'class-stupidity' what hope could there be for 'the small local middle-class men who scarcely ever look beyond the bounds of their boroughs'. Noting the recent failure of such men to accept the candidacy of a miners' leader at Stoke, the paper lamented that '[t]his prejudice by employers and shopkeepers against Trade Unionists and Co-operators cannot, we fear, be rooted out', and argued that 'if these blind and brutal prejudices against working men and trade unions cannot be overcome in the Liberal Party, it will be the duty of the working men of the country to separate from that party'. Significantly, they would do so in order to establish 'a new party capable of understanding Liberal principles and working out a Liberal policy useful and creditable to the nation.'[40] Here, at least, ideological divisions were much less important than social-cum-organisational divisions. Nor was this an isolated outburst. In August 1876 *The Bee-Hive* was again attacking the 'fortunate and fussy shopkeepers and manufacturers' who dominated local Liberalism in the constituencies, using their power to foist 'rich incapables' upon the electors.[41]

An account by a Liberal candidate defeated at the 1885 General Election, tells the same story of dissension and animosity. Chosen by the newly created Liberal Association of 'Wallsborough' (despite hardly considering himself to be a Liberal at all), the candidate quickly finds himself spurned by local Liberals whose 'fad' he had ignored in his election address, and publicly attacked by members of the borough Radical Club.[42] Divisions of this sort could dominate a town's Liberal politics for decades. Dewsbury, in west Yorkshire, is a classic example. There had long been tensions between the different factions of the town's Liberal movement, and with the achievement of borough status in 1867 these quickly found institutional expression, as well-to-do local Liberals and the Dewsbury Trades Council selected rival Liberal candidates to

---

[40] *The Bee-Hive*, 27 February 1875.   [41] *Ibid.*, 12 August 1876.
[42] A defeated candidate, 'My contested election', *Fortnightly Review*, 39 (Jan.-June 1886), pp. 93–101.

contest the new borough.[43] The Trades Council denounced the selection of the west country coal owner Handel Cossham by a self-appointed committee of prominent Liberals, and upheld the principle of selection by open public meeting. Their chosen candidate, the Chartist veteran Ernest Jones, overwhelmingly won the support of the 15,000 towns-folk who gathered in Dewsbury Market Place for a special selection meeting, but the Cossham camp refused to accept the decision.[44] Thereafter battle-lines became confused. Jones withdrew to concentrate on his Manchester candidacy, but his supporters refused to give up. Instead they persuaded local Conservative leaders to back John Simon, the radical Jewish lawyer, as an alternative 'independent Liberal' candidate. Fighting in the name of 'Simon and No Dictation' and 'Simon and Liberty', this 'strange union', as Cossham subsequently described it, of 'the Tories, the ultra trade unionists, the Chartists and the Catholics' won by 3,392 votes to 2,923 on an 89 per cent poll.[45] In 1874 Simon retained the seat, again in a straight fight with a rival Liberal candidate (J. Charles Cox), and again relying both on Conservative and Radical support.[46] As at the previous election the rhetoric of 'independence' was very much to the fore, with both the 'Simonites' and their Tory allies denouncing the borough's Liberal 'clique' for trying to usurp the electoral freedom of independent voters. Significantly at the declaration Simon went out of his way to attribute his victory to 'the working men of Dewsbury', observing that 'they brought him there in 1868, they had stood by him ever since, and their courage and steadfastness had won him the election of 1874'.[47]

By 1880 Simon's opponents (still known as the 'Cosshamites') had formed a 'Liberal 300' on the Birmingham model, which again chose a rival candidate (the Lancashire manufacturer and temperance advocate William Hoyle). Simon refused to acknowledge the legitimacy of this Caucus selection ballot, claiming that he derived his mandate from the near unanimous vote of confidence passed at his recent annual meeting attended by 6–7,000 townsfolk, in contrast to 'the two or three hundred

---

[43] This account of Dewsbury borough politics draws from Christopher J. James, *MP for Dewsbury: one hundred years of Parliamentary representation* (Brighouse, 1970), pp. 65–83.

[44] For a discussion of Jones's political manoeuverings at this time, see Anthony D. Taylor, 'Ernest Jones: his later career and the structure of Manchester politics, 1861–1869', Unpublished MA thesis, University of Birmingham, 1984, *passim*, and on Dewsbury, pp. 52, 76–8.   [45] *Ibid.*, pp. 79–80.

[46] *Dewsbury Reporter*, 31 January and 7 February 1874. Cox's election agent explicitly accused Simon of 'coquetting' with both the Tories and the extreme Radicals. See also James, *MP for Dewsbury*, pp. 83–6.

[47] *Dewsbury Reporter*, 7 February 1874.

gentlemen' who had 'formed themselves into an association'.[48] This time there was also a popular Conservative candidate, but Simon again survived – by 345 votes on an 85 per cent poll. Again Simon portrayed himself as the working-man's champion against the power and wealth of the town's Liberal elite. He denounced the 'Cosshamites' for their faddist views on temperance, and proclaimed that together they would 'vindicate the powers of the working classes of the borough, and show that they formed part of the Liberal party, and were not to be lightly ignored by a small section of gentlemen who took up one particular question as their hobby'.[49] Only after this third contest was a reconciliation finally brokered between the MP, his diverse supporters, and the powerful Liberal leadership which dominated municipal life in Dewsbury. In 1888 a champion of the local Liberal elite, mine-owner and woollen manufacturer Mark Oldroyd, finally became MP for the borough, but within less than a decade official Liberalism faced a new challenge to its authority – this time from the emergent Independent Labour Party which took up the old cries of 'independence' and 'no dictation' in support of the Bradford socialist Edward Hartley.[50]

The Dewsbury case is interesting because it reminds us of the inherent ambiguity of many 'democratic' innovations in party organisation after 1867. L. A. Atherley Jones, one of the politicians interviewed by the Dewsbury 'Liberal 300' before the 1880 General Election, later lamented that local politicians had sought to unseat Simon 'because he was not sufficiently submissive to the will of the local Liberal Caucus'.[51] At issue were two contrasting conceptions of democratic representation. Simon, like other Liberal opponents of the 'Caucus', upheld the importance of a direct relationship between politician and constituents, rather than one mediated through party organisations. Like Joseph Cowen at Newcastle, that other great scourge of the caucus, Simon continued to hold an

---

[48] *Dewsbury Chronicle*, 28 February and 6, 13, 20 and 27 March, 3 April 1880. See also James, *MP for Dewsbury*, pp. 91–4.

[49] *Dewsbury Chronicle*, 20 March 1880.

[50] James, *MP for Dewsbury*, p. 120. Later Harry Quelch fought the seat for the SDF (in 1902), and then Ben Turner for Labour (in 1906 and 1908), each time unsuccessfully. See Martin Crick, 'Labour alliance or socialist unity? The Independent Labour Party in the heavy woollen areas of West Yorkshire, c. 1893–1902', in K. Laybourn and D. James (eds.), *'The rising sun of socialism': the Independent Labour Party in the textile district of the West Riding of Yorkshire between 1890 and 1914* (Bradford, 1991); also Ben Turner, *About myself, 1863–1930* (London, 1930), pp. 232–4; and David Howell, *British workers and the Independent Labour Party, 1888–1906* (Manchester, 1983), pp. 200–1.

[51] L. A. Atherley-Jones, *Looking back: reminiscences of a political career* (London, 1925), p. 21. Atherley-Jones also suggests that the treatment of Joseph Cowen greatly weakened Liberalism in Newcastle in the later nineteenth century (*ibid.*, p. 24).

annual open public meeting where as many as 10,000 people, voters and
non-voters, men and women, might attend to hear an account of his work
as borough MP.[52] Other opponents of the 'caucus' were less fundamentalist – they accepted the need for more formal political structures,
but questioned the representativeness of the new organisations. George
Potter's *Industrial Review*, successor to *The Bee-Hive*, was perhaps predictably critical of the caucus in the wake of the editor's rejection by the
Liberal Hundred at the Peterborough by-election of 1878, but many trade
union leaders shared the belief that 'caucus' organisation would make
Radical and Labour candidatures more difficult in most constituencies.[53]
In Birmingham during the 1870s trade union leaders who were strongly
Liberal in their sympathies, none the less sought to organise a Labour
association, and run their own independent Labour candidates in order
to preserve some independence from Chamberlain's powerful political
machine.[54] Similarly Pelling argues that the decision to establish the
Democratic Federation in 1881 (forerunner of the socialist SDF) was in
large part a reaction against Chamberlain and the new Caucus politics
which were coming to dominate Radicalism – hence Cowen's prominent
role in the early stages.[55]

On the other hand, there were also many Radicals who saw the new
constituency organisations as a means of undermining the political power
of the shadowy, self-nominated 'Liberal Committees' which had traditionally controlled the representation of many constituencies. *Reynolds's*
certainly argued as much at the 1885 General Election, when it held up
Chamberlain's firm grip on Birmingham politics as an example to

[52] *Dewsbury Chronicle*, 13 and 20 March 1880; James, *MP for Dewsbury*, pp. 90–1. On
Cowen's use of the annual meeting see, E. R. Jones, *The life and speeches of Joseph Cowen
MP* (London, nd [1885]), and Waitt, 'Newcastle politics', esp. pp. 157, 207, 209–10, 225,
244–5, which also charts Cowen's emergence as the political champion of a large but very
diverse coalition of marginalised 'out groups'. Waitt offers a stridently anti-Cowen analysis, but provides little explanation for the Cowenites' final break with the Caucus in late
1880 (p. 155). See also Biagini, *Liberty, retrenchment and reform*, pp. 328–37 (esp. 335–7),
and Roland Quinault, 'John Bright and Joseph Chamberlain', *Historical Journal*, 28
(1985), pp. 623–46 (esp. 628–9).

[53] *Industrial Review*, 2 November 1878; see Henry Pelling, *America and the British Left: from
Bright to Bevan* (London, 1956), pp. 44–8.

[54] See W. A. Dalley, *The life story of W. J. Davis, J.P.* (Birmingham, 1914), pp. 44–64; Asa
Briggs, *History of Birmingham, vol. II: borough and city, 1865–1938* (London, 1952), pp.
192–4; and C. Green, 'Birmingham politics, 1873–1891: the local basis of change', *Midland
History*, 2 (1973), pp. 84–98. See also Mark Netherley, 'Electoral politics in Bristol,
1885–1914', Unpublished MPhil. thesis, University of Wales, Lampeter, 1990, pp. 153–4.

[55] See Henry Pelling, *The origins of the Labour party, 1880–1900* (Oxford, 1954), pp. 16–18; see
also M. S. Wilkins, 'The non-socialist origins of England's first important Socialist
organisation', *International Review of Social History*, 4 (1959), pp. 199–207, and Waitt,
'Newcastle politics', pp. 162, 171, 191.

Radicals elsewhere in the country.[56] By December 1886, however, in the wake of the great Liberal schism and Chamberlain's break with the party, the paper was lamenting that so few Liberal leaders appeared to recognise that 'something more is wanted for the development of a healthy Liberalism than mere party organisation or caucus construction'.[57] After 1886 few Radicals saw organisation as a panacea for their political woes, though most acknowledged its necessity in an emergent mass democracy.[58] Initially optimism was relatively high, not many Liberals celebrated the recent schism in the party ranks, but on the other hand few considered it likely to be permanent either.[59] In a collection of essays published soon after Salisbury's 1886 election victory, Jacob Bright could argue that '[t]o be in opposition, to suffer adversity, does much to teach and strengthen', though Thomas Burt was perhaps more triumphalist, arguing that since the Radicals would now be in the ascendent they could dominate the formation of party policy.[60] As we shall see below, when the editor of this collection published a second volume on the future of Radicalism in the early 1890s this optimism, even complacency, had evaporated. Instead the emphasis was on the need to forge a 'New Party', which would reinvigorate Radical-Liberalism by tapping into the energy and enthusiasm of the recent 'labour revival'.[61] The fact that the political face of the 'labour revival' was in part a revolt against the stranglehold of caucus organisation within the Liberal party, merely underlines the extent to which the perfection of organisation was no longer seen as the key to Radical success.[62]

[56] *Reynolds's Newspaper*, 29 November 1885.
[57] *Ibid.*, 19 December 1886. The paper was commending Labouchere as the exceptional Liberal leader who *could* see beyond mere organisation. He too was a keen advocate of the caucus, however; see his essay 'Radicals and Whigs', *Fortnightly Review*, 35 (Jan.-June 1884) p. 210, and his contribution to A. Reid (ed.), *The new Liberal programme: contributed by representatives of the Liberal Party* (1886), pp. 7–8.
[58] On the attitudes of the Liberal intelligentsia, see Paolo Pombeni, 'Starting in reason, ending in passion: Bryce, Lowell, Ostrogorski and the problem of democracy', *Historical Journal*, 37 (1994), pp. 319–41, esp. pp. 322, 332–41.
[59] See Michael Hurst, *Joseph Chamberlain and Liberal reunion: the round table conference of 1887* (London, 1967); also P. C. Griffiths, 'The Caucus and the Liberal party in 1886', *History*, 61 (1976), pp. 183–97, and Graham Goodlad, 'Gladstone and his rivals: popular perceptions of party leadership in the political crisis of 1885–86', in Biagini and Reid (eds.), *Currents of Radicalism*.
[60] Reid (ed.), *New Liberal programme*, pp. 18 and 47. Though see Thomas Burt, *Pitman and privy councillor: an autobiography with supplementary chapters by Aaron Watson* (London, 1924), pp. 213–14, where Burt takes a very conciliatory line towards Whig politics.
[61] Andrew Reid (ed.), *The new party: described by some of its members* (London, 1894), discussed more fully below, chapter 8, pp. 201–2.
[62] This is, of course, an important theme in Pelling, *Origins of the Labour party*, see also the discussion in chapter 9 below.

IV

So far the discussion of party organisation and the role of political elites has focused overwhelmingly on the attitudes of a highly politicised minority – those political activists who, except in their most pessimistic moments, claimed to articulate the 'authentic' voice of urban popular politics. Perhaps of more fundamental importance, however, is the question of the impact of party organisation on popular politics as a whole in the years between 1867 and 1914. Historians analysing 'the rise of party' after 1867 have tended to fall into two camps – those who stress how the growth of formal party organisation completed the 'taming' of popular politics,[63] and those who stress how party organisation was able to integrate the new electors of 1867 and 1885, so that they posed little threat to the existing political and social status quo.[64] The first approach stresses the world that was lost with the rise of party, while the second focuses more on the world that was created (albeit often from a critical perspective). They are, of course, two sides of the same story, though the first approach undoubtedly lays greater emphasis on the highly developed political traditions of non-electors before 1867.

It would be wrong to suggest that these accounts of 'the rise of party' are wholly misplaced. The period after 1867 did witness a great expansion of permanent party organization in the constituencies – driven in large part by the greatly increased scale of registration work and canvassing, and by the consequences of the Secret Ballot Act of 1872, and the Corrupt Practices Act of 1883. Equally there is no denying that during this period local parties began to develop an elaborate 'social' dimension as they sought to attract party members, and to fête potential voters. But, if this much is not in question, how we should interpret these developments certainly is. Do they amount to 'the taming of popular politics' – the 'socialization' of the new electors on terms dictated by an established political elite? Most accounts of late nineteenth-century popular politics certainly suggest that they do, but I would like to offer an alternative interpretation, one which stresses the *incompleteness* of party control. Throughout this period party elites were obliged to engage with, and adapt to, aspects of popular culture but dimly understood, and in some measure feared. By this reading, we should be highly sceptical about politicians' frequent claims for the 'educational' and 'improving' function of their political clubs or their party social events. Most political leaders had read their Bagehot – they knew that they were meant to be moulding

---

[63] E.g. Vernon, *Politics and the people*.

[64] E.g. Garrard, 'Parties, members and voters'; Hanham, *Elections and party management*; Vincent, *Formation of the Liberal party*; Joyce, *Visions of the people*.

the new democracy – bolstering its supposed natural deference, whilst instilling a sense of how to use the new franchise 'wisely'.[65] The intellectual consensus around the need to educate the new electors, or 'our new masters', was so strong that we should hardly be surprised if politicians echoed these sentiments when setting up new party organisations. But nor should we take them at their word, as John Garrard appears to do in his influential article 'Parties, members and voters' (still the clearest statement of the 'socialization' thesis).[66] For example, when the Wolverhampton Tories opened the town's first Working Men's Conservative Club in 1884, local leaders spoke of the valuable contribution the club would make to the education and 'improvement' of the working classes. In contrast, however, contemporary accounts of the working-men's clubs set up in the 1880s stress their fine surroundings, excellent facilities for billiards and other games, and the ready-supply of good cheap beer.[67] Significantly, just months after the town's first working-men's club opened a leading local Conservative prophesied that 'the 1,200 "horny-handed sons of toil" in their working men's club' would win the Borough for Hickman – the prospective Conservative candidate and an important local industrialist.[68] It was of course no accident that the previous year had seen the passing of the Corrupt Practices Act, which drastically reduced the number of paid election workers a candidate might hire. As an internal party paper on 'The condition of the Conservative Party in the Midland Counties' had acknowledged immediately after the Act was passed, the new conditions made it imperative that in future local politicians should be able to call on the services of *volunteer* workers. This, the report concluded, meant setting up new mass organizations, regardless of the consequent danger of encouraging an 'abundance of zeal' among the rank and file which might challenge traditional party structures.[69] Here, at least, the mass party was seen as an

---

[65] Walter Bagehot, 'The English Constitution' (1867) in Norman St John-Stevas (ed.), *The collected works of Walter Bagehot*, II vols. (London, 1974), V, pp. 165–409, esp. the introduction to the second edition of 1872 (*ibid.*, pp. 169–74). Also Jon Roper, *Democracy and its critics: Anglo-American democratic thought in the nineteenth century* (London, 1989), pp. 152–6.

[66] John Garrard, 'Parties, members and voters', esp. pp. 149, 153–61, though he does accept that practice did not always follow theory in club organisation.

[67] See *[Wolverhampton] Evening Express*, 19 Jan. 1884; for discussion of the clubs' facilities, see *Midland Counties Express*, 15 February 1896. Also Keeton, *Liberal Attorney-General*, p. 82 which records Robson's opposition to teetotal working mens' clubs at South Shields on the grounds that they could never rival the attractions of the Tory alternative.

[68] *Wolverhampton Evening Express*, 21 April 1884.

[69] 'The condition of the Conservative Party in the Midland Counties' published as part of *The Seventeenth Annual Conference Report of the National Union of Conservative and Constitutional Associations*, 1883 (Micro Methods Microfilm edn). The report explicitly notes that prior to the Act 'we have had to depend to a very great extent upon paid canvassers'.

explicit threat to the authority and control of established political leaders, only electoral necessity could justify its adoption.[70]

These arguments do not, however, undermine the approach to the rise of party which places more stress on the management of popular politics than on the education (or 'socialisation') of the new electors. Clearly working-men's clubs and political festivals *were* usually initiated from above, by professional party politicians. It is less clear, however, that party leaders were always able to control the political character of their creations. The fears of Midland Tories in 1883 were by no means unfounded. Political clubs, including those nominally dependent on wealthy political patrons, could provide organisational resources for independent political activity 'from below'. For instance, in Wolverhampton, the Tory clubs set up in the early 1880s ran an independent 'Tory-Labour' candidate for the borough council in 1891 despite receiving little or no support from the local party leadership.[71] Mike Savage has told a similar story for Preston Conservatism in the later nineteenth century, while even an organisation such as the British Brothers League in the East End of London could put unwelcome pressure on the politicians who controlled local Tory politics.[72] As we have already seen, Liberal organisations were yet more susceptible to internal dissension and 'pressure from below'.

One is therefore forced to ask why, if party leaders so frequently failed to control their own members, we should imagine that they were able to establish control over popular politics as a whole. No less than in their relations with their own rank and file, party leaders found that their relations with the wider electorate had to be continuously negotiated and renegotiated. Particularly important here was the ambiguity introduced into relations between 'leaders' and 'led' by the fact that large numbers of politicians continued to uphold the notion that open public meetings, especially meetings of one's constituents, represented an important source of political legitimacy. Hence the elaborate intellectual contortions politicians frequently found themselves performing when trying to distinguish between 'true' and 'false' expressions of public opinion. A classic example of this is Gladstone's response to the metropolitan pro-war, or 'Jingo', demonstrations of 1878. Gladstone argued that the influential Guildhall meeting supporting Disraeli's policy was called without proper notice, and that it was packed with suburban supporters of the Government brought into the City for the occasion (supporters

---

[70] John Gorst took a more positive view of the 'real' associations likely to be encouraged by the 1883 Act, see his article 'Elections of the future', *The Fortnightly Review*, 24 (1883), pp. 690–99, esp. pp. 697–9. The article was published just as he bowed out of the 'fourth party' crusade for Tory democracy.   [71] See above chapter 5, p. 112.

[72] Savage, *The dynamics of working class politics,* pp. 138–44; David Feldman, 'The importance of being English: Jewish immigration and the decay of Liberal England', in Feldman and Stedman Jones, *Metropolis: London*, esp. pp. 67–75.

who had previously been used to break up anti-war meetings held elsewhere in the capital).[73] During the tumult of a contested election partisan local newspapers frequently placed great emphasis on their candidate's ability to hold genuinely open public meetings. Any private (or 'ticketed') meetings held by an opponent were said to reflect his lack of popular support (and his lack of 'pluck'), while the disruption of an opponent's meeting was frequently portrayed as evidence of the electors' honest outrage, rather than of organised rowdyism.[74]

Although Gladstone was convinced that in 1878 the jingos use of organised intimidation and violence had prevented the 'true' expression of public feeling, it is clear that the use of physical force remained a central, and widely tolerated, element of popular politics down to the First World War. Moreover, as the widespread disturbances of the 1880 election indicate, these 'politics of disruption' were deployed at least as readily by Liberals as by Conservatives.[75] The physical control of civic space – of public squares, meeting halls, factory gates or polling-day crowds – remained central to the symbolism of political legitimacy for politicians, as much as for their supporters.[76] Writing on the eve of the First World War, Robert Tressell could still portray a Parliamentary by-election as a period of disorder and misrule in which bands of Liberal and Tory working men engaged in bloody battles on the streets of the normally peaceable seaside town of 'Mugsborough'. In Tressell's account, the objective of the rival gangs of partisans is to establish control of the town's Grand Parade long enough to hold an election rally with the fountain as their platform.[77] Joseph Howes' aptly titled book, *Twenty-five years*

---

[73] Gladstone, 'Electoral facts', p. 958–9.

[74] For good examples, see *South Durham and Cleveland Mercury*, 21 September 1900 (the Hartlepools); *Burnely Express and Clitheroe Division Advertiser*, 26 September 1900; *[Wolverhampton] Express and Star*, 27 and 30 April, 1 May 1908.

[75] See Cornelius O'Leary, *The elimination of corrupt practices in British elections*, (Oxford, 1962), pp. 121–4, 132–57; Donald Richter, 'The role of mob riot in Victorian elections, 1865–1885', *Victorian Studies*, 15 (1971), pp. 19–28, esp. p. 22, and his *Riotous Victorians* (Athens, Ohio, 1981), p. 66–8. Richter makes use of William Saunders, *The new Parliament, 1880* (London, 1880). On the Edwardian period, see Clarke, *Lancashire and the New Liberalism*, pp. 137–43, which suggests that disruption was simply a barometer of public opinion by the 1900s.

[76] For useful discussions of the political symbolism of urban space in nineteenth-century Britain see Vernon, *Politics and the people*, esp. pp. 64–70, 208–50, and Anthony Taylor, '"Common stealers", "land-grabbers" and "Jerry-builders": space, popular radicalism and the politics of public access in London, 1848–1880', *International Review of Social History*, 40 (1995), pp. 383–407; see also Jon Lawrence, 'The dynamics of urban politics, 1867–1914', in Lawrence and Taylor (eds.), *Party, state and society*.

[77] Robert Tressell, *The ragged-trousered philanthropists* (Panther ed., London, 1965), pp. 533–4. Having regrouped after an earlier drubbing by the Tories, the Liberal gang are said to have 'swooped down upon the Tory meeting. They overturned the platform, recaptured their torches, tore the enemy's banner to tatters and drove them from their position. Then the Liberals in their turn paraded the streets singing "Has anyone seen a Tory flag?"' (*ibid.*, p. 534).

fight with the Tories, published in 1907, chronicles countless similar examples of the 'politics of disruption', presenting such skirmishes as the basic fare of late Victorian popular politics, rather than as something exceptional.[78] Similarly, in his autobiography *My life's battles*, Will Thorne recalls that in the 1880s 'political fights were usually physical fights between the opposing parties in the constituencies, and in these I was compelled to take part on many occasions'.[79]

Whilst it is true that political meetings were often highly controlled affairs by the late nineteenth century, not least thanks to the frequent use of 'ticketing', hired party stewards and the services of the local constabulary, such control tended to break down at times of great political excitement such as elections. Then meetings ceased to be stage-managed affairs intended solely to boost the morale of party activists and provide good copy for the daily press; they became, instead, the focal point of elaborate, and sometimes bloody, struggles to establish a party's claim to political legitimacy in a constituency. The rational democracy described by Colin Matthew and others thus represented only one facet of Victorian party politics.[80] Indeed if this were not so, it would be difficult to explain why so many Liberal intellectuals had become doubtful about the prospects of reconciling popular government with *efficient* government by the 1880s,[81] or why by the turn of the century so many British Radicals could be heard lamenting the 'irrationalism' and crowd mentality of the emergent mass society.[82] It would also be difficult to understand why political leaders felt obliged to rely so heavily on 'stunts' and crude slogans during elections. Edwardian popular politics were dominated by highly charged political cries such as Chinese slavery, 'We want eight' [dreadnoughts], and, of course, the famous 'big loaf'/'little loaf' of 1906. During elections constituencies were often awash with propaganda of the

[78] Joseph Howes, *Twenty-five years' fight with the Tories* (Morecambe, 1907), A. L. Lowell was convinced little had changed by the Edwardian period, see his *The Government of England*, 2 vols (London, 1908), II, pp. 63–5.

[79] Will Thorne, *My life's battles*, (London, nd [1925]), pp. 43, 54, 201–5.

[80] H. C. G. Matthew, 'Rhetoric and politics in Great Britain, 1860–1950', in P. J. Waller (ed.), *Politics and social change in modern Britain: essays presented to A. F. Thompson*, (Brighton, 1987); also H.C.G. Matthew, R. I. McKibbin and J. A. McKay, 'The franchise factor in the rise of the Labour party', *English Historical Review*, 91 (1976), pp. 723–52, esp. pp. 748–9.

[81] See Christopher Harvie, *The lights of Liberalism: University Liberals and the challenge of democracy, 1860–86* (London, 1976), esp. p. 13, 218–42; John Roach, 'Liberalism and the Victorian intelligentsia', *Cambridge Historical Journal*, 13 (1957), pp. 58–81; Pombeni, 'Starting in reason'; Henry Maine, *Popular government: four essays* (London, 1885). Also Brian Harrison, *Separate spheres: the opposition to women's suffrage in Britain* (London, 1978), pp. 187–8.

[82] See John Hobson, *The psychology of Jingoism* (London, 1901); Graham Wallas, *Human nature in politics* (London, 1908); Ramsay MacDonald, *Socialism and government*, 2 vols. (London, 1909), I, pp. xxvi, 108; II, p. 2; and *Parliament and democracy* (London, 1920), esp. pp. 3–7 and 63–8.

crudest form. Recalling his by-election campaign at Wolverhampton East in 1908, L. S. Amery describes how 'The Imperial Tariff Committee and the Free Trade Union, naturally set up their headquarters in the division, with shop windows displaying dumped foreign goods or revolting illustrations of Germans feeding on horseflesh and black bread.'[83]

V

The main studies of electoral violence in nineteenth-century Britain make little attempt to explain the widespread acceptance of, and frequent connivance in, 'the politics of disruption'. Concerned primarily with delineating long-term trends in the incidence of electoral violence, they tend to treat electoral disturbances, either as outbursts of politics 'from below', or as the result of crude manipulation by unscrupulous members of the political elite, rather than as phenomena which embody the ambiguities inherent in the relationship between 'leaders' and 'led' in the Victorian polity.[84] Cornelius O'Leary undoubtedly exaggerates the decline of political violence by focusing on the sharp reduction in the frequency of election petitions after 1880. Petitions alleging intimidation had always been difficult to sustain (O'Leary himself notes twenty election riots in 1880, only one of which resulted in a petition) – from the mid-1880s they also became prohibitively expensive for all but the most wealthy and determined candidate.[85] O'Leary believes that electoral behaviour changed dramatically in the later nineteenth century, because society as a whole changed – becoming much less tolerant both of bribery and corruption, and of public displays of licence and physical intimidation.[86] And yet as he himself acknowledges, and as many contemporaries observed, there was very little public clamour for the reform of electoral practices during the 1870s and 1880s.[87] Indeed, as late as 1911 an election court judge could lament the large numbers of electors who felt no shame in accepting a bribe.[88] There is little reason to believe that attitudes

---

[83] Amery, *My political life*, I, p. 331.

[84] For the decline in violence, see O'Leary, *Elimination of corrupt practices*, and Vernon, *Politics and the people*, p. 229; for an emphasis on pressure from below, Richter, *Riotous Victorians*, ch. 5, and his 'Role of mob riot'; for elite manipulation, K. T. Hoppen, 'Grammars of electoral violence in nineteenth-century England and Ireland', *English Historical Review*, 109 (1994), pp. 597–620.

[85] O'Leary, *Elimination of corrupt practices*, pp. 121–4; on the cost of petitions, see *ibid.*, p. 202; also Richter, *Riotous Victorians*, p. 67, and Gwyn, *Cost of politics*, pp. 85–7.

[86] See especially, O'Leary, *Elimination of corrupt practices*, pp. 177 and 233.

[87] *Ibid.*, p. 177; see *Blackwood's Edinburgh Magazine*, 134 (1883), pp. 728 and 738; Gwyn, *Cost of politics*, pp. 72 and 77. For a discussion of Mill's fight for 'purity of election' at Westminster in the 1860s, see Pippa Norris, 'John Stuart Mill versus bigotry, bribery and beer', *Corruption and Reform: an International Journal*, 1 (1986), pp. 79–100.

[88] *Controverted Elections (Judgements)* (PP1911, vol. LXI), Nottingham East, December 1910, p. 3. Also Gwyn, *Cost of politics*, p. 77.

towards electoral intimidation had undergone a more thorough sea-change since the 1880s. O'Leary argues that after 1883 '[p]ublic drunken-ness was almost a thing of the past; and likewise organized intimidation' – thanks in part to the growth of the caucus which relied on 'enthusiasm of a disciplined and orderly kind'.[89] This seems misconceived – more formal organisation often simply improved the efficiency with which the 'politics of disruption' could be directed against one's opponents. Just as Gladstone complained of a concerted attempt by jingo politicians to organise the disruption of anti-war meetings in 1878, so Birmingham Tories frequently complained of attempts by Chamberlain's Radical lieutenants to organise violent attacks on their public meetings.[90] In Birmingham under the caucus, even attempts to use 'ticketing' to prevent disruption often failed, as in 1884, when a mass meeting at Aston called to support the Tory position during the stalemate over franchise reform was broken up by thousands of Liberals protesting against a 'Tory picnic being considered an expression of the voice of the Midlands'. The Liberals' principal objection appears to have been that local Tories were trying to pass off a closed, 'ticketed' meeting as a manifestation of the 'public' sentiment of Birmingham and the surrounding districts.[91] In 1901 similar tactics were used by Unionists when Lloyd George visited the city – sandwich men were said to have paraded the streets calling on people to defend the King, the Government and Chamberlain against the 'Brum Boers'.[92] Even after the resulting riot had left one protester dead, and many more injured, the local Unionist press could be found arguing that in defying the mood of the city the Liberals had 'courted the disaster they experienced'.[93]

According to some interpretations, orchestration rendered electoral violence an 'anachronistic and irrelevant aspect of public life' – sustained only by the liberal distribution of free beer and cash, and by the 'irrecover-able personal antagonisms' of participants.[94] This argument, which is echoed in James Vernon's recent emphasis on the 'taming' of popular pol-

---

[89] O'Leary, *Elimination of corrupt practices*, p. 208; see also Hoppen, 'Grammars of electoral violence', p. 620, which attributes a similar role to Parnell and the Irish Nationalist Party in the 'taming' of Irish popular politics; and Vernon, *Politics and the people*, esp. 177–82, 225–9, 336–9.

[90] For instance, see Thomas Wright, *The life of Colonel Fred Burnaby* (London, 1908), p. 236, which alleges that in October 1884 Birmingham Liberals issued a circular stating 'Churchill leaves the Exchange Rooms at 10.30; meet him and greet him', similar allegations are published in *The Times*, 27 October, and 4, 10 November 1884.

[91] *The Times*, 14 October 1884.

[92] *The Times*, 21 December 1901.

[93] *Birmingham Daily Mail*, 19 December 1901, cited in Richard Price, *An imperial war and the British working class: working-class attitudes and reactions to the Boer War, 1899–1902* (London, 1972), p. 142.   [94] Hoppen, 'Grammars of electoral violence', pp. 605–6.

itics, is unhelpful. Rather than dismiss British electoral violence as 'a collusive – even conservative – activity', because of its strong partisanship, and its failure to challenge an elite-dominated political system, we need to understand how politicians were able to mobilise popular enthusiasm at particular moments, and how the demands of popular mobilisation in turn helped to shape both the form and the content of party politics in the constituencies.[95] It may well be that politics were becoming less violent in the later nineteenth century, after all, historians seem more or less agreed that other forms of *public* violence were declining rapidly from the 1870s.[96] More interesting, given these broader societal trends, is the fact that so many politicians continued to connive in the 'politics of disruption', whilst most others seem to have accepted that such controlled displays of intimidation and violence were a natural facet of the 'game' of electoral politics. As we shall see in chapter 9, this was certainly how most pioneers of the labour movement recalled late Victorian elections – much to their disgust, for more often than not they were the victims, not the perpetrators, of the 'politics of disruption'.[97]

The great political excitement surrounding the South African war of 1899–1902, and the controversy caused by the activities of so-called 'pro-Boers' and their opponents, brought the question of political disruption to new prominence. It seems clear that in many districts local Conservatives seized on the jingoistic mood of public opinion to revenge themselves for years of Radical rowdyism and disruption.[98] Across the

[95] *Ibid.*, p. 607. Hoppen's argument hinges on a comparison with the much more ferocious violence of nineteenth-century Irish elections, without ever discussing the political implications of Ireland being a nation under occupation. It should be noted that there *were* English examples of non-partisan electoral violence directed at disrupting the electoral process itself, rather than influencing its outcome; see *Report of the Select Committee on Parliamentary and Municipal Elections (Hours of Polling)*, PP1878, vol. XIII, Q2522 where a representative of the Manchester Working Men's Conservative Association claims that 'respectable' workers of *both* parties dread a (Saint) Monday poll because of the disruption by 'idle drunken fellows'; also Richter, *Riotous Victorians*, p. 68, who characteristically dismisses such incidents as 'outbursts of sheer ebullience'.

[96] See V. A. C. Gatrell, 'The decline of theft and violence in Victorian and Edwardian England', in V. A. C. Gatrell, B. Lenman and G. Parker (eds.), *Crime and the law: the social history of crime in western Europe since 1500* (London, 1980); V. A. C. Gatrell and T. B. Hadden, 'Criminal statistics and their interpretation', in E. A. Wrigley (ed.), *Nineteenth-century society: essays in the use of quantitative methods for the study of social data* (Cambridge, 1972); and David Woods, 'Community violence', in John Benson (ed.), *The working class in England, 1875–1914* (London, 1985), which offers a note of caution by highlighting the hidden nature of much violence, especially within the home.

[97] See George Lansbury, *Looking backwards – and forwards* (London, 1935), pp. 69–70. Will Thorne's, *My life's battles*, is aberrant in this respect. See p. 202 where he recalls taking part in systematic attempts to break up Liberal meetings at West Ham during the 1890s in order to frustrate Liberal plans to bring out a candidate against Hardie.

[98] This happened even in radical Northampton, home of Bradlaugh and Labouchere, see Price, *An imperial war*, pp. 147–8.

country peace meetings were broken up, and prominent anti-war activists became the targets of great hostility. In the spring of 1900 the Liberals forced a debate on the matter in the House of Commons. Sir Robert Threshie Reid produced a catalogue of attacks on opponents of the war, including a number of cases where suspected 'pro-Boers' and their families had been attacked and injured by angry 'mobs'.[99] Whilst only one Conservative MP actually claimed to be 'delighted at this exhibition of feeling', many pointed out that Radicals were simply being repaid in kind for years of rowdy disruption.[100] William Redmond, speaking for the Irish Nationalists, echoed this sentiment arguing 'I should be the last person in the world to complain myself or sympathise with Liberal members who complain of the storming of an election meeting and the taking of the platform. I think that is one of the most interesting features of electioneering.'[101] If elections were reformed, argued Redmond, 'political life would have lost much of its charm'. Clearly in Redmond's mind election 'rows' were quite legitimate, but wanton attacks on private meetings, and assaults on individuals and their families in their homes most definitely were not. Campbell-Bannerman, summing up for the Liberals, largely accepted this position, since he too focused on the right of individuals to hold *private* meetings to discuss their views, however unpopular they might be. He seems to have accepted that *public* meetings would be liable to disruption, just as election meetings often were. Interestingly, Campbell-Bannerman suggested that in this respect English custom differed markedly from Scottish, since he suggested that, 'during the excitement of a general election ... meetings are, I believe, in this country, not in mine, broken up by both sides'.[102]

Perhaps significantly, although George Lansbury was active in east end politics for over half a century, his recollections of political disruption mainly relate to his early days as a Radical activist in Bow during the 1880s. They neatly capture the flavour of the 'politics of disruption' at this time. Lansbury recalls how party activists organised the disruption of Tory meetings in the locality, and how they were able to thwart their opponents attempts at retaliation by hiring local 'heavies' to defend Liberal speakers and to despatch hecklers.[103] Examples of the 'politics of disruption' which presumably presented few problems for the well-to-do

---

[99] *Parliamentary Debates*, 4th ser., LXXX (1900), cols. 940–986, 'Right of free speech: disturbances directed against opponents of the war in South Africa'. Reid lists twenty-nine disturbances, including serious rioting at Scarborough, Stratford, and Midhurst. Industrial districts mentioned include Sheffield, West Bromwich, Northampton, Gateshead, Glasgow, Dundee, Derby and parts of east and south-east London (cols. 941–4).   [100] *Ibid.*, cols. 959 (Balfour); 968–9 (Bartley); 971 (Coghill).
[101] *Ibid.*, col. 973.   [102] *Ibid.*, cols 978–80.
[103] For instance, George Lansbury, *My life* (London, 1928), pp. 85 and 89.

patrons of Bow Liberalism. But Lansbury also recalls how, during the early 1880s, East End Radical and Irish activists turned this strategy against their own Liberal MP in protest at his support for the Government's policy of coercion in Ireland. At a meeting attended by what he terms 'a whole crowd of notabilities' he describes how

> a small crowd on one side of the hall rose and, to the music and words of *God Save Ireland*, marched as one man to the platform, picking up on their way Fanny Parnell and holding her aloft, just brushed Buxton, Bryce and their friends off the platform. No one was hit, no one was hurt; all that happened was that a group of earnest men and women had refused to hear a defence of coercion and persecution in Ireland.[104]

Far from suggesting a 'simple love of disorder', or 'irrecoverable personal antagonisms', this incident suggests a highly controlled and purposive use of physical force, which relied for its effect on the ability of Radical activists to appropriate the practices of party political conflict for other ends. In other words, far from being an 'anachronistic and irrelevant aspect of public life', the stylized repertoire of election violence and intimidation could be used to legitimate genuinely radical and subversive forms of popular politics.[105] Interestingly, Hoppen cites William Albery's study of Horsham to help establish his claim that English election mobs largely consisted of 'toughs hired for the day',[106] but even in this ancient Sussex town electoral violence could be highly purposive – as when anti-temperance Liberals prevented a potential Liberal candidate, brought to the town by the local branch of the United Kingdom Alliance, from addressing a meeting intended to promote his candidacy.[107]

It would, however, be wrong to imply that attempts to appropriate the politics of disruption went unchallenged. Indeed during the late nineteenth century there were a number of high-profile confrontations over the right to free speech and public meeting which can be read as attempts to delineate 'legitimate' from 'illegitimate' manifestations of public

---

[104] *Ibid.*, p. 86. *The Times*, 25 January 1882 describes a similar incident involving the disruption of a meeting held by Bryce at the Bow and Bromley Institute, though it suggests that only a small minority of Irish militants were involved.

[105] Quotations from Richter, *Riotous Victorians*, p. 165, and Hoppen, 'Grammars of electoral violence', p. 605.

[106] Hoppen, 'Grammars of electoral violence', p. 606, he notes that at Horsham party strife 'seems largely to have been sustained by artificial respiration involving the transmission of large amounts of oxygenating cash', citing Albery, *Parliamentary history*, pp. 330–491.

[107] Albery, *Parliamentary history*, p. 454; there are echoes here of the 'Skeleton Army' attacks on the early Salvation Army, see Victor Bailey, 'Salvation Army riots, the "Skeleton Army" and legal authority in the provincial town', in A. P. Donajgrodzki (ed.), *Social control in nineteenth-century Britain* (London, 1977). The 'legitimation' of popular violence by magistrates and others in authority is noted, but seen simply as a facet of 'social control'.

opinion. Such struggles had long been a feature of London popular politics,[108] and in the mid-1880s the metropolitan police went to great lengths to curtail the right of socialist agitators, and their libertarian supporters, from holding political meetings in public places such as Dodd Street in the East End, and most controversially, Trafalgar Square in the West End.[109] But even here one needs to be careful about assuming any simple model of elite control. Both in 1885 and 1887 it seems that the initiative for controlling spontaneous manifestations of 'the politics of civic space' came, not from party politicians, but from the police themselves – apparently in response to pressure from local ratepayers. Indeed it is noticeable that the Home Office, under first Cross and later Matthews, was decidedly reluctant to give the police full backing in their attempts to stop the socialist gatherings – primarily because of its greater sensitivity to issues of free speech and the right to public meeting.[110] And at the trial of Burns and Cunninghame-Graham, the Attorney-General went out of his way to stress that the right to public meeting was not in question, only the right to hold meetings anywhere one liked – though in itself this undoubtedly marked a significant limitation to the boundaries of popular politics.[111] It is certainly difficult not to conclude that the police felt themselves empowered to take a firm line against political disturbances which were 'unauthorised' and radical, whilst often proving remarkably tolerant of 'traditional' forms of disturbance associated with elections, party politics, and the antics of privileged students.[112]

VI

If physical force, and the threat of physical force, was an ever present feature of popular politics before the First World War, this was in part because professional politicians were frequently mythologised for their acts of bravery and strength in facing down the 'politics of disruption'.

[108] See Taylor, '"Common stealers"'.
[109] See Richter, *Riotous Victorians*, pp. 95–7 and 133–62; for Radical/SDF cooperation at this time, see F. W. Soutter, *Recollections of a labour pioneer* (London, 1923), pp. 128–56. For general context see Judith Walkowitz, *City of dreadful delight: narratives of sexual danger in late Victorian Britain* (London, 1992), chs. 1 and 2.   [110] See *ibid.*, pp. 97–8 and 159.
[111] *The Times*, 17 January 1888, the Attorney General stressed the statutory right to hold meetings in the capital's four great public parks: Battersea Park, Victoria Park, Regent's Park and Hyde Park – and argued that the Trafalgar Square demonstration should therefore have been diverted to one of these locations once the police voiced their fears about public order; also Richter, *Riotous Victorians*, p. 153.
[112] See Gilbert McAllister, *James Maxton: the portrait of a rebel* (London, 1935), pp. 6–8, on the reluctance of Glasgow police to intervene in battles between Liberal and Tory students; or Stewart, *J. Keir Hardie*, pp. 254 and 256, and John Hodges, *My adventures as a Labour leader* (London, nd [1924]), p. 30 on Hardie as the victim of 'ragging' by Oxbridge students.

Colonel Fred Burnaby, the famous soldier and adventurer, was the subject of particularly colourful myth-making after he was killed in action on the expedition to relieve Gordon at Khartoum. A strong Conservative and imperialist he had fought Chamberlain and the Liberal caucus at Birmingham during the 1880 General Election – a pretty hopeless prospect. Subsequent biographies draw little distinction between his super-human feats on the field of battle and his exploits as a Parliamentary candidate. For instance a study of his life published in 1908 tells of him silencing two hecklers at a difficult meeting in Wolverhampton by leaning over the platform and pulling them out of the audience – one on each arm. According to the account, he 'carried them so suspended to the back of the platform. Depositing one in a chair, he said, "You sit there, little man!", and then carrying the other, still at the end of his extended arm, three yards further, he dropped him into another chair with "and you sit there, little man".'[113] At another meeting, this time in Leicester, he is described sorting out a disruptive 'party of roughs' at the back of the hall by leaping into the audience in order to confront the ringleader. We are told that, 'singling out his man he [Burnaby] ploughed his way through the crowd and felled him with a terrific blow'. As a general fight developed, Burnaby is described 'revelling in the melée, [he] struck out right and left – and every man who came within reach of his terrible fist fell sprawling – so that in a minute or two there was a clear space of six or seven feet around him.'[114] Now these accounts of Burnaby's exploits may of course be no more than late Victorian equivalents of the urban myth – but, if so, this would simply strengthen the point that, down to the First World War, popular politics were routinely *represented* through a language which glorified the exploits of the male hero who was able to quell, even 'civilize' the mob (this was the reassuring side of the story for well-to-do readers). Thus at another point in the Burnaby story we are told how our hero won the hearts of a 'seething' and hostile mob simply by showing he had no fear of them.[115] Violence itself was not 'manly' by this code – only when 'provoked' (a much used and slippery concept) was a man right to defend his person, and his 'honour' by force. Thus John Wilson, the Durham miners' leader, recalls the 'unmanly acts'

---

[113] Wright, *Life of Burnaby*, pp. 163–4.
[114] *Ibid.*, p. 164, there are similarly colourful accounts of his clashes with Birmingham Liberalism in the early 1880s, see pp. 167, 236, 239–40.
[115] *Ibid.*, p. 239. Again the parallel with standard Victorian and Edwardian accounts of heroic imperialists subduing native peoples is striking. Masculinity is discussed in the latter context in Catherine Hall, *White, male and middle class: explorations in Feminism and history* (Cambridge, 1992), ch. 10, and John Tosh, 'What should historians do with masculinity? Reflections on nineteenth-century Britain', *History Workshop Journal*, 38 (1994), pp. 179–202.

of hired roughs brought into North Durham in 1874 to disrupt polling, but he is much more understanding of the violent reaction of local Liberal working men, commenting that the Tories 'had called into operation a power they could not allay'.[116] Similarly, at Southwark West in 1900, the Unionist press denounced local 'roughs' for 'supplementing legitimate criticism of free speech with brutal violence' at an election rally. After a motion had been passed to expel a group of hecklers, Harry Newton, the Tory candidate's son, apparently 'carried the ringleader out in his arms by main force'. But if this was legitimate 'manly force' according to the *South London Observer*, the subsequent attack on Newton by half a dozen 'roughs' most definitely was not. By outnumbering Newton, and by fighting 'dirty' (they pushed his head through a glass door), the 'roughs' asserted an alien code of masculinity which was unequivocally denounced by the paper as 'brutal' and 'unmanly'.[117] But if elaborate codes surrounded, and to some extent circumscribed, male electoral violence, it remains clear that before the First World War popular politics were inextricably linked with definitions of 'manliness' which stressed physical strength and bravery.[118]

When 'suffragette' protesters began disrupting political meetings in the 1900s they were thus consciously appropriating the rituals of (male) popular politics to highlight their own exclusion from political power. Rather than accept their allotted role of 'decorating' the platform at ticketed meetings, suffragettes sought to exploit the 'politics of disruption' to force their cause onto a political agenda dominated by male concerns. Annie Kenney recalls how Liberal stewards used considerable force to prevent her and Christabel Pankhurst from asking questions of ministers at the General Election in 1905/6.[119] Sympathetic accounts describe women protesters being attacked by members of the audience, and even indecently assaulted, whenever they tried to use the high-profile, but far from revolutionary tactic, of demanding the right to put questions from the floor at public meetings.[120] Attempts to organise rival 'indignation

---

[116] John Wilson, *Memories of a labour leader* (Caliban edn, Firle, 1980), pp. 231–5.
[117] *South London Observer*, 30 October 1900; for other good examples of the elaborate and varied codes of behaviour which surrounded the 'politics of disruption', see Howes, *Twenty-five years fight*, pp. 216–17, 232–4, 267, 302–3.
[118] For useful discussions of these codes, see Michael Roper and John Tosh, *Manful assertions: masculinities in Britain since 1800* (London, 1991), esp. intro., and Tosh, 'What should historians do with masculinity'; see also J. A. Mangan and James Walvin (eds.), *Manliness and morality: middle-class masculinity in Britain and America, 1800–1940* (Manchester, 1987).
[119] Annie Kenney, *Memories of a militant* (London, 1924), pp. 35, 47–8.
[120] Many commentators noted that disturbances at meetings usually derived from the platform's refusal to accept questions from the floor, and excessively aggressive stewarding, see Lansbury, *Looking backwards*, p. 69.

meetings' were often treated no less brutally by opponents of the suffrage.[121] Women thus found that the traditional political tactics of disruption and mass protest were effectively denied them by the willingness of their opponents to use physical violence. This was in part because violence was still integral to English popular politics, as the early socialists had frequently discovered to their cost, but also because the case against women's suffrage still drew on the argument that citizenship rights were derived from the ability to bear arms in defence of the state. Some went further, arguing that majorities could only legislate over minorities because they reserved the right physically to coerce that minority.[122] In these circumstances, it is perhaps not surprising that suffragette biographies frequently recall having to rely on male sympathisers, often socialist working-men, to provide physical protection at public meetings.[123] Nor is it surprising that the 'militants' increasingly shifted away from the politics of disruption and mass protest after 1909 – more individualist forms of protest such as stone-throwing had the advantage of swift arrest.[124] However, they also represented a retreat from the earlier tactic of challenging male dominance of public political space head-on.[125]

Interestingly, much was done to de-legitimize the role of violence in politics after the First World War. Politicians went to great lengths to denounce the 'macho' face of public politics, and to deny that it could bestow legitimacy on a political party. The disruption of meetings, battles to raise the party colours, intimidation by aggressive crowds all continued, but they were now more universally demonised in mainstream party politics.[126] Three main factors may lie behind this apparent shift in the character of British politics. Firstly, it seems likely that the desire to de-

[121] See A. E. Metcalfe, *Woman's effort: a chronicle of British women's fifty years struggle for citizenship, 1865–1914* (Oxford, 1917), pp. 24, 51–2, 81–2, 135; Hannah Mitchell, *The hard way up: the autobiography of Hannah Mitchell, suffragette and rebel* (Virago edn, London, 1977), pp. 136–57; Lisa Tickner, *The spectacle of women: imagery of the suffrage campaign, 1907–14* (London, 1987), pp. 144–5.

[122] See Harrison, *Separate spheres*, pp. 73–8, 114–15.

[123] E.g. Mitchell, *The hard way up*, pp. 138, 151–7; Metcalfe, *Women's effort*, pp. 52, 135, 166; Tickner, *The spectacle of women*, p. 145.

[124] See Constance Rover, *Women's suffrage and party politics in Britain, 1866–1914* (London, 1967), pp. 80–1; Andrew Rosen, *'Rise up women! The militant campaign of the Women's Social and Political Union, 1903–1914* (London, 1974), pp. 142 and 165; Sandra Stanley Holton, *Feminism and democracy: women's suffrage and reform politics in Britain, 1900–1918* (Cambridge, 1986), pp. 47–8; Harrison, *Separate spheres*, pp. 187–8.

[125] These ideas are explored more fully in Jon Lawrence, 'Contesting the male polity: the suffragettes and the politics of disruption', in Amanda Vickery (ed.), *Women's privilege, women's rights* (forthcoming, Univ. of Stanford Press).

[126] Though see Henry Snell, *Men, movements and myself* (London, 1938), p. 205 where he recalls how Captain Robert Gee, war-hero and victor over MacDonald at the famous Woolwich East by-election of 1921, 'was always ready to challenge any one who corrected or interrupted him to come upon the platform to fight'.

legitimise political violence was part of a much broader desire to restabilise society after the traumas of war, and to purge public life of 'masculinist fantasies'. The sheer scale and brutality of the Great War led many to fear that civil society itself might have been irrevocably brutalised – and the social upheavals of 1919–1920 did little to quell such fears.[127] Secondly, the growth of far Right and far Left politics, both on the continent and at home, seemed to many to underline the dangers of war producing a brutalised polity. As 'the politics of disruption' came to be seen as the special tactic of fascist and communist groups, so they increasingly became unavailable to mainstream politicians (though this argument must certainly be qualified given the Tories' apparent willingness to use British 'Fascisti' as stewards in the late 1920s).[128] Rhetorical opposition to intimidation was more vocal than ever – Conservatives regularly denounced Labour as a party of macho 'bully-boys' determined to debase the character of British politics,[129] while Labour, in turn, had long presented itself as the one party committed to creating a rational, educated electorate, rather than simply appealing to voters' lowest instincts.[130] Finally, there was also the influence of partial female enfranchisement in 1918. The political parties were very unsure how to address the new female electorate, and decidedly fearful of how it might vote.[131] Many felt that electoral politics would have to be 'feminised', either to avoid alienating the new voters, or to make it possible to brand one's opponents as macho and aggressive.

However, I do not wish simply to push forward the timing of the 'triumph of party' to after the First World War. There were significant changes after 1918 – not least the much more concerted attempt to delegitimise the political crowd, but also the new scope for political parties to operate as mediators between an enlarged state and a changed (and enlarged) electorate. But it remains doubtful whether such a strongly teleological concept as the 'triumph of party' could be helpful even for

---

[127] Susan Kingsley Kent, *Making peace: the reconstruction of gender in inter-war Britain* (Princeton, New Jersey, 1993); Sandra Gilbert, 'Soldier's heart: literary men, literary women, and the Great War', in Margaret Higonnet et al. (eds.), *Behind the lines: gender and the two world wars* (New Haven, 1987).

[128] I am indebted to David Jarvis of Emmanuel College, Cambridge for this information.

[129] See David Jarvis, 'Mrs Maggs and Betty: the Conservative appeal to women voters in the 1920s', *Twentieth-Century British History*, 5 (1994), pp. 129–52.

[130] See below, chapter 9; also Bernard Barker, 'The anatomy of reformism: the social and political ideas of the Labour leadership in Yorkshire', *International Review of Social History*, 18 (1973), pp. 1–27.

[131] See Martin Pugh, *Women and the women's movement in Britain, 1914–1959* (Basingstoke, 1992), chs. 5 and 6; David Jarvis, 'British Conservatism and class politics in the 1920s', *English Historical Review*, 111 (1996), pp. 59–84, and 'The shaping of the Conservative electoral hegemony, 1918–39', in Lawrence and Taylor (eds.), *Party, state and society*.

this later period. For the years before the First World War, where the concept is usually short-hand for the demise of popular politics and the unproblematic 'socialization' of the new electors, it must be judged profoundly unhelpful. These were years of great trial and tribulation for Britain's political parties – none was at ease with the emerging 'mass democracy', least of all the fledgling Labour party, which foresaw a polity blighted by mass apathy and ignorance. Many Liberal and Conservative politicians were no less pessimistic, but their great fear was that rational self-interest must eventually triumph among the new propertyless electors, and that when it did they would inevitably use their political power to overthrow the rights and privileges of the propertied. Democracy, they argued, must mean socialism unless the established political parties could act decisively to construct an alternative politics which could appeal to workers' material interests. Misplaced or not, this was the logic which lay behind the increasingly programmatic character of Edwardian party politics as both Liberal and Conservative politicians sought to devise ways of boosting government revenue in order to fund state social legislation.[132] The following chapters examine the 'tribulations of party' in greater detail – focusing first on the fortunes of the Liberals in the wake of the Home Rule split of 1886, and then on the problems faced by Labour as it sought to assert its claim to be the 'real' people's party prior to the First World War.

[132] See Clarke, *Lancashire and the New Liberalism*, esp. pp. 153–97 and 343–64; and *Liberals and social democrats* (Cambridge, 1980). On the difficulties which beset Conservative attempts to develop an advanced social programme, see especially E. H. H. Green, *The crisis of Conservatism: the politics, economics and ideology of the British Conservative party, 1880–1914* (London, 1995), and 'Radical Conservatism: the electoral genesis of tariff reform', *Historical Journal*, 28 (1986), pp. 667–92; Avner Offer, *Property and politics, 1870–1914: landownership, law, ideology and urban development in England* (Cambridge, 1981), esp. part V; and Jane Ridley, 'The Unionist Social Reform Committee 1911–1914: wets before the deluge', *Historical Journal*, 30 (1987), pp. 391–413.

8 The fall and rise of popular Liberalism, 1886–1906

I

This chapter re-examines a familiar subject: the precipitate decline and eventual recovery of popular Liberalism between the Home Rule crisis of 1886 and the landslide electoral victory of 1906. The aim is not to retrace the pre-history of 'New Liberalism', but to study the Liberals' 'wilderness years' for their own sake. How did the party respond to electoral and ministerial failure, and how did these failures impact upon semi-detached sections of the Liberal coalition such as metropolitan Radicals and organised labour? In essence it is argued that the political defeats of these years proved decisive, not only to the growth of independent Labour politics, but also to shaping the whole political outlook of the socialist and Radical left before 1914.

The chapter begins by reiterating the argument that the great Liberal schism of 1886 helped Conservatives to demonize their political opponents as no more than a sectarian, 'faddist'-dominated rump. Under the influence of political nonconformity, it was argued, the Liberals had turned their backs on the tolerant, freedom-loving traditions of their past in favour of the harsher instincts of the moral reformer. There is no doubt that the political voice of nonconformity was at its most strident in these years, but despite this even the nonconformist electorate seems to have wavered in its support for Liberalism at the polls.[1] By the early 1890s there were clear signs of a revolt against the nonconformist moral agenda from within the Liberal party, but there were also signs of a growing pessimism about the prospects for democracy in Britain. Many interpreted the ascendency of jingoism and Toryism as confirmation of the inherently 'irrational' character of the mass electorate. The disappointments of the minority Liberal Government of 1892–95, and the crushing rejection of 'Newcastle' style politics by the electorate at the subsequent General

---

[1] See D. W. Bebbington, *The nonconformist conscience: Chapel and politics, 1870–1914* (London, 1982), and 'Nonconformity and electoral sociology, 1867–1918', *Historical Journal*, 27 (1984), pp. 633–56.

Election greatly reinforced these sentiments. Indeed, it is argued that in many respects the nadir of Liberal fortunes came in 1895, rather than in 1886, or even 1900. Moreover, it was responses to this defeat, especially within the labour movement, which did most to shape the character of Edwardian 'Progressivism'. Many on the left came to believe that a progressive popular politics needed to be anchored in the organisational strength and rational aspirations of the labour movement. This was especially true within socialist groupings such as the ILP, where the leadership, if not necessarily the membership, came to believe that a combination of an electoral alliance with trade unionism and state socialism offered the best prospect for educating workers out of jingoism and Toryism. These themes are explored more fully in chapter nine, here more attention is devoted to explaining why Liberals drew the same lessons more slowly and fittingly after 1895. Newcastle style 'programme' politics might have been rejected after the 1895 debâcle, but there was little sign of any systematic attempt to redefine the party's relationship with organised labour until after the 1900 election, and little interest in the prospects of using state-directed social and economic reforms to 'rationalise' the mass electorate until after 1906. By then it was clear that the Liberal and Labour parties were following distinct, if for the moment inter-locked, political trajectories. Labour's aspirations had been born out of the political failures of the preceding two decades, but it was far from clear that they could now be satisfied by the political triumphs of Edwardian 'Progressivism'.

II

As Henry Broadhurst, the Lib–Lab MP and Gladstonian loyalist observed, when the Liberal party split over Home Rule for Ireland in 1886 'few Liberals realised how cohesive would prove the elements of Toryism and Dissenting Liberalism which went to make up the new Unionist Party'.[2] Faith in Gladstone's moral judgement, and anxiety about the prospects of a revitalised Conservatism helped to ensure that, whatever their private views on the Irish question, most rank and file Liberals remained loyal to 'the cause' in the difficult election of 1886.[3] Discussing the party crisis which lead him to abandon his Birmingham seat to fight a Liberal defector at Nottingham, Broadhurst recalls that 'I never wavered

[2] Henry Broadhurst, *Henry Broadhurst MP: the story of his life from a stonemason's bench to the Treasury Bench told by himself* (London, 1901), p. 207.
[3] See Graham Goodlad, 'Gladstone and his rivals: popular Liberal perceptions of the party leadership in the political crisis of 1885–1886', in Eugenio Biagini and Alastair Reid (eds.), *Currents of Radicalism: popular radicalism, organised labour and party politics in Britain, 1850–1914* (Cambridge, 1991).

for a moment in what I considered my duty – loyalty to the great leader of the Liberal party'.[4] At the same time, more semi-detached sections of Radical-Liberal opinion, such as *Reynolds's Newspaper*, chose to forget their profound frustrations with the Liberal Government of 1880–85, as they threw themselves wholeheartedly into the 'Gladstonian' crusade for Home Rule.[5]

Though resoundingly beaten by the combined forces of Unionism, it would be wrong to present 1886 as an electoral (as opposed to a political) disaster for the Liberals. In many constituencies Unionism had won by default. In part this was because Gladstonian loyalists hoped that by avoiding a contest they might avoid deepening the schism in party ranks, leaving the way open for a dissenting MP to return to the fold. Indeed sometimes, as at Wolverhampton South, local Liberals insisted that despite their MP's break with Gladstone over Home Rule, they still considered him to be a *bona fide* Liberal.[6] In all, the Conservatives recorded a net gain of sixty-six seats, accounted for largely by the great turnover of seats in England.[7] In addition Liberal Unionists won a total of seventy-nine seats (more than a third unopposed) – giving the combined Unionist parties an overall majority of sixty.[8] It is hardly surprising, therefore, that James Cornford should find that the diverging fortunes of Liberalism in different regions after 1886 owed much to the relative strength or weakness of Liberal Unionism in each area.[9] An analysis of election results for English single-member boroughs shows that the average Liberal vote fell from 47.2 per cent in 1885, to 46.5 per cent across the four elections of 1886, 1892, 1895 and 1900.[10] However, this modest decline rather understates the impact of schism on the party since in 1885 the Liberals had left only one English borough seat uncontested, whereas at the subsequent four General Elections on average the party left thirty-three seats uncon-

---

[4] Broadhurst, *Story of his life*, p. 198.
[5] *Reynolds's Newspaper*, 20 June and 4 July 1886, see also above, chapter 7, pp. 171–3.
[6] Many Wolverhampton activists maintained this fiction into the 1890s, even though Villiers, their 'Liberal' MP was frequently paired with Gladstone at divisions.
[7] The party made a net gain of just three seats in Ireland, Scotland and Wales combined, Michael Kinnear, *The British voter: an atlas and survey since 1885* (2nd edn, Tiptree, 1981), pp. 13–17.
[8] *Ibid.*, p. 17. On their own the Conservatives were thus twenty seats short of an overall majority.
[9] See James Cornford, 'Aggregate election data and British party alignments, 1885–1910', in E. Allardt and S. Rokkan (eds.), *Mass politics: studies in political sociology* (New York, 1970), pp. 108–9.
[10] For details of this data-set, see Jon Lawrence and Jane Elliott, 'Parliamentary election results reconsidered: an analysis of borough elections, 1885–1910', *Parliamentary History*, 16, 1 (1997), [E. H. H. Green (ed.), *An age of transition*], pp. 18–28; here the analysis makes no allowance for the changing number of uncontested seats, or for the intervention of third-party candidates.

tested.[11] If one compares seats fought by the Liberals both in 1885 and in 1900, the party vote fell more sharply, from 50.3 per cent in 1885 to just 43.7 per cent fifteen years later.[12]

As these findings might suggest, the decline of constituency organisation certainly played its part in Liberal difficulties. In some areas the defection of wealthy patrons exposed the extent to which, even after the Corrupt Practices Act of 1883, money had been essential to the smooth workings of the party machine. Even where radical enthusiasm had been enough to capture a seat from the Unionists in 1886, the local party often experienced serious decline in subsequent years. As we have seen, this was the case in Sir William Plowden's seat of Wolverhampton West, it was also Broadhurst's experience at Nottingham West, where the local mine-owner and Liberal defector Colonel Seely transformed a minority of 849 in 1886 into a majority of 301 at the subsequent election.[13] In all, the Liberals lost eleven seats in the English boroughs at the 1892 election, and their percentage vote fell in thirty-five of the 140 single-member seats contested in both 1886 and 1892.[14] But to understand the mixed fortunes of English Liberalism in this period we need to look beyond questions of organisation, important though these undoubtedly were, to focus directly on the political appeals of Unionism and Liberalism. After all, even if one accepts that political defections often played a significant part in Liberal decline, one must still explain why these were so much more frequent in some areas than in others.

III

Privately many Unionist leaders undoubtedly remained fearful of democracy and anxious about the prospects for economy and Empire,[15] but this did not translate itself into the adversarial world of party propaganda. On the contrary, buoyed by the disarray of their opponents over Home Rule, Unionist propaganda appeared confident, even strident, in its condemna-

[11] T. P. O'Connor, the Irish Nationalist, was left unopposed at Liverpool Scotland at all five elections.

[12] In all 122 single-member English boroughs had a contest involving a Liberal (or Lib-Lab) at both elections.

[13] Broadhurst, *Story of his life*, p. 241. Broadhurst described the local Liberal organisation as wanting cohesion and 'greatly inferior' to 1886, he also claimed registration work had been neglected since the previous election.

[14] This includes two losses to independent Labour candidates who subsequently accepted the Liberal Whip (Burns and Wilson). Other notable losses included Walsall and Wednesbury in the west Midlands, and Stockton-on-Tees and Newcastle (one seat) in the north-east.

[15] See especially, E. H. H. Green, *The crisis of Conservatism: the politics, economics and ideology of the British Conservative party, 1880–1914* (London, 1995).

tion of the Gladstonian enemy, and in its celebration of the patriotic good sense of the English voter. As I have discussed elsewhere, the Unionist critique of 'Gladstonianism' involved three key inter-locking elements: firstly, the charge that, thanks in large part to the innovation of 'caucus' organisation, the Liberal party had been hijacked by nonconformist 'faddists'; secondly, the charge that as a result, instead of championing the people's liberties, Liberalism increasingly wished to reform their habits; and thirdly, the charge that Liberal 'faddists' placed party interests and their own moral sensibilities above the national interest in foreign and imperial affairs.[16] At heart, therefore, Unionist politics represented a rejection of the influence of militant nonconformity in British party politics. In effect, Unionists charged their opponents with wishing to construct a 'nonconformist state' where the 'pleasures of the people' (and especially of 'honest working *men*') would be strictly regulated, and the commercial and imperial interests of the country neglected.

Given the nature of the Unionist appeal it would seem reasonable to assume that Liberalism would prove most resilient in areas of nonconformist strength. In practice this is a very difficult proposition to test, not least because of the difficulty of obtaining robust data on denominational allegiance at a constituency level.[17] Using Michael Kinnear's data on the distribution of nonconformists in 1922 for those constituencies where boundary changes did not make comparison impossible, it was decided to investigate the relationship between Liberal partisanship and nonconformity in the English boroughs.[18] Looking only at constituencies fought at each election between 1885 and 1900, the first striking finding was that out of the twenty constituencies where under 6 per cent of the population appear to have been active nonconformists, only four actually saw contests at each election. In other words, where nonconformity was particularly weak the Liberals frequently failed to mount a consistent electoral challenge between 1885 and 1900.[19] There is also evidence of a positive relationship between high levels of nonconformity and Liberal voting, both in 1885, and in the four elections fought after the Home Rule split. However, whilst in 1885 the relationship is statistically significant,

[16] Jon Lawrence, 'Class and gender in the making of urban Toryism, 1880–1914', *English Historical Review*, 108 (1993), p. 635.
[17] And the difficulties of then interpreting such data, see Hugh McLeod, *Religion and the working class in nineteenth-century Britain* (London, 1984), pp. 13–16,, also Robert Moore, *Pit-men, preachers and politics: the effects of Methodism in a Durham mining community* (Cambridge, 1974), pp. 69 and 240.   [18] Kinnear, *British voter*, pp. 125–9.
[19] The Liberals fought 45 per cent of the borough constituencies with over 6 per cent nonconformists at every election between 1885 and 1900, but only 20 per cent of those with under 6 per cent nonconformists.

this is not so when taking the elections of 1886–1900 *en bloc*.[20] Moreover, if one looks only at the relationship between *change* in the Liberal vote after 1885 and nonconformity, one finds, perhaps unexpectedly, that the Liberal vote fell more sharply in the more strongly nonconformist seats.[21] Given the nature of data involved, and the small number of seats fought at every election, one needs to be cautious when interpreting these findings, but they clearly offer little support to the hypothesis that strong nonconformity insulated the Liberal vote against erosion in the wake of the Home Rule split. But then as D. W. Bebbington has argued, some nonconformist communities were drawn to Unionism after 1886 because anti-Catholic traditions remained extremely powerful – the nonconformist vote was by no means monolithic.[22]

Perhaps equally surprising is the fact that Unionist political ascendancy does not appear to have relied simply upon low turnout, Liberal abstentions and manipulation of the electoral register.[23] Outside the south-east of England, turnout varied little between Conservative and Liberal won seats, except in 1886, when Conservative seats registered a higher turnout, and 1906, when Liberal seats did so. Except in 1900, turnout was also broadly comparable in seats won by the two parties in the south-east, but in the 'khaki' election of that year Conservative-won seats registered an average turnout of just 64.8 per cent, while in Liberal-won seats the figure was 73.8 per cent.[24] However, even in the 'khaki' election the story is complicated by the fact that the fall in voter turnout appears to have been concentrated in constituencies which were already Conservative in 1885. There is also little evidence that Conservative electoral success was

---

[20] Given the nature of the data it was decided to divide the sample into two groups at the median value for nonconformity (9.3 per cent). The data were analysed using SPSS; employing the pooled variance estimate for the t statistic, Student's t was calculated to have a value of −2.94 (with an associated significance of 0.005) for nonconformity against Liberal vote in 1885, and a value of −1.81 (0.075 significance) for nonconformity against Liberal vote 1886–1900 inclusive.

[21] The Liberal vote fell on average by 1.7 per cent in constituencies with lower levels of nonconformity, and by 4.2 per cent in the group with higher levels. Employing the pooled variance estimate, Student's t was calculated to have a value of −2.12 (with an associated significance of 0.038).

[22] Bebbington, 'Nonconformity and electoral sociology', pp. 648–52.

[23] See James Cornford, 'The transformation of Conservatism in the late nineteenth century', *Victorian Studies*, 7 (1963), pp. 35–66; and 'The adoption of mass organisation by the British Conservative party', in E. Allardt and Y. Litlunen (eds.), *Cleavages, ideologies and party systems: contributions to comparative political sociology* (Helsinki, 1964); P. Marsh, *The discipline of popular government: Lord Salisbury's domestic statecraft, 1881–1902* (Hassocks, 1978), and E. H. H. Green, 'Radical Conservatism: the electoral genesis of tariff reform', *Historical Journal*, 28 (1985), pp. 667–92.

[24] See Lawrence and Elliott, 'Parliamentary election results', pp. 22–4 and table 2. The findings refer only to single-member borough constituencies.

linked to neglect of the electoral register, and hence lower levels of enfranchisement, in 'working-class' seats (broadly defined).[25] Taken together these findings tend to suggest that organisational weakness was more a consequence, than a cause, of the Liberal malaise after 1886.

All this begs the obvious question: why did the Liberals prove so inept at countering the Unionist case in the late 1880s and 1890s, and why did their fortunes improve so dramatically in later years? One simple, if not especially illuminating, answer must be that many Liberal leaders, both national and local, believed passionately in the policies which their critics sought to demonise as the blueprint for a 'nonconformist' state. In addition, many Liberals of a less fundamentalist temperament accepted that they could hardly ignore the widespread demand from within their party for policies such as local option (i.e. liquor controls) or disestablishment of the Church in Wales. Even so, by the late 1880s, when prospects of Liberal union had been dashed, there were already many within the party voicing doubts about 'the future of Liberalism', and registering their disquiet at the increasingly sectarian nature of the party's programme. In 1889, L. A. Atherley-Jones, Liberal MP for the mining seat of Durham North-West and son of the Chartist leader Ernest Jones, began an early discussion of 'new Liberalism' by arguing that the party was stifling internal debate and saddling itself with a set of measures which, though worthy, were 'not calculated to kindle the enthusiasm of English artisans and labourers'.[26] Atherley-Jones argued that English voters were 'wonderfully indifferent' to Gladstone's efforts to 'Bulgarianise' the Home Rule issue, and insisted that the party's future depended upon giving voice to the yet inarticulate demands of the masses for a better life. It must, he argued, develop policies to secure 'for our people a wider diffusion of physical comfort'.[27] In response to these heresies, George Russell (Liberal MP for Aylesbury 1880–85 and Biggleswade 1892–95), insisted that whilst most Liberals had merely 'suspended judgement' on the question of Home Rule in 1886, they now understood why it had to be their first policy. On the other hand, Russell was prepared to accept that there was little enthusiasm for the policy among working people, and he also accepted that the party's future depended on recognising the need for 'social reform' and breaking 'the bondage of wire-pullers and caucus-mongers'.[28] The prominent Congregationalist James Guinness Rogers took a more uncompromising line. Home Rule was not negotiable, he

---

[25] *Ibid.*, pp. 24–6.
[26] L. A. Atherley-Jones, 'The New Liberalism', *Nineteenth Century*, 26 (August 1889), pp. 186–93 (p. 192).   [27] *Ibid.*, pp. 189 and 192.
[28] George W. E. Russell, 'The New Liberalism: a response', *Nineteenth Century*, 26 (September, 1889), pp. 492–9 (esp. pp. 497–9). Russell had been defeated at Fulham in 1885 and 1886.

insisted, and if Atherley-Jones was right that the masses were not interested in the issue then 'so much the worse for the masses'.[29]

Most practical Liberal politicians found it more difficult to dismiss
popular opinion out of hand, but there is little doubt that they were
becoming increasingly anxious about the temperament and political
instincts of 'the Democracy' (as Radicals usually preferred to call 'the
masses'). In his contribution to Andrew Reid's collection of essays on 'the
new Liberal programme', published in the wake of the 1886 defeat,
Labouchere bemoaned the fact that the people were 'cajoled by the
contemptible trash talked by Primrose Knights and Dames', and suggested that they would 'forego their birthright for the sake of the free teas,
the conjurors, the rope-dancers, the fire-works and the comic singers
which are provided for them at Primrose League and Conservative fêtes'.
But despite his harsh words Labouchere did not doubt that once
Liberalism embraced a genuinely Radical programme the people would
again rally to its cause.[30] By the mid 1890s few Radicals were likely to
echo this breezy optimism. *Reynolds's Newspaper*, which had long proclaimed 'Government of the People, by the People, for the People' across
its masthead, now talked of the need to educate 'the indifferent English
working masses' and argued that 'the English people are naturally
inclined to Conservatism' – indeed, it claimed that the urban and rural
poor were 'among the most ignorantly brutal and vicious in existence'.[31]
The Liberal intelligentsia, so prominent in its support for popular government in 1867, was also developing grave doubts about the direction, and
even the wisdom, of the democratic impulse. At college high tables, no
less than on the imaginary barricades of London's Jacobin journalists,
pessimism was very much the mood of the age in Liberal circles.[32]

IV

When Andrew Reid came to edit a second volume of essays on the future
of radical politics in 1894, neither he, nor many of his contributors, had
much doubt that the Liberal party was a spent force. Enigmatically titled

[29] J. Guinness Rogers, 'The middle class and the New Liberalism', *Nineteenth Century*, 26
(October, 1889), pp. 710–20 (esp. p. 711).
[30] Andrew Reid (ed.), *The new Liberal programme: contributed by representatives of the Liberal
party* (London, 1886), pp. 13–14. Labouchere called on the party to 'substitute a programme for a name' (i.e. Gladstone). He advocated justice for Ireland, progressive taxation, Church disestablishment, land reforms and abolition of the House of Lords (p. 9).
[31] *Reynolds's Newspaper*, 12 February and 24 September 1893.
[32] Christopher Harvie, *The lights of Liberalism: University Liberals and the challenge of democracy, 1860–86* (London, 1976), esp. chs. 1, 6 and 9, and John Roach, 'Liberalism and the
Victorian Intelligentsia', *Cambridge Historical Journal*, 13 (1957), pp. 58–81. For a good
example of the metropolitan Radicals' Jacobin romanticism, see William Thompson's
portrait of Robespierre in *Reynolds's Newspaper*, 16 April 1899.

'the New Party', his second collection had as its dominant theme a heart-felt desire to see radical politics revitalised by the raw enthusiasm and energy of the new labour and socialist politics. Reid himself dismissed the Liberals as 'the Tinkering Party – the Fainting Party – the Expiring Party', arguing that 'for a century they have been tricking the people'.[33] Like many metropolitan Radicals Reid was already a strident advocate of the state regulation of hours and wages, and he argued that the New Party would fight for the 'Three Eights': a legal eight-hour day, an eight shilling minimum daily wage, and a minimum hiring period of eight months for any labourer (the last measure was intended to end the curse of casual employment once and for all). Indeed he went further, arguing that across large swathes of industry the state should not be content simply to regu-late capitalism, it should intervene and assume direct control of the work-shop.[34] Of course, Reid's problem was that there was no 'New Party' – only a widely expressed aspiration for some new political force capable of reigniting the radical enthusiasm of 'the masses'. In his contribution to the collection Keir Hardie, perhaps not surprisingly, insisted that the New Party had already been established at Bradford the previous year and was known as 'the ILP'. However, most contributors, including socialists such as Robert Blatchford, were clearly looking for something more transcendental – a new movement, a new source of idealism – not just a new political organisation.[35]

With its calls to rename the Liberals the 'Isocratic Party' (committed to equality of *political* power), or to follow the teachings of the early Church by embracing 'the gospel of the poor', there is something 'other-worldly', and at times frankly ridiculous about Reid's collection.[36] It should not, however, be dismissed out of hand. For all its idiosyncrasies – and they are many – it captures the impatient, frustrated mood of many sections of the Liberal movement by the mid 1890s. Disillusioned by the failures of the minority Liberal administration elected in 1892, by the division among the party's leaders and by the disarray in the country, many activists, not all of them ultra-Radicals by any means, had come to despair of their party. The ultra-Radicals, like the socialists with whom they had so much in common, had largely abandoned hope in the Liberal party even before its return to power in 1892. For instance, *Reynolds's Newspaper*, like the metropolitan Radicalism it was steeped in, had been calling for collec-tivist social policies, including the legal Eight Hour Day, since the mid

---

[33] Andrew Reid (ed.), *The New Party: described by some of its members* (London, 1894), pp. 421 and 424.   [34] *Ibid.*, pp. 438 and 432.   [35] *Ibid.*, pp. 1, 13, 74, 376, 416.

[36] *Ibid.*, pp. 1–2, 51, 74. In contrast, Reid's own contribution is rather modish, but often seems rather insincere, as when he announces 'we are vitalists. Our aim is to vitalise society. We shall vitalise the poor with food and vitalise the rich by want' (p. 431).

1880s.[37] By 1892 the paper had no doubt that the Liberals' failure to secure a working majority was the direct result of the 'obstinate refusal' of party 'wire-pullers to recognise the growing Democratic Labour Vote'.[38] Though it would later clash bitterly with Hardie, at this stage *Reynolds's* still hoped that the explosion of interest in labour politics, associated with the growth in general trades unions and the propagandist efforts of the socialists, would lead to the development of a new democratic political force on the left of British politics. In August 1892 the paper was celebrating the return of 'a distinct Labour party of three to the House of Commons', and looking forward to the imminent

absorption of the 'haves', embracing the so-called 'moderate Liberals' and Conservatives, into one undivided party of monopolists, as against those of the 'have nots', who under the banner of Collectivism, will include Radicals, Trade Unionists, Socialists and well nigh the whole of the Labour army. It is from the inherent probability of this development that the formation of a distinct Labour party at the present moment derives its extreme importance.[39]

A year later *Reynolds's* voiced its criticism of Gladstone's ministry by arguing that 'absolutely nothing has been done for the English democracy', and that 'the Liberals have constantly filled us with hopes, and as frequently falsified their promises'.[40] While on the eve of the 1895 election the paper was arguing that the historic Liberal ideals of 'peace, retrenchment and reform' and 'civil and religious liberty for all' had become obsolete – *Reynolds's* claimed that 'these ideas no longer move us, and we are waiting for the new thought which will mould a new party – and carry it to new victories'.[41] Many voices from *within* the Liberal Coalition could be heard to echo these sentiments. For instance, William Saunders, MP for

[37] For example, *Reynolds's Newspaper*, 20 June 1886, which outlines policies Radicals should expect candidates to endorse. For discussion of this metropolitan Radicalism, see Michael Barker, *Gladstone and Radicalism: the reconstruction of Liberal policy in Britain, 1885–94* (Hassocks, 1975), pp. 138–54, which focuses on its relations with the National Liberal Federation; Jon Lawrence, 'Popular Radicalism and the socialist revival in Britain', *Journal of British Studies*, 31 (1992), pp. 163–86; and Willard Wolfe, *From Radicalism to Socialism: men and ideas in the formation of Fabian socialist doctrines, 1881–1889* (New Haven, Conn., 1975), which examines the impact of this Radical tradition on the Fabians' development from ethical to collectivist socialism. These new politics were very much constructed within the context of the intense metropolitan debates on the 'social question' which raged throughout the 1880s, see especially Gareth Stedman Jones, *Outcast London: a study in the relationship between classes in Victorian soicety* (Penguin edn, London, 1984), and Judith Walkowitz, *City of dreadful delight: narratives of sexual danger in late-Victorian London* (London, 1992).   [38] *Reynolds's Newspaper*, 17 July 1892.

[39] *Ibid.*, 28 August 1892. *Reynolds's* counted Burns, Hardie and Sam Woods (not Havelock Wilson) as its new 'Parliamentary Labour Party', and contrasted their purpose with the 'awful example' of Henry Broadhurst. Henry Fowler made a similar prediction about the realignment of party politics in the late 1890s, see E. H. Fowler, *The Life of Henry Hartley Fowler, First Viscount Wolverhampton* (London, 1912), p. 439.

[40] *Ibid.*, 6 August and 24 September 1893.   [41] *Reynolds's Newspaper*, 16 June 1895.

Walworth and another London Radical, published a pamphlet chronicling the Liberal Government's failures during its first year in office. Saunders' argument was uncompromising: he attacked the Liberal Cabinet as a bastion of 'class privileges', and claimed Home Rule had been foisted upon the party by Gladstone and his allies as a ploy to prevent Liberalism from tackling social questions which alone could restore its popular mandate.[42]

Feeling was also running strongly against the Liberals within sections of the socialist and labour movement which had previously taken a fairly pragmatic view of the question of political independence. The London Fabians published *To Your Tents Oh Israel!* in November 1893, a pamphlet cataloguing the Liberals' many failures in office and calling for a policy of strict political independence along the lines of the recently formed ILP.[43] In 1894 Ramsay MacDonald, long connected with socialism as an ethical movement, finally and famously announced his complete disillusionment with the Liberal party and threw in his lot with 'the Independents'.[44] The wider trade union movement also appeared to be distancing itself from organised Liberalism. In 1893 the Trades Union Congress approved plans to finance independent labour candidates pledged to a socialist programme, while at Norwich the following year Congress supported an amendment, brought forward by Hardie of the ILP and James MacDonald of the SDF, calling for the nationalisation of the means of production, distribution and exchange.[45]

Clearly the Liberals' political problems were being compounded by their inability to satisfy the aspirations of a politically more assertive labour movement. The character of this emergent Labour politics is discussed more fully in the next chapter, here I wish only to discuss why the problem appeared so intractable to Liberal strategists. As David Powell has argued, the Liberal ministries of 1892 to 1895 were not wholly indifferent to the claims of labour as an 'interest', hence the many trade unionists appointed as local magistrates or given government posts concerned with the regulation of factories and with industrial relations.[46]

---

[42] William Saunders, *The political situation: how it strikes a Radical* (London, nd [1893]), esp. pp. 7, 17, 30.
[43] [Shaw and Webb], 'To your tents, Oh Israel!', *Fortnightly Review*, 323 (November, 1893), pp. 569–89, later incorporated into Shaw's 'A plan of campign for Labour' (*Fabian Tract No. 49*, London, 1894), see A. M. MacBriar, *Fabian socialism and English politics, 1884–1918* (Cambridge, 1962), pp. 249–50.
[44] David Marquand, *Ramsay MacDonald* (London, 1977), pp. 34–7.
[45] See David Howell, *British workers and the Independent Labour party, 1888–1906* (Manchester, 1983), pp. 124–5; Trades Union Congress, *T.U.C Annual Report, 1894* (Norwich), 53–5.
[46] David Powell, 'The Liberal Ministries and Labour, 1892–1895', *History*, 68 (1983), pp. 408–26.

Such developments were widely welcomed in trade union circles, but they could not hope to stifle the call for trade unionists to have a much larger presence within Parliament itself. Here the Liberal 'wire-pullers' had a problem. The decentralized character of Liberal organisation meant that national party agents could exert little influence over local branches – except where the latter were weak and hence in need of central assistance.[47] However, in these cases Liberalism was also likely to be *electorally* weak, offering little prospect of Parliamentary success for any 'labour' man nominated by the centre. In fact, in such areas the problem was not that local Liberals tended to shun labour, often they were more than happy to embrace its causes and support its candidates, rather it was that 'Liberal-Labour' candidates were coming to recognise that electoral success depended on *not* being associated with Liberalism. We have seen this clearly in the case of Wolverhampton, where the growth of working-class Conservatism after 1886 increasingly put Lib-Lab leaders on the defensive (chapter 5). Similarly, when John Hodge fought Preston for Labour at a by-election in 1903 he made frequent and full-blooded attacks on the Liberals and their failed Newcastle programme, despite himself being a life-long Liberal activist. When Henderson complained, apparently fearful that the party would lose both Liberal votes and the support of wealthy Liberal patrons, Hodge retorted that it was Tory votes they needed if they were ever to win Preston and towns like it.[48]

Of course the reverse of this was that in areas where Liberalism remained strong, local parties tended to be indifferent to the pleadings of central party 'fixers', and deeply hostile to the idea that their 'nonconformist agenda' (for want of a better phrase) should be overturned in favour of social policies which would raise taxes and perhaps threaten commerce. In areas such as west Yorkshire or south Wales most Liberal leaders remained implacably hostile to claims for increased labour representation and 'advanced' social policies, though even here there were important exceptions such as W.P. Byles, the Bradford newspaper proprietor, who challenged 'official' Liberalism at Spen Valley in 1892 (suceessfully) and again at Leeds East in 1900 (this time unsuccessfully).[49] Yorkshire and

---

[47] See H. V. Emy, *Liberals, Radicals and social politics, 1892–1914* (Cambridge, 1973), pp. 71–93 (esp. p. 72).

[48] John Hodge, *Workman's cottage to Windsor Castle* (London, 1938), p. 148.

[49] See Keith Laybourn and Jack Reynolds, *Liberalism and the rise of Labour, 1890–1918*, (London, 1984), esp. chs 4 and 6; K. O. Morgan, 'The New Liberalism and the challenge of Labour: the Welsh experience', in K. D. Brown (ed.), *Essays in anti-Labour history* (London, 1974); Robert Perks, 'The New Liberalism and the challenge of Labour in the West Riding of Yorkshire, 1885–1914 – with special reference to Huddersfield', Unpubl. PhD thesis, Huddersfield Polytechnic, 1985. On W. P. Byles, see Laybourn and Reynolds, *Rise of Labour*, pp. 84–8; *Yorkshire Evening Post*, 13 and 17 September 1900; and *The Times*, 14 and 18 September 1900.

south Wales also produced 'Lib–Lab' miners' MPs such as Ben Pickard and William Abraham (better known as 'Mabon') who were strongly independent in their politics, and (whatever their views on socialism) broadly sympathetic to the new 'labour platform', with its emphasis on the state regulation of the working day and of wage rates.[50] These men were the representatives of powerful trade unions which had long since captured the 'caucus' and made it their own. Their success was an inspiration to many, not least among the rising generation of socialists, but it was the product of peculiar circumstances – the dominance of a constituency by a single union and its officials – which could not simply be reproduced elsewhere.[51]

V

So far the focus has been very much on the problems of Liberalism, and on the many internal voices calling for change if the party's decline was not to prove irreversible. I wish now to turn to public voices which might be said to be of a more 'official' character by examining party propaganda produced by the Liberal Publication Department (established in 1887).[52] We know that the volume of such propaganda, and its importance to party leaders, was increasing rapidly during the early 1890s, but we know much less about how it was viewed, either by local party branches or by the electors for whom it was intended.[53] The focus of the following discussion must therefore concentrate on the construction rather than the reception of political discourse. In particular, on whether such 'official' sources articulated similar anxieties about the political instincts of 'the Democracy', and the weaknesses of the Liberal programme to those expressed by many back-bench MPs, Liberal intellectuals and Radical journalists. Whilst the style of much of this propaganda makes it difficult

---

[50] See John Shepherd, 'Labour and Parliament: the Lib–Labs as the first working-class MPs, 1885–1906', in Biagini and Reid (eds.), *Currents of radicalism*.

[51] For sympathetic accounts of the early Lib-Lab leaders by socialists, see Robert Smillie, *My life for labour* (London, 1924), pp. 62–3; James Sexton, *Sir James Sexton, agitator: the life of the dockers' MP, an autobiography* (London, 1936), p. 133; Henry Snell, *Men, movements and myself* (London, 1938), pp. 64, 139–40, 144. In 1906, commenting on the new intake of Labour MPs, the *Review of Reviews*, February 1906, commented that the Lib–Lab miners were 'miners first, labour men second, and Liberals third', unlike men such as Burns 'who form an integral part of the Liberal party'.

[52] In the following discussion I make use of the collections of Liberal party leaflets and pamphlets held at the British Library; Bristol University Library (National Liberal Club Archive, DM668); and Cambridge University Library. As reference I give the title and serial number, and indicate the library at which the leaflet was consulted.

[53] On the growing importance of centrally produced propaganda at this time, see Bryce to Geake, 29 April 1892 (Geake Papers, Bristol University Library, Special Collections, DM 668).

to resist the temptation to speculate on its likely ability to persuade the doubting voter, I fully accept that this is no more than speculation – propaganda of this sort cannot give us a window onto popular mentalities, though it may tell us much about how political activists perceived the popular mind.

As one might expect of an organisation which had been jointly founded by the National Liberation Federation and the Liberal Central Association, the Liberal Publication Department made strong efforts to promote official party policy. Potentially unpopular policies such as local option and Welsh Disestablishment were defended, though interestingly very little was said about Home Rule for Ireland considering how completely it dominated the Liberal agenda at Westminster in the first half of the 1890s.[54] When discussed at all, the main virtue of Home Rule was said to be that it would finally settle 'the Irish question'. More tangentially, some effort was made to turn the issue against the Unionists by charging them with inciting rebellion in Ulster, while there were also efforts to suggest that the policy was simply part of a broader Liberal commitment to the extension of self-government. Since 'Home Rule all Round' (or devolution) remained a controversial issue within the party, emphasis was placed instead on 'Home Rule for the village' (the introduction of parish councils to the more prosaically-minded).[55]

Liberal propagandists of the early 1890s spent a great deal of time rehearsing the great Liberal reforms of previous governments. A pamphlet on taxation and the working-classes published during the 1892 election devoted most of its time to chronicling measures passed between twenty and fifty years earlier to reduce duties on consumables such as tea, tobacco, sugar and paper.[56] Remarkably, another pamphlet informed trade unionists that it was the Liberals who had repealed the Combination Laws in 1824.[57] Often such appeals to history were used to emphasise that only the (Gladstonian) Liberals were true heirs to this

[54] Good examples include 'The Liberal programme: temperance reform' (No. 1575) – 1892; 'The disestablishment and disendowment of the Church of England in Wales' (No. 1658), 'The Local Option Bill' (No. 1679), and 'Local option: what it is and what it is not' (No. 1680) – all 1894. However, Home Rule was still placed at the top of the leaflet advertising the Newcastle Programme; see 'The Newcastle Programme: as endorsed by the National Liberal Federation' (No. 1589) – 1892; see also 'The elector's choice of two Irish policies' (No. 1595) – also 1892 – with its less than ringing slogan 'Home Rule or sham county councils?' (all leaflets at BL).

[55] For these themes see 'The real issue' (No. 1697) – from 1895; and 'A Tory incitement to rebellion' (No. 1596); and 'The Liberal Programme: parish councils or Home Rule for the village' (No. 1572) – both 1892 (all at BL).

[56] 'What the Liberal party has done to relieve the working classes of taxation' (No. 1594) – 1892 (BL).

[57] 'The Liberal Programme: amendment of the factory and workshop acts' (No. 1598) – 1892 (BL).

great political tradition – 'Liberal Unionism', it was suggested, was simply a 'dodge to deceive the electorate', or 'a farce and a fraud'.[58] But if the party was bullish in its denunciation of Liberal Unionism, it was often much more uncertain and faltering when it came to explaining its own policies – especially in 1895, after the frustrations of three years in office. For instance, a long pamphlet detailing the Unionist party's 'black record' of obstructionism adds, apparently as an afterthought to raise dampened spirits: 'the Liberal party did actually pass a large number of important measures . . . but the above Record shows the reason why even more was not done'.[59]

If tone was often a problem, so was style. Though later Liberal propaganda would successfully adopt a very punchy, populist style, in these early years the output from the publication department was often impossibly wordy. For instance, in 1894 the emboldened 'slogan' at the foot of a leaflet on the 'wreck of the Employers' Liability Bill' declared that 'The responsibility for the destruction done to the lives and health of thousands of British citizens, for the misery of widows and orphans left unprovided for, rests upon the heads of the Party which has drawn the keystone from the arch.'[60] Even less successful were leaflets, such as the one published after the 1894 budget, which tried to offer political instruction in the form of imaginary dialogues between working-men electors. In 'Working-men and the budget' a Liberal working-man tries to explain to his rather slow Tory colleague that it would be 'the rich man', not 'the working-man' who would pay increased death duties. Like a skit on early television advertising, the leaflet concludes with the Tory working-man declaring, 'Well, now you've explained it to me, I agree with you that THE BUDGET IS AFTER ALL A REAL WORKING-MAN'S BUDGET.'[61] Overall, the Liberal propaganda of the early 1890s suggests a party acutely conscious of a gulf between its own ideals and aspirations, and popular feeling. Confidence in the traditions of popular democracy had not wholly disappeared. The Local Government Act of 1894 was hailed as the 'New Liberal Charter', bringing 'democratic freedom' to 'the very door of the agricultural labourer and village artisan'. Parliamentary opposition to 'one man, one vote' was said to reveal the tories' historic

---

[58] 'A farce and a fraud' (No. 1690) – 1895 (BL). This leaflet ends by declaring: 'You can only vote for the party of Progress and Reform – the Party which in the past has secured civil liberty and religious freedom – by VOTING for the LIBERAL CANDIDATE' (original emphasis). See also, 'What Liberal Unionists, when they were Liberals, thought of the House of Lords' (No. 1631) – 1894 (BL); and 'The farce of Liberal Unionism' (No. 1668) – 1895 (Bristol University).

[59] 'The Black Record of the Unionist Party, 1892–1895' (No. 1695) – 1895 (BL).

[60] 'The wreck of the Employers' Liability Bill' (No. 1638) – 1894 (BL). For equally prolix appeals, see 'The Liberal Programme: temperance reform' (No. 1575), and 'The Liberal Programme: amendment of the factory and workshop acts' (No. 1598) – both 1892 (BL).

[61] 'Working-men and the budget' (No. 1646) – 1894 (BL) – original emphasis.

'distrust of the people'.[62] But at other times a different note was sounded. Workers were told that the payment of MPs would complete 'the *gift* of the franchise made by the Liberals', and that bills which had fallen because of opposition in the Lords 'show a real insight into, an understanding of, a sympathy with, the needs and trials of the lives of the masses.'[63]

Liberal languages of social description were often no less awkward. One pamphlet asked the rhetorical question: 'What has been done for the factory hand, the Artisan and other Trade Worker?' before reproducing a long list of Liberal-inspired health and safety measures.[64] Many made clumsy use of flattery in their appeals to the intelligence, patriotism and respectability of working-men electors.[65] But, however infelicitous in execution, such propaganda demonstrates that 'official' Liberalism had no doubt that its political future depended on closing the apparent gulf between its own agenda and the 'needs and trials of the masses'. The Newcastle Programme may have made relatively few concessions to the new labour sentiment,[66] but when, in 1894, the party published a leaflet outlining its achievements in office 'labour' issues were very much to the fore. On the other hand, when the same pamphlet outlined twenty 'things to be done' labour issues were again much less prominent – only employer liability made it into the 'top five', and there were no concessions to labour's increasingly collectivist spirit on questions of wages, hours or social welfare.[67] When, during the 1895 General Election, Liberal propagandists asked for their party to be given the chance to prove that 'they recognise the crying needs of the People, and that their first and foremost policy is to do them justice', it was clear that rhetorical flourish would have to stand in for substantial policy commitments.[68]

---

[62] 'The new Liberal Charter' (No. 1628); 'One man, one vote' (No.1645) – both 1894 (BL). This legislation involved abolishing plural voting and reducing the residency requirements for voter registration, it did not involve tackling the problem of 'some men, no votes'.

[63] 'The Liberal programme: payment of members' (No. 1583) – 1892 (emphasis added); 'The Liberal Government and the People' (No. 1700) – 1895 (both BL).   [64] *Ibid.*

[65] For instance, 'Agricultural labourers and the Liberal Party' (No. 1534) – ?1891; 'One man, one vote' (No. 1645) – 1894 (both BL).

[66] The exceptions were commitments to extend the factory acts, and to fund both election expenses and salaries for MPs.

[67] 'What the Liberal party had done, and what it intends to do' (No. 1629) – 1894 (BL). 'labour' measures listed included the appointment of working-class magistrates and factory inspectors, the regulation of hours for railway servants and government workers, increased wages for government workers and ending bans on their trade union membership, creating a Labour Department at the Board of Trade and appointing a Royal Commission into the aged poor. Commitments on payment of expenses and MPs' salaries, and extension of the factory acts were renewed. Also mentioned was amendment of the law of conspiracy, and creation of a new conciliation and arbitration courts.

[68] 'The Liberal Government and the People' (No. 1700) – 1895 (BL).

VI

Despite the party's poor showing at the so-called 'Khaki' election of 1900, in many respects the crushing defeat of 1895 can still be said to have marked a turning point in Liberal fortunes. Though, as will be seen, this was more because of its impact on the labour movement, and especially on the influence of the ILP, than because Liberalism itself was suddenly transformed. In all the Unionist parties had made a net gain of 96 seats since 1892, giving them an overall majority of 152. For the first time since 1874, the Conservatives now had an outright Parliamentary majority, irrespective of other parties.[69] The Liberal vote fell in all but 22 of the 140 single-member English boroughs contested in both 1892 and 1895, and in 60 of these contests it fell by over 5 percentage points. In a number of high-profile constituencies, including Bradford West, Halifax, Manchester North-East, and Rochdale ILP intervention meant that the Unionist candidate won on a minority poll.[70]

Party ultra-loyalists such as the itinerant orator and controvertist Joseph Howes blamed defeat on poor organisation and the lack of educational work – indeed Howes insisted that 'we never had a better Government than the last one'.[71] Most Liberals were more reflexive, but just as no clear issue had emerged to give unity to the campaign, so no clear explanation now emerged for the failure of that campaign.[72] The *Manchester Guardian* focused initially on the disruptive impact of the Independent Labour Party, not so much in the high-profile cases where its intervention had allowed a Unionist to win the seat on a minority poll, but in the more general sense that the new party denuded the Liberals of many key activists, whilst simultaneously frightening more timid voters into the arms of the Unionists.[73] Overall, however, the paper remained

---

[69] Kinnear, *British voter*, pp. 22–5, the Conservatives had a majority of twelve over all other parties.

[70] The same was true at Salford South, where the SDF had intervened, and a plausible case could also be made that socialist intervention had contributed to the loss of Liberal seats at the double-member boroughs of Southampton, Newcastle-upon-Tyne and Northampton.

[71] Joseph Howes, *Twenty-five years fight with the tories* (Leeds, 1907), pp. 316–18 (quoting his letters of the time to the *Daily News*).

[72] See *Reynolds's Newspaper*, 14 July 1895, where Gracchus reviews the many Liberal 'crusades' (Home Rule, abolition of the Lords, local option, fiscal reform) being floated by different party leaders during the campaign, before concluding that the party should throw its weight behind reform of election procedures, voter registration and the franchise. According to Gracchus it would then at least have a built-in explanation for its defeat – the unjust electoral system.

[73] *Manchester Guardian*, 19 July 1895. See also J. Guinness Rogers, 'The General Election: what does it all mean?', *Nineteenth Century*, 38 (August, 1895), pp. 177–87, which offers a broadly similar analysis.

remarkably sanguine about Liberal prospects, arguing that 'the present exceptional combination of adverse circumstances cannot recur . . . before many years are over the Liberal Party, which has now reverted to its 1874, will once more find its 1880'.[74] *The Daily Chronicle* was also critical of the ILP, suggesting that so far it had 'done nothing but mischief', but the paper was equally clear, firstly that the ILP was no more than 'a ripple on the wave of reaction' which had engulfed Liberalism, and secondly, that intransigent local Liberal parties must carry much of the blame for the breakdown in relations with Labour in the industrial districts of the north. The newspaper attacked the 'fatuity' of running Liberal candidates against strong Labour men such as Lister at Halifax and Jowett at Bradford, lamented the reluctance of Wigan Liberals to support the Lib–Lab miners' leader Thomas Aspinwall, and argued that Newcastle would not have been lost if a local working-man Liberal had been run alongside Morley to spike the ILP's guns.[75]

Reynolds's Newspaper, on the other hand, was intensely hostile towards the ILP and its 'wrecking tactics' at the recent election. Putting to one side, at least for the moment, its own grave reservations about the reforming credentials of the out-going government, *Reynolds's* adopted a language of unquestioning Liberal partisanship. Having apparently used organised intimidation to drive the ILP from the field at Limehouse (though to no avail as the seat was still lost), William Thompson then used his editorship of *Reynolds's* to continue the attack by different means.[76] In an editorial entitled 'the Keir Hardie bubble burst', Thompson celebrated Liberal gains at Bolton and Huddersfield which had been achieved despite ILP interventions 'designed to hurt the Liberals'. Even the strong ILP candidatures of Lister, Jowett and Burgess (at Leicester) were disparaged.[77] More controversially, Thompson also resurrected the 'Tory Gold' charges which had surrounded many socialist candidatures in the 1880s.[78] Noting that the ILP had been short of funds

[74] *Ibid.*, 22 July 1895. It was an attitude widespread in Liberal circles in the aftermath of 1895, see D. A. Hamer, *Liberal politics in the age of Gladstone and Rosebery: a study in leadership and policy* (Oxford, 1972), pp. 240–3.
[75] *Daily Chronicle*, 16 and 19 July 1895. The paper did not refer directly to the abortive attempts to select Arthur Henderson as Morley's Lib–Lab running mate in 1895. See E.I. Waitt, 'John Morley, Joseph Cowen and Robert Spence Watson: Liberal divisions in Newcastle politics, 1873–1895', Unpubl. PhD thesis, University of Manchester, 1972, pp. 402, 415–21b, 438, 446–9. The Conservatives already held one of the two seats.
[76] On Limehouse, see *Labour Leader*, 13 July 1895. Herbert Samuel won the seat for the Conservatives overturning a Liberal majority of 170 in 1892. On Thompson, who became editor of *Reynolds's* in February 1894, see *The dictionary of national biography, supplement, 1901–1911* (Oxford edn, 1920), pp. 506–7.
[77] *Reynolds's Newspaper*, 21 July 1895.
[78] Henry Pelling, *Origins of the Labour party, 1880–1900* (2nd edn, Oxford, 1965), pp. 40–1.

up to the eve of the poll, he declared, 'we want to know where the money came [from] at the last moment for several candidates who were hastily and suspiciously adopted. Did these sums, or did they not, come, directly or indirectly, from the Tory party?'[79]

Such charges were neither new, nor unexpected. The fledgling party had gone to considerable lengths to disassociate itself from Maltman Barry, the central figure in the original 'Tory Gold' scandals, and from H. H. Champion, editor of the *Labour Elector*, and one of Barry's closest allies.[80] Predictably such caution was not enough to prevent *Reynolds's* from running frequent stories painting the ILP as a 'Tory plot'. Indeed, after the 1895 election, the paper printed correspondence from Barry in which he claimed to have been the central figure behind the ILP's formation in 1893.[81]

To be fair, the ILP made little attempt to smooth relations with political Radicalism during this period. On the contrary, Hardie and the ILP leadership rejoiced in 'the rout' of Liberalism. The *Labour Leader* talked of the party's 'proud, exultant elation' at its contribution to Liberal defeat, and claimed that in major industrial centres such as Derby, Newcastle, Nottingham, London, Bradford and Glasgow the ILP had 'destroyed Liberalism'.[82] By August 1895, though still celebrating the ILP's part in 'the wreck of a great party', Hardie was also warning of the dangers of Liberal revival. Chief among these dangers, according to Hardie, would be the temptation for many in the ILP to strike 'secret deals' with the Liberals in order to secure the return of socialist candidates to Westminster. Hardie predicted that there would be 'a party inside the ILP anxious to make terms', but made it clear that he, for one, would clear out of the movement before compromising its independence in this way.[83] Clearly 'progressivism' – even in its loosest sense – was not part of Hardie's vocabulary in the mid 1890s.[84]

Criticism in the Radical press could perhaps be dismissed as partisan and predictable. More damaging to the ILP was criticism from within the trade union and socialist movements. Hence the decision of the National Administrative Council of the ILP, made immediately after the election,

---

[79] *Reynolds's Newspaper*, 21 July 1895.
[80] See Pelling, *Origins*, pp. 40, 57, 149–50; Howell, *British workers*, pp. 302, 378–9.
[81] *Reynolds's Newspaper*, 1 and 8 March 1896. The story was still being used by the party to denounce 'divisive' ILP candidatures at the 1905 election, *ibid.*, 31 December 1905. Barry stood (unsuccessfully) as a Conservative at Morpeth in 1895, challenging the Lib–Lab miners' leader Thomas Burt.   [82] *Labour Leader*, 20 and 27 July 1895.
[83] *Labour Leader*, 3 August 1895.
[84] Radicals were also angered by ILP indifference to democratic reforms, see below, chapter 9, pp. 261–2, and Lawrence, 'Popular Radicalism', p. 177.

to ask 'that the treasurer of election fund in each constituency contested by the ILP be requested to supply at once a financial statement showing the sources of income and expenditure, the same *to be published in labor* [*sic*] *papers*, and included in the annual report of the NAC'.[85] The Fabian Society showed little interest in 'Tory Gold' scares, but it was quick to denounce 'frivolous candidatures' in the name of socialism. Retreating swiftly from the position adopted in *To your tents, oh Israel!*, the Fabians argued that such candidatures 'give great offence, and discredit the party in whose name they are undertaken', stating bluntly that

> any third candidate who is not well supported will not only be beaten himself, but may also involve in his defeat the better of the two candidates competing with him. Under such circumstances, the Fabian Society throws its weight against the third candidate, whether he calls himself a Socialist or not, in order to secure the victory to the better of the two candidates between whom the contest really lies.[86]

With Fabian politics increasingly detached from Labour politics after 1895, it is doubtful whether pronouncements of this nature carried much direct influence. Their significance lies rather in the extent to which they encapsulate changing attitudes within the wider labour movement at this time. Most important of all, of course, were attitudes within the trade union movement.

In many respects identification with the aspirations of organised labour was a defining feature of ILP politics in the 1890s. The young activists in their red ties who became such a feature of trade union meetings during this period were mainly 'ILPers' – as were the rising generation of socialist trade union leaders such as Robert Smillie of the miners, George Barnes of the engineers, Freddie Richards of the boot and shoe workers, Ben Tillett and James Sexton of the dockers, Allan Gee and Ben Turner of the woollen workers, or J. R. Clynes and Pete Curran of the gasworkers.[87] Hence the controversy caused at the 1895 Trades Union Congress in Cardiff when, in his report on behalf of the Parliamentary Committee, Sam Woods argued that the result of the recent general election demonstrated that 'among the working classes there are too many "faddists",

---

[85] NAC Minutes, 13 August 1895 (ILP Minute Books, 1893–1909, micro-film collection, CUL) (emphasis added).

[86] Fabian Tract No.70 [Bernard Shaw], *Report on Fabian policy and resolutions*, (London, 1896). In contrast, see Fabian Tract No. 64 [MacDonald], *How to lose and how to win an election* (London, 1895), which says little about three-cornered contests (MacDonald was involved in one at Southampton), focusing instead on questions of organisation, especially voter registration and canvassing.

[87] This dimension of ILP politics is explored most thoroughly in Howell, *British workers*, chs. 1 to 6, and p. 331.

and each "fad" has got its followers, and, as a result, the working-class vote of the country is broken up into factions.' Woods, who had lost his own seat as Lib–Lab MP for Lancashire, Ince in 'the rout', was careful not to attack the ILP by name, but few doubted the meaning of his comments – certainly not Pete Curran, who called on the references to 'fads' and 'faddists' to be excluded from the report.[88] More controversial still was the address by the Cardiff shipwright John Jenkins as president of Congress. Jenkins displayed none of Woods' restraint, and launched a stinging attack on the ILP's role at the 1895 election. The result of the ILP's 'hopeless electioneering campaign' was, he argued, 'to convert the term "labour" candidate into a by-word of reproach and mistrust'. Developing Woods' critique of sectarianism, he deplored the fact that the ILP had 'harassed and opposed genuine trade unionists who happened to be Liberals'. Finally, Jenkins raised the spectre of 'Tory Gold' by questioning how such a small party could have funded so many hopeless contests.[89]

Of the two Lib–Labs, Woods and Jenkins, it was undoubtedly Woods who most nearly embodied the mood of trade unionism in 1895. All sides were agreed that the influence of party politicians and 'wire-pullers' must be expunged from congress; all agreed that trade unionists must find unity in politics if their influence was to be felt at Westminster.[90] Partisanship – whether Lib–Lab, Tory or ILP – was strongly deprecated by speakers as diverse as James Mawdsley, the Tory cotton spinners' leader, Ben Tillett, the ILP dockers' leader, and William Inskip, the Lib-Lab boot and shoe workers' leader.[91] At the same time, few delegates, even among the 'ILPers', echoed the triumphalism of Hardie and the *Labour Leader* at the demise of the Liberal Government. On the contrary, in rejecting Jenkins' allegations, Pete Curran made a point of denying that the ILP could be held to blame for 'the recent *defeat*' in the political arena.[92]

There is little doubt that the ILP experienced a period of prolonged decline after 'the defeat' of 1895. National membership figures are notoriously difficult to interpret, but suggest a sharp drop after the 1895 election, followed by recovery until 1898, and then a more serious decline in

---

[88] *TUC Annual Report, 1895* (Cardiff), p. 26. For a colourful, but not wholly accurate, report of the proceedings, see *Reynolds's Newspaper*, 8 September 1895. For once the paper's sympathies lay unequivocally with the 'old unionists'.

[89] *TUC Annual Report, 1895* (Cardiff), pp. 28–9.

[90] These themes are explored more fully in chapter 9 which looks in detail at the significance of the debate which surrounded changes to the standing orders of congress in 1895.   [91] *TUC Annual Report, 1895* (Cardiff), pp. 34–6.

[92] *Ibid.*, p. 31 (emphasis added).

membership reversed only after the 1906 election.[93] In Bradford membership of the party had halved within a year of the election, while at Glasgow the party all but disappeared after controversies thrown up by the 1895 election (the ILP apparently borrowed money from a local wine merchant to finance its six candidates – all of whom polled poorly).[94] During these years many ILP leaders, such as Tillett, Clynes and Barnes, became increasingly immersed in trade union affairs, almost to the exclusion of party politics.[95] Even in 1895 there were signs that many trade union leaders rejected the polarised model of the 'old guard' against the 'new'. For instance, Tillett and Inskip cooperated across the political divide to block a call for the Parliamentary Committee to support Lister at Halifax.[96] Indeed, by removing high-profile party political figures such as Burns, Hardie and Broadhurst from Congress, the new standing orders introduced in 1895 probably strengthened the cause of independent labour within the trade union movement. The *Labour Leader* recognised this from the outset, arguing that 'the disposition towards self-reliance' characteristic of the 1895 Congress suggested 'a mental attitude which makes for independent Labourism'.[97]

Gradually the ILP itself came to voice the sort of pragmatic political language necessary for the construction of a broad labour coalition based on trade union foundations. When Sam Woods stood as a Lib–Lab candidate at the Walthamstow by-election of February 1897 the *Labour Leader* offered its best wishes, recognising that though no ILPer, Woods was 'less slavishly Liberal than some of his colleagues'.[98] For substantive support Woods relied mainly on Lib–Lab stalwarts such as Havelock Wilson and Bill Steadman, though Will Crooks and the Poplar Labour League also rallied to his cause.[99] The new attitude of conciliation was by no means always reciprocated in Lib–Lab circles. At Halifax a month later,

---

[93] See Howell, *British workers*, pp. 328–9.

[94] See Laybourn and Reynolds, *Rise of Labour*, p. 89; William Martin Haddow, *My seventy years* (Glasgow, 1943), pp. 39–40; Howell, *British workers*, pp. 161–2; also Perks, 'New Liberalism: Huddersfield', pp. 216, 233–4. The Glasgow party had originally assured the NAC that its campaign was to be funded by the income from 'the prospective bazaar', rather than from a loan against the expected profits, *ILP Archive*, NAC Minutes, 3 July 1895 [Harvester microfilm].

[95] Howell, *British workers*, pp. 115 and 331; George N. Barnes, *From workshop to War Cabinet* (London, 1923), p. 45; Ben Tillett, *Memories and reflections* (London, 1931), pp. 89 and 116.

[96] Trades Union Congress, *Parliamentary Committee minutes, 1888–1922*, Reel 1, 10 July 1895 [Harvester microfilm edn].   [97] *Labour Leader*, 7 September 1895.

[98] *Labour Leader*, 30 January 1897.

[99] See *Daily News*, 2 February 1897; *Reynolds's Newspaper*, 31 January 1897. For the background to the contest, see John Shepherd, 'A Lancashire miner in Walthamstow: Sam Woods and the by-election of 1897', *Essex Journal*, 22 (1987), pp. 11–14.

Broadhurst, Pickard and Fenwick all intervened in opposition to Tom Mann's candidature, while the Sheffield Brightside and Barnsley by-elections in August and October 1897 respectively were even more rancorous.[100] Such confrontations owed at least as much to organisational as political rivalries – both the ILP and the Yorkshire Miners Association laid claim to political influence over the industrial constituencies of Yorkshire, and neither was yet prepared to compromise over its sphere of influence. Elsewhere such institutional rivalries were generally much less intense, and in turn the distinctions between 'Lib–Lab', Labour and socialist politicians proved to be less clearly defined and more mutable.[101] Certainly by the late 1890s a life-long Liberal such as John Hodge had little difficulty accepting the decision of his union, the Steel Smelters, to back independent Labour representation. Like many trade unionists, Hodge accepted 'independence' as the logical outcome of the twin failings of Liberalism: its electoral weakness, and its apparent indifference to labour representation.[102]

Even *Reynolds's Newspaper* was mellowing a little by the late 1890s. For instance, it was even prepared to support joint ILP/SDF plans to bring forward Joseph Burgess as a socialist candidate at Blackburn when a by-election seemed imminent in early 1897. Perhaps partly in recognition of his claim to have run with, rather than against, Henry Broadhurst in contests for the double-member constituency of Leicester, *Reynolds's* described Burgess as 'a Lancashire man, an ex-cotton operative, and a sound Democrat – very different to some of the faddists who at times masquerade as ILP candidates.'[103] Even before the outbreak of the South African war, *Reynolds's* was coming to recognise that it had more in common with the ILP than with the bulk of the Liberal party – though it never abandoned its deep dislike of Hardie. In August 1899 the paper was trying to promote a 'New Chartist League', and in the process called on readers to support such good 'radical democrats' as George Lansbury, Will Thorne, Richard Bell, Pete Curran, Ramsay MacDonald, Sidney Webb and Harry Quelch.[104] Not for the first, or the last, time *Reynolds's*

---

[100] Howell, *British workers*, pp. 19–20, 192–3, 273–4, and 331; David Rubinstein, 'The Independent Labour party and the Yorkshire miners: the Barnsley by-election of 1897', *International Review of Social History*, 23 (1978), pp. 102–34.

[101] See Jon Lawrence, 'Popular politics and the limitations of party: Wolverhampton, 1867–1900', and Pat Thane, 'Labour and local politics: radicalism, democracy and social reform, 1880–1914', both in Biagini and Reid (eds.), *Currents of radicalism*.

[102] Hodge, *Workman's cottage*, pp. 137–42, 145–51.

[103] *Reynolds's Newspaper*, 24 January 1897. Also Broadhurst, *Story of his life*, p. 248; Howell, *British workers*, pp. 60 and 217; Bill Lancaster, *Radicalism, cooperation and socialism: Leicester working-class politics, 1860–1906* (Leicester, 1987), pp. 124–5 and 132–3.

[104] *Reynolds's Newspaper*, 27 August 1899.

great hope was 'the union of Radicals and Socialists' to secure full democracy as a prelude to thorough-going social reform.[105]

VII

As John Hodge's experiences should remind us, the 1895 'rout' influenced labour attitudes more profoundly than Liberal. Initially divided, both in their explanations of the 'wave of reaction' which had swept them from power, and in their assessment of how easily lost ground might be recovered, Liberals showed few signs of developing a political consensus throughout the late 1890s. The debate on 'the future of Liberalism' continued unabated during this period, but it seemed to make little impact either on official party policy, or on the temper of local Liberalism.[106] Liberal leaders continued to search for the single issue which would unify and re-energise their party, but they could agree on little beyond the need to avoid repeating the mistakes of the Newcastle Programme, with its mass of competing, and largely unrealisable, sectional policy commitments.[107] Campbell-Bannerman, who assumed the leadership in 1899, favoured a cautious policy of consolidation – reconfirming the party's faith in its political roots rather than beginning again with a 'clean slate', as both the ultra-Radicals and Rosebery and the Liberal Imperialists advocated.[108]

A brief analysis of Liberal propaganda in the late 1890s reinforces this picture of a party gripped by an essentially negative, reactive mentality. Not only is there no evidence of innovation in party policy, either on labour questions, or on any other issue of the moment, there is in fact no discussion of Liberal policy at all. There could be no more striking testimony to the party's determination to shed the legacy of programmatic politics than this silence. Instead, party propaganda of the late 1890s concentrates almost exclusively on attacking the Unionist record in government. Two issues predominate: firstly, claims that Salisbury's

---

[105] *Ibid.*, 15 January, 13 and 27 August 1899; the programme of the National Democratic League, launched by Thompson through *Reynolds's* in October 1900, was broadly similar. For socialist reactions to the League, see Logie Barrow and Ian Bullock, *Democratic ideas and the British labour movement, 1880–1914* (Cambridge, 1996), pp. 141–6. *Reynolds's* continued to promote the League down to the 1906 election, see *Reynolds's Newspaper*, 10 December 1905.

[106] See Emy, *Liberals, Radicals and social politics*, pp. 67–71.

[107] Hamer, *Liberal politics*, chs. 9 and 10.

[108] *Ibid.*, ch. 11 and pp. 291–303; Emy, *Liberals, Radicals and social politics*, pp. 70, 137–8. For an ultra position see *Reynolds's Newspaper*, 13 August 1899, which denounced most of the shadow cabinet as 'feeble and reactionary Whigs', or *ibid.*, 3 December 1899, where Fowler is described as 'the dreary emblem of the Nonconformist conscience'.

Government was subsidising its political friends in the Anglican clergy, the gentry, and the drink trade, at the taxpayers' expense;[109] and secondly, claims that Chamberlain had reneged on the promise, made at the 1895 election, to initiate a major 'social programme' if returned to power.[110] These issues were pursued in a slightly more punchy, populist style than had been characteristic of Liberal propaganda in the early nineties. For instance, in 1897 the party published, in quick succession, three pamphlets entitled: 'The landlords' Government', 'Taking care of their friends' and 'The rich man's party'.[111] By 1900 it was using cartoons to drive its message home. For instance, the leaflet 'Part of the pantomime', depicts Salisbury, dressed as a jester, defacing a copy of Chamberlain's 1895 social programme, while a second, called 'Pasting over the old promises', shows Chamberlain sticking a large poster of a soldier with the slogan 'Vote for khaki!!" on top of earlier election posters promising social reform.[112]

By focusing on Chamberlain's betrayal of social reform Liberals were able to reiterate their old message that only *real* Liberals could be trusted to deliver reform, without actually having to make any firm pledges of their own on social policy. Indeed, with sound finance and retrenchment still central planks of Liberal propaganda, there was little scope for such pledges.[113] Just occasionally there was an attempt to suggest how the money wasted on the Government's political friends might be put to better use, but even then tax reduction was given as much emphasis as expenditure on pensions, the unemployed or education.[114] More funda-

---

[109] For good examples, see 'A Tory MP on two Tory Bills' (No. 1724), and 'Robbing Peter to pay Paul' (No. 1727), both attacking the Agricultural Rating Bill – 1897; 'The new Church dole' (No. 1809), attacking the Clerical Tithes Bill – 1899; and more generally, 'How the Tory Government has spent your money' (No. 1780) – 1898 (all BL).

[110] For good examples, see 'The Tories and Old Age Pensions' (No.1708) – 1896 (Bristol); 'Dropping the social programme' (No. 1743) – 1897 (BL); 'The social programme: four years' performance' (No. 1817) – 1899 (BL). Liberals claimed that Chamberlain had pledged reform on eight issues: (i) workmen's dwellings, (ii) alien immigration, (iii) old age pensions, (iv) shorter hours in shops, (v) workmen's compensation, (vi) miners' eight hour day, (vii) temperance reform, and (viii) conciliation in trade disputes.

[111] 'The landlords' Government' (No. 1733); 'Taking care of their friends' (No. 1734); 'The rich man's party' (No. 1735) – all 1896 (BL).

[112] In 'Part of the pantomime' (No. 1832) Salisbury has written 'nonsense! free indulgence for ever!' over Chamberlain's slogan 'Temperance a virtue', and 'Rubbish! think of the poor consumer' over his claim that 'Long hours are injurious to shop assistants'; 'Pasting over the old promises' (No.1833), is reproduced from the *Westminster Gazette* – both 1900 (BL). As early as 1897 Liberals were arguing that Chamberlain's imperialist vision had led him to abandon social policy as 'of minor importance, too parochial for me now', see 'Dropping the social programme' (No. 1743) – 1897 (BL).

[113] For instance, see 'Liberal v. Tory Expenditure: Liberal economy and Tory extravagance' (No. 1785) – 1898, which includes the slogan: 'Electors! If you favour Economy: VOTE for LIBERAL CANDIDATES'. Also 'An utterly bad budget' (No. 1799) – 1899 (both BL).

[114] See 'How the Tory Government has spent your money' (No.1780) – 1898 (BL).

mentally, it is important to recognise what Liberals meant when they spoke of the need for 'social reform'. Like most contemporaries, they continued to place as much, if not more, emphasis on the need to reform social behaviour, as on the need to reform the structure of society.[115] Hence the prominence given to the temperance issue in criticism of the Tories' failed 'social programme'.[116] The influence of 'new Liberalism' on party propaganda was minimal. On the contrary, almost the only leaflets to carry a positive message about the virtues of Liberalism were locked in a nostalgic frame of reference. A pamphlet published to coincide with Queen Victoria's diamond jubilee began by attributing the constitutional settlement of 1688 to the 'liberal spirit', and then spent most of its time rehearsing the reforming triumphs of the mid nineteenth century.[117] Perhaps not surprisingly, Gladstone's death the following year gave the cue for another wave of Liberal nostalgia.[118] Clearly the propagandists at the Liberal Publications Department had no interest in wiping the party slate clean – on the contrary, in the present troubled times they saw the past as their one trump card. Certainly it gave them their only positive cry. Hence the 1898 pamphlet 'Liberalism in the Queen's reign', which ends with a call on voters to

> support the party which has always stood for
> PROGRESS
> CIVIL AND RELIGIOUS LIBERTY
> AND
> EQUALITY OF OPPORTUNITY[119]

Despite the Liberals' decisive defeat in the so-called 'khaki election' of 1900, and the continuing divisions within the party over strategy, there is evidence that party fortunes were beginning to improve by the late 1890s.[120] The increasingly pragmatic mood in labour circles, including within the ILP, was also helpful. Nor was the 1900 election a complete

[115] For a good example of an Edwardian critique of social reform conceived as the reform of working-class behaviour and morality, see Stephen Reynolds, Bob Wooley and Tom Wooley, *Seems So! A working-class view of politics* (London, 1911).

[116] For example, 'Broken pledges: temperance reform' (No. 1705) – 1896, which quotes Salisbury reminding pro-temperance Bishops of the importance of 'individual liberty'; also 'Part of the pantomime' (No. 1832) – 1900 (both BL).

[117] 'What Liberalism has done for us during the record reign' (No. 1766) – 1897 (BL).

[118] 'Our leaders' legacy' (No. 1790) – 1898 (BL).

[119] 'Liberalism in the Queen's reign' (No. 1792) – 1898 (BL).

[120] On the favourable by-election trend for the Liberals prior to the outbreak of the war in South Africa see J. P. D. Dunbabin, 'Parliamentary elections in Great Britain, 1868–1900: a psephological note', *English Historical Review*, 81 (1966), pp. 82–99, esp. pp. 93 and 99.

disaster for the party. The Liberals registered a net gain of eight seats on their 1895 performance, although this still left the combined Unionist parties with an overall majority of 134 in the Commons.[121] The Liberals made some important gains, though these were often in traditionally Liberal seats where the party had performed exceptionally poorly in 1895.[122] Overall, the party's performance was very uneven. In some districts there had been a strong revival in party fortunes which appears to have anticipated the more general recovery experienced by the party in the early 1900s. Elsewhere, the Liberal vote slumped even on 1895.[123] But why should the chronology of Liberal revival be so uneven?[124] Party propaganda can offer few clues here. Most literature produced during the campaign was defensive. It tried to neutralise 'khaki fever' by arguing that Salisbury's incompetent Government must not be allowed to hide behind the bravery of 'Tommy Atkins'.[125] The party's only other theme was to reiterate the critique of Tory misrule developed over the preceding five years.[126]

As Salisbury had intended, turnout was low in 1900, thanks in large part to the age of the electoral register in force, but this cannot explain the Liberals' uneven performance.[127] There are also strong grounds for doubting the suggestion that localised improvements in Liberal voter registration provide the key since there is no evidence, at least in the English boroughs, of a correlation between growth in the Liberal vote and

---

[121] Kinnear, *British voter*, pp. 24–7. In these calculations I have counted Bell's return at Derby as a Liberal gain though he was returned under the auspices of the newly formed Labour Representation Committee.

[122] For instance, at Camberwell North, Crewe, Camborne, Derby, Haggerston, Northampton, Northants Mid, Oldham, Otley, Radcliffe-cum-Farnworth, Stroud and Westbury.

[123] An analysis of Liberal candidacies in the English boroughs indicates that the party's vote rose by over 5 per cent on its 1895 level in nine constituencies, but that it fell by over 5 per cent in thirty-three constituencies (excluding seats left uncontested at either election). In two cases (Dewsbury and Huddersfield) the improved Liberal performance can be attributed wholly to the withdrawal of the ILP since 1895.

[124] There is a strong *negative* correlation between growth in the Liberal vote in the English boroughs between 1895 and 1900, and its growth between 1900 and 1910, see Lawrence and Elliott, 'Parliamentary election results', p. 26.

[125] See especially, 'Why I shall dissolve Parliament in October' (No. 1841), 'Hustling it on: what a khaki election means' (No. 1851), and 'Hiding behind "Bobs"' (No. 1852) – all 1900 (BL). The last leaflet carries the slogan 'Electors – Don't be deceived. The bravery of Tommy Atkins and the Generalship of Lord Roberts are the property not of the Tory Party, but of the whole nation.'

[126] For example, 'Ask your wife' [to tell you what the war and Tory doles mean] (No. 1846), and 'Waiting in vain' (No. 1845), which depicts two old men waiting for their promised old age pensions, while parson and landlord slink off with the Tory gold – both 1900 (BL).

[127] It may not even have been a vital factor in the *size* of Liberal defeat, see Lawrence and Elliott, 'Parliamentary election results', pp. 22–4.

rising levels of enfranchisement.[128] It seems most likely, therefore, that specifically political factors must have played a large part in the unevenness of Liberal recovery. The problem is determining which factors proved most important, and whether they can be said to anticipate the factors which underpinned the more general revival in Liberal fortunes *after* 1900. Inevitably this is a very difficult issue to resolve. It has often been argued that the Liberals fared relatively well in Wales because here the 'Jingo' tide flowed less powerfully than in either England or Scotland.[129] But it is much harder to identify clear geographical patterns influencing the party's fortunes within England. The Liberals did poorly in many metropolitan seats – especially in socially mixed divisions such as Hammersmith and St Pancras – but even here the party's fortunes varied dramatically in adjacent and broadly similar constituencies. Thus in Camberwell North the Liberal vote rose by nearly thirteen per cent, whereas in Bermondsey it was unchanged and in Deptford it fell by six per cent. Similarly in the industrial north-east, like London a region where the war factor is often said to have proved damaging for the Liberals, the pattern is again very uneven. The Liberal vote fell heavily at Morpeth (down 19.9 per cent), Middlesbrough (down 9.0 per cent) and Stockton-on-Tees (down 4.5 per cent), but it rose sharply at South Shields (up 13.6 per cent) and the Hartlepools (up 8.9 per cent). Undoubtedly a candidate's attitude to the war played its part here. Both Thomas Burt at Morpeth and Havelock Wilson at Middlesbrough were outspoken critics of the Government's policy in South Africa – as was fellow Lib–Lab Fred Maddison, soundly beaten in the normally ultra-safe Liberal seat of Sheffield Brightside.[130] On the other hand, strong Liberal performances such as Robson's at South Shields or Furness's at the Hartlepools, were often associated with imperialist candidates who fully supported the Government's war policy.[131]

---

[128] *Ibid.*, pp. 24–6, the possibility of such a relationship was suggested, rather tentatively, in James Cornford, 'Aggregate election data and British party alignments, 1885–1910', in E. Allardt and S. Rokkan (eds.), *Mass politics: studies in political sociology* (New York, 1970), pp. 115–16.

[129] Henry Pelling, 'British labour and British imperialism', in his *Popular politics and society in late Victorian Britain* (2nd edn, London, 1979), esp. pp. 92–3, and Kinnear, *British voter*, p. 26, though see K. O. Morgan, *Wales in British politics, 1868–1922* (2nd edn, Cardiff, 1970), pp. 178–81, and 'Wales and the Boer War', in his *Modern Wales: politics, places and people* (Cardiff, 1995), pp. 46–58 – first published in the *Welsh History Review* for 1969.

[130] See *South Durham and Cleveland Mercury*, 28 September 1900; *Shields Daily Gazette*, 4 October 1900; *Yorkshire Evening Post*, 4 October 1900. Wilson was not explicitly anti-war, but much of his campaign was taken up with allegations that Chamberlain had fomented the war for personal gain.

[131] *Shields Daily Gazette*, 26 September 1900, and *South Durham and Cleveland Mercury*, 5 October 1900.

Similarly, at Camberwell North Dr T. J. Macnamara went out of his way to counter the dangers of war enthusiasm by stressing that he was 'a man born and brought up in the ranks of the regiment that defended Kimberley – a man whose father went through the Crimea with the same regiment' – as such, he suggested, it was quite unthinkable that he would act to undo the soldiers' good work against the Boers in South Africa.[132]

There were exceptions to this pattern, of course. At Stockton-on-Tees Samuel's claim to have backed the Government's war policy did not save him from defeat, while at Battersea John Burns enjoyed a slightly increased majority despite strongly opposing the war, and at Shoreditch W. R. Cremer, the Radical internationalist, actually regained the seat he had lost in 1895.[133] Social reform does not appear to have been a decisive issue for the Liberals in 1900. Some of the most successful Liberal candidates did have strong credentials as reformers – for example Robson had sponsored the Half Timers' Act – but most were quite cautious in their attitude to radical new measures.[134] At Walsall, Sir Arthur Hayter declined to support calls from the local Trades Council for the payment of MPs and for universal state pensions, but this did not prevent him from regaining the seat.[135] On the other hand, many Liberal candidates directed fierce criticism at the failure of the outgoing Government to deliver significant social reform. At the Hartlepools, Sir Christopher Furness made much of his opponent's vote to exclude seamen from the recent workmen's compensation legislation, while at Camberwell North Macnamara was scathing about Tory broken promises on social reform.[136] Clearly the war was by no means the only factor influencing Liberal success and failure in 1900, but it was the dominant theme of the election, in part because few Liberals had any alternative political cries to raise against their opponents.[137]

This ambiguous approach to social reform continued to characterise Liberal propaganda in the wake of the 1900 defeat. As before, Chamberlain was pilloried for abandoning promised social reforms,

---

[132] *South London Observer*, 29 September 1900, see also *Walsall Advertiser*, 22 September 1900 for Sir Arthur Hayter's strongly imperialist (and successful) Liberal campaign in a town doing very well from war-related Government orders.

[133] See Elizabeth Enstam, 'The "Khaki" election of 1900 in the United Kingdom', Unpubl. PhD thesis, Duke University, North Carolina, 1967, pp. 171–2; Pelling, 'British labour and British imperialism', p. 94.

[134] *Shields Daily Gazette*, 1 October 1900.   [135] *Walsall Advertiser*, 29 September 1900.

[136] See *South Durham and Cleveland Mercury*, 5 October 1900; *South London Observer*, 29 September 1900. Significantly neither man made any substantial pledges of his own on social policy.

[137] Enstam, 'The "khaki" election', argues strongly against the war as the sole factor explaining Liberal defeat, placing much weight on Liberal organisational failures.

whilst little was said about the Liberals' own policy intentions.[138] By mid 1902, however, there were signs of change. A leaflet attacking Tory 'doles' to landlords and clergy argued that the Liberals would spend this money not on tax reduction, as in the past, but on much-needed social reforms such as old-age pensions, unemployment relief and better access to higher education.[139] That said, party propaganda was still dominated by the defence of traditional Liberal causes, especially non-denominational education and free trade.[140] Government policy on such issues presented the Liberals with strong cards to play – and increasingly they played them with flair (and a highly populist flourish). As early as 1902 the party issued a pamphlet depicting Hicks Beach, the Unionist Chancellor, as a rat 'nibbling at the big loaf [in] the poor man's cupboard'.[141] Later the so-called 'Chinese slavery' issue proved an equally successful vehicle for Liberal populism. Here humanitarian concern for the plight of Chinese labourers who had been separated from their families, mistreated and stripped of their freedom frequently merged with overt racism encapsulated in the fear that the imperialist vision of 'the new colony as a white man's country' was to be sacrificed in the pursuit of quick profits.[142] Thus in 1904 a Liberal leaflet asked, 'will you allow these Chinese to come as slaves and take the bread out of the mouth of the British workman?'.[143] During the 1906 election the Liberal press showed even less restraint in exploiting the issue. For instance, *Reynolds's Newspaper* not only presented Chinese slavery purely as a race issue, they also insisted that it was the result of a conspiracy between Tory politicians and Jewish financiers. The paper characterised Joseph Chamberlain, the erstwhile Colonial Secretary, as 'the Rt. Hon. Chowseph Chamerstein', and labelled the Tories as 'the pro-pigtail party'.[144]

---

[138] For example, 'The cast off child' (No. 1870), and 'Mr Chamberlain's social programme' (No. 1875) – both 1901; and 'Mr Chamberlain's social programme' (No. 1883) – 1902 (all BL).

[139] 'How the Tory Government has spent your money' (No. 1885), 1902 (BL). On the growing influence of 'social Radicalism' within the central machinery of Liberal politics after 1901 see Emy, *Liberals, Radicals and social politics*, pp. 71, 77–8.

[140] Good examples include 'The Education Bill' (No. 1887), 'The bread and pudding tax' (No. 1899) – both 1902 (BL); and 'The bad old days of protection' (No. 1993) – 1904 (BUL).   [141] 'In the poor man's cupboard' (No. 1898) – 1902 (BL).

[142] See Sydney Buxton, 'The supersession of whites by Chinese', *Liberal Magazine*, August 1904, p. 439, for examples displaying more humanitarian concerns (though still often mixed with racism) see *ibid.*, April 1904, p. 175; October 1905, pp. 526–31 and November 1905, pp. 590–3.

[143] 'Chinese slavery in a British colony' (No. 1989), also 'Chinese labour: truth at last' (No. 2015), both 1904 (BUL).

[144] *Reynolds's Newspaper*, 31 December 1905, the paper also reproduced a cartoon from the *Morning Leader* showing the number of European, African and Chinese workers in South African mines, the caption read 'Do you see the long line of yellow men? Do you see the long line of kaffirs? Then look at the figures representing the white men.'

In many respects the unscrupulous exploitation of the 'Chinese slavery' issue during the 1906 election marked the culmination of a long learning process for Liberal politicians. For years the party had been forced on to the defensive by Tory populism. The party's 'nonconformist' agenda of temperance reform and Church disestablishment had been reviled by their opponents, and in 1900 the 'jingo' card had been exploited to the full against them. The apparent transformation in the temperament of 'the Democracy' proved profoundly disillusioning for many radicals – Hobson's was by no means the only voice decrying the pathological state of the modern 'mass-mind'.[145] But whereas Hobson and his like might call on politicians and the press to help mould an educated, 'rational' democracy, others learnt a very different lesson from Liberalism's *fin de siècle* defeats. They learnt that politicians must address electors as they are, not as they would like them to be. That they must highlight the issues calculated to inflict most damage on their political opponents, whilst avoiding controversies which might divide their own forces. The circumstances of 1905–1906 made it relatively easy to put these lessons into practice. The defence of free trade was a gift to Liberal propagandists – images of the 'big loaf' of free trade alongside the 'little loaf' of protection could easily overshadow residual anxieties about nonconformist-inspired moral reforms. Indeed it is interesting to note that even the education issue, which had done so much to excite nonconformist anger since 1902, was presented, not as a denominational issue, but as yet another example of how the Unionist Government had deceived the electorate during the 'khaki' election of 1900. Just as they had subsequently imported Chinese 'slaves' into the South African mines, so, it was suggested, they had also gone back on their pledge that patriotic Liberals could vote Unionist on the war issue without fear that the Government would use its majority to force through controversial domestic legislation inimical to Liberal interests. Both the Education Act and the 1904 Licensing Act were said to be gross breaches of political faith, but very little was said in party propaganda about how, or even whether, an incoming Liberal administration would reverse such measures.[146]

Despite the fact that the Liberals won the election of 1906 largely by mobilising the electorate to defend traditional Liberal causes, there can be little doubt that politics were changing rapidly in Edwardian Britain.

---

[145] J. A. Hobson, *The psychology of Jingoism* (London, 1901); L. T. Hobhouse, *Democracy and reaction* (London, 1904); Graham Wallas, *Human nature in politics* (London, 1908); and generally Miles Taylor, 'Patriotism, history and the left in twentieth-century Britain', *Historical Journal*, 33 (1990) pp. 971–87.

[146] See *Liberal Magazine*, February 1905, p. 15.

Politicians from the two main parties, and socialists such as MacDonald and Hardie, were increasingly fearful about the likely trajectory of democratic politics. Paradoxically, whilst many on the Right heralded the changing tenor of labour as proof that rational self-interest must eventually triumph among the masses, and that the result would be socialism and the overthrow of property, many on the left remained marked by the defeats of the preceding two decades and feared that the masses might be hopelessly *irrational*, forever to be deluded by the allure of patriotism and royal ceremony, and by the appeals of unscrupulous demagogues.[147] Significantly proponents of both positions tended to argue for greater state-directed social reform, either to head-off the emergence of class politics and socialism, or to create the conditions within which a genuinely rational (and hence liberal) democracy might emerge. Whatever their leaders' views, many supporters of tariff reform were convinced that the policy would allow Unionists to fund a substantial programme of social reform. As organised nonconformity began to turn away from party politics and mass protest after 1906,[148] so Liberals too gave more and more thought to the scope for constructive social policies. Lloyd George's innovative fiscal policies might be targeted at the Radicals' traditional political enemies, but their purpose was new and forward-looking: to fund social reforms such as old age pensions without compromising politically sensitive expenditure commitments such as naval expansion. By the late 1900s Britain had taken a decisive shift, not simply towards reforms to benefit the socially disadvantaged, but towards centralized and programmatic party politics. Both developments proved invaluable for the Labour party. Social reform, so long an issue above or even outside party politics, was now coming to form the core of partisan controversy.[149] At the same time, the shift to a more programmatic and state-centred politics potentially created political opportunities for a Labour party which still tended to favour municipal over state socialism, and communal over class interests.[150] In the age of tariff reform and 'New Liberalism' it seemed at least plausible that Labour might emerge as the party most strongly committed

[147] On the fears of the Right, see especially Green, 'Radical Conservatism', and *Crisis of Conservatism*, esp. chs. 4 and 10. Such views were also to be found within the Liberal party, for instance in Churchill's defence of social reform.

[148] Bebbington, *The nonconformist conscience*, esp. pp. 154–60.

[149] On attitudes to social reform in the later nineteenth century, see Peter Ghosh, 'Style and substance in Disraelian social reform, *c.* 1860–80', in P. J. Waller (ed.), *Politics and social change in modern Britain: essays presented to A. F. Thompson* (Brighton, 1987); and A. S. Wohl, *The eternal slum: housing and social policy in Victorian London* (London, 1977), pp. 226–30 and 235–49, which discusses how Salisbury took up the housing issue in part to embarrass Gladstonian Liberals.

[150] For instance, see Thane, 'Labour and local politics', in Biagini and Reid (eds.), *Currents of radicalism*.

to the defence of locality, and most firmly rooted in the 'politics of place'. However, Labour was, from the outset, a very heterogeneous political party, shaped by diverse and at times conflicting political traditions and impulses. As we shall see in the following chapter, it was not easy for Labour to present itself as the alternative to national or programmatic politics just as it was not easy for Labour to present itself unequivocally as the 'party of the people'.

9   Labour roots, Labour voices, Labour myths

I

This chapter will explore three facets of early Labour politics: their social base, their ideology and their mythology. Picking up on the closing themes of the last chapter, the discussion begins by exploring Labour's ability to offer a new 'politics of place' in response to the increasingly centralised and programmatic tenor of British politics after 1900. In recent years much has been made of the local factors which shaped the development of Labour politics between the late nineteenth century and the Second World War. At a theoretical level, Mike Savage's work has been especially influential in this respect,[1] although the two most substantial historical studies to register this new sensitivity to local political traditions and local social structures are without doubt David Howell's *British workers and the Independent Labour Party* and Duncan Tanner's *Political change and the Labour party*.[2] This work has provided a valuable corrective to an older historiographical tradition which saw Labour as an intrinsically national, centralised and 'statist' party – in short, as the epitome of 'modern' class-based politics.[3] That said, the pendulum may now have swung too far in the opposite direction – certainly in the work of Savage one is often presented with a picture of organic local Labour parties, rooted in their com-

---

[1] E.g. Mike Savage, 'Understanding political alignments in contemporary Britain: do localities matter?', *Political Geography Quarterly*, 6 (1987), pp. 53–76; 'Urban politics and the rise of the Labour party, 1919–1939', in L. Jamieson and H. Corr (eds.), *State, private life and political change*, Explorations in Sociology, No. 32 (Basingstoke, 1990); and 'Urban history and social class: two paradigms', *Urban History*, 20 (1993), pp. 61–77.

[2] David Howell, *British workers and Independent Labour party, 1888–1906* (Manchester, 1983), esp. part 2; Duncan Tanner, *Political change and the Labour party, 1900–1918* (Cambridge, 1990). I am not suggesting that these studies reduce Labour politics solely to a question of local context and the peculiarities of place, *contra* Stephen Berger, 'The decline of Liberalism and the rise of Labour: the regional approach', *Parliamentary History*, 12 (1993), pp. 84–92.

[3] E.g. John Vincent, *Pollbooks: how Victorians voted* (Cambridge, 1967); Henry Pelling, 'Labour and the downfall of Liberalism', in his *Popular politics and society in late Victorian Britain* (2nd edn, London, 1979); Peter Clarke, *Lancashire and the new Liberalism* (Cambridge, 1971); Ross McKibbin, *The evolution of the Labour Party, 1910–1922* (Oxford, 1974).

munities and unproblematically espousing their interests which, frankly, does not ring true either for the pre- or post-war periods.[4] As this chapter seeks to demonstrate, local Labour parties frequently found it extremely difficult to develop coherent 'localist' appeals – not least because their Parliamentary candidates were often union-backed 'carpet-baggers', while their own loyalties were as much to national organisations (the party and the union), as to local identities and customs. The logic which drove Henderson to suggest that for purposes of party organisation Wales be divided into two regions based on Liverpool and Bristol was perhaps extreme, but it was none the less indicative of a strand of Labour thinking which perceived local identities as backward and dangerous (even when they were the identities of an entire nation).[5] The great irony here, it is suggested, was that from the 1880s onwards urban communities, and especially predominantly working-class neighbourhoods, were becoming more stable, both demographically and residentially. In theory they increasingly provided ideal environments within which an 'organic', working-class politics based on local identities might develop – in practice this proved very difficult to achieve.

Besides considering the politics of locality within the Labour party, and the related issue of how Labour fared in traditionally Tory districts where such politics had always had a strong appeal, the chapter also looks at other aspects of early Labour party ideology. The discussion does not pretend to be exhaustive (it is doubtful whether any study could be genuinely exhaustive, and certain that a whole volume would be required simply to encompass the diverse strands of Labour ideology before 1914).[6] The intention is rather to focus on themes which provide an insight into the intellectual origins, and political trajectory, of Labour down to the early 1920s. Attitudes to centralisation, and to the representation of 'community' are clearly important here, but so too is an understanding of how 'anti-party' traditions rapidly collapsed after 1900, and how the notion of 'independence', so central to the break with Liberalism in the 1890s, came to be reinterpreted in later years.

The final section of the chapter takes us into different, and less well-charted waters. It changes the focus away from Labour's ideas about politics, and on to its ideas about itself. Autobiography, and early popular

---

[4] In his more recent work Savage himself has become increasingly critical of locality theories, see, 'Space, networks and class formation' in Neville Kirk, (ed.), *Social class and Marxism: defences and challenges* (Basingstoke, 1996), and 'Some thoughts on space and locality in sociological theory and research', *CCSR [Manchester] Occasional Papers*, 12 (1997), pp. 18–28.   [5] McKibbin, *Evolution*, pp. 168–9 and 174–5.

[6] A recent monograph has been devoted to one aspect of pre-war socialist and labour ideology, see Logie Barrow and Ian Bullock, *Democratic ideas and the British labour movement, 1880–1914* (Cambridge, 1996).

biographies are used to explore what might be termed 'Labour subjectivities'. Here biographies are read, not for the 'facts' they convey about the rise of Labour, but for the insights they offer into the mental universe of Labour in this formative period, and especially into the narratives Labour activists constructed to explain their party's emergence within the British political system.[7] Particular attention will therefore be devoted to Labour's 'foundation myths' – for example, stories of the party's 'pioneers' (or 'founding fathers'), and how they struggled to uphold 'the cause' against the indifference and hostility of the masses. These powerful myths of struggle, independence and belonging helped to reassure party members of the 'authenticity' of their vision of popular politics. These were, at least in part, myths of consolation which helped, not only to explain the party's tortured progress, but to obscure many of the ambiguities at the heart of its claim to represent working people. Auto/biography, it is therefore argued, can offer important, and much neglected insights into the central theme of the present study – namely, the complex, and often highly ambiguous relationship between politicians and the people they claim to represent.[8]

II

We turn first to the question of Labour and locality. Taken together, the work of Howell and Tanner suggests that one facet of the call for independent labour representation was a conscious revolt *against* the nationalisation of politics in the late Victorian and Edwardian period. There is no doubt that local Labour politicians did frequently espouse what might be termed a politics of community – contrasting their own concern for, and understanding of, the locality and its needs with the remoteness of London's political elites. Their claim was simple: Labour leaders were uniquely qualified by birth, experience or local knowledge to defend the interests of the locality from an increasingly hostile and interventionist national state. Indeed, Alun Howkins has argued that one of Labour's greatest strengths before the First World War was that its political leaders

---

[7] At other points these books are read in a more traditional manner – that is as essentially representational, both of the lives that form their principal subject, and of wider political and social realities. It is this approach, combined with the desire to *de*mystify auto/biography, which has so far dominated the historiography, for instance see Duncan Tanner, 'Socialist pioneers and the art of political biography', *Twentieth Century British History*, 4 (1993), pp. 284–91, and Kenneth Morgan, 'From eulogy to elegy: Welsh political biography' in his *Modern Wales: politics, places and people* (Cardiff, 1995).

[8] My reading of these life stories has been most strongly influenced by Raphael Samuel and Paul Thompson (eds.), *The myths we live by* (London, 1990); Carolyn Steedman, *Landscape for a good woman: a story of two lives* (London, 1986); and Liz Stanley, *The auto/biographical I: the theory and practice of feminist autobiography* (Manchester, 1992).

tended to be rooted in the communities they represented, whereas the champions of the 'New Liberalism' were often carpet-baggers foisted on constituencies they hardly knew.[9] This whole emphasis on the 'politics of locality' must not, however, be pushed too far. From the outset many Labour politicians believed that the local and the particular must be transcended, not championed, if Labour was to transform politics and break the hold of the old parties. The strongest proponent of this argument was probably Ramsay MacDonald, for whom local interests were all but synonymous with the corrupting influence of wealth – with the nursing of constituencies and the debasement of voters.[10] In 1909 he even recommended that Britain adopt the party list system of proportional representation on the grounds that it would 'eliminate personalities except in so far as they are national' (though MacDonald acknowledged that popular suspicion of party would in practice make the system unworkable in Britain).[11] Interestingly, in the wake of the Great War, when his assessment of popular politics was at its most pessimistic, MacDonald modified these views considerably. He began to lament the break up of interest communities, which he claimed had been greatly accelerated by the creation of new 'purely artificial' constituencies in 1918 in order to create electorates of equal size. MacDonald argued that identification with community had been undermined, and that 'the electorate has been dissolved into separate individuals'.[12] Socialist priorities were clear, suggested MacDonald: to rebuild social 'contacts', to forge a new sense of 'civic unity', and to reassert 'the community idea'.[13]

MacDonald was perhaps unusual in the pre-war labour movement for the stridency with which he advocated centralisation and the dominance of party, but there were in any case many practical barriers to the development of a viable 'localist' Labour politics. Even if the cultural and physical gulf between Labour activists and the mass of the working population did not undermine the project from the outset,[14] the financial and organisational frailties of local Labour parties could make it very difficult for them to mount a credible campaign from their own resources. Before the First World War many local parties were simply too small and too poor to sustain a Parliamentary campaign unaided. Moreover, Labour activists generally cherished their links to national organisations with national political

---

[9] Alun Howkins, 'Edwardian Liberalism and industrial unrest: a class view of the decline of Liberalism', *History Workshop Journal*, 4 (1977), pp. 143–61.

[10] Ramsay MacDonald, *Socialism and government*, 2 vols. (London, 1909), I, pp. 48, 137, 146–7, 159; II, pp. 1, 7, 10.

[11] *Ibid.*, I, pp. 146–7. The Social Democratic Party also advocated the party list system, see *Justice*, 7 December 1912.

[12] Ramsay MacDonald, *Parliament and democracy* (London, 1920), pp. 3–5.

[13] *Ibid.*, pp. 35, 68, 71.

[14] See chapter 6 on 'Labour and the working class' at Wolverhampton.

agendas – whether industrial or political – and these were often assiduously cultivated in order to attract outside candidates with guarantees of sponsorship. By selecting the nominee of a powerful national trade union a local party might hope to cover the cost, not simply of the election itself, but of a full-time election agent, and perhaps even of a local Labour newspaper (as at Wolverhampton after Walkden of the RCA was nominated).

The Steel Smelters Union embraced independent labour representation in 1899, setting up a fund to sponsor Ayrshire-born John Hodge as their Parliamentary candidate. Within months he was being interviewed by 'the long-haired intellectuals' of the St Rollox ILP (Glasgow), though he finally chose to fight the Welsh mining seat of Gower. Unsuccessful here in 1900, Hodge then contested Preston at a by-election in 1903, before finally being returned to Parliament for Gorton, near Manchester, at the 1906 General Election.[15] Such was the itinerant life of the sponsored parliamentary candidate. Though it should perhaps be noted that Hodge had lived in Manchester for fourteen years when he won Gorton, just as Arthur Henderson, another Scot, had lived in the north-east for many years before winning at Barnard Castle in 1903.[16] Overall just over half the twenty-two trade-union sponsored Labour (LRC) MPs elected in 1906 lived either in their constituency, or in a neighbouring constituency (see table 9.1).[17] Fewer could claim to have been born locally – just eight hailed from the county they now represented.[18]

Interestingly, figures for MPs sponsored by ILP branches and local Labour Representation Committees are broadly similar – exactly half lived locally, and the same proportion could claim local birth (table 9.1).[19] This represented something of a departure from earlier practice. During the 1890s, ILP branches had shown a strong tendency to prefer well-known national celebrities as candidates rather than local political

---

[15] John Hodge, *Workman's cottage to Windsor Castle* (London, 1938), pp. 137–9, 141–2, 145–8, 151.

[16] He had in fact lived in the region for nearly thirty years, and in Barnard Castle itself for the previous seven years. However, after the 1906 election he moved his family to Clapham: see Edwin A. Jenkins, *From foundry to Foreign Office: the romantic life story of the Rt. Hon. Arthur Henderson, MP* (London, 1933), p. 12; *Dictionary of labour biography*, I, p. 161; similarly, Walter Hudson, Labour MP for Newcastle-Upon-Tyne (1906–18) moved his family home to Stockwell on election to Parliament (*ibid.*, II, p. 199).

[17] Thus Henderson counts as a local resident even though he moved immediately after the election.

[18] For the sources used in this analysis see table 9.1. Where constituencies were close to the border between two counties, for instance Newcastle, birth in either county has been accepted. These figures include J. W. Taylor of the Durham miners, who won Chester-le-Street as an independent, but immediately took the Labour whip.

[19] The four 'locals' are not identical in each case. James Parker had been born in Lincolnshire, but lived in his Halifax constituency; Will Crooks (the only successful candidate run by a local LRC) was a Londoner by birth, but lived at Poplar, some distance from his Woolwich constituency.

Table 9.1 *The proportion of Labour and Liberal-Labour MPs born locally, and living locally, in 1906*

	Local born[a]	Local resident[b]
All Labour (LRC) MPs	12 (30)[c]	16 (30)
trade union sponsored	8 (22)	12 (22)
ILP/LRC sponsored	4 (8)	4 (8)
All Lib–Lab MPs	12 (27)	10 (27)
Lib–Lab Miners	9 (13)	8 (13)
other Lib–Labs	3 (14)	2 (14)

Notes:
[a] Local born: constituency in same county as MP was born (see note 18).
[b] Local resident: maintained home in same constituency or adjacent constituency at time of 1906 General Election.
[c] Figures in parentheses: total number in group/sub-group.
Sources: The Dictionary of Labour Biography, vols. 1–9; M. Stenton and S. Lees, *Who's who of British members of Parliament*, II and III; *Dod's parliamentary Companion*, 1906; F. W. S. Craig, *British Parliamentary election results, 1885–1918*; *The Ordnance Survey Gazetteer of Great Britain* (Southampton, 1987), and associated Landranger maps; Kinnear, *The British voter*; Bealey and Pelling, *Labour and politics*, Tanner, *Political change*; Shepherd, 'Labour and Parliament'; plus individual biographies and autobiographies.

leaders (though Halifax was a notable exception in this respect).[20] Hardie's political wanderings are well documented: after the famous by-election of 1888 in his native Lanarkshire, he fought West Ham South in 1892 (successfully), then Bradford East at a by-election in 1896, and Preston in 1900, before finally unseating Pritchard Morgan to become the junior member for Merthyr (also in 1900). Others proved no less nomadic. Robert Smillie, the Scottish miners' leader (and an Ulsterman by birth) fought Parliamentary contests at Mid-Lanark (1894 and twice in 1910), Glasgow, Camlachie (1895), North-East Lanark (1901), Paisley (1906), and Cockermouth (1906) – all unsuccessfully – and finally won the Northumberland mining seat of Morpeth in 1923.[21] Ben Tillett, a

[20] At Halifax, the first independent Labour champion was John Lister, a local manufacturer and landowner with strong Radical-Liberal credentials, though at the by-election of 1897 the party turned to Tom Mann before returning to a local champion in 1900 by selecting their party secretary James Parker. See Patricia Dawson, 'The Halifax Independent Labour movement: Labour and Liberalism, 1890–1914', in K. Laybourn and D. James (eds.), *'The rising sun of socialism': the Independent Labour Party in the textile district of the West Riding of Yorkshire between 1890 and 1914* (Bradford, 1991), and Howell, *British workers*, pp. 180–99.

[21] Robert Smillie, *My life for labour* (London, 1924). Smillie was a resident of Larkhall in Lanarkshire – he received sponsorship from the Scottish Miners Federation in many of these contests.

Bristolian by birth, fought Bradford West (1892 and 1895), Eccles (1906), and Swansea (1910), before winning Salford North as an unofficial Labour candidate in 1917.[22]

Overall, therefore, it is quite difficult to argue that Labour was demonstrably less reliant on the political 'carpet-bagger' than its Liberal and Conservative opponents. If one compares the Labour MPs with their twenty-seven Lib–Lab counterparts of the 1906 Parliament there is little difference in the proportion of each group born locally or living locally (table 9.1).[23] On the other hand, the Labour MPs returned under the auspices of the LRC were much less closely identified with the localities they represented than the thirteen miners' MPs who formed the solid core of the Lib–Lab group (table 9.1).[24] For men like John Wilson of the Durham miners, or William Abraham ('Mabon') of the South Wales miners, local identities were the bedrock of politics. In his autobiography Wilson makes no apologies for his political parochialism, arguing that '[w]ith me Durham has held the chief place, and it does so yet'. Unwavering in his loyalty to the north-east miners' unions in their resistance to the legal eight hour day, Wilson clearly took pride in prioritizing the interests of '[t]he people amongst whom I was born and . . . among whom I have lived and struggled after a better life' above wider conceptions of political interest.[25] Here was the politics of place in the raw, and in many respects it was a creed reviled as selfish and sectional by the champions of a more universal conception of labour politics within the ILP and the fledgling Labour party. MacDonald was also a prominent critic of this brand of particularism. For instance, in an article for the *Railway Review* in 1901, MacDonald observed that whilst Ben Pickard and the Miners Federation might talk of setting up a special fund to run as many as seventy miners' candidates at the next election, no one should forget that, 'for political purposes all trade unionists are as one. There are no engineers, or carpenters, or boot and shoe operatives, but only wage-earners and toilers when we come to consider necessary laws for the protection and benefit of

---

[22] Ben Tillett, *Memories and reflections* (London, 1931) – though he says little about his political, as opposed to his trade union, exploits; see also Jonathan Schneer, *Ben Tillett: portrait of a labour leader* (London, 1982), pp. 62–76, 108–11, 127–8, 139–45, 191–3. Tillett was sponsored by the London dockers in 1906, see Frank Bealey and Henry Pelling, *Labour and politics, 1900–1906: a history of the Labour Representation Committee* (London, 1958), pp. 266 and 291.

[23] 'Lib-Lab' MPs have been designated following Craig, *British Parliamentary election results, 1885–1918* which gives a slightly higher figure than the twenty-four Liberal–Labour MPs suggested in Bealey and Pelling, *Labour and politics*, p. 274, following *The Times*, 30 January 1906.

[24] Three miners' MPs were identified with the LRC grouping – Walsh and Glover of the Lancashire and Cheshire miners, and Taylor from the traditional Lib–Lab stronghold of Durham.

[25] John Wilson, *Memories of a labour leader* (1910; Caliban reprint, Firle, 1980) p. 18.

labour'.[26] Even here, however, the critique was qualified – in the same article MacDonald observed that Richard Bell, the railway servants' new Labour MP, had already paid back the cost of his return by securing important amendments to the Great Eastern Railway company's parliamentary legislation.[27] Though its ultimate ambition might be a broader and more inclusive conception of labour, MacDonald knew that, in the short-term, labour representation could not succeed unless it was seen to be a sound business proposition for unions and their members.[28]

As MacDonald acknowledged in his 1901 article, the miners constituted a special case within Labour representation. If one excludes the miners' representatives, Lib–Lab MPs were actually significantly less likely to possess strong local roots than their counter-parts in the LRC.[29] Indeed, Henry Broadhurst, the son of an Oxford stone mason, described himself as a 'carpet-bagger pure and simple' when he chose to give up his seat at Bordesley in Birmingham in order to fight a Liberal Unionist renegade at Nottingham in 1886.[30] Previously Broadhurst had represented the double member borough of Stoke (1880–85), and after his defeat at Nottingham in 1892 he fought a by-election at Great Grimsby in 1893, before finally securing a new seat at the Leicester by-election of 1894. But Broadhurst, who was a close friend of Schnadhorst, secretary to the National Liberal Federation, appears, like many Lib–Lab MPs, to have been heavily dependent on the good-will and assistance of Liberal party headquarters.[31] Only the miners' MPs represented the politics of locality in an unadulterated form. Only they could hope to control a constituency simply through force of numbers, political enthusiasm and organisational discipline. The miners' greatest strength was that, except in Lancashire and parts of central Scotland, union leaders and union members shared a common

[26] *Railway Review*, 7 June 1901; for a discussion of 'solidarity' rather than 'independence' as the defining feature of the new Labour politics, see Bealey and Pelling, *Labour and politics*, pp. 189–90.

[27] *Railway Review*, 7 June 1901, and *ibid.*, 1 and 22 March 1901 for details of Bell's interventions on behalf of his union. It should also be remembered that in the great battles over the legal eight-hour day within the TUC in the early 1890s representatives of the new Labour creed such as Keir Hardie were often prepared to accept the right of the north-east miners' unions, or the cotton unions, to claim the right of exemption from general labour legislation; see Trades Union Congress, *Annual Report, 1891*, pp. 53–4.

[28] For the best discussion of this wider vision within the Edwardian Parliamentary Labour Party, see Pat Thane, 'The Labour party and state welfare' in Kenneth D. Brown (ed.), *The first Labour party, 1906–14* (London, 1985).

[29] Of fourteen non-mining Lib–Labs, only three were born in the county they represented, and just two lived in, or adjacent to, their constituency (table 9.1).

[30] Henry Broadhurst, *Henry Broadhurst MP: the story of his life from a stonemason's bench to the Treasury bench* (London, 1901), p. 200.

[31] See Broadhurst, *Story of his life*, pp. 177, 183, 218, and 237; and John Shepherd, 'Labour and Parliament: the Lib–Labs as the first working-class MPs, 1885–1906', in Eugenio Biagini and Alastair Reid (eds.), *Currents of radicalism: popular radicalism, organised labour and party politics in Britain, 1850–1914* (Cambridge, 1991), pp. 193 and 196.

heritage in political radicalism. Unity was not imposed through the union lodge, it was rooted in the political traditions of the coalfields themselves. When, in exceptional circumstances, union leaders found themselves at odds with the political convictions of their members, the relationship could swiftly break down. Hence Thomas Burt's difficulties at Morpeth during the Boer War, or the poor performance of official union candidates in Derbyshire after 1910 where most miners appear to have remained loyal to Liberalism even after their union affiliated to the Labour party.[32]

In theory, at least, the politics of locality could as easily be articulated by an 'outsider', as by a politician born and bred in a community. In practice local patriotisms often proved more difficult to break down. Jack Jones recalls how community leaders in Merthyr tried to discredit socialism as the creed of 'agitators from other parts' who had been disowned by their own people but still hoped to 'mislead the people of Merthyr'. On the other hand, he suggests that few people took much heed of such warnings, especially during the great coal strike of 1898 when Hardie was able to touch the sympathies of the Welsh miners in ways that their own leaders could not.[33] In this period of crisis and privation, Hardie was able to focus on the universality of the miners' plight to great effect, but socialist denunciations of *poverty* and the horrors of the slums were not always so successful. When Freddie Richards spoke out in Parliament against the appalling slums of Wolverhampton, local Tories condemned him as an outsider who had insulted the town and its people before the nation. Unlike Sir Alfred Hickman, whom he had defeated in 1906, Richards was said to know nothing of the town's traditions, and to have done nothing of substance to promote its improvement.[34] George Lansbury recalls that the early socialist propagandists often faced the same problem. During the Walworth by-election of 1895 Harry Quelch, the Southwark SDF leader, called on the locals to 'come out of their bug-hutches and slums and fight for Socialism'. According to Lansbury, 'a man in the crowd, who looked as if he had come straight from a slum, rushed to knock him [Quelch] off the stool, shouting "You lying —, call my — home a slum and bug-hutch!" '[35]

Sometimes the problems of the outsider were more basic. When Philip

[32] See R. G. Gregory, *The miners and British politics, 1906–1914* (Oxford, 1968), pp. 144–67; J. E. Williams, *The Derbyshire miners* (London, 1962), chs. 12 and 21. Another example would be C. B. Stanton's victory at Merthyr in 1915 – he defeated the miners' official Labour candidate by over 4,000 votes on a strong pro-war platform.

[33] Jack Jones, *Unfinished journey* (London, 1938), pp. 78 and 85–6.

[34] *Express and Star*, 11 July 1905, January 1906, 26 and 28 October 1907. Walkden found himself embroiled in a similar controversy a few years later, see *ibid.*, 5, 7 and 10 May 1913.

[35] George Lansbury, *My life* (London, 1928), p. 111; also *Looking backwards – and forwards* (London, 1935), p. 80, where Lansbury recalls that it was 'only in this election that we really discovered the strength of the ignorance and prejudice that we had to combat'.

Snowden contested Wakefield at a by-election in 1902 he not only found that the town had no Labour organisation to support him, but was even obliged to bring his own chairman to introduce him to the constituency.[36] Moreover, when it came to attempts to politicise poverty, even politicians with strong local connections had to tread with care. Standing as the Labour candidate in a particularly deprived inner-city ward, James Sexton, the Liverpool dockers' leader, tells of using a magic-lantern display to contrast the slum housing of the local dockers with the splendid homes inhabited by their employers. The stunt caused great controversy, but according to Sexton the dockers still voted heavily against him because 'they resented this exposure of their poverty'.[37] According to Sexton they were 'prisoners hugging their chains', but the problem for Labour was that they were also citizens (and voters) whom the party could ill-afford to alienate.

As Sexton well knew, it was extremely difficult to construct a viable Labour politics in districts such as inner-city Liverpool where the population was not only extremely poor, but also industrially disorganised, occupationally diverse and politically divided by religion and ethnicity. Liverpool presented an extreme, though not *wholly* insuperable, case,[38] but in most cities and towns Labour politicians found that political success depended partly on brokering alliances between diverse and potentially antagonistic groups, and partly on the painstaking process of constructing a sense of shared political identity. It was not a case simply of articulating a pre-existing 'Labourist' consciousness within the community. Indeed even on the coalfields community identities had to be constructed – they were not simply implicit within the productive relations of the mining industry – and it follows that miners' politics were similarly the product of active processes of cultural endeavour.[39] The politics of locality were made – they did not simply happen.

---

[36] Philip Snowden, *An autobiography*, 2 vols. (London, 1934), I, p. 108.

[37] James Sexton, *Sir James Sexton agitator: the life of the dockers' MP* (London, 1936), pp. 167–8. It should, however, be noted that though Sexton's local connections were strong, he was not a native of the city (he had been born at Newcastle, and grew up in St Helens), and as dockers' leader he lived outside the city at Halewood village.

[38] See Sam Davies, *Liverpool Labour: social and political influences on the development of the Labour party in Liverpool, 1900–1939* (Keele, 1996); also Joan Smith, 'Labour tradition in Glasgow and LIverpool', *History Workshop Journal*, 17 (1984), pp. 32–56; and 'Class, skill and sectarianism in Glasgow and Liverpool, 1880–1914', in R. J. Morris (ed.), *Class, power and social structure in British nineteenth-century cities* (Leicester, 1986).

[39] See David Gilbert, 'Imagined communities and mining communities', *Labour History Review*, 60, 2 (1995), pp. 147–55; also *Class, community and collective action: social change in two British coalfields, 1850–1926* (Oxford, 1992). For an interesting discussion of the interaction of community identities and political/class identities, see Raymond Williams, 'The ragged-arsed philanthropists', in David Alfred (ed.), *The Robert Tressell lectures, 1981–88* (Rochester, 1988), pp. 24–6.

III

The most successful exponents of 'localist' Labour politics appear to have embraced two quite distinct, but complementary, political roles: within their communities they were political trouble-shooters, always available to resolve a dispute, to take up a cause, or to give advice; on the national stage they were the lone figures defending their communities against the ignorance and hostility of malign outside forces. Before the First World War it was London, where on the whole Labour was still very weak, that produced the most notable examples of this type of localist politics. Burns and Thorne, veterans of the SDF agitations of the 1880s, subsequently built powerful local bases for themselves in Battersea and West Ham respectively.[40] In the mid 1920s it was Thorne's proud boast to 'still live among my people – dockers, labourers, casual workers in many queer and unpleasant trades'. The phrase 'my people' is perhaps somewhat ambiguous here – conveying the sense both of 'my folk' and of 'my subjects'. It is an ambiguity intensified by Thorne's blunt statement that East London stands for 'all that is mean and ugly'.[41] This tension between paternalism, and what one might call 'organicism' – that is the claim to be simultaneously 'of the people' and yet also their political leader – ran through community-based Labour politics in London. Both Lansbury at Bow, and Crooks at Poplar, probably the two most important metropolitan Labour leaders before 1914, could be said to embody this tension. Ben Tillett recalls Crooks as a Londoner straight out of Dickens – born and brought up in Poplar, where he continued to live, Crooks was probably as close to being an 'organic' Labour leader as England has come.[42] A biography of Crooks published in 1911 portrays him unequivocally as a man of the people. Distinct from almost all other Labour MPs, it claims, Crooks stood out as 'a representative who represents . . . He is really like the people for whom he stands.'[43] The book makes much of Crooks' work among the poor children of Poplar, his efforts to promote workers' education through an informal 'college' at the dock-gates, and his campaigns to humanise the local poor law. But perhaps most significant is the claim that Crooks' Poplar home was the first port-of-call for any local resident in trouble – there is even a story of Crooks being woken in the middle of the

[40] Burns lived at Clapham, Thorne at Plaistow.
[41] Will Thorne, *My life's battle* (London, 1925), p. 13. Thorne was born at Hockley, near Birmingham, and came to London in the 1880s.
[42] Tillett, *Memories and recollections*, p. 171. He brackets Crooks with Billy Steadman, the barge-builder and prominent Lib–Lab, whom he recalls as 'a cockney of cockneys . . . born and bred on the Thames'.
[43] George Haw, *From workhouse to Westminster: the life story of Will Crooks, MP* (London, 1911), p. xvii. The quotation is from G. K. Chesterton's introduction.

night by a man who wanted Crooks to take him to the doctors and explain his case.[44]

There is little doubt that Crooks was immensely popular throughout East London. When he died, in 1921, there appears to have been a spontaneous outpouring of grief – tens of thousands lined the streets of Poplar on the day of his funeral, and local schools and factories remained closed.[45] But even Crooks remained acutely conscious of the ease with which popular acclaim, and his status as a local leader, might be undermined. For instance, in the mid 1900s he felt obliged to turn down the chance to move to a larger, more comfortable house because he knew that, '[m]y friends among the working people would fear I was deserting their class, and would not come to me as freely as they come now', and that his enemies would say 'look at that fellow Crooks; he's making his pile out of us'.[46]

Though born in Suffolk, and initially raised in 'Kentish' London, George Lansbury also lived in East London for almost the whole of his life – moving there, with his parents, in 1868, when he was nine.[47] This long association with the East End, and especially with Bow, was central to Lansbury's political identity. Like Crooks, Lansbury was renowned for keeping an open-door for those in need. Raymond Postgate, Lansbury's son-in-law and an early biographer, suggests that 'He was, in Bow itself, a sort of universal consultant – doing by himself the work which 'Citizen's Advice Bureaux' try to do today. Almost daily the house in Bow was called upon by men and women who were in legal, personal or financial difficulties and wanted 'G.L.' (the initials were by now commonly used) to advise and help.'[48] In the wake of Lansbury's failed attempt to seek re-election for Bow and Bromley as an independent Labour and pro-suffrage candidate in 1912 the question of locality was to still very much to the fore. Lansbury himself later admitted that the contest had confused many of his local supporters, but at the time the *Daily Herald* (not yet under his editorship but strongly under his influence), insisted that despite the defeat Lansbury could still count on the loyalty, and the love, of the people of Bow. The paper even claimed to overhear two women in the declaration crowd saying of Blair, Lansbury's victorious Tory opponent, "e don't live in Bow, not 'e. 'E'll go back to 'is 'Ermitage, dahn in Middlesex'.[49]

---

[44] *Ibid.*, p. 146, and generally, pp. 80, 113, 153, 212.

[45] *The Times*, 9 and 10 June 1921; also Henry Snell, *Men, movements and myself* (London, 1938), p. 204.   [46] Haw, *Life story of Will Crooks*, p. 83.

[47] See Lansbury, *My life*, pp. 15–26.

[48] Raymond Postgate, *The life of George Lansbury* (London, 1951), p. 104. Postgate is writing of the late 1900s.

[49] *Daily Herald*, 27 November 1912; Lansbury, *My life*, p. 121. On Lansbury and the *Herald*, see R. J. Holton, '*Daily Herald* v. *Daily Citizen*: the struggle for a Labour daily in relation to "the Labour unrest" ', *International Review of Social History*, 19 (1974), pp. 347–76.

But Labour politics in Bow, and in the borough of Poplar as a whole, consisted of more than offering a mixture of philanthropy and citizens' advice. No less important was Labour's role on the national political stage. Here, leaders such as Lansbury and Crooks – or Thorne at West Ham – presented themselves as the authentic voice of a marginalised and unjustly served people. As James Gillespie has demonstrated, Labour politics in Poplar were premised above all on the defence of the local community – especially through the campaign to secure the equalisation of the burden of poor relief within London. The aim, even before post-war unemployment raised the stakes, was to construct a cross-class alliance within Poplar in order to overcome the resistance of penny-pinching West End boroughs and an unsympathetic state.[50] But for Lansbury, defence of locality went hand-in-hand with a strongly 'statist' approach to social welfare, hence his endorsement of the 'minority report' of the Royal Commission on the Poor Laws.[51] Defending the report's findings in a debate with Harry Quelch, the veteran SDF leader, Lansbury insisted that local control of poor relief had to be sacrificed in order to ensure two more fundamental principles: uniformity of treatment and equality of sacrifice. Only the central state could deliver these twin principles.[52] Thus 'Poplarism', as it became known in the 1920s, was essentially a desperate strategy to use Labour's local power base to try and force government to embrace a more liberal conception of its social responsibilities. The great irony was that centralisation – once Lansbury's 'rational' solution to the social problem – became the means by which successive Tory-dominated governments effectively blunted Labour's 'localist' challenge. Labour's problem between the wars was that, except perhaps in the General Election of 1929, the party found it very difficult to present itself as a genuinely national political force.[53] For most of the period its support remained highly localized.[54] 'Localist' politics – whether they involved the dogged defence of an embattled community as at Poplar, West Ham or

[50] James Gillespie, 'Poplarism and proletarianism: unemployment and Labour politics in London, 1918–34', in David Feldman and Gareth Stedman Jones (eds.), *Metropolis: London histories and representations since 1800* (London, 1989). John Marriott has painted a similar picture of Labour politics in West Ham between the wars; see his *The culture of labourism: the East End between the wars* (Edinburgh, 1991).

[51] *Report of the Royal Commission on the Poor Laws and Relief of Distress* (Minority Report), PP1909 Cd.4499 vol. XXXVIII, pp. 721–1238.

[52] *The Poor Law Minority Report: a debate between George Lansbury and Harry Quelch (20–21 September 1910)* (London, nd [1910]), pp. 6–7, 8, 12.

[53] For a stimulating discussion of Labour's near breakthrough in 1929, see Duncan Tanner, 'Class voting and radical politics: the Liberal and Labour parties, 1910–31', in Lawrence and Taylor (eds.), *Party, state and society*.

[54] John Turner, *British politics and the Great War, 1915–1918* (New Haven, Conn., 1992), chs. 10 and 11; though for a somewhat different emphasis, see Tony Adams, 'Labour and the First World War: economy, politics and the erosion of local peculiarity?', *Journal of Regional and Local Studies*, 10 (1990), pp. 23–47.

the Rhondda, or the provision of innovative social services through the local state – were never likely to solve this basic problem.[55] Labour's fortune, in a sense, was that a second global war allowed it to 'nationalise' its politics in a way that the first most definitely had not. During the First World War Labour's influence over the management of the home front was partial at best, and trade unionists remained suspicious of the state and unconvinced about the practicality of defending their members through political as opposed to industrial strategies.[56] During the Second World War Labour dominated the home front, especially through the colossal figure of Bevin at the Ministry of Labour.[57] The context was set, at last, for the nationalization of Labour politics. But that, as they say, is another story.

IV

So far the emphasis in this discussion has been on political languages, and on the practical strategies of local Labour politicians. But political success depended on more than this – it depended, as well, on the social context within which Labour politics were being developed. In this respect histories of Labour politics have tended to focus overwhelmingly on one factor – occupational structure. Clearly occupation *was* important, specific trades, such as miners or shoemakers, often developed strong, autonomous political cultures which party leaders might hope to tap into.[58] Many of the tensions in the pre-war Labour movement over the extent and the nature of state intervention undoubtedly had their roots in

---

[55] Marriott, *Culture of labourism*; Mike Savage, 'Urban politics and the rise of Labour party, 1919–39', in Jamieson and Carr (eds.), *State, private life and political change*, 'Urban history and social class: two paradigms', *Urban History*, 20 (1993), pp. 61–77; and 'The rise of the Labour party in local perspective', *Journal of Regional and Local Studies*, 10 (1990), pp. 1–16. For the Communist party, see Stuart MacIntyre, *Little Moscows: communism and working-class militancy in inter-war Britain* (London, 1980).

[56] See especially Turner, *British politics*, ch. 10, and Martin Jacques, 'The emergence of "responsible" trade unionism: a study of the "new direction" in TUC policy, 1926–1935', Unpubl. PhD thesis, University of Cambridge, 1977. For a contrasting view of Labour and the state during and after the war, see Alastair Reid, 'Dilution, trade unionism and the state in Britain during the First World War', in S. Tolliday and J. Zeitlin (eds.), *Shopfloor bargaining and the state: historical and comparative perspectives* (Cambridge, 1985).

[57] Alan Bullock, *The life and times of Ernest Bevin, vol. II: Minister of Labour, 1940–1945* (London, 1967).

[58] For example, Eric Hobsbawm and Joan Scott, 'Political shoemakers', in Hobsbawm, *Worlds of labour: further studies in the history of labour* (London, 1984); Alan Campbell, *The Lanarkshire miners: a social history of their trade unions, 1775–1874* (Edinburgh, 1979); Robert Colls, *The pitmen of the northern coalfield: work, culture and protest, 1790–1850* (Manchester, 1987); Williams, 'Ragged-arsed philanthropists'; Duncan Tanner, 'The Labour party and electoral politics in the coalfields, 1910–47', in A. R. Campbell, N. Fishman and D. Howell (eds.), *Miners, unions and politics* (Aldershot, 1996).

these distinctive occupational cultures and the political voice they found through the trade union wing of the Labour coalition. Mike Savage has identified three distinct forms of working-class politics: economistic, mutualist and statist, which he argues can be mapped back to the specific labour market experiences of different occupational groups.[59] The distinctions are perhaps a little too neat here – there was, in particular, considerable common ground on the need for systematic state intervention on behalf of those who could not help themselves – but the general point is well made.[60] Occupational structure could be equally important in relation to the capacity for political mobilisation – workers in occupations offering reasonable wages, relative security, and some margin for leisure were much better placed to participate in all forms of sustained associational activity – including political activism. Similarly, where the occupational structure was relatively homogeneous politicians might find it much easier both to broker political alliances and to construct a coherent language through which to articulate the interests and aspirations of the community. Here the contrast between the coalfield communities of Durham or south Wales, on the one hand, and the casualized, shifting and socially diverse communities of London or Liverpool, on the other, could hardly be greater. Ultimately, as we have seen, both types of community could sustain Labour politics – but political mobilisation took very different forms in the two environments.

The coalfields and the sprawling cities were not, however, socially distinct in every respect. One characteristic the cities shared with most coalfield communities by the turn of the century was a remarkable degree of 'demographic stability'.[61] Immigration into the south Wales coalfield remained high down to 1914, but even here one finds approximately 60 per cent of the population to be local born in districts such as Aberdare and Merthyr, though in the Rhondda the figure was much lower, at just 47 per cent.[62] At Wigan, on the Lancashire coalfield, nearly 70 per cent of the population was local born.[63] The great cities showed a similar degree of demographic stability by the turn of the century. Two-thirds of Londoners had been born within the London County Council area, and

---

[59] Michael Savage, *The dynamics of working-class politics: the labour movement in Preston, 1880–1940* (Cambridge, 1987), the approach is discussed more fully in chapter 3. See also Alastair Reid, *Social classes and social relations in Britain, 1850–1914* (Basingstoke, 1992), esp. pp. 60–2.

[60] Thane, 'Labour and state welfare'; Sheila Blackburn, 'Working-class attitudes to social reform: Black Country chainmakers and anti-sweating legislation, 1880–1930', *International Review of Social History*, 33 (1988), pp. 42–69.

[61] This theme is discussed more fully in Jon Lawrence, 'The dynamics of urban politics, 1867–1914', in Lawrence and Taylor (eds.), *Party, state and society*.

[62] *Census of England and Wales, 1911*, vol. IX (Birthplaces), PP1913 Cd.7017 vol. LXXVIII, pp. 108–10.   [63] *Ibid.*, pp. 40–2.

in the poor districts of the East End the figure was even higher. Though mythology presented such districts as home to shifting populations of itinerant migrants, the census shows that by 1911 over 85 per cent of the population of Bethnal Green and Shoreditch was London-born, compared with levels of under 60 per cent for most West End and suburban boroughs (and just 48.1 per cent for affluent Westminster).[64] However, demographic stability rarely meant settled residential patterns. Home ownership was rare, except in a few areas with well developed traditions of mutualist provision, and most families moved house regularly, though often within a very limited geographical area.[65] Such conditions might still make it difficult for political parties to sustain a strong organisational base, but demographic stability did at least create a social environment in which appeals to local identities, and to the defence of the local community, were likely to have some resonance.

If early Labour politics did possess a strong organic or 'localist' dimension it would seem reasonable to expect that the party would prove particularly dynamic in such areas of high 'demographic stability'. It is, however, extremely difficult to test this proposition. For one thing, the MacDonald-Gladstone pact of 1903 distorted the geography of Labour politics – often Labour was allowed a free-run, not in its own areas of greatest strength, but in areas of conspicuous Liberal weakness (as at Wolverhampton West).[66] Similarly the 'Caxton Hall Concordat' of 1905 effectively set in stone the existing geography of Lib–Lab and LRC politics, and represented a formal recognition of the 'Labour' credentials of both groupings.[67] To some extent these problems can be overcome by measuring Labour strength in terms of the number of Parliamentary candidatures (as opposed to victories), and by including Lib–Lab as well as socialist and LRC/Labour candidatures in the total. However, many practical problems remain. For one thing, census data on place of birth and residence exist for municipal not parliamentary districts. We can therefore include only constituencies where there is an approximate match between the two – London, and the great provincial cities must necessarily be excluded. We know that in 1911 almost 70 per cent of Liverpudlians

---

[64] London County Council, *London statistics, vol. 25: 1914–1915* (London, 1919), plate 4 (between pp. 48 and 49). On myths of East End demography, see Gareth Stedman Jones, *Outcast London: a study in the relationship between classes in Victorian society* (Penguin edn, 1984), pp. 133–51.

[65] R. Dennis, 'Stability and change in urban communities: a geographical perspective', in J. Johnson and G. Pooley (eds.), *The structure of nineteenth-century cities* (London, 1982).

[66] On the pact generally, see Bealey and Pelling, *Labour and politics*, pp. 143–6, 156–9, 287–92, 298–9; Tanner, *Political change*, pp. 21–2; on the confusions caused by the pact in the north-west, see *ibid.*, pp. 140–9.

[67] Bealey and Pelling, *Labour and politics*, pp. 209–11, 263–4 – the agreement related only to Lib–Lab candidates endorsed by the Parliamentary Committee of the TUC.

were natives of their city, but we have no idea how this varied between, say, the inner-city (and strongly Irish) division of Scotland, and the affluent, suburban district of East Toxteth.[68] A second problem is that in Edwardian Britain levels of geographical mobility carried a definite, though as yet unquantifiable, class dimension – with manual workers, on average, less mobile than non-manual and professional workers (though in industrial 'boom towns' such as Devonport and Barrow those locally born still represented a minority of the population in 1911).[69] Most towns dominated by 'outsiders' were either burgeoning suburban districts such as Croydon or fashionable resorts such as Hastings, Brighton, and Bath.[70] On the other hand, the towns where over 70 per cent of the population had been born locally were all important industrial centres: Preston, St Helens, Dudley, Sunderland, Hanley and Stoke (table 9.2).[71]

Clearly we need to show caution when trying to determine the meaning of any relationship between 'demographic stability' and the incidence of Labour candidacies. Superficially, the relationship appears strong – in constituencies with none, one or two Labour candidacies between 1885 and December 1910, on average 54.5 per cent of the population was local-born, whereas in constituencies with three or more Labour candidacies the figure was 63.2 per cent local-born. The difference between the two groups was found to be statistically highly significant, though this should not be read as implying that demographic factors alone determined the frequency of Labour candidacies – clearly many other factors were at work.[72]

There is, of course, a second measure of demographic stability – namely the proportion of people born in a community who subsequently remain resident there. Often the two measures overlap very neatly – Canterbury, Bath, Exeter and Brighton show low levels of stability by

[68] *Census of England and Wales, 1911*, vol. IX (Birthplaces), p. 33, and Davies, *Liverpool Labour*, pp. 197–231.

[69] *Census of England and Wales, 1911*, vol. IX (Birthplaces), pp. 12 and 27, locals constituted 44.0 per cent of the population at Devonport and 49.9 per cent at Barrow. The figure for Aston, near Birmingham, was just 8.0 per cent, but this was a separate town only in law, and has therefore be omitted from the analysis in table 9.2. This discussion is confined, throughout, to the English provincial boroughs returning one or two MPs, the cities have necessarily been excluded.

[70] *Ibid.*, pp. 75–6 and 84–8 – locals constituted 33.9 per cent of the population at Croydon, 43.2 per cent at Hastings, 47.8 per cent at Brighton, and 48.5 per cent at Bath. Other towns where locals were in a minority included Canterbury, Lincoln, and Reading.

[71] *Ibid.*, pp. 15, 33, 36, 78–9, 93–4 – the highest figures were for Hanley/Stoke at 75.3 per cent. Moreover, the Potteries also recorded the second highest level for a second measure of demographic stability – the percentage of those born locally and still resident (75.7 per cent). Leicester was even higher at 76.1 per cent (*Ibid.*, p. 39).

[72] The data were analysed using SPSSx; employing the pooled variance estimate for the t statistic, Student's t was calculated to have a value of -4.04 with an associated significance of less than 0.001.

Table 9.2 *'Demographic stability' and the incidence of labour candidacies before the First World War*

Rank Order	Constituency name[a]	% population born locally[b]	% 'locals' still resident[b]	No. Labour candidates[c]
1=	Stoke-on-Trent	75.3	75.7	3
1=	Hanley	75.3	75.7	4
3	Sunderland[d]	73.3	65.9	4
4	Dudley	71.9	52.4	1
5	St Helens	71.6	73.8	3
6	Preston[d]	70.5	67.0	6
7	Wigan	69.2	62.5	5
8	Norwich[d]	68.8	67.4	3
9	Bolton[d]	67.9	73.8	4
10	West Bromwich	67.8	58.9	0
11	Blackburn[d]	67.5	73.6	4
12	Warrington	66.0	68.7	0
13	Halifax[d]	65.7	64.4	5
14	Walsall	64.9	67.9	0
15	Oldham[d]	63.8	69.8	0
16	South Shields	62.7	71.5	0
17	Great Yarmouth	62.5	60.7	0
18	Leicester[d]	62.3	76.1	8
19	Huddersfield	62.2	67.8	4
20	Bury	62.0	60.1	0
21	Rochdale	61.0	67.3	5
22	Northampton[d]	60.6	66.6	6
23	Burnley	59.3	74.4	6
24	Tynemouth	59.1	62.3	0
25	Dewsbury	57.8	61.6	2
26=	Derby[d]	57.6	64.4	4
26=	Newcastle-u-Tyne[d]	57.6	63.7	4
28	Worcester	56.9	51.6	0
29	The Hartlepools	56.5	70.4	0
30	Stockport[d]	56.1	73.2	3
31	York[d]	55.9	58.0	1
32=	Ipswich[d]	55.7	60.9	0
32=	Stockton-on-Tees	55.7	53.9	1
34	Chester	55.3	44.3	0
35	Wakefield	53.6	53.0	2
36=	Gateshead	53.3	61.7	2
36=	Gloucester	53.3	50.9	0
38	Birkenhead	53.2	65.7	2
39	Southampton[d]	52.8	61.8	3
40	Coventry	52.4	72.9	0
41	Middlesbrough	51.9	64.7	6
42	Plymouth[d]	51.5	57.4	0
43	Oxford	51.3	53.1	0

Table 9.2 (*cont.*)

Rank Order	Constituency name[a]	% population born locally[b]	% 'locals' still resident[b]	No. Labour candidates[c]
44	Portsmouth[d]	50.9	67.8	2
45	Great Grimsby	50.6	65.8	1
46	Darlington	50.4	59.8	2
47	Exeter	50.0	45.6	0
48	Barrow-in-Furness	49.9	67.6	4
49	Reading	49.4	55.8	0
50	Bath[d]	49.1	40.8	0
51	Brighton[d]	48.5	52.4	0
52	Lincoln	47.8	57.5	0
53	Canterbury	46.3	40.2	0
54	Devonport[d]	44.0	53.9	0
55	Hastings	43.2	55.5	0
56	Croydon	33.9	59.5	1

Notes:
[a] Single and double-member provincial English boroughs.
[b] Census data on birthplace relate to municipal not parliamentary boundaries. It proved impossible to find even an approximate match for some boroughs, these have therefore been excluded from the analysis.
[c] Includes Labour/LRC, Liberal-Labour, Independent Labour, and other socialist candidacies at General Elections between 1885 and 1910.
[d] Double-member constituency.
Sources: F. W. S. Craig, *British parliamentary election results, 1885–1918*; *Census of England and Wales, 1911*, vol. IX, (Birthplaces), PP1913 Cd.7017 vol. LXXVIII.

both measures, just as St Helens and the towns of the Potteries record high levels by both. There were, however, exceptions. Areas experiencing rapid growth through immigration such as Barrow, Coventry, or Portsmouth might contain large numbers of people born outside the town, but their economic dynamism meant that those born there tended to stay.[73] Conversely areas in economic decline such as the Black Country towns of Dudley and West Bromwich might be dominated by locals, but thanks to emigration barely half those born locally remained resident (table 9.2).[74] As the study of Labour's failures in the depressed

[73] Thus Barrow appears 48th out of the 56 English boroughs analysed in terms of the proportion of the population born locally, but 17th out of 56 in terms of the proportion of locals still resident in their town of birth. Comparable figures for Coventry are 40th and 9th respectively, and for Portsmouth 44th and 16th.
[74] Dudley: 71.9 per cent of residents born locally, but only 52.4 per cent Dudley-born still resident; West Bromwich: 67.8 per cent of residents born locally; and 58.9 of 'locals' still resident.

Table 9.3 *The changing strength of Conservatism in the English regions (percentage of contests won)*

Increased Conservative Strength			Decreased Conservative Strength		
Region[a]	1892–1910(J)	1922–29 & 1935 (Scaled[b])	Region	1892–1910(J)	1922–29 & 1935 (Scaled[c])
Wessex	78	79	Sth East[c]	85	71
Bristol	57	57	West Mids	78	66
Central	52	68	LCC	63	51
East Anglia	47	62	Lancastria	56	50
East Midlands	40	49	Peak Don	32	19
Devon/Cornwall	39	59			
Yorkshire	36	41			
Northern England	26	32			

Notes:

[a] Regions based on Pelling, *Social geography*.

[b] Conservative inter-war victories scaled to be comparable with 1892–1910 period, (see Dunbabin, pp. 246–7).

[c] Excluding the London County Council area.

Sources: Calculated from figures in J. P. D. Dunbabin, 'British elections in the nineteenth and twentieth centuries: a regional approach', *English Historical Review*, 95 (1980), pp. 241–67, tables 2 & 3.

iron-making districts of east Wolverhampton has suggested, this demographic instability may well have been an important factor constraining Labour's development across the Black Country before the First World War.

V

Districts such as the Black Country, south and west Lancashire, industrial west Scotland or East London, are often portrayed as areas where Labour success depended on the party's ability to tap the support of working-class Tories at least as much as that of disillusioned radicals.[75] A regional analysis of partisanship before and after the First World War suggests that during the 1920s and 1930s the Conservative party did indeed lose ground in areas traditionally associated with working-class Toryism (see table 9.3).[76] This was very much against the general trend of the

---

[75] The evidence is carefully assessed in Tanner, *Political change*, pp. 144–6, 154–5, 158–60, 162–96.

[76] Table 9.3 refers only to the English regions, but west Scotland showed a similar pattern; after scaling, Tory victories fell from 50 per cent of contests, to 33 per cent between the pre- and post-war periods, Dunbabin, 'British elections', pp. 247 and 251.

inter-war period – Conservative strength increased in most regions, including many such as the east Midlands, East Anglia and Yorkshire long associated with popular radicalism. The trend is suggestive, but no more. Certainly it cannot confirm whether Labour prospered in former Tory strongholds because it was able to develop a viable 'localist' politics to rival the increasingly national and programmatic politics of Conservatism. There are, in any case, a number of methodological problems with a long-term comparison of this nature. The altered franchise is one, especially in London, where pre-war residence requirements kept many poor householders off the register.[77] The proliferation of three-way contests after 1918 is another, since this must have altered patterns of partisanship in many constituencies. We must therefore be careful about drawing conclusions. Labour may well have captured a portion of the traditional working-class Tory vote, but its failure to make more significant headway in cities such as Liverpool and Birmingham (except in 1929) must surely remind us not to overstate this argument.

The question of whether Labour was able to tap a reservoir of working-class Tory support can also be explored by analyzing the impact of Labour candidacies on patterns of partisanship at constituency level before 1914. Again there are methodological problems to overcome, not least variations in the turnout and size of electorate between elections. Table 9.4 summarises the results of an analysis of English single member constituencies which experienced at least one three-party contest involving Labour between 1900 and 1914.[78] Since the aim is to find a rough estimate of the impact of Labour intervention or withdrawal on the vote of the other two parties, the analysis excludes constituencies which saw a three-way contest at each election after 1900 (e.g. Rochdale), and also where the Liberals intervened in a previous two-way Labour-Conservative fight (e.g. Hanley, 1912). Party votes were compared at adjacent contested elections,[79] and allowance was made for the expected 'swing' of opinion between elections when classifying constituencies. Overall, in just over half the cases the analysis suggested a straight shift of support between Liberal and Labour (Group One). Many of these seats were in Liberal heartlands such as the north east and west Yorkshire

---

[77] Paul Thompson, *Socialists, Liberals and Radicals: the struggle for London, 1885–1914* (London, 1967), pp. 68–72; Tanner, *Political change*, pp. 103–5.

[78] The analysis excludes four-party contests (e.g. Jarrow, 1907), and seats where the Labour/socialist candidate received less than 10 per cent of the poll. Seats such as Morley, in west Yorkshire, where a three-cornered contest (January 1910) followed an unopposed return (1906) are also excluded because the interval between elections is too great to make comparison meaningful.

[79] The shortest period between elections was always preferred, hence fifteen of the thirty-nine cases concern the December 1910 election. Each constituency therefore appears only once in the table.

Table 9.4 *The impact of Labour and socialist candidacies on partisanship in three-party contests in England, 1900–1914*

Group one: straight Labour/Liberal shift (20)
Ashton-under-Lyne (1906–W); Barnard Castle, Co. Durham (1903–I); Bermondsey (1910J–W); Bishop Auckland, Co. Durham (1910J–I); Bow & Bromley (1910J–I); Cockermouth (1910D–W); Crewe (1912–I); Dewsbury (1910J–W); Durham north-west (1914–I); Gateshead (1910D–W); Gravesend (1910J–W); Great Grimsby (1910J–W); Holmfirth (1910J–I); Houghton-le-Spring, Co. Durham (1913–I); Keighley (1910J–W); Leeds south (1910D–I); Poplar (1914–I); Pudsey (1910J–W); Stockton-on-Tees (1910J–W); Whitehaven (1910J–I).

Group Two: predominantly Labour/Liberal shift (9)
Bradford East (1910D–W); Bristol East (1910D–W); Chester-le-Street (1906–I); Deptford[a] (1906–I); Hull West (1907–I); Leigh (1910D–W); Manchester south-west (1910D–W); Middlesbrough (1910D–W); Wigan (1906–I).

Group Three: approximately equal shift (7)
Burnley (1906–I); Croydon[b] (1910J–W); Eccles (1910D–W); Huddersfield (1906–I); Hyde, Cheshire (1910D–W); Salford west (1910D–W); Shoreditch, Haggerston (1910D–W).

Group Four: predominantly Labour/Conservative shift (3)
Carlisle (1910D–W); Colne Valley (1910D–W); Spen Valley (1910D–W).

Notes:
I   Labour/socialist *intervention.*
W Labour/socialist *withdrawal.*
[a] Independent Liberal in 1906 polling under 10 per cent.
[b] Ignores intermediate by-election when Labour polled under 10 per cent.
Sources: Craig, *British Parliamentary election results, 1885–1918*; Tanner, *Political change*; Bealey and Pelling, *Labour and politics*; Pelling, *Social geography*; Kinnear, *British voter*; Douglas, 'Labour in decline'.

where 'Progressivism' met with much resistance, at least in part because the two parties were fighting for a common constituency. Even in this group, however, one also finds a small number of seats from areas traditionally associated with working-class Toryism: notably Ashton-under-Lyne, Gravesend, Whitehaven and, to a lesser extent, Stockton and Bermondsey. Here at least, Labour had not obviously created a political identity capable of capturing sections of the working-class electorate traditionally hostile to Liberalism. The second group of constituencies is more disparate. These are the constituencies where the shift in the party vote appears to have occurred mainly, but not exclusively, between the two 'progressive' parties.[80] Four of the nine are city constituencies (com-

---

[80] In these constituencies the change in the Liberal vote was equivalent to between 60 and 75 per cent of the Labour vote at the three-party contest (after allowances for changes in turnout and the expected swing between elections).

pared with only one out of twenty in the first group), and four are constituencies generally assumed to have had a sizeable working-class Tory vote in the 1890s (Deptford, Wigan, Leigh and Manchester south-west).[81] The third group, representing seven constituencies, includes the cases where Labour interventions (or withdrawals) appear to have affected the vote of the other two parties more or less equally. Of these only Burnley and Huddersfield would normally be considered Liberal strongholds – and in both cases there is evidence of a strong minority tradition of working-class Conservatism with its roots in the 'Radical Toryism' of Oastler and Stephens.[82] This is probably not the explanation for the three northern constituencies in the final category – seats where support for Labour appears to have had more affinity with Conservative than Liberal voting. Unlike the seats in Group Three, these were all Liberal strongholds, and there is some suggestion that in these cases defeat in a three-way contest at the January 1910 election led local socialists to seek revenge on their Liberal foes at the December election by voting Tory.[83]

An analysis of this sort must necessarily be treated with caution. Inevitably it can make little allowance for the specific local context which shaped election contests – local disillusionment with a specific candidate, local responses to the forced withdrawal of a candidate, and the like. Voters clearly respond differently to party appeals at different elections. For instance, on the basis of the 1906 election Leeds South would be classified in Group Four – Labour intervened, the Tory vote fell from 48.8 per cent in 1900, to just 17.2 per cent, and Labour polled 32.6 per cent. In December 1910 Labour intervened again; this time the Liberal vote fell by 19.1 per cent (on its January 1910 level) and Labour polled 21.5 per cent.[84] Clearly, context could be all. Overall, the analysis provides some evidence, through the seats in groups two and three, that Labour was able to make inroads into working-class Tory support before the First World War. But, as with the comparison of long-term shifts in regional allegiance, it would be rash to suggest that it represents conclusive proof of Labour's ability to exploit the political vacuum created by the changing face of Conservatism in the early twentieth century.

---

[81] There was also a tradition of Labour candidates tapping Tory support in Bristol East, see M. C. Neathey, 'Electoral politics in Bristol, 1885–1910', Unpublished MPhil, University of Wales, Lampeter, 1990, pp. 174, 197–205.

[82] See Robert Perks, 'The New Liberalism and the challenge of Labour in the west Riding of Yorkshire, 1885–1914 – with special reference to Huddersfield', Unpublished PhD, Huddersfield Polytechnic, 1985, pp. 132, 224–5, 553; *Burnley Express and Clitheroe Division Advertiser*, 6 October 1900, which gives a breakdown of party vote by ward.

[83] Pelling, *Social geography*, p. 304; Tanner, *Political change*, pp. 264 and 274.

[84] The seat appears in Group One because there was a shorter interval between the elections of 1910.

VI

We turn now to the question of attitudes to 'party', and to the meaning of 'independence' in pre-war Labour politics. As in debates on the politics of locality, one finds a great diversity of views within the labour movement. As we have already noted, Ramsay MacDonald could be as unequivocal in his defence of party as in his championing of programmatic, national politics. But even he was prepared to denounce the pernicious influence of the 'caucus' in modern politics. Like Hardie at mid Lanark or Hodge at St Rollox, MacDonald had experienced rejection by the Liberal party machine,[85] he also understood the power of anti-caucus rhetoric in labour circles. Though, perhaps characteristically, MacDonald blamed the rise of the caucus, not on cunning party wire-pullers, but on the quiescence and carelessness of the masses who allowed their rights to be usurped by secret committees.[86] The solution, he suggested, was to ensure that executive committees were 'kept properly subordinate to party opinion'.[87] Clearly the caucus and the party were very different bodies in MacDonald's mind. Not everyone within the labour movement accepted this nice distinction. For many the call for independent Labour politics involved a much more wholesale rejection of party politics as they had developed since the mid-nineteenth century. Among the ethical socialists some eschewed involvement in electoral politics and all forms of party organisation from the outset.[88] They were, however, very much a minority, even among the socialist 'evangelists'. More typical were the many advocates of independent Labour politics who saw themselves as pioneering a new type of party politics. Drawing heavily on popular traditions which conceived of 'independence' in terms of resistance to party dictation, they had considerable influence over the initial development of Labour as a separate political force. But by 1914, as we shall see, their influence within the labour movement had all but disappeared.

Suspicion of party had a long pedigree in labour circles. We have already discussed the anxieties felt by many trade union leaders at the rise of caucus politics in the 1870s.[89] Another facet of this suspicion was the

[85] See David Marquand, *Ramsay MacDonald* (London, 1977), pp. 34–7 on the circumstances which ultimately led MacDonald to stand as an ILP candidate at Southampton in 1895. For Hodge at St Rollox, see his *Workman's cottage*, p. 139.

[86] MacDonald, *Socialism and government*, II, pp. 23–4.

[87] *Ibid.*, p. 27 – hence his insistence that the selection of Parliamentary candidates should be in the hands of special representative conferences rather than inner committees (pp. 25–6).

[88] Stephen Yeo, 'A new life: the religion of socialism in Britain, 1883–1896', *History Workshop Journal*, 4 (1977), pp. 5–56. For a good example of this fundamentalist tradition see, Anon., *Robert Weare of Bristol, Liverpool and Wallasey: an appreciation, and four of his essays* (Manchester, nd, [1921]), esp. pp. 43 and 47.

[89] See above, chapter 7, pp. 173–6.

widespread dislike of canvassing, which many felt allowed party leaders to circumvent the ballot and exert undue influence over voters. When Thomas Burt fought Morpeth in 1874 he refused to allow any canvassing on his behalf.[90] The fledgling Scottish Labour party took the same line more than a decade later, arguing that it was morally wrong to canvass electors.[91] Many Edwardian socialists remained committed to outlawing canvassing on these grounds, and some continued to avoid taking any personal part in the work, but after 1900 few local parties were prepared to abandon canvassing on principle.[92] Recalling this early disdain for canvassing from the perspective of 1940s Glasgow – where the machine had long dominated local Labour politics – Martin Haddow is intensely cynical about idealists who could have trusted in the 'intelligence' and 'independence' of the average elector. His cynicism tells us much about how far Labour politics had travelled by this time.[93]

The resonances of 'independence' as a political cry were undoubtedly especially strong within the trade union movement. Only a minority of trade unions were genuinely non-political, but many were hostile to open partisanship, partly because they feared dividing the membership along party lines, and partly because they feared allegations that the union had been 'nobbled' by party wire-pullers. John Hodge of the steel-smelters union, expressed this sentiment clearly in his presidential address to the 1892 Trades Union Congress at Glasgow. Though privately a prominent Liberal activist,[94] Hodge counselled against *any* party exerting influence within the unions,

Our unions are being used by faddists for the purposes of airing their political crochets or advancing their own individual ambitions. We must have none of this. Our unions must be kept free from political intriguers. Our unions contain men of both of the great political parties in the State, and it would be disgraceful and dishonourable if a majority of either political party were to use the prestige of these unions on behalf of any or either of our great political parties. If we are to have a Labour party, let it be distinct from our unions, for so soon as we begin to make our unions political hotbeds, so soon will disintegration set in.[95]

[90] Burt, *Pitman and privy councillor*, p. 215.   [91] Haddow, *My seventy years*, p. 34.

[92] See *Justice*, 25 February 1911; Snell, *Men, movements and myself*, p. 188. For an early pamphlet stressing the importance of thorough canvassing to electoral politics, see Fabian Tract No. 64 [Ramsay MacDonald], *How to lose and how to win an election* (London, 1895), which warns socialists that public meetings might be useful to 'educate and stir up the people, but *canvassing gets votes*' (original emphasis).

[93] Haddow, *My seventy years*, pp. 34–5. For an historical account of this transition locally, see Alan McKinlay, 'Labour and locality: Labour politics on Clydeside, 1900–1939', *Journal of Regional and Local Studies*, 10 (1990), pp. 48–59, also Alastair Reid, 'Glasgow socialism', *Social History*, 11 (1986), pp. 82–97.

[94] See Hodge, *Workman's cottage*, pp. 94, 115–16, 137. After moving to Manchester in 1892 he soon became president of the local ward Liberal party, and was on the constituency executive committee. He even sat as a Liberal councillor for Cheetham in the later 1890s.

[95] Trades Union Congress, *TUC Annual Report, 1892* (Glasgow), p. 29.

Hodge certainly intended his criticisms to apply to socialist politicians as much as anyone else. As his abiding hostility to the ILP indicates, his conception of 'independence' was not their's – his concern was not so much with breaking the hold of the caucus over electoral politics, as with breaking the influence of political outsiders over the unions.[96]

This powerful trade union tradition of 'independence' was as likely to work against the 'ILPers' as for them in the 1890s. At the 1891 TUC, Keir Hardie failed to secure support for a proposed scheme to finance independent Labour representation, but a simple amendment calling on the Labour Electoral Association to work 'independent of party politics' was passed by 256 votes to 26.[97] As we have seen, in the wake of the Tories' resounding election victory of 1895, the ILP came under sustained attack within the TUC (chapter 8). John Jenkins, as president of Congress, insisted that until the party published full accounts for the recent election 'doubts of the genuineness and "independence" of the Independent Labour Party might well be entertained by the great body of trade unionists. It would be looked upon as a foil of party political wire-pullers.'[98]

Neither Jenkins nor Hodge can be dismissed simply as Lib–Lab apologists, despite ILP claims to the contrary.[99] Both sat as Labour MPs in the 1900s – Hodge for Gorton and Jenkins for Chatham in Kent. Their suspicions that political 'intriguers' were trying to manipulate the unions were genuine, but when their own unions embraced independent labour representation neither had any qualms about the new departure.[100] In any case, Jenkins and the ILP were something of a side-show at the 1895 Congress. Far more important was the Parliamentary Committee's decision to reform the standing orders of Congress, and to insist that their recommendations be debated and voted upon according to the new rules and procedures. Both sides presented the issue as a crusade against political intrigue – both sides insisted that the continued independence of the unions was at stake. Pete Curran of the gas workers detected party 'wire-pulling and intriguing' behind the new standing orders, while Ben Tillett, another ILP stalwart, denounced the 'Brummagem methods' of the Parliamentary Committee. Tillett, for one, had no doubt that 'it was the politicians, the voice and hand of the party politicians, that had been at the bottom of this, as in the address of the president [Jenkins]'.[101]

---

[96] See Hodge, *Workman's cottage*, pp. 137, 156–7, 165, 261–3.
[97] Trades Union Congress, *TUC Annual Report, 1891* (Newcastle), pp. 86–7.
[98] Trades Union Congress, *TUC Annual Report, 1895* (Cardiff), pp. 28–9.
[99] See *Labour Leader*, 7 September 1895, which notes of Jenkins, 'two years ago he inclined towards the ILP, but a judiciously timed magistracy settled his hash, and now he can be relied upon by the Liberal Caucus. None the less, he is a good sort . . .'.
[100] For Jenkins, see *Dictionary of labour biography*, IV, pp. 109–10; also Hodge, *Workman's cottage*, pp. 137–48.
[101] Trades Union Congress, *TUC Annual Report, 1895* (Cardiff), pp. 34 and 36.

Supporters of the new regulations couched their arguments in a similar language. William Inskip, of the boot and shoe workers, welcomed the chance to purge congress of self-seeking politicians, while James Mawdsley, the Tory cotton spinners' leader, argued that,

> it was time they showed they were neither a Labour Electoral Congress, nor an Independent Labour Party Congress, nor a Liberal nor a Conservative Congress, but a Labour Congress (Applause). They met there to do work on behalf of labour through duly-appointed labour men, and not through men who had somehow managed to cling to the skirts of the Labour party.[102]

As each side sought to denounce their opponents as 'lick-spittles of party', or self-seeking careerists, it was hardly surprising that the common ground between them tended to be obscured. In fact, this was far from being a straight fight between the old guard and the new. John Burns backed reform of the standing orders, though he would thereby be excluded from Congress, while Henry Broadhurst, the veteran Lib–Lab MP (who would also be excluded) was a vociferous opponent arguing, in good Whig fashion, that Congress should hand their constitution down 'to future generations unsullied and untouched'.[103] Moreover, socialist opponents like Tillett actually welcomed the exclusion of 'mere professional politicians' such as Burns, Broadhurst and Hardie – their primary objection was to the unconstitutional methods used by the Parliamentary Committee to introduce the new procedures (significantly Hodge voiced similar concerns).[104] One can therefore argue that despite the ill-tempered exchanges of the 1895 Congress, an underlying consensus already existed about the need to break the influence of party politics, and to uphold the independence of the unions. It was this consensus which ultimately formed the bed-rock for the formation of the Labour Representation Committee, and the eventual emergence of a distinct Parliamentary Labour Party. Though that is not to suggest that either was in any sense an inevitable consequence of the trade union movement's instinctive suspicion of party and its pride in political independence.[105]

Most trade unionists might agree with Tillett that unity depended on expunging 'the damnable party political spirit' from their ranks, but it was

---

[102] *Ibid.*, p. 34. Cowey, the Lib–Lab Yorkshire miners' leader and, like Mawdsley, a member of the Parliamentary Committee, took a non-political rather than a non-party line by arguing that 'they had no right to introduce politics into the Congress business' (*ibid.*).

[103] *Ibid.*, p. 37; Trades Union Congress, *Parliamentary Committee Minutes* (Microfilm ed.), 1888–1922, Reel 1, 6 February 1895; Howell, *British workers and the ILP*, pp. 125–6.

[104] *Ibid.*, pp. 34–6; *Reynolds's Newspaper*, 8 September 1895 (Hodge had been re-elected to the Parliamentary Committee of the TUC in 1895).

[105] The essential contingency surrounding the emergence of a distinct Parliamentary Labour Party between 1899 and 1906 is still brought out most clearly in Bealey and Pelling, *Labour and politics*.

much less clear how this could be reconciled with the widespread recognition that trade unions also need a strong political voice at Westminster.[106] There was a powerful tension here. In the early years this tension was obscured, partly by a political rhetoric which portrayed 'Labour', not as a new political party, but as an alternative to party politics, and partly by the rudimentary nature of Labour organisation.[107] Thus in his election address at Leeds South in 1895 Arthur Shaw, the ILP candidate, called for a programme to help 'the struggling shopkeeper and wage-earner' (itself an interesting cross-class appeal), and insisted that 'to carry the main points in this programme it is necessary that there should be independence on the part of members of Parliament. The cry of "Party!", "Party"! has broken down, and against that I raise the cry of "Principle!"'.[108] Similarly, John Lister at Halifax represented his candidacy as a bid to thwart 'the set determination of the wire-pullers of the Halifax Liberal Association to resist the just claims of the working-class electors'.[109] Such anti-party rhetoric became more difficult to sustain after the formation of the LRC in 1900. Gradually, but inexorably, 'Labour' became more and more clearly the label of a political party, rather than simply the vague aspiration of assorted individuals in revolt against the established party political system. Indeed, in some respects, with its powerful National Executive Committee, and its ethos of solidarity and collective discipline derived from the unions, Labour represented the epitome of the centralisation of politics.[110] Even if Labour was much more than simply the political mouthpiece of the union's corporate interests – and it was – this could not alter the fact that the Edwardian Labour party was a hostile environment for the anti-party tradition.

Perhaps significantly after 1906 anti-party sentiment was largely confined to the radical left of the party, where it merged into a critique of 'Progressivism' as a betrayal of political independence. Within the ILP discontent was strong even before the twin elections of 1910 underscored the extent of PLP support for the Liberals. Victor Grayson, Fred Jowett and the authors of the so-called 'Green Manifesto' all challenged the cautious parliamentary and electoral strategy of the PLP, arguing that even within the ILP oligarchy had triumphed over party democracy.[111] This

---

[106] *Ibid.*, p. 36.
[107] See the discussion of Wolverhampton Labour politics in the 1890s, above chapter 6, p. 141.
[108] *National Liberal Club Archive*, DM 668, General Election Addresses (1895) Box 1, Leeds South (Bristol University Library).   [109] *Ibid.*, (1895), Box 1, Halifax.
[110] See especially, Tanner, *Political change*, ch. 3; McKibbin, *Evolution*.
[111] See Tanner, *Political change*, pp. 51–6; Barrow and Bullock, *Democratic ideas*, pp. 196–208; Dylan Morris, 'Labour or socialism? Opposition and dissent within the ILP 1906–14: with special reference to the Lancashire division', Unpubl. PhD thesis, University of Manchester, 1982, esp. chs 6, 8, 12 and 13.

hostility to the direction of Labour politics intensified after 1910, but by 1912 it was already clear that the malcontents were both politically marginal and ideologically divided. The problems facing the 'left opposition' before the war can be seen especially clearly in the events surrounding George Lansbury's decision, in late 1912, to resign his seat at Bow and Bromley and fight a by-election as an Independent Labour and pro-suffrage candidate.

The resulting contest is usually portrayed as an aberration – the product of Lansbury's eccentric, even sentimental, attachment to woman's suffrage. In fact it was about much more than votes for women. Lansbury was in revolt against the PLP and the whole strategy of 'progressive' co-operation. In his election address Lansbury made free use of anti-party rhetoric: 'believe me', he wrote, 'we have been caucus-ridden and party-driven too long'.[112] Acting as his political mouthpiece throughout the campaign, the *Daily Herald* consistently linked hostility to party with the cry of 'independence'. Comparing Lansbury's fate to that of Victor Grayson it concluded that 'any man who won't side with the Caucus in their coquetting with the Liberals must be persecuted.'[113] The paper called on voters to give Lansbury 'a free hand in Parliament unfettered by party "loyalty" ', and described him as 'the first and only quite complete and genuine Democrat in the Parliamentary field'.[114] In an editorial on the eve of poll the paper declared that 'above all he is the soul of independence. He is against caucus, conservatism, stagnation, temporising, everything that checks militant enthusiasm and delays progress.'[115] Here the language of independence merged into a syndicalist hymn to spontaneity and direct action – underlining the strange mixture of traditional and avant garde themes which were interwoven in left politics at this time.

Ill-feeling came to a head after Lansbury's defeat. The NEC was quick to issue a statement which refuted Lansbury's main charges against the PLP by declaring that 'there is no caucus in the Labour party'. Far from being dragooned by party whips, it insisted, the Labour group continued to uphold the principle that all key issues should be decided on a free vote. If Lansbury's example was generally adopted there could be no hope 'of realising either the political or industrial unity of the workers as a means of their liberation'.[116] The *Labour Leader* took a similar line, arguing that most European socialists were surprised that the Labour group imposed so little collective discipline on its members.[117] Lansbury,

[112] *Daily Herald*, 15 November 1912.   [113] *Ibid.*, 8 November 1912.
[114] *Ibid.*, 18 and 25 November 1912.   [115] *Ibid.*, 25 November 1912.
[116] *Ibid.*, 27 November 1912.
[117] *Labour Leader*, 5 December 1912. The paper noted that the other five dissidents over National Insurance (Hardie, Snowden, Jowett, O'Grady and Thorne) remained loyal members of the PLP.

however, was unrepentant. He hoped the contest would be seen as 'a first step towards a really independent Labour movement' – socialism, he insisted, could never be obtained 'by creating any party or caucus'.[118] Writing in the *Labour Leader* he vowed to remain out of Parliament

until Bow and Bromley, or some other place cares to send me back unfettered and unbound to any party. I am quite certain that the party system in this country (which the Labour party is bent on influencing) is the greatest hindrance to democratic progress . . . machine made politics have been proved in America and other countries to be the very worst kind of politics.[119]

Lansbury was strongly influenced by the critique of the party system and Liberal welfare legislation then being advanced by Hilaire Belloc and Cecil and G. K. Chesterton.[120] He was not alone – their radical libertarianism was widely discussed among left-wing critics of MacDonald and the Labour leadership in the years after 1910, but few socialists were prepared to accept their anti-party arguments so completely.[121] Hyndman's social democrats might attack the existing party system as a 'vast engine of corruption and misrepresentation', but their goal remained the *improvement* of party machinery, not its overthrow.[122] Like MacDonald, they supported the party-list system as a means of curbing personal influence in politics.[123] And also like MacDonald, they had little time for Lansbury's brand of 'conscience' politics. Rejecting his case against the PLP, *Justice* insisted that 'the chief defect of the Labour party has not been a too rigid discipline, or too strict a caucus rule, but altogether too much liberty and latitude, and too little regard for the decisions of the party conferences'.[124]

Similar views predominated within the Labour party itself. Trade unionists objected, not only because many could not accept that 'independence' demanded denying their own strong 'Progressivist' instincts, but also because Lansbury's actions cut across even more fundamental instincts – namely the need for loyalty and disciplne within organisations. MacDonald, as we have seen, was no less unequivocal in his defence of

---

[118] *Daily Herald*, 28 November 1912.   [119] *Labour Leader*, 5 December 1912.

[120] They gave him strong support during the by-election at Bow, e.g. *Daily Herald*, 16 November 1912. See especially Hilaire Belloc and Cecil Chesterton, *The party system* (London, 1911), Hilaire Belloc, *The servile state* (London, 1912), and 'The end of the Labour party', in *The Eye-witness*, 20 June 1911, pp. 135–6.

[121] See *Justice*, 25 February 1911, 16 November and 28 December 1912; *Daily Herald*, 8 November 1912; C. E. Smith, 'The servile state' and J. L. McCallum, 'The party system', both in *The Socialist Review*, April 1913; *Labour Leader*, 3 February 1911. Also James Hinton, *The first shop stewards' movement* (London, 1973).

[122] *Justice*, 25 February 1911 and 16 November 1912, which denounced the Liberals' national insurance scheme as a 'Prudential, Employers' Federation, Lloyd George, Labour party combination for the enslavement of the workers'.

[123] *Ibid.*, 7 December 1912.   [124] *Ibid.*, 28 December 1912.

party and party discipline – more surprising, perhaps, was that most of his left-wing critics took the same view. Lansbury's emphasis on the need to overthrow old party structures as a prelude to building new forms of socialist organisation often seemed positively reckless to activists who had devoted great time and energy to developing local party machines, which now formed the basis of their own power and influence within the movement.[125] Perhaps inevitably, they too tended to focus on the perfection of party machinery (on achieving 'internal democracy'), rather than on its destruction. So much so, in fact, that by the early 1920s it was right-wing Labour figures such as George Barnes or John Hodge who were most vociferous in their denunciations of the 'sinister . . . tendency of the party machine'.[126] Within Labour circles, at least, the 'triumph of party' was clearly complete.

VII

Finally, we turn to an analysis of Labour mythology – to the stories which the party told itself about its origins and its rise to political prominence through accounts of the movement's early 'pioneers'. The primary source for this discussion will be the autobiographies and popular biographies of early Labour politicians. Until now I have treated such sources as basically representational, both of the lives they describe, and of the wider social context in which they are embedded. I now wish to adopt a very different approach, one which focuses less on content, and more on form by stressing the mythological function of these early life stories.[127] By 'mythology' I do not mean untruths, but rather shared stories about the party's origins and development which, regardless of their veracity, take on a life of their own within the collective identity and historical consciousness of party activists.[128] In the present discussion I wish to focus specifically on what might be termed Labour's 'foundation myths' – for these stories of the party's early political struggles did much to mould

---

[125] Morris, 'Labour or socialism?', pp. 334 and 367–9.
[126] See George N. Barnes, *From workshop to War Cabinet* (London, 1923), p. 203; Hodge, *Workman's cottage*, pp. 261–3.
[127] In defence of this methodological (and apparent epistemological) eclecticism I would argue that such texts work at many different levels, and may therefore legitimately be read through many different 'frames'. For examples of such readings, see, Carolyn Steedman, *Childhood, culture and class in Britain: Margaret McMillan, 1860–1931* (London, 1990); and from a more 'realist' perspective, J. P. Roos, 'The true life revisited: autobiography and referentiality after the "posts"', *Auto/Biography*, 3 (1994), pp. 1–16.
[128] The most stimulating discussion of this remains Samuel and Thompson (eds.), *The myths we live by*, intro.; but see also Agnes Hankiss, 'Ontologies of the self: on the mythological rearranging of one's life history', in Daniel Bertaux (ed.), *Biography and society: the life history approach to the social sciences* (Beverley Hills, Calif., 1981).

Labour 'mentalities' down to the 1940s (when war and the trials of office created new subjects for myth-making).[129] And if little distinction is made between biography and autobiography, this is simply because little exists at the mythological level: both forms of writing seek to make sense of (and generally give narrative form to) the complex web of events and experiences surrounding the emergence of the Labour party. Necessarily both are therefore fictions, that is more or less coherent (and explanatory) stories about the past.[130] As we will see, many of the stories Labour told itself could be said to be stories of consolation – they told of struggle, of unflinching independence, but also of belonging – Labour, in its own mythology, was often the embodiment of the virtues and aspirations of 'the common people'. Labour mythology thus legitimated the party's claim to represent the people – even to be 'the people', despite the fact that in practice, as we have seen, Labour politics had often been constructed on only the shakiest basis within local communities.

One thing which immediately stands out in these accounts of early Labour politics, is the very different nature of the myths which developed around the movement's male and female 'pioneers'. Though women such as Enid Stacy, Carrie Martyn, and Katherine Conway played a central part in the socialist evangelism of the early 1890s, and were clearly immensely popular, they do not feature prominently in subsequent narratives about 'the rise of Labour'. Moreover, when they are present, it is generally in the guise of tragic 'martyrs': middle-class women who broke with family and friends in order to take up the 'people's' cause, but then succumbed to the terrible hardship of their chosen life of self-sacrifice.[131] Labour men, in contrast, are generally presented as heroic figures locked in battle with the forces of ignorance and corruption. Bruce Glasier is recalled as socialism's 'lone scout and chief apostle', unbowed either by the hostility of the crowd, or by the rigours, and enforced poverty, of the

[129] This is not to resurrect an 'essentialist' view of political parties, only to suggest that whilst parties may indeed be evolving, and ever-shifting, coalitions made up of very diverse ideological groupings (cf. Gareth Stedman Jones, *Languages of class: studies in English working-class history, 1832–1982*, pp. 243–8); they are also organisations with historical traditions (and *mythologies*) which help to shape what is possible in practical politics.

[130] For discussions which challenge the long-established distinction between biography and autobiography see, Steedman, *Margaret McMillan*, pp. 243–7; Norman K. Denzin, *Interpretive biography*, Sage Qualitative Research Methods series, vol. 17 (Newbury Park, Calif., 1989), esp. pp. 17–26; and Stanley, *Auto/biographical*, I, *passim*.

[131] For instance, see Smillie, *My life*, p. 305 (Stacy, Martyn and Eleanor Marx); Tom Mann, *Tom Mann's memoirs* (1923; MacGibbon & Kee reprint, 1967), p. 102 (Martyn). 'Survivors', women such as Conway, Margaret McMillan, or Annie Besant appear much less frequently, though see Hannah Mitchell, *The hard way up: the autobiography of Hannah Mitchell, rebel and suffragette* (London, 1977), pp. 86, 118–19. Inspired early in life by Katherine Conway, she none the less resented the way many 'lady' socialists ignored working-class women such as her.

itinerant evangelist's life.[132] Pugnacious figures such as Will Thorne, Ben Tillett or Joe Toole present themselves as manly heroes who helped make socialism through the very force of their personality, and many popular biographies adopt a similarly epic mode.[133] There was, however, an alternative mode for representing the male hero which approximated more closely to the stories of female martyrs. Men such as Keir Hardie or Will Crooks were celebrated for their manly virtue and bravery, but their extraordinary exploits on behalf of the movement were said to have been possible only at great personal sacrifice. Snowden recalls how Hardie wore himself out through selfless exertion, while the second half of Stewart's popular biography is haunted by the spectre of Hardie's premature death.[134] According to MacDonald, that most accomplished of myth-makers, Hardie epitomised 'those miraculous endurances of the men who defied hardship in the blank wilderness, the untangled forest, the endless snowfield . . . the exhaustion of soul and body which had to be undergone between 1890 and 1900 in order to create a Labour movement'.[135] Indeed, in Labour mythology Hardie is presented as the party's great male martyr – killed, not simply by a life of hardship and self-sacrifice, but by the crushing ingratitude both of the masses, and of the labour movement he had done so much to build, at the outbreak of war in 1914.[136]

In general Labour's 'founding fathers' are presented very much as 'men apart': wholly incorruptible, indifferent to petty criticism and undaunted by popular disdain. Early in their lives they are depicted as struggling to uphold principle and truth within the old Liberal party, only to be frustrated by the machinations of party agents.[137] Thus Lansbury claims that

---

[132] Haddow, *My seventy years*, p. 169.

[133] Thorne, *My life's battles*, p. 57; Tillett, *Memories and reflections*, pp. 188–9; Joseph Toole, *Fighting through life* (London, 1935), pp. 85–7 and 155. MacDonald was often treated in this vein before 1931, see Herbert Tracey (ed.), *The book of the Labour Party: its history, growth and leaders*, 3 vols. (London, nd [1925]), III, pp. 118–41; 'Iconoclast', *The man of tomorrow: J. Ramsay MacDonald* (2nd edn, London, 1924), pp. 59–134 (where the Great War and the Woolwich by-election carry undertones of the martyr's travails).

[134] See Snowden, *An autobiography*, I, p. 75; William Stewart, *J. Keir Hardie: a biography* (2nd edn, London, 1925), pp. 195, 198, 258, 346, 366. Also Haw, *Workhouse to Westminster*, p. 69 (Crooks). Hardie was not averse to describing his life in this tragic key, see Emrys Hughes (ed.), *Keir Hardie's speeches and writings: from 1888 to 1915* (3rd edn, Glasgow, nd [1928?]), p. 124.

[135] Stewart, *Keir Hardie*, p. xxii (MacDonald's introduction). On MacDonald's understanding of the role myth could play in the project of party-building, see Rodney Barker, 'Political myth: Ramsay MacDonald and the Labour Party', *History*, 61 (1976), pp. 46–56.

[136] *Ibid.*, pp. xxvi and 364–7. See also Sexton, *Agitator*, p. 239; Haddow, *My seventy years*, p. 119; Emrys Hughes, *Keir Hardie: a pictorial biography* (London, 1950), p. 78 (quoting Shaw); Tracey (ed.), *Book of the Labour Party*, III, p. 116.

[137] For instance, Stewart, *Keir Hardie*, p. 39.

the experience of being denied a hearing at the National Liberal Federation conference in 1889 'ended my connection with Liberalism'.[138] After the decisive 'break' with Liberalism many accounts then focus on the stubborn refusal of the pioneers to be swayed from their chosen path either by flattery or by bribery on the part of the established parties. As with the stories of heroic sacrifice and martyrdom, Christian imagery is very much to the fore – here through the theme of temptation. Thus Hardie describes how during the mid-Lanark by-election 'a baronet was sent down from London' to offer him a safe seat and a salary of £300 per year if only he withdraw from the contest in favour of the official Liberal candidate. Describing how he refused the offer, Hardie concludes 'I have never had reason to regret following the steep, straight path of duty.'[139] Similarly Lansbury and Tillett recall being offered safe seats and secure incomes if only they would run as 'Liberal' candidates.[140] But again it is Hardie who embodies this mythic political purity – in popular biographies he is the 'miner who stood out alone for so long – dour, determined, implacable, incorruptible – among the shams of the politics of his day'; the 'incorruptible man of the common people, who, in his own person, symbolised the idea of independence'.[141]

Another important theme of these early life stories is the hero's 'leap into the unknown' on breaking with the Liberal party. Again 'the masses' are generally presented as hostile and ignorant, so wedded to the bread and circuses of old-style party politics that they vilify the pioneers' determination to uphold the 'truth' and the 'independence' of their new politics. Thus in a short piece marking his fiftieth birthday, Hardie recalls how, in the name of socialism, he had faced 'the turmoil of a contested election. Howls, curses, execrations, peltings with mud and stones; one poor solitary figure knocked and buffeted about bodily and mentally, and yet compelled to go forward by he knew not what.'[142] Frank Hodges, the Welsh miners' leader, recalls being chased out of a nearby village when trying to preach 'the word', a scene common to many early Labour

[138] Lansbury, *My life*, p. 73. The story is, of course, more complicated in every respect, but that is hardly the point.

[139] Hughes (ed.), *Speeches and writings*, p. 124 (Hardie was writing in 1906). For popular biographical accounts of the episode, see Stewart, *Keir Hardie*, pp. 43–4; Hughes, *Pictorial biography*, pp. 26–7; and *Keir Hardie* (London, 1956), pp. 42–3. Equally frequently repeated are the stories of Hardie declining $100,000 from an American millionaire who wanted the ILP to back bi-metalism, and his refusal to accept £300 per year from two elderly Scottish women after his election in 1892.

[140] Lansbury, *My life*, pp. 64 and 74–5; Tillett, *Memories and reflections*, p. 192. Tillett claims to have been offered Battersea in 1892, thereby suggesting that from the outset Burns was a creature of the Liberal party.

[141] Hughes, *Pictorial biography*, p. 3; Stewart, *Keir Hardie*, p. 394.

[142] In Hughes (ed.), *Speeches and writings*, p. 124.

biographies.[143] Even Joe Toole recalls that during his first local election he was denounced by the parish priest while attending mass, and booed by the crowd at the declaration – though characteristically he adds that within fifteen years he was sitting at Westminster as MP for the same south Salford district.[144]

On this reading, Labour's 'foundation myths' placed great emphasis on personal conscience, political independence and an abhorrence of populist 'mob oratory'. Such unifying myths tended to ignore many of the tensions within the emergent party – tensions over party democracy, over parliamentary strategy and even over the extent to which Labour should appeal to workers as they were, rather than as they *wished them to become*. As we have seen, the Edwardian Labour party was emerging as a highly centralised, and increasingly disciplined organisation. It was also emerging as a party more determined than any before to reshape popular politics – to reform 'the Democracy' through education. Hardie's picture of an election is symptomatic of a widespread (though not universal) revulsion at the tumultuous, even violent, world of late Victorian popular politics. Socialists such as Hardie and MacDonald had long argued that what Britain needed was not more democracy, but more education – why, they suggested, prioritize the creation of yet more ignorant, frivolous electors, surely it would be better to focus energy on securing the social reforms, and the cultural enlightenment, necessary for the growth of a truly 'rational' democracy. When the SDF had organised a mass demonstration in favour of universal suffrage in 1893, Hardie's response was to accuse the party of 'placing themselves in line with mere Radicalism'.[145] Writing in 1909 MacDonald went further, suggesting that few now feared democracy because 'the conquest of Democracy by its enemies has proved to be possible, and . . . the weakness of Democracy has come to be understood'.[146] As we have seen, MacDonald's pessimism was at its most intense in the aftermath of the First World War, and the bitter election of 1918 (the first fought under universal suffrage, at least for men). In 1919 he described how 'the governing classes' had come to understand the weakness of democracy, namely that 'the masses'

[143] Frank Hodges, *My adventures as a labour leader* (London, nd [1924]), p. 24. Also Smillie, *Life for labour*, pp. 108–12; Tillett, *Memories and recollections*, pp. 188–9; Lansbury, *Looking backwards and forwards*, pp. 70 and 80; Thorne, *Life's battle*, pp. 54 and 57.

[144] Toole, *Fighting through life*, pp. 100–1.

[145] *Justice*, 21 October 1893.

[146] MacDonald, *Socialism and government*, I, p. xxvi, later he rejects the traditional Radical case for institutional reforms by insisting that 'the people themselves require enlightenment . . . If a change of system were really to show that the people have been wide-awake all the while, the revelation would be a miracle' (*ibid.*, p. 108).

could be stirred into passion by things which were trivial, they could be easily deceived, they were fond of dramatic representations, and were very credulous, mental habits and the world as they found it held them in bondage, they were absolutely tame, very obedient and very suspicious of new leaders and willing to believe anything against them . . . the effect of having the vote was not to make them consider what they could do with it, but to make them enjoy an election.[147]

Like many Left intellectuals of his age, MacDonald was convinced that social and political progress could only be achieved if the people themselves were first reformed. Labour's first objective must be the creation of a rational polity, and this would only be possible if, as well as taming popular politics, one also educated 'the masses'.[148] Hardie took the same view. Writing in 1906 he warned of the dire consequences, should a would-be socialist candidate

ever forget that *he* is a pioneer and sink to the level of a mere vote-hunting, popularity seeking candidate, then *he* is in a more false position than either Liberal or Conservative. The main part of their business is to mislead the people. They find out [what] questions are most likely to excite the prejudices and appeal to the passions of the mob, and they play upon these as though they were matters of life and death . . .[149]

Philip Snowden was another Labour 'pioneer' to share this vision, hence his disparaging assessment of Victor Grayson, a predecessor as MP for Colne Valley, that he 'was essentially the mob orator'.[150] Even 'pioneers' of a more pugnacious stamp such as Sexton, Thorne or Tillett placed great stress on the movement's mission 'to educate democracy' – according to Tillett '[i]t was our gospel, proclaimed at the street corners, that set in motion the new forces of social redemption . . . it was a period of brain storm, as well as of physical violence, for it stirred up the alleys of the slums.'[151]

Thus socialist 'revivalists' such as Snowden or MacDonald, and socialist street-fighters such as Thorne or Tillett shared a common faith, not only in education, but in their own qualifications as educators. But it would be too easy to dismiss this determination to transform the culture and the habits of the poor simply as patronising or coercive. Certainly it frequently carried such overtones, and there is no doubt that the party's reforming zeal greatly complicated its relationship with many voters, but,

[147] Ramsay MacDonald, *Parliament and revolution* (1919), in Bernard Barker (ed.), *Ramsay MacDonald's political writings* (London, 1972), pp. 221–2.
[148] See MacDonald, *Socialism and Government*, I, p. xxviii, II, 130–2; and *Parliament and democracy*, pp. 63–7; Barker (ed.), *MacDonald's political writings*, pp. 162, 223 and 226.
[149] Hughes (ed.), *Speeches and writings*, p. 122 (emphasis added).
[150] Snowden, *Autobiography*, I, p. 169.
[151] Tillett, *Memories and recollections*, pp. 238 and 188–9; also Sexton, *Agitator*, pp. 110–11; Thorne, *My life's battles*, p. 54.

for all that, the mission to educate was inspired by great idealism and humanitarianism.[152] On the whole, I would suggest, the more cerebral and pacific version of the mission to educate predominated within the labour movement, especially after 1918 – in part, one suspects, thanks to the sheer strength of the autodidact tradition throughout the movement.[153] Writing in support of Lansbury during the 1912 Bow and Bromley by-election, Sylvia Pankhurst summed up the belief that socialism (especially a 'feminised' socialism) would be able to transcend the vulgar, violent world of Edwardian electoral politics. According to Pankhurst, the most uplifting aspect of Lansbury's campaign was that

There are no fierce, jostling crowds of men and youths frantically waving party colours and booing and howling down their opponents' speeches. There is no mud and stone-throwing, none of the heat and violence that are so common; yet there are more meetings, and larger meetings than at other elections.[154]

Pankhurst herself may reasonably be seen as something of a marginal figure within the British labour movement, but the vision she outlined of 'the democracy' transformed was anything but marginal. Labour's identity, strongly shaped by the mythology which grew up around the party's 'founding fathers', encapsulated the tension at the heart of the Labour project: the wish both to speak for the people, and to change them.

---

[152] For a careful analysis of the complexities and tensions within such a reforming impulse, see Steedman, *Margaret McMillan*.
[153] For examples from labour autobiographies, see Mann, *Tom Mann's memoirs*, pp. 17, 20, 48; Snell, *Men, movements and myself*, pp. 43–4; Sexton, *Agitator*, pp. 217–22; Ben Turner, *About myself, 1863–1930* (London, 1930), p. 27; and even Toole, *Fighting through life*, pp. 80, 88.   [154] *Daily Herald*, 25 November 1912.

Conclusion

A recurrent theme of the present study has been the dynamic tension which frequently existed between organised party politics and the wider populace. Popular mistrust of party probably had its roots in opposition to the secretive committees of Whig or Tory politicians who often controlled political representation in the eighteenth and early nineteenth centuries. By the mid-Victorian period, however, it had become an important constraint on the emergence of a truly hegemonic Liberalism in many districts. Despite strong popular support for Liberalism as a movement of 'progress' and 'reform', suspicion of the party 'wire-puller', and from the 1870s of the party 'caucus', placed a break on the full integration of Radicalism within the Liberal coalition. Among trade unionists, who were for the most part profoundly Radical in outlook, mistrust of party ran especially strong, hence the great emphasis placed on 'independence', and the widespread suspicion shown towards leaders such as Howell or Broadhurst who appeared to have sacrificed this independence. From the later 1880s the inflexibility shown by local Liberal parties towards calls for greater labour representation undoubtedly played an important part in the growth of an alternative 'independent' Labour politics. This should not, however, obscure the fact that labour's break with Liberalism and the Caucus had its roots in a long-term distrust of party, and in the unresolved tensions between Radicalism and 'official' Liberalism. It was, after all, among Radical activists that advocates of the new labour politics found most of their 'converts' in the early 1890s.

Yet, as we have seen, anti-party traditions did not flourish in the Edwardian Labour party. By then Labour too had been forced to take up the trappings of party, and to face head-on the dilemmas of representation. Indeed, Labour faced these dilemmas in a particularly acute form, since it claimed the right not only to speak for the people but also to change them in its own image. As we have seen, Labour leaders had a particularly strong sense of their mission to educate and reform 'the Democracy' – the people must be made fit to build socialism. As a result

264

the desire to 'tame' popular politics was very strong in Labour circles, much more so than among Tory or Liberal politicians, who if anything were discovering an increasingly populist style prior to the First World War. Not only did many party politicians continue to accept the legitimacy of the politics of disruption, but they often seemed to eschew any explicit ambition to change the people they claimed to represent. In many respects the hallmark of Tory success in the 1880s and 1890s had been the party's willingness, not only to accept the people as they were, but even to celebrate some of their least loved characteristics. As Liberalism came more fully under the sway of the nonconformist conscience after 1886, so Tories found it easier to present themselves as the champions of the 'respectable' working man who wanted to enjoy the honest pleasures of pub, race-track or music hall free from interference. The Liberals adapted only slowly to the new politics, but by the early 1900s they too began to find a strongly populist voice by exploiting issues such as 'Chinese slavery' and dear food.

Politics were changing in other ways at this time. Many politicians remained deeply uncertain about the likely consequences of mass democracy – anxious that democracy must mean either the triumph of ignorance over reason (a fear apparently strongest on the Left from the later 1880s), or the triumph of material self-interest over civic responsibility. Though different, both scenarios appeared to conjure up a bleak political future characterised by the eclipse of what we would now call the rational public sphere. The growth of Labour politics was widely read as confirming the destructive forces at work within the polity. It was taken as axiomatic by most political observers that Labour threatened to reduce politics to questions of class interest and class loyalty.[1] And whilst there is little doubt that this represented a serious misreading of Edwardian Labour politics, which remained strongly committed both to 'reason' and to the *defeat* of class interest, what matters in politics is often perception, rather than substance. Politicians feared that they stood on the brink of a new order: not only might the anonymous masses out-vote intellect and ability, but class interest could provide those masses with a new and dangerous cohesion. What was new was not the presence of 'class' – for decades party politicians had rehearsed their hymns of praise to the peculiar virtues of the 'honest' working man – but the fear that class might emerge as an independent force capable of overturning the rights of property. Politicians within both major parties became keen to find policies which would avert this threat, and in the process also contain the poten-

---

[1] For a rather sober analysis along these lines, see A. L. Lowell, *The government of England*, 2 vols. (1908; London, 1921), I, p. 453; II, pp. 122–6 and 533.

tial *electoral* threat posed by Labour. Herein lay the great appeal of tariff reform for many Conservatives, since it held up the prospect of funding social reforms out of import revenues, rather than domestic taxation.[2] The delicate balance between state collectivism and voluntarism at the heart of 'New Liberalism' can similarly be seen as a skilful political response to frustrate the growth of full-bloodied class politics.[3]

Historians have tended to assume that Edwardian party politicians were right to see themselves as faced by inexorable forces of 'modernisation' which predetermined the realignment of politics along the fault-lines of class and material interest. But should we really take this so much for granted? In particular, should we really accept contemporary assessments of the character of Labour politics at face value? Political observers saw Labour politicians as threatening the 'rise of class politics' as much because of who they were as what they stood for. As we have seen, there is little reason to believe either that structural changes within economy and society had created a new material base for class politics or that the Labour party perceived itself as a new type of party based on the solidarities of working-class life. This is not to suggest that consciousness of class was not highly developed in late Victorian and Edwardian England, only to insist that Labour was ill-placed to translate such consciousness into a new form of class-based political identity. Not only did Labour have to compete against highly developed Conservative and Liberal appeals to the putative interests of the English working *man* (gender, as much as class, shaped pre-war popular politics), but its activists were in any case only marginally more representative, in the literal sense, of the average working man, than the traditional party politician. Indeed, given the constant tension within Labour politics between the desire to represent and the desire to reform, Labour's claim simply to be 'speaking for the people' was if anything more problematic than that of their opponents.

In theory, the determination of Liberal and Tory politicians to head off the 'threat' of class by embracing more programmatic, state-centred politics created a political space which Labour could exploit by presenting itself as the champion of local communities. In some respects this was to prove an important, if ultimately rather self-limiting, aspect of Labour's appeal between the wars, but before 1914 the 'politics of place' appear to have remained under-developed, despite widespread interest in municipal socialism, Labour's own communitarian ethos, and considerable

[2] E. H. H. Green, 'Radical Conservatism: the electoral genesis of tariff reform', *Historical Journal*, 28 (1985), pp. 667–92; and *The crisis of Conservatism: the politics, economics and ideology of the British Conservative party, 1880–1914* (London, 1995), pp. 184–253 and 274–80.
[3] Peter Clarke, *Lancashire and the New Liberalism* (Cambridge, 1971), and *Liberals and social democrats* (Cambridge, 1978); also Michael Freeden, *The new liberalism* (Oxford, 1978).

popular suspicion towards the dirigiste style of Edwardian social policy. Labour's inability to exploit the 'politics of place' more successfully can in part be attributed to the constraints of the 'Progressive Alliance', which tended to exchange local autonomy for Parliamentary representation. No less important was the fact that local Liberal and Conservative politics often remained highly resistant to the shifting currents of national politics, and had no intention of abdicating the 'politics of place' to Labour. But perhaps most decisive of all, was the shaky basis of Labour's credentials to be the party of locality in most parts of the country before 1914. In Wolverhampton, as we have seen, not only did the geography of Labour activism bear little relationship to the geography of class, but Labour also suffered because of its reliance on 'outsiders' as Parliamentary champions, and because its attempts to expose the horrors of the slums could easily be denounced as shameful attacks on the town and its people. Labour's claims to embody civic 'patriotism' were easily challenged, not just in Wolverhampton, but across the country.

By questioning conventional notions both of the rise of class politics and the triumph of party this study has sought to challenge the strongly teleological approach to British politics epitomized by the concept of 'modernisation'. Politics were changing in the years before the First World War, but the changes taking place were extremely complex. By imposing upon them sociological models such as 'modernisation', which assume a strictly linear course of development, we lose sight of this complexity. Seeing change as linear and progressive leads naturally to the assumption that inexorable external forces are at work, rooted in society and economy, and that the fortunes of political parties are determined largely by developments at this 'deeper' level. That parties are, in effect, simply the vehicles through which pre-existing social constituencies find political expression. In contrast, the present study has insisted on recognising the active role parties play, not simply by adapting to change, but by interpreting it through language, and influencing it through policy. At the same time, however, it has also insisted that precisely because parties do not simply represent, in some unmediated sense, the interests of their constituents, their claim to represent is always problematic – that it can be sustained only by constant processes of negotiation and renegotiation. It is by studying these processes, by concentrating our critical attention on the ambiguity inherent in the claim to 'speak for the people', that we can hope to understand both the role of party and the dynamics of popular politics more fully.

Select Bibliography

PRIVATE PAPERS

BISHOPSGATE INSTITUTE (LONDON)
George Howell Collection (Reform League Archive).

BRISTOL UNIVERSITY LIBRARY
National Liberal Club Archive, including Geoffrey Mander Papers (DM668/16455).

BRITISH LIBRARY
Cobden Papers, (BL Add MS 43 662).

BRITISH LIBRARY OF POLITICAL AND ECONOMIC SCIENCE
Local Fabian Society Collection, Coll. Misc. 375, vol. 5.
Thornely/Villiers Correspondence, SR 1094 (2 vols).
Webb Trade Union Collection.

CLUB AND INSTITUTE UNION (LONDON)
Annual Reports of the Working Men's Club and Institute Union.
Unfiled correspondence of B. T. Hall.

WOLVERHAMPTON REFERENCE LIBRARY
Census enumerators' returns for Wolverhampton, 1881, [sample].
Villiers/McIllwraith Correspondence.
Wolverhampton Labour party minutes (1907–).
Wolverhampton Methodist Archive.

OFFICIAL PAPERS
Census of Great Britain, 1851, vol. I.
Census of England and Wales, 1871, vol. III.

Census of England and Wales, 1881, vol. I.
Census of England and Wales, 1891, vol. I.
Census of England and Wales, 1901, Essex and Stafford vols.
Census of England and Wales, 1911, vols. III and IX.
Controverted Elections (Judgements), PP1911, LXI.
General Register Office (Great Britain), *Quarterly Return for Marriages, Births and Deaths, 1905* (HMSO, London, 1905), part 2.
London County Council, *London statistics, vol. 25: 1914–1915* (London, 1919).
Minutes of Evidence taken at Wolverhampton on Inquiry into Proceedings, May 1835, PP1835, XLVI p. 245f.
Minutes of evidence taken before the Fair Wages Committee, PP1908, Cd. 4423, XXXIV.
Parliamentary Debates, 4th and 5th series.
Religious Worship in England and Wales, PP1852–53, XXXIX.
Report of an Enquiry by the Board of Trade into Working-Class Rents, Housing and Retail Prices and Standard Rates of Wages in the United Kingdom, PP1908, Cd.3864, CVII.
Report of the Royal Commission on the Poor Laws and Relief of Distress (Minority Report), PP1909, Cd.4499, XXXVIII.
Report of the Select Committee on Parliamentary and Municipal Elections [Hours of Polling], PP1878, XIII.
Reports of the Royal Commission on the Depression of Trade and Industry, PP1886, Cd. 4621, XXI; PP1886, Cd. 4715, XXII, pt I; PP1886, Cd. 4797, XXIII.
Return of Municipal Boroughs, Part I: England and Wales, PP1884–85, LXVII.
Return Relating to School Fees, PP1875, LIX.
Returns Relating to Electors, 1886, 1891, 1901, and 1911.
Schools Aided by Parliamentary Grants, PP1852–53, LXXIX.

ORGANISATIONAL RECORDS

Conservative Party, *Annual Conference Reports of the National Union of Conservative and Constitutional Associations* (Micro Methods Microfilm edition, CUL).
Independent Labour Party, *NAC Minutes* (ILP Minute Books, 1893–1909, microfilm collection, CUL).
Liberal Party, *National Liberal Federation records* (Harvester microfilm, CUL).
Liberal Party, *Leaflets and pamphlets* (BL; Bristol University Library; CUL).
Trades Union Congress, *Parliamentary Committee Minutes* (Microfilm ed.), 1888–1922, Reel I (CUL).
Trades Union Congress, *Annual reports* (1891–1901).

NEWSPAPERS AND JOURNALS

NATIONAL

Daily Chronicle
Daily Herald
Daily News

Manchester Guardian
Northern Star
Reynolds's Newspaper
The Times

LOCAL

Birmingham Daily Mail
Burnley Express and Clitheroe Division Advertiser
Dewsbury Chronicle
Dewsbury Reporter
Midland Counties Evening Express
Midland Counties Express
Midland Evening News
Midland Examiner and Wolverhampton Times
Miner and Workmen's Examiner
Shields Daily Gazette
South Durham and Cleveland Mercury
South London Observer
Staffordshire Advertiser
Walsall Advertiser
Wolverhampton Chronicle
Wolverhampton Evening Express
[Wolverhampton] Express and Star
Yorkshire Evening Post

PERIODICALS/JOURNALS

The Bee-Hive
Birmingham Workman's Times
Blackwood's Edinburgh Magazine
The Charter
Club and Institute Journal
The Commonwealth
The Eye-witness
Fabian News
Fortnightly Review
Industrial Review
Justice
Labour Leader
Labour Prophet
Liberal Magazine
Marxist Quarterly
The Metal Worker
Monthly Journal of Gas, Municipal and General Workers
Nineteenth Century
National Reformer
Primrose League Gazette

Quarterly Review
Railway Review
The Republican
Review of Reviews
Socialist Review
Wolverhampton Worker
Workers' Union Record
Workman's Times

REFERENCE WORKS

Alfred Hinde's Wolverhampton Street map (Wolverhampton, 1910 and 1923).
Baptist Handbook (London, 1860–).
Bellamy, J., and Saville, J. (eds.), *The Dictionary of Labour Biography*, vols 1–9 (London, 1972–).
Congregational Yearbook (London, 1847–).
Craig, F. W. S., *British Parliamentary election results, 1832–1885* (2nd edn, Aldershot, 1989).
  British Parliamentary election results, 1885–1918 (2nd edn, Aldershot, 1989).
Crocker's Post Office Wolverhampton and district directory (Birmingham, 1884).
Dictionary of national biography and supplements.
Dod's Parliamentary companion, 1906.
Kinnear, M., *The British voter: an atlas and survey since 1885* (2nd edn, Tiptree, 1981).
The Liberal and Radical Yearbook, 1887 (Harvester reprint, Brighton, 1974).
McCalmont's parliamentary poll book: British election results, 1832–1918 (8th edn, Brighton, 1971).
Marsh, A. and Ryan, V. (eds.), *Historical directory of trade unions*, I (Farnborough, 1980).
Newspaper press directory (London, 1877).
Ordnance Survey one inch to one mile maps, first series (London, 1834 and 1858).
Ordnance Survey six inch to one mile map of Wolverhampton (Southampton, 1886).
Ordnance Survey Gazetteer of Great Britain (Southampton, 1987).
Smith, H. S., *The Parliaments of England from 1715 to 1847* (2nd edn, Chichester, 1973).
Spennells Wolverhampton Directory, 1921–22 (Wolverhampton, 1921).
Steen and Beckett's plan of the town and borough of Wolverhampton in the county of Stafford [220 feet to an inch] (Wolverhampton, 1871) [CUL].
Stenton, M. and Lees, S., *Who's who of British members of Parliament*, vols. II and III.
Tracey, H. (ed.), *The book of the Labour Party: its history, growth and leaders*, 3 vols. (London, nd [1925]).
Wolverhampton Red Books (Wolverhampton, 1892–1914).

CONTEMPORARY WORKS (PRE-1914)

Anon., *The Poor Law Minority Report: a debate between George Lansbury and Harry Quelch (20–21 September 1910)* (London, nd [1910]).

Bagehot, W., 'The English Constitution' (1867) in Norman St John-Stevas (ed.), *The collected works of Walter Bagehot*, V (London, 1974).

Bell, F., *At the works: a study of a manufacturing town* (London, 1907).

Belloc, H., *Mr Clutterbuck's election* (London, 1908).

Belloc, H., *The servile state* (London, 1912).

Belloc, H., and Chesterton, C., *The party system* (London, 1911).

Booth, C., *Labour and life of the people*, 2 vols + App. (3rd edn, London, 1891).

Colmer, J. (ed.), *The collected works of Samuel Taylor Coleridge, volume 10: On the Constitution of the Church and State* (1976; 1st published in 1829).

de Rousiers, P., *The labour question in Britain*, trans. F. L. D. Herbertson (London 1896).

Fabian Tracts:

No. 49: [Shaw] 'A plan of campaign for Labour' (London, 1894).

No. 64: [MacDonald], *How to lose and how to win an election* (London, 1895).

No. 70: [Shaw], *Report on Fabian policy and resolutions* (London, 1896).

Fletcher, T., *Local slums: our black stains* (nd, press cuttings, WRL).

Gissing, G., *The nether world* (London, 1889).

Green, J. R., *A short history of the English people* (1874).

Hammond, B. and Hammond, J., *The village labourer, 1760–1832: a study in the government of England before the Reform Bill* (1911).

Hardie, J. K., *My confession of faith in the Labour Alliance* (London, nd, [1909]).

Hinde, A., *A handy history of Wolverhampton and guide to the district*, (Wolverhampton, 1884).

Hobhouse, L. T., *Democracy and reaction* (London, 1904).

Hobson, J. A., *The psychology of Jingoism* (London, 1901).

Hutcheon, W. (ed.), *Whigs and Whiggism: political writings by Benjamin Disraeli* (1913).

Jeffcock, J. T., *Original Wolverhampton guide and visitor's handbook* (2nd edn, Wolverhampton, 1884).

Jephson, H., *The platform: its rise and progress*, 2 vols. (1892).

Jones, B., *Co-operative production*, 2 vols. (Oxford, 1894).

Jones, W.H., *The Congregational churches of Wolverhampton, 1664–1894* (London, 1894).

The story of the japan, tin-plate working and iron-braziers trades, bicycle and galvanizing trades and enamelware manufacture in Wolverhampton and district (London, 1900).

Lowell, A. L., *The Government of England* (1908; 2 vols. London 1921).

May, T. E, *The constitutional history of England since the accession of George the Third, 1760–1860*, 2 vols. (1861–63).

MacDonald, R., *Socialism and government*, 2 vols. (London, 1909).

Parliament and democracy (London, 1920).

Maine, H., *Popular government: four essays* (London, 1885).

Mann, H., *Religious worship in England and Wales* (London, 1854).

Mearns, A., *The statistics of attendance at public worship* (London, 1882).

Ostrogorski, M., *Democracy and the organisation of political parties*, 2 vols. (1902).

Pratt, A. C., *Black Country churches* (London, 1891).

Reeves, M. P., *Round about a pound a week* (1913; London, 1979).

Reid, A. (ed.), *The new Liberal programme: contributed by representatives of the Liberal party* (London, 1886).

The New Party: described by some of its members (London, 1894).

Reynolds, S., Wooley B., and Wooley, T., *Seems So! A working-class view of politics* (London, 1911).

Rowntree, B. S., *Poverty: a study of town life* (London, 1901).

Saunders, W., *The new Parliament, 1880* (London, 1880).

The political situation: how it strikes a Radical (London, nd [1893]).

Stubbs, W., *The constitutional history of England in its origin and development*, 3 vols. (Oxford, 1866).

Tressell, R., *The ragged-trousered philanthropists* (1955; Panther edn, London, 1965).

Wallas, G., *Human nature in politics* (London, 1908).

Webb, B., *The co-operative movement in Great Britain* (1891).

Webb, B., and Webb, S., *The history of trade unionism* (1894).

Industrial democracy (1897).

Wright, T. [A Journeyman Engineer], *Some habits and customs of the working classes* (London, 1867).

The Great Unwashed (London, 1868).

Our new masters (London, 1873).

AUTO/BIOGRAPHY

Amery, L. S., *My political life, vol. I: England before the storm, 1896–1914* (London, 1953).

Anon., *The Free Trade speeches of the Right Hon. Charles Pelham Villiers MP – with a political memoir* (London, 1883).

Robert Weare of Bristol, Liverpool and Wallasey: an appreciation, and four of his essays (Manchester, nd [1921]).

Atherley-Jones, L. A., *Looking back: reminiscences of a political career* (London, 1925).

Barnes, G. N., *From workshop to War Cabinet* (London, 1923).

Benn, E., *Happier days: recollections and reflections* (London, 1949).

Broadhurst, H., *Henry Broadhurst MP: the story of his life from a stonemason's bench to the Treasury bench* (London, 1901).

Bullock, A., *The life and times of Ernest Bevin, vol. II: Minister of Labour, 1940–1945* (London, 1967).

Burt, T., *Pitman and privy councillor: an autobiography with supplementary chapters by Aaron Watson* (London, 1924).

Dalley, W. A., *The life story of W. J. Davis, J. P.* (Birmingham, 1914).

Fowler, E. H., *The life story of Henry Hartley Fowler, First Viscount Wolverhampton* (London, 1912).

Haddow, W. M., *My seventy years* (Glasgow, 1943).

Haw, G., *From workhouse to Westminster: the life story of Will Crooks, MP* (London, 1911).

Henderson, W. O., *Charles Pelham Villiers and the Repeal of the Corn Laws* (Oxford, 1975).

Hodge, J., *Workman's cottage to Windsor Castle* (London, 1938).

Hodges, F., *My adventures as a labour leader* (London, nd [1924]).

Howes, J., *Twenty-five years fight with the Tories* (Leeds, 1907).

Hughes, E., *Keir Hardie: a pictorial biography* (London, 1950).

Hughes, E. (ed.), *Keir Hardie's speeches and writings: from 1888 to 1915* (3rd edn, Glasgow, nd [1928?]).

'Iconaclast', *The man of tomorrow: J. Ramsay MacDonald*, (2nd edn, London, 1924).

Jenkins, E. A., *From foundry to Foreign Office: the romantic life story of the Rt Hon. Arthur Henderson, MP* (London, 1933).

Jones, E. R., *The life and speeches of Joseph Cowen MP* (London, nd [1885]).

Jones, J., *Unfinished journey* (London, 1938).

Keeton, G. W., *A Liberal Attorney-General: being the life of Lord Robson of Jesmond, (1852–1918)* (London, 1949).

Kenney, A., *Memories of a militant* (London, 1924).

Lansbury, G., *My life* (London, 1928).

  Looking backwards – and forwards (London, 1935).

Leventhal, F. M., *Respectable Radical: George Howell and Victorian working-class politics* (London, 1971).

McAllister, G., *James Maxton: the portrait of a rebel* (London, 1935).

Mann, T., *Tom Mann's memoirs* (1923; MacGibbon & Kee reprint, 1967)

Marquand, D., *Ramsay MacDonald* (London, 1977).

Maxwell, R., *The life and letters of George William Frederick, Fourth Earl of Clarendon*, 2 vols. (London, 1913).

Mitchell, H., *The hard way up: the autobiography of Hannah Mitchell, rebel and suffragette* (London, 1977).

Postgate, R., *The life of George Lansbury* (London, 1951).

Roberts, R., *The classic slum: Salford life in the first quarter of the century* (Pelican edn, London, 1973).

  A ragged schooling: growing up in the classic slum (Fontana edn, London, 1978).

Schneer, J., *Ben Tillett: portrait of a labour leader* (London, 1982).

Sexton, J., *Sir James Sexton agitator: the life of the dockers' MP* (London, 1936).

Smillie, R., *My life for labour* (London, 1924).

Snell, H., *Men, movements and myself* (London, 1938).

Snowden, P., *An autobiography*, 2 vols. (London, 1934).

Soutter, F. W., *Recollections of a labour pioneer* (London, 1923).

Steedman, C., *Landscape for a good woman: a story of two lives* (London, 1986).

  Childhood, culture and class in Britain: Margaret McMillan, 1860–1931 (London, 1990).

Stewart, W., *J. Keir Hardie: a biography* (2nd edn, London, 1925).

Thorne, W., *My life's battle* (London, 1925).

Tillett, B., *Memories and reflections* (London, 1931).

Toole, J., *Fighting through life* (London, 1935).

Trollope, A., *An autobiography* (Williams and Norgate edn, London, 1946).

Turner, B., *About myself, 1863–1930* (London, 1930).

Wilson, J., *Memories of a labour leader* (1910; Caliban reprint, Firle, 1980).

Wright, T., *The life of Colonel Fred Burnaby* (London, 1908).

THESES

Barnsby, G., 'The working class movement in the Black Country, 1815–1867', MA thesis, University of Birmingham, 1966.

Enstam, E., 'The "Khaki" election of 1900 in the United Kingdom', PhD thesis, Duke University, North Carolina, 1967.

Jacques, M., 'The emergence of "responsible" trade unionism: a study of the "new direction in TUC policy, 1926–1935', PhD thesis, University of Cambridge, 1977.

Kent, G. B., 'Party politics in the county of Staffordshire during the years 1830 to 1847', MA thesis, University of Birmingham, 1959.

Lawrence, J., 'Party politics and the people: continuity and change in the political history of Wolverhampton, 1815–1914', PhD thesis, University of Cambridge, 1989.

Manai, M. A., 'Electoral politics in mid-nineteenth-century Lancashire', PhD thesis, University of Lancaster, 1991.

Morris, D., 'Labour or socialism? Opposition and dissent within the ILP 1906–14: with special reference to the Lancashire division', PhD thesis, Manchester, 1982.

Neathey, M. C., 'Electoral politics in Bristol, 1885–1910', M.Phil thesis, University of Wales, Lampeter, 1990.

Perks, R., 'The New Liberalism and the challenge of Labour in the west Riding of Yorkshire, 1885–1914 – with special reference to Huddersfield', PhD thesis, Huddersfield, 1985.

Scott, G., ' "The working-class women's most active and democratic movement": the Women's Co-operative Guild from 1883 to 1950', PhD thesis, University of Sussex, 1988.

Tanner, D. M., 'Political alignment in England and Wales, c.1906–22', PhD thesis, University College, London, 1985.

Taylor, A., 'Ernest Jones: his later career and the structure of Manchester politics, 1861–1869', MA thesis, University of Birmingham , 1984.

Taylor, E., 'The working-class movement in the Black Country, 1863–1914', PhD thesis, University of Keele, 1974.

Tunsiri, V., 'The party politics of the Black Country and neighbourhood, 1832–1867', MA thesis, University of Birmingham, 1964.

Waitt, E. I., 'John Morley, Joseph Cowen and Robert Spence Watson: Liberal divisions in Newcastle politics, 1873–1895', PhD thesis, Manchester, 1972.

Wright, R. A., 'Liberal party organisation and politics in Birmingham, Coventry and Wolverhampton – with special reference to the development of independent Labour politics', PhD thesis, University of Birmingham, 1978.

Index

Aberdare, 241
Abraham, W. (Mabon), 206, 233
activists, political (role of), 47–8, 61, 66–7
Adams, J., 114, 117
Albery, W., 187
Althusser, L., 20
Amery, L. S., 183
Anglicanism, and politics, 101–3, 124–5, 218
Anson, Hon. G., 77n
Anti-Corn Law League, 78
anti-semitism and Left, 223
artisan cultures, 26–7, 37
Artizans' Dwellings Act, 173
Ashton-under-Lyne, 57, 248
Aspinwall, T., 211
associational life, development of, 30; and politics, 47–8, 66, 241
Aston (Birmingham), 184, 243n
Atherley Jones, L. A., 175, 200–1
Attwood, T., 74
autobiography, readings of, 228–9, 257–63
autodidact culture, 66, 263
Aylesbury, 200

Bagehot, W., 178
Baker, T. G., 117–19
Bantock, A. B., 87, 156
Barker, B., 147n
Barker, Fred, 143
Barker, J., 76
Barnard Castle, 231
Barnes, G., 149, 213, 215, 257
Barnsby, G., 74
Barnsley (by-election, 1897), 216
Barrow in Furness, 243–5
Barry, M., 212
Bath, 243
Battersea, 222, 237
Bayliss, S., 104
Beard, J., 28, 37n
Bebbington, D. W., 199

The Bee-Hive, 82, 170–73, 176
Bell, R., 216, 220n, 234
Belloc, H., 256
Benbow, J., 77
Benn, E., 167
Bent, A., 147
Berelson, B., 21
Bermondsey, 32n, 167, 221, 248
Besant, A., 258n
Bethell, Sir R., 80
Bethnal Green, 242
Beverley, 166–7
Bevin, E, 240
Biagini, E., 41, 46–8, 53, 169
Biggleswade, 200
Bilston, 73, 78n, 79, 81, 154
Birkenhead, 33
Birmingham, 32, 33n, 34, 73n, 86, 166n, 237n, 247; Bordesley constituency, 105n, 195, 234; early labour politics, 176; Reform League, 85–6; role of caucus, 184, 189
Birmingham Centre for Contemporary Cultural Studies, 20
Black Country, 74, 79; politics of, 99, 245–6
Blackburn, 216
Blair, R., 238
Blatchford, R., 202
Board of Trade, cost of living inquiry, 30–5
Boden, A., 143
Boer War, (see South African war)
Bolton, 211
Booth, C., 31n, 152
Bourdieu, P., 18, 64n
Bow and Bromley, 186–7, 237–9; by-election (1912), 255–6, 263
Bradford, 202, 205, 212, 215; East (constituency), 232; West (constituency), 210–11, 233
Bradlaugh, C., 114, 185n
Brand, A. G., 96